TOWARD ENLIGHTENMENT . . .

One of the main reasons Man is on Earth is to become increasingly more self-realized. The important task then is to find a method for such progressive awareness. Astrology is one such means.

The proper method for its use is revealed in

THE HOROSCOPE,
THE ROAD
AND
ITS TRAVELERS

Bantam Books by Alan Oken

AS ABOVE, SO BELOW
THE HOROSCOPE, THE ROAD AND ITS TRAVELERS

The Horoscope, The Road and Its Travelers

ALAN OKEN

BANTAM BOOKS · TORONTO · NEW YORK · LONDON

RLI: $\dfrac{\text{VLM 10 (VLR 9–12)}}{\text{IL 10-adult}}$

THE HOROSCOPE, THE ROAD AND ITS TRAVELERS
A Bantam Book / published September 1974
2nd printing
3rd printing

Published simultaneously in the United States and Canada

Bantam Books are published by Bantam Books, Inc. Its trade-
mark, consisting of the words "Bantam Books" and the
portrayal of a bantam, is registered in the United States
Patent Office and in other countries. Marca Registrada. Bantam
Books, Inc., 666 Fifth Avenue, New York, New York 10019.

PRINTED IN THE UNITED STATES OF AMERICA

This book is dedicated to
M.C., D., J.C., and the Reader

Acknowledgments

The author is deeply indebted to Karen Oken, who kept him strong enough to finish his task; to Felissa Rose, whose help and understanding of planetary influences eased the course which this book had to take in order to reach its present form; to Tobi Sanders, my guardian angel and dear friend; and to all the many friends and students whose encouragement and goodwill are a constant source of inspiration, love, and support.

CONTENTS

Foreword

PART I: The Horoscope

1. Astrology: The Cosmic Tool   3
2. The Astrologer: Artist and Scientist   9
3. The Natal Chart and the Importance of
   Birth Data   14
4. The Tools of the Trade   22
5. Symbology   30
6. The Planetary Energies   34
7. The Zodiacal Principles   65
8. The Planets in the Signs   86
9. The Pattern of the Houses and the Ascendant   102
10. The Planets in the Houses   115

PART II: The Road: Chart Erection and Interpretation

Note   139
11. Time: Universal Factor   140
12. The Wheel of Life   153
13. The Planetary Blueprint   168
14. The Geometry of the Spheres   193
15. Interplanetary Relationships   217
16. Planetary Pictures   265
17. Interpretation: The First Steps   277
18. Interpretation: The Second Steps   286
19. Prognostication: Free Will or Destiny?   296

PART III: The Travelers: Seven Delineations

Note   315

20. Carl Jung: Voice of the Collective Unconscious   316
21. Isadora Duncan: Voice of the Muses   326
22. Joseph Stalin: Voice of the Ego   335
23. Angela Davis: Voice of the Revolution   346
24. Harry Houdini: Voice of Illusion   355
25. Greta Garbo: Voice of a Woman   364
26. Edgar Cayce: Voice of the Spirit   375

Appendix: Answers to Exercises   385
Bibliography   390
Index   391

FOREWORD

The Horoscope: The Road and Its Travelers is addressed to four types of readers:

1. To the curious individual, who knows that there is more to astrology (and to life) than what he or she reads in the newspapers.

2. To the beginning student, who has very little technical background in astrology but who feels drawn to the planetary lights for possible illumination.

3. To the intermediate student, who can erect the horoscope but who could profit from some shortcuts in calculations and a systematic interpretive technique.

4. To the advanced student or professional, who is always seeking additional insights and opinions about astrological fundamentals, occult philosophy, and interesting nativities.

The purpose of the present work is to present astrology both as a spiritual path toward the expansion of one's understanding of Universal Law and as a practical tool for helping others through the use and interpretation of the horoscope. This book has been written to satisfy the many thousands of individuals who have been asking for a text which would fuse these two elements into a cohesive whole. It is the author's sincere hope that the volume has accomplished its objective.

New York City
1st day of Pisces, 1973

PART 1

The Horoscope

I.

ASTROLOGY: THE COSMIC TOOL

Each of us who reads these words (and the one who writes them) is seeking to grow and evolve. For many of us the world of our personal existence as well as the realm of activities beyond our individual interests are a mass of relative unknowns. The seeker of enLightenment desires to make comprehensible the many laws of creation which are at work both in his own life and in the Life of the Universal Being.

The questions which now arise are: How is this accomplished? How is a greater level of consciousness achieved? How can I find a key which will help me to unlock some of the so-called Hidden Mysteries?

Mankind has had its philosophers and seekers throughout most of its existence. In the past, these were comparatively few in number, but we now find that millions of individuals are actively pursuing many varied paths toward the Light. This has been especially true during the past decade. This upsurge in the search for understanding has led to the rise in popularity of the Eastern religions; the new renaissance of interest in the teachings of Jesus; the proliferation of "New Age" churches, organizations, and sects; and the great multitude of students of the occult sciences.

People are realizing that there exists in the world a tremendous, invisible power. This power can be tapped by each of us and used for the creative good and well-being of our fellow Man. The inherent dangers in the misuse of this fount of energy, however, are as great as is the positive potential available from its proper channeling. This is comparable to the harnessing of atomic energy: nuclear power can give heat and light to a city of a million inhabitants or destroy it in an instant, for

3

it is the direction and purpose of this energy which determine its ultimate manifestation and destiny.

It therefore becomes apparent that the seeker must be given, along with the access to Light, the means to use it and the spiritual understanding necessary to insure his or her welfare and safety. The mastery of a technique which gives greater consciousness and the spiritual awareness to know how to apply this consciousness are two different things. One must accompany the other or increased chaos is the result. Consciousness entails responsibility, and the mishandling of such responsibility will result in the annihilation of that consciousness.

No better example of such misuse can be given than the experience of those thousands of our brothers and sisters who first experimented with and then went on to abuse the latent power contained within mind-expanding drugs. It is true that, for many, these chemicals did unlock certain areas of perception not normally given to Man, at least not at the present stage of human evolution. Though these individuals had the vision, they had neither the spiritual attunement nor the training to creatively direct this input of high-voltage energy into their daily life experience. Knowledge may have been there, but wisdom was absent. The result was similar to the reaction when 200 volts of electricity are put through a conductor made to handle only 100. The conductor blows, becoming inoperable, often beyond repair. In short, a whole generation of minds (nervous systems) were blown. Such is the feedback from the misuse of energy, from the misdirection of consciousness.

One of the main reasons for Man's presence on Earth is for him to become increasingly more self-realized. The important task then is to find a means and a method for such progressive awareness which combines safety and effectiveness. Astrology is one such means, and it is hoped that this book will in part provide the method for its proper use. It is vital to state at the outset that the reader should study the material contained within this volume slowly. He or she should digest each chapter completely, answering all the questions and exercise material found at the end of most chapters before proceeding. The reading of one book will produce neither an enlightened soul nor a competent astrologer; but then again, the primary purpose of this work is not to create astrologers (although more would be welcomed) but to provide a means through which individual awareness of the Universe is safely broadened, deepened, and made more permanent.

What, then, is astrology, and how can modern Man use it to manifest his latent higher consciousness?

Astrology is a system of thought. It is a philosophical doctrine which serves to incorporate certain (though not all) absolutes at work in our solar system through its own symbolic language and principles. In essence, astrology is a vehicle for an ancient teaching. It endeavors to show that there is an intimate relationship among all the plans of nature: mineral, vegetable, animal, human, planetary, and galactic.[1] Students who have become intimately familiar with the patterns of these relationships will be able to understand and time their cycles of cause and effect. This synchronicity is the basis of the astrologer's predictive work.

Many individuals come to know astrology through grossly misleading newspaper columns. These are to the true astrologer as instant pea soup is to the Cordon Bleu chef or kitsch to the connoisseur of Italian Renaissance painting. Yet the astrologer and occultist understands the reasons for astrology's past image in the popular media and its present, although still rather cloudy, resurgence.

Astrology and most other philosophic systems and religions have a dual nature. At the center of the system there is a body of principles upon which the credo is founded. Known only to initiates and some priests, it is called the *inner temple,* or the *esoteric teaching.* Then there are the many levels of the diluted forms of these occult aspects of a specific doctrine, which are

---

[1] This particular pattern, which we call "The Law of Correspondences," was the basis for the first volume of this trilogy, *As Above, So Below.*

taught and given out to the masses.[2] The latter take the
form of dogma, tradition, and symbolic rituals. They
are collectively called the *outer temple,* or the *exoteric
teaching.* In the case of certain state religions, such as
Catholicism in the Middle Ages and Hinduism until
very recent times, the outer temple was used to maintain temporal power over the masses.

In remote antiquity the priests used astrology to
time harvest cycles. Thus a little of the vastness contained within the teachings was allowed to be employed
by Man so that he could live in harmony with nature,
propagate his own kind, husband his animals, and
consequently help the state to prosper. In its inner aspect, however, astrology was and is a factor that serves
to reveal the greater evolutionary cycles of our planet,
the races of Man who live upon its surface, and the
solar system in general. With the coming of increasingly
larger and more complex civilizations, astrologers were
employed by the rulers of many kingdoms to time the
latter's various wars of expansion and conquest as well
as to help select favorable periods for other affairs of
state.

As Mankind began to develop its intellectual capaci-
ties, the numerous uses to which astrology was applied
were gradually replaced by the scientific devices and
systems of thought invented through the awakening
mental faculties. The consciously rational mind of the
scientist, therefore, predominated over the latent intuitional faculties and the emotional control of the people
by the priests. Power then passed temporarily from the
philosophers and theologians to the technicians and
industrialists. The development of a finely tuned intellect—reason—is a definite necessity for the future
evolution of Western Man's higher faculties of consciousness. Intellect is the perception which leads to
judgment. Proper judgment comes from a balanced
and objective approach to life. The acquisition of this
kind of outlook on life necessitates a depersonalization

---

[2] The term "occult" should be clearly understood by the student.
It simply means "hidden (knowledge)," with the connotation that
such information may involve nonphysical forces known only to a
very few.

of desire, so that individual considerations are viewed as only one of a myriad of factors in a given situation. This is a principal requirement for the safe handling of the higher level of consciousness to which we aspire.

Today we find the natural sciences fulfilling a great service to the collective race of Man by their investigations into the physical aspects of being. This activity is of vital importance, for quite obviously we live on Earth, and our vital nature acts through the physical body. But life exists on many levels, most of which lie beyond the scope of both presently evolved physical senses and technology. Many of today's scientists are becoming aware of this situation and as a result are more frequently becoming involved with research in the various forms of ESP phenomena.

The general public is also becoming increasingly preoccupied with the (currently) unseen. Armed but not satisfied with reason alone, people are turning their interests inward to the Soul and outward to religion and the occult. But in order for the latter to be useful in the present era, orthodoxy and astrology must be reshaped to meet modern Man's needs and the prevailing trends of thought. Old-fashioned socioreligious dogma as well as certain prevailing vestiges of medieval astrology are no longer the viable forms through which Man can evolve. This does not mean that the teachings of Master Jesus and those of the occultists should be abandoned. The compassionate Love of which Jesus spoke and the Laws of Being contained within the body of astrological symbolism are alive and well. It is the traditions within which these teachings are cloaked and the consciousness of many of the spokesmen of these various doctrines which require a breath of new life. And this new life is coming, for the Age of Aquarius (that is, the Age of Man's [Further] Enlightenment) is approaching; the human race must evolve to be able to incorporate these new vibrations into its collective consciousness. Thus some of the doctrines contained within astrology's "inner temple" are now allowed to be presented to the masses, for we are presently in a position to begin to understand and utilize them.

In order to grasp the principles which comprise the system of astrological teachings, the student must begin to use certain faculties of the mind which have heretofore lain dormant, been partially conscious, or remained undirected. It will not be enough to memorize the meaning of, let us say, Mercury in the twelve astrological signs. This is an important step, but memorization is only an intellectual function. The student must digest the *essence* of Mercury and of the twelve signs, wordlessly, from a conceptual point of view. Once this has been accomplished, the student can choose any words at his command to describe something he knows "inside" himself. This mastery takes training: memory development, including learning a new vocabulary, followed by the awakening and the disciplining of the intuitional aspects of mind. In addition, the student must also become familiar with some of the Laws of Being contained within the astrological system, so that he or she can make proper use of the newly acquired awareness, language, and talents.

With the relative accomplishment of these goals in mind, this text material, its lessons and exercises, is offered to the reader.

2.

THE ASTROLOGER: ARTIST AND SCIENTIST

The astrological profession is composed of thousands of individuals, each with a different opinion about his or her chosen field and about life itself. At any astrological convention, for example (and these are regularly conducted in all parts of the world), great arguments will arise about the true nature of astrology, its predictive, diagnostic, and interpretive methodologies, and its role in today's world.

At the present time two types of astrologers prevail within the astrological community, each group emphasizing its own particular calling as either artists (the more mystical esotericists) or scientists (the more pragmatic and technical exotericists). There are even a few astrologers, such as Dane Rudhyar, who have managed to combine the two.

The astrologer-artist sees astronomy as the framework on which his delineation of the horoscope is based. The signs of the Zodiac are his canvas; the planets, his colored pigments; and the intuitional and rational aspects of mind, his paintbrushes—that is, the instruments with which he will synthesize and shade his colors in order accurately to render the "astroportrait" of his subject. For inspiration, the astrologer-artist draws upon the Source of Light through the psychic forces of his particular type of sensitivity.

The astrologer-scientist endeavors to bring together and harmonize the more technical aspects of physics, astronomy, and psychology within astrological symbolism. He is more attracted to the use of logical deduction and reason in the interpretation of a chart than he is to the use of the more psychic aspects of mind.

9

In today's progressively mechanized and computerized world, the number of astrologer-scientists is increasing. During the past two decades there has been a growing trend among many astrologers to either greatly improve upon or completely discontinue the use of traditional methods of horoscope calculation and interpretation. One of the most respected and best-known of these scientific astrologers is Dr. Reinhold Ebertin, who, with his associates, founded the Cosmobiological Institute in West Germany. Cosmobiology uses a completely different mathematical approach to the natal horoscope. The results of Dr. Ebertin's work have proven quite accurate, and many other astrologers have incorporated certain aspects of his cosmobiological methodology into their own interpretive techniques.[1]

The uses to which astrology can be applied are as varied as the backgrounds and interests of the astrologers themselves. A practitioner whose primary objective in reading charts is to provide guidance in such everyday events as the choice of a vocation or the timing of a vacation will interpret the horoscope with these goals in mind. The psychologist or psychiatrist using astrology as an aid toward a better understanding of his patient—such as Carl G. Jung, H. F. Darling, and Zipporah Dobyns—will interpret the map in terms of personality structure and natural behavioral patterns or use it to forecast a coming psychological crisis in someone's life. The esoteric astrologer may use the chart as a guide to interpreting the subject's reincarnation cycle, the political astrologer may explain planetary motions in terms of their consequences on international affairs, while the meteorological astrologer may weigh the relative positions of Mars, Jupiter, and Uranus to judge the severity of a coming thunderstorm.

Needless to say, the vast majority of astronomers and other members of the natural-scientific community classify astrology as neither art nor science. In their most benevolent terminology, they simply refer to it as a pseudoscience. More usually, they perfunctorily dis-

---

[1] Cosmobiology and other nontraditional and newly developing astrological methods are treated in *Astrology, Evolution and Revolution*, Volume III in this series.

miss our 6000 years of recorded data, research, observations, and experimentations as bunk. They also categorize some of history's greatest astrologers—such as Sir Isaac Newton and Tycho Brahe—as "astronomers," finding myriad explanations to rationalize and excuse these men's participation in and contribution to astrology. In the case of Newton, Brahe, and even Kepler, the truth of their professional calling was that they were both astronomers and astrologers, for it was not until late in the seventeenth century that the two really began to go their separate ways.

This attitude on the part of the natural scientist is quite understandable, for the points of reference dividing the physicist from the metaphysicist are based on research conducted in two polarized, though inseparably related, spheres. The astronomer-natural scientist seeks to measure the cosmos through such factors as distance, chemical components, orbital speeds, and temperature. His understanding of consciousness and evolution, in the occult sense of these terms, is either nonexistent or discarded as "unreasonable." The astrologer-occult scientist also recognizes the validity of the physical structures and locations of the planets in the solar system, and he uses this data in his calculation and interpretation of the horoscope; but more important to him than physical coordinates is his comprehension of the solar system (and the entire Universe of Universes) as a manifestation of the Great Plan of Creation. The occultist seeks to understand and *work with* those invisible aspects of interplanetary relationships which are the causal factors behind the physical events in all the kingdoms of nature.

The occultist respects the theories and efforts of the natural scientific community to explain the purpose and composition of the Universe. But he knows that their knowledge without his vision is incomplete. It is as incomplete as is his vision without the practical applications toward which the natural scientists labor for the benefit of Mankind and our planet. It is only through the union of the physical and the metaphysical laws and communities that Man may obtain the necessary perspective on the relationship between the visible and the invisible; between the past, present and future; between cause and effect; and between life and so-called death.

Pollution, for example, is the result of the lack of understanding of the Law of Collective Responsibility on the part of all Mankind for the well-being of our Mother, the Earth. It is also in part the backlash of unbalanced vibrations of greed and social corruption, a violation of the Law of Reciprocity. In effect, pollution is the excreta of digested negative thoughts and emotions.

Sir Isaac Newton observed and conducted lengthy experiments with physical phenomena. One result of his efforts took form in his Laws of Motion, the Third of which states that "For every action, there is an equal and opposite reaction." The astrologer-occultist refers to this Law as the Law of Karma and does not limit its application to the physical world of appearances. He knows that Karma and Newton's Third Law are operable on many levels, including the planes of thought and emotion. For example, the projection of fear upon a normal dog will result in the dog's efforts to master the human. The projection of mastery, accompanied by love, on the other hand, will result in a wagging of the tail, obedience, and perhaps a friendly nuzzle by a cold nose. Human nature is such that Man learns about collective responsibility only by seeing the garbage piling up in front of his own door and the fish dying in his local lake. He learns about reciprocity when he is taken advantage of by corrupt neighbors, and he learns about Karma when he consistently bumps his head against the same door in his attempt to pass an impenetrable barrier. When the Laws of Being become completely ingrained in the collective consciousness of the human race, Man will finally have learned his lesson and will have the pleasure and wisdom without the pain and suffering. Collectively, this will take eons, but individually a great deal can be done in one lifetime—your lifetime.

As Mankind evolves, an increasing number of aspects of the Eternal Life Force are made manifest on Earth. The human race will provide scientists to create the proper machines and instruments to coincide with these revelations, doctors capable of meeting the medical needs of Man in space, and legislators and philosophers whose duty it will be to formulate the various governmental structures of "New Age" Man. The human race will also produce astrologers and occultists equipped with the sensitivity to adjust, adapt, and interpet the eternal Laws of Being to Man's ever-changing state. You and I are now being affected and conditioned by this evolutionary process.

3.

THE NATAL CHART AND THE IMPORTANCE OF BIRTH DATA

The term *natal astrology* can, in a very broad sense, be applied to the birth of anything—an idea, a corporation, an animal, or a person. In this volume, however, we are primarily concerned with that aspect of natal work which relates to a person's birth, life, death, and personal evolution. (For an outline of astrology's other major divisions and a further consideration of natal astrology, see *As Above, So Below*, Chapters 2 and 3.) The natal horoscope is also referred to as the natal chart, the nativity, the natal map, the natal figure, the natus, and the geniture. All these terms are completely interchangeable and are equally valid. A very common term for the person for whom the natus is cast (or erected or set up) is *native*.

No matter what the specific interest, personal objective, or ultimate goal toward which you apply astrology, the basis for your work rests in the correct calculation of the natal horoscope. This is a comparatively easy task, since the calculations involved consist for the most part of simple addition and subtraction. The truly difficult job of formulating the tables upon which the simple calculations are based has—fortunately—already been done by previous astrologers, astronomers, and mathematicians. Once you learn to use these tables carefully you only have to make sure that your addition and subtraction are correct.

You should therefore immediately wipe out of your mind any misconception concerning the difficulty of the numerical processes. You should look forward to such calculations as the first step toward the mental discipline necessary to perfect the true skill of the astrologer—the interpretation of a natal figure.

The word *natal* is derived from the Latin word for birth. *Horoscope* is a hybrid of two words: Latin *ora,* meaning "hour," and Greek *scopos,* meaning "to view." Thus the term *natal horoscope* can be literally interpreted as "the view of the hour of birth." This "view" reveals aspects of the universal forces at work in our solar system as embodied in the constitution and consciousness of one human being. The total interplay of all these energies naturally results in the creation of the entire human race and the stages of evolution through which it has been and is evolving. This is why all of us, collectively, are one huge family of Man, each with his or her own particular "family traits."

In order to erect a chart for a specific nativity, the astrologer requires some fundamental information and the proper equipment. He must know the exact date of birth (month, day, and year), the place of birth (city or town), and the given time of birth. It is also vital that he know the sex of the individual, so that his interpretation can be modified accordingly.

1. Date of Birth. The movements of the planets in relation to the Earth are constantly changing. It is therefore essential that the exact date of birth be ascertained in order to determine the specific nature of the planetary influences on a person's life. The planets refer, of course, to the quality of a person's various life energies—physical, emotional and mental.

2. Place of Birth. As the Earth revolves around its axis during the twenty-four hours of its daily journey, all the different latitudes and longitudes of its surface come in contact with the Zodiac of Signs.[1] The loca-

---

[1] The Zodiac of Signs is synonymous with the "ecliptic"—i.e. the actual—orbit of the Earth around the Sun. 0 degrees of Aries is indicated by the point where the equator of the Earth intersects with the plane of the ecliptic. The joining of these two points in space occurs each year at the vernal equinox (now about March 21). The first 30-degree segment is called Aries, the second 30-degree sector is called Taurus, and so on through the twelve signs (= 360 degrees of the Earth's yearly passage). Because of the Procession of the Equinoxes this starting point differs slightly with each year (about 50 seconds of arc backward through the Zodiac

tion of the birth is directly concerned with determining the "House structure" of the horoscope. The Houses are the fields of life's activities—career, marriage, children, and so forth—which all of Mankind holds in common. The twelve Houses are divided in the horoscope by lines called *cusps;* these segments of the map and their interpretations are explained in chap. 8 (see also Diagram 1).

3. Time of Birth. Along with the place, the exact time of birth is essential to the proper erection of the horoscope. The time factor enables the astrologer both to locate the exact relationship of a specific point on the Earth's surface to the great circle of the heavens and to properly calculate the positions of the planets in relation to the signs and Houses.

The signs are the fields of energy through which the planets operate. Thus Mercury (which represents the rational mental faculties) in Aries (the sign of impulsive behavior) functions quite distinctly from Mercury in Taurus (the sign of cautious behavior). The role and effect of the signs is treated in Chapter 6, as is the relationship between planets and signs. In effect, the interpretation of a horoscope is based on the interplay between the planets, the signs, and the Houses.

Certain other questions arise in regard to the time of birth.

When is the actual time of birth determined? Most astrologers agree that the birth takes place when the newborn infant draws its first independent breath. It can therefore be assumed that most recorded birth times—if, indeed, the time is recorded at all—are slightly inaccurate, since the officiating doctor, nurse, or midwife most probably notes the time of birth as taking place somewhere around the first cry, perhaps at the severance of the umbilical cord, after the baby

---

of the Constellations). The Zodiac of the Signs and the Zodiac of the Constellations are two different circles and should not be confused. The latter refers to the various formations of the fixed stars, which lie in a huge circle within which all the planets of the solar system (except Pluto) revolve in concentric orbits around the Sun.

is shown to its mother, or at any number of different moments. For the beginning astrologer, this possibility of inaccuracy should not be taken too seriously, since an accurate character portrait of an individual can be read from a natal chart even though there may be a small error in the time of birth. (In most cases an error of four minutes or less is quite tolerable.) What suffers most from inaccuracy are the progressions and transits. These constitute certain methods of prediction, the use of which is dealt with later on in the text (see chap. 19). It is more correct to erect a chart for sunrise of the day of birth than for a grossly approximate time of birth.

It is therefore understandable that one of the severest criticisms of astrology as an exact science is just this factor of the relative accuracy of times of birth. How can a precise interpretation be developed from imprecise data? It is on this point that astrology should be considered as an art and as an instrument through which intuition plays a large part in determining accuracy. This is why the development of the higher mental forces is so important to astrological work (as well as to personal evolution).

Let us suppose that someone consults an astrologer and claims 8:00 A.M. as his time of birth. The astrologer immediately becomes suspicious, since it is quite possible that the time was rounded off from, let us say, 7:55 or 8:06. A further complication arises when the cast map reveals that the rising sign is 29 degrees Taurus. If the actual birth had occurred just five minutes later than the time given, the Ascendant (First House cusp) would be 0 degrees Gemini (see chap. 9). It is then that the astrologer should ask certain questions of the native in order to determine whether Taurus or Gemini rises. If the astrologer knows the characteristics of these two signs, he or she will have no trouble in ascertaining the correct one.

What does the astrologer do when, as is frequently the case (especially with people born before World War II), the native states that he or she was born "sometime in the morning" or "after my father came home from work"? In such situations several choices are open. For a skilled practitioner, "rectification" of the map may be the answer. This very difficult process, which demands great ability and long experience, consists of matching up certain major events in a person's life—such as a marriage, the death of a loved one, or a giant step either forward or backward in the career—with the astrological forces at work at the time of the events. These are then related to the planetary positions for the day of birth so that a true Ascendant (and subsequent House cusps) may be found. The beginner need not deal with the methods of rectification, for they, as well as the total "feel" of astrology, will come along in the natural course of events. I know that at the outset astrology may appear to be one incomprehensible jigsaw puzzle. But keep the faith, for the puzzle gradually puts itself together. All that is needed is time, the desire to learn, and the patience to keep things going while you do.

The astrologer who rectifies a map is like a physician who specializes in diagnostic work. When a patient exhibits an unknown ailment, the doctor looks at the symptoms, examines the patient's medical and family history, makes certain tests, and comes up with his opinion on the nature of the disease. He then prescribes the appropriate treatment. If the patient responds favorably, the diagnosis can be considered correct. The same goes for rectification. After closely examining the native's life and physical appearance (and, if possible, the charts of the native's immediate family), the astrologer suggests a horoscope pattern and "prescribes" the House positions. (This process assumes, of course, that the subject knows his or her exact day of birth, for without it rectification is practically impossible.)

After testing the map with the course of past events in the person's life and with future events over a period of weeks or months, the rectifying astrologer will see if such occurrences match with his "prescription." If they do not, he makes certain adjustments in the components of his astrological medicine and tests again. If they do, he knows that his diagnosis of his client's case is accurate. In both cases, medical and astrological, what is at work—is it science or art, intuition or logic?

One would venture to say that it is a combination of all these elements, harmoniously linked together.

Should the actual time of birth be unknown and the astrologer either chooses not to rectify and/or wants to obtain an idea of an individual's planetary positions, three other methods may be employed. These are the natural chart, the approximate sunrise chart, and the exact sunrise chart. Let us draw up each of these three types of natal figures using November 21, 1950, as the date of birth in all three cases. Do not be upset if you cannot interpret or even decipher the symbols in the charts. This is not expected at this point. Just make yourself familiar with what a cast horoscope looks like and believe that before long you will be able to read it as you are now reading these words.

1. The Natural Chart.   This is simply erected by following the natural order of the signs around the horoscope wheel. Thus the cusp of the First House is 0 Aries, the Second is 0 Taurus, the Third House cusp is 0 Gemini, and so on. Next one takes the planets as they appear in the ephemeris (a table of planetary positions) for the day of birth and without any further calculation places them accordingly in the chart.

2. The Approximate Solar Chart.   This chart uses the degree of the Sun's position for noon, Greenwich Mean Time (GMT). In our example (Diagram 2) this is 28° Scorpio 37'. We take this to be the cusp of the First House. The other cusps are then set up as follows: Second House, 28° Sagittarius 37'; Third House, 28° Capricorn 37'; and so forth. Thus the Sun and its degree are seen to be rising at the Ascendant of the map. The other planets are also inserted into the wheel according to their noon, GMT, positions, so that neither the place of birth nor further calculations are required.

3. The Exact Sunrise Chart.   Such a chart is calculated for the true time of the Sun's rising at the latitude and longitude of birth. The chart is cast as if this time were the actual moment of birth. Therefore we will have to add to our example date of November 21,

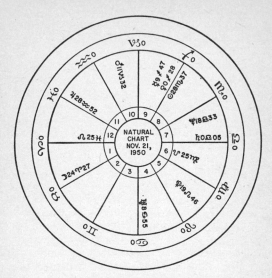

Diagram 1: The Natural Chart.

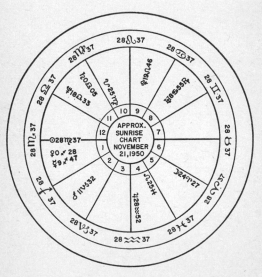

Diagram 2: The Approximate Solar Chart.

1950, a hypothetical place of birth—New York City—
and 6:54 A.M. (EST)—the actual sunrise time—as the
time of birth. We must then erect and adjust the map
accordingly, as shown in Diagram 3.

All three sunrise charts are symbolic. They are based
on the principle that, as the rays of the Sun color and
give life to the entire day, so all individuals born on
any given day will share some characteristics. How they
apply these traits and their degree of consciousness of
these traits—that is, their Selves—depends, of course,
on the individual's personal level of evolution.

The above is even more evident in judging charts of
"astrological twins"—two or more individuals born not
only on the same day, but at the same time and in the
same place. In these cases the intuition of the astrologer must once again come into play. It then becomes
his or her task to "tune in" to the differences in consciousness (as well as the hereditary and socioeconomic factors) of the individuals concerned and thus
present a viable interpretation of the horoscopes before him.

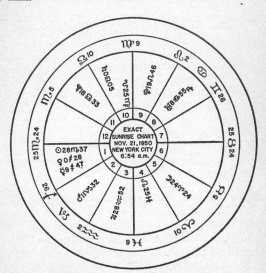

Diagram 3: The Exact Sunrise Chart.

4.

THE TOOLS OF THE TRADE

The required materials for casting the natal figure are listed below now but the time when you will really need them has been placed later on in this volume (see Part II). This will give you ample time to search out the various books and tables (and perhaps, in some cases, to allow you to save enough "green energy" to purchase them). At the same time you will be able to continue to assimilate the principles outlined in this work and, if possible, in *As Above, So Below* as well. Thus when the time comes to begin to calculate the horoscope, you will already have the necessary background and materials to benefit from your efforts right away.

Let us first itemize the entire "toolbox" and then proceed to discuss each item in detail:

Absolute Requirements
1. The birth data.
2. An ephemeris for the year of birth.
3. A Table of Houses.
4. An atlas with a gazetteer.
5. Chart forms (horoscope blanks).
6. Ruler, compass, colored pens or pencils.
7. A large spiral notebook with lined paper.
8. A place to study.

Optional Though Highly Recommended Materials
9. Time-factor tables.
   a. Time Changes in the United States.
   b. Time Changes in Canada and Mexico.
   c. Time Changes in the World.
10. The Table of Diurnal Planetary Motion.
11. Geographical-factor tables.
   a. Longitudes and Latitudes in the United States.

    b. Longitudes and Latitudes throughout the World (except USA).

12. Astronomical texts.
    a. The Astrologer's Astronomical Handbook.
    b. Simplified Astronomy for Astrologers.

A. Absolute Requirements

1. The Birth Date. In addition to what has already been discussed in the previous chapter, it is also important that the astrologer ascertain the source of the birth information as well as *the kind of time* (or Time Zone) in which it was recorded—that is, E(astern) S(tandard) T(ime); C(entral) S(tandard) T(ime); W(ar) T(ime), and so on.

2. Ephemeris For the Year of Birth. An ephemeris is a table which lists the positions of the planets for any given day. Ephemerides also list the time and zodiacal degree of new and full moons and eclipses and contain many other valuable and essential items necessary for horoscopic work. There are several different sets of ephemerides with which the student should become familiar:

    a. The most complete is RAPHAEL'S EPHEMERIS, published by W. Foulsham & Co., Ltd., Yeovil Road, Slough, Bucks, England. Raphael's has been issued annually since 1860. Back issues of this ephemeris may be difficult to acquire, and the separate purchase of each volume can become quite costly. These excellent tables are calculated for noon, GMT.

    b. THE SIMPLIFIED SCIENTIFIC EPHEMERIS (The Rosicrucian Fellowship, Oceanside, California) is also published annually. Fortunately these tables are also compiled in ten-year volumes, beginning with 1900–1910 and continuing through 1960–1969; the cost of each book is very reasonable. Although these volumes are quite clear, extremely easy to read, and economical, several printing errors have been found in the calculations. A careful and trained eye can spot them, however, and in some cases the editors have inserted errata slips correcting them. These tables are calculated for noon, GMT.

c. The volumes in DIE DEUTSCHE EPHEMERIDE (Otto Wilhelm Barth-Verlag, Weilheim/Obb., West Germany) are noted for their accuracy and portability; no knowledge of German is required. The six hard-bound volumes, beginning with 1850 and ending with 1980, are moderately priced. There are two major drawbacks to their use, however. The position of Pluto is not listed in all years previous to 1960. Second, they are not nearly as complete as either the Raphael or the Rosicrucian series. Another feature of these books which should be noted (though it is certainly not a drawback) is that these ephemerides are calculated for noon, GMT, until 1930, after which they are figured for midnight, GMT. Those who choose this series can obtain separately printed Pluto ephemerides from various publishers (The Aries Press, for example).

3. Table of Houses. Tables of Houses reveal the signs on the cusps of the Houses of the horoscope for the various latitudes of the globe. There are several different types:

a. RAPHAEL'S TABLE OF HOUSES FOR NORTHERN LATITUDES 2°–50° (also latitude 59° 56′) can be difficult to read because the print is very small. But it is inexpensive and dependably accurate. In this as in all other Tables of Houses, northern latitudes can be easily converted into those for the southern hemisphere (see chap. 13).

b. A/P TABLE OF HOUSES (Aries Press, 1035 West Lake Street, Chicago, Illinois) is basically the same as Raphael's, but the print is larger and the cost double (but surely worth it). The table is bound in hard covers.

c. DALTON'S TABLE OF HOUSES FOR NORTHERN LATITUDES 22°–60° offers a beautifully constructed table with large print. It is hard-bound and quite reasonably priced. It gives the degrees on all cusps (except the Tenth and Fourth) to a fraction of a degree (nice but unnecessary in most cases). Its major drawback is that it is of no help in casting maps for people born in the lower latitudes (such as the Caribbean and Mexico). Its major advantage is that it provides House cusps for everyone born in countries situated about latitude 50°

north (parts of England as well as Scandinavia, Scotland, parts of Russia, and the like).

d. SIMPLIFIED SCIENTIFIC TABLE OF HOUSES (The Rosicrucian Fellowship) is about the best bet. It covers all latitudes from 1° to 66° north. In addition, there is a gazetteer and a table listing the geographic location of many towns and cities in this country and abroad. Its typeface is large and its cost is low.

4. Atlas. In order to set up the wheel properly, the astrologer must determine the exact longitude and latitude of birth. This can be found fairly accurately through the use of the coordinate lines found on most maps. This method, however, allows for errors. The better atlases have a gazetteer section with exact listings, but these are costly. If the student can obtain them, the best aids in this area of his work are the geographic-factor tables.

5. Chart Forms. It is important to use a well-apportioned horoscope blank on which to insert the positions of the planets, signs, and Houses. These forms can be purchased in any occult bookshop; they can also be ordered through the Rosicrucian Fellowship and the Faculty of Astrological Studies, 15 New Bridge Street, London. You can also make your own horoscope blanks by using a compass and ruler. The size of your wheel will depend on personal preference, but it should be large enough for all the necessary data to be clearly legible.

In addition to the horoscope blank, it is a good idea to have a complete calculation form. This will provide the astrologer with a quick reference to certain information to which he will often refer during the course of casting and reading the chart. This step-by-step data sheet also helps in spotting and avoiding errors. Such a form, as well as a sample horoscope blank, will be found at the beginning of Chapter 13. To make things easier for the student who plans to cast many horoscopes, he or she is advised to copy the forms out of the book and then have them either mimeographed or photocopied.

6. Ruler, Compass, Colored Pens or Pencils. The student will also find it handy to keep at hand a scribbling pad as well as a folder or divider in which completed horoscopes can be filed for future reference.

7. Large Notebook. Those special features of each horoscope which the student finds particularly interesting and/or important should be jotted down for further reference. In this way you may further personalize your own approach to astrology.

8. Place to Study. Your work will require (and thereby train you in) concentration and contemplation (as well as occasional meditation). It is therefore important that you have a little corner set aside in some room wherein you may study and keep your astrological materials and books. Your special place will begin to acquire vibrations of its own, and you will find it a source of comfort to you. The more you work and contemplate in your particular spot, the easier your studies will become as time goes on. So choose and maintain your place of study with care.

B. Optional Though Highly Recommended Materials

9. Time-Factor Tables. One impediment to obtaining an accurate time of birth is the legislated use of Daylight Savings Time (DST) by the various federal, state, and local authorities. The following three books have enormously helped the astrologer in solving most of his problems with time, and a great debt is owed to the compiler of this essential information, Doris Chase Doane. The books are: *Time Changes in the United States* (and supplement); *Time Changes in Canada and Mexico* (both published by The Church of Light, P.O. Box 1525, Main Office, Los Angeles, California 90053); and *Time Changes in the World (Except Canada, Mexico and the U.S.A.)* (published by Professional Astrologers Incorporated, P.O. Box 2616, Hollywood, California 90028).

10. Table of Diurnal Planetary Motion (American Federation of Astrologers, 6 Library Court, Washington, D.C. 20003). The Table of Diurnal Planetary Motion saves the astrologer a great deal of time and work. Its purpose is to provide the necessary calculations in order to find the exact positions of the planets for the given time of birth (see Chapter 14). If this table is not used, the student will have to employ logarithms in order to obtain the required data. Logarithms as used in astrology are rather uncomplicated, but they do add extra steps and can be a source of arithmetic error. The erection of the horoscope through the use of this table as well as through logarithmic functions are both covered in this volume.

11. Geographical-Factor Tables. As we previously explained, the gathering of the longitude and latitude of the place of birth through the use of an atlas is often inaccurate. The following two tables largely eliminate the problem, besides providing other essential data helpful in casting the most accurate possible horoscope. They are *Longitudes and Latitudes in the United States* (American Federation of Astrologers) and *Longitudes and Latitudes through the World* (National Astrological Library, 631 East Capital Street, Washington, D.C. 20003).

12. Astronomical Texts. Two books furnish an extremely valuable addition to any astrologer's library, for they completely clarify any astronomical problems he may encounter. They are *The Astrologer's Astronomical Handbook* by Jeff Mayo (L. N. Fowler & Co., Ltd., Stuart House, 1 Tudor Street, London, E.C. 4) and *Simplified Astronomy for Astrologers* by LCDR. David Williams (American Federation of Astrologers).

Before proceeding further, answer the following questions to make sure that you have understood the principles stated so far and that you have memorized the key words and phrases and are thus ready to continue. If you are encountering any difficulty with any question, search for the correct response in the pages of the first four chapters.

QUESTIONS FOR CHAPTER 1.

1. What is the difference between the microcosm and the macrocosm?
2. What is the difference between knowledge and wisdom?
3. Give two or more definitions for "astrology" as it is used in the context of this material.
4. What is meant by the Law of Correspondences?
5. What is meant by the term "the collective consciousness of Man"?

QUESTIONS FOR CHAPTER 2.

1. What is the difference in point of view about the Cosmos separating the natural scientist from the occult scientist?
2. What does the natural scientist need in order to make his "vision" complete?
3. What does the occult scientist need in this respect?
4. What is meant by the "Law of Collective Responsibility"? Give an example.
5. What is meant by the "Law of Reciprocity"? Give an example.
6. What is meant by the "Law of Karma"? Give an example from your own life showing Karma at work.
7. Is Mankind still in the process of evolving? Give an example.

QUESTIONS FOR CHAPTER 3.

1. What is meant by "natal astrology"?
2. Give at least four other terms for "natal chart."
3. What is the term for an individual for whom a natal chart is cast?
4. What information is required in order to cast an accurate horoscope?
5. Why is each of these factors important?
6. What is meant by a cusp?
7. What is meant by rectification?
8. What are three alternatives to rectification if the time of birth is unknown?

9. What are "astrological twins," and how do they differ?

QUESTIONS FOR CHAPTER 4.

1. What is meant by "kind of time" or "time zone"?
2. What is an ephemeris?
3. What is a Table of Houses?

5.

SYMBOLOGY

Astrology has its own particular language. Some of these words and phrases, such as "cusp," "native," and "setting up the wheel," should already be familiar. Others, such as "trine," "declination," and (the horrendous) "sesquiquadrate" will be added to your vocabulary as we go along.

Astrology also has its own symbolic shorthand. A symbol serves a very important function both in astrology and in the development of the intuitional faculties. The trained astrologer only has to see the symbol for, let us say, Mars in Scorpio (♂ ♏) to instantaneously and wordlessly understand a concept which, if it were to be explained verbally, could take hundreds of words. The student can imagine what it must be like to quietly hold in one's mind the entire delineation of a natal chart just by glancing at thirty-odd symbols for a few minutes.

It is not enough, however, to grasp the entire picture of a person's life structure on the intuitional level. The true astrologer (at least one who wishes to work in a personal sense with others) must be able to have the necessary faculty for communicating verbally what is known or felt wordlessly. The higher and lower mental faculties (one's personal vocabulary and its use) must be taught to cooperate instantaneously with one another; the mastery of symbology is part of this training.

Some of the symbols of astrological shorthand, such as the glyphs (that is, the symbols) for the planets, are used to represent various abstract and occult principles. Others, such as those which stand for the spatial relationships existing between the planets—the aspects— are space-saving as well as communicative. There are also those figures which are pure abbreviations, such as the older (though still used) form of the symbol for Pluto (♇). The latter is a combination of the first two letters of the planet itself as well as the initials of the man credited with its discovery, Percival Lowell. Thus P + L = ♇. Finally, there are the glyphs for the signs of the Zodiac. These serve a dual purpose: they are both pictographs of the parts of the human body and/ or the animal each of the signs represents and ideographs of the metaphysical principles for which they stand.

It is important to learn all these symbols by heart and to contemplate each of them in order to glean as many of their various interpretations as possible. The more one comes to an intimate understanding of the symbols, the more profound is one's comprehension and appreciation of astrology.

We will not treat all of the symbols in this chapter; it seems preferable to meet most of them as we progress along the astrological road. The student should, however, at this juncture know the symbols within the symbols—that is, those individual components which make up the more complex emblems of the planets and the signs.

A. The Circle: Spirit

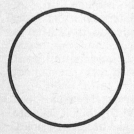

The circle represents the totality of all the energy in the Cosmos. Like Creation itself, it is eternal and infinite. It is a perfect shape, for it has no beginning and no end and contains within itself the vivifying potential of all Creation. The circle stands for the Father Spirit which provides the spark of life and consciousness to everything in the Universe. It is absolute; it is The Absolute. For example, it is the LIFE of a tree.

B. The Semicircle: Soul

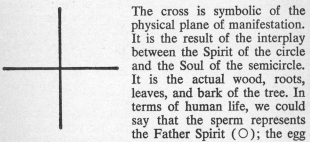

The semicircle represents the duality of existence because it takes the essence of Life and gives to it a form. The semicircle represents that which is created from the great un-manifest (the circle). The purpose of the semicircle is finite, for within it is the potential for the growth of all classes and types of manifestation. The semicircle is the Mother Soul, providing for all kinds of being, the form surrounding the spark of Life of the Father Spirit. For example, it is the REALM of the vegetable kingdom which produces the tree which contains the Life of the Absolute.

C. The Cross: Matter

The cross is symbolic of the physical plane of manifestation. It is the result of the interplay between the Spirit of the circle and the Soul of the semicircle. It is the actual wood, roots, leaves, and bark of the tree. In terms of human life, we could say that the sperm represents the Father Spirit (○); the egg (which is entered and activated by the sperm and in turn surrounds it) represents the Mother Soul (☽); and the human being who is finally born out of the womb of its natural mother and onto the surface of Mother Earth (who Herself receives the spark of Life from Father Sun and produces Nature in all its forms) represents the cross.

D. The Dot

The dot stands for the aperture through which the rays of creativity pour out from the Absolute Source, the Sun. It is the symbolic point where the infinite becomes the finite. It is a beginning, a place of primary manifestation.

E. The Rod

The vertical rod stands for the authority (or force) of the Absolute. It is symbolic of a ray of the Sun (the Lord of our solar system). As a horizontal line, the rod signifies a linking of the life force existing between two separate elements or factors within a total symbological statement (for example, Pisces = ⅓).

EXERCISE.

With a compass and ruler, draw each of these symbols on a separate white index card. Quietly contemplate the symbols by looking at each card for a few minutes. After each contemplation, write down in your notebook, next to the symbol, your impression of what each one signifies.

OPTIONAL EXERCISE.

Meditate on each of the symbols, holding one after the other in your mind's eye. Relax for a few moments between symbols by taking a few deep breaths. Inhale through the nose deeply and slowly until the lungs are filled (without strain), hold the breath for a short interval, then gradually release the breath, once again *through the nose*. Some of you may wish to use a count to time your breathing. In other words, inhale to the count of four, hold the breath for four more counts, then exhale to the count of four. Your meditation should be preceded and ended by several of these deep breaths.

After meditating on these five symbols, you may wish to write down some additional impressions in your notebook. Do this, however, after you have completed the *entire* meditation.

6.

THE PLANETARY ENERGIES

We have spoken at some length about the Great Plan of Creation both in this and in other works. We have shown that the events which occur on Earth have their corresponding indicators in the "book" of the heavenly movements. The language of astrology can definitely help to decipher this celestial handwriting and make some of the Plan known.

Everything in the Universe is energy. Energy is what constitutes the matter of the atom. The apparent differences in the appearance of, let us say, water, ice, and vapor are due to their individual densities of energy. The number of possible manifestations which may crystallize as a result of the interplay of the various energies at work in the Cosmos is as infinite as is the Cosmos Itself. Astrology can help the seeker of Light to decode this seemingly impossible complex world of energy in which he lives. It does this by giving the student a system which neatly categorizes almost all phases of Man's existence through the use of universally applicable symbols. Ten of these major life principles at work in your life and mine are represented by the *planets*.

What is the nature of the physical relationship which exists between the planets and the Earth? It is quite obvious that the Sun affects life on Earth. As for the Moon, it is well known that she is directly responsible for the ebb and flow of the tides. In addition, says the astrologer, our Moon's twenty-eight-day cycle is related to a woman's menstrual period and to the rhythm of labor pains in childbirth. Sociologists and criminologists have shown that more crimes of violence are committed during a full moon than at any other time of the month. This datum corroborates the astrological dictum that the Moon is directly associated with Man's emotional nature.

The Moon is so close to us—a mere quarter of a million miles away—that it becomes plausible, even for the most diligent skeptic, to believe in her influence on the world of Nature. But what of Venus, for example? Can she send "rays" of energy to the Earth which are received by Man and Nature as direct influences on behavior? Can Pluto, located some 3,500 million miles from Earth, affect the destinies of nations and the lives of individuals?

The offered explanation will make a great deal of sense to those who are metaphysically oriented but who might like some rational reassurance added to their intuition. What follows will already be familiar to people who have some background in yoga, especially those branches known as Hatha and Kundalini.

The human organism is constructed as an exact miniature duplicate of the solar system.[1] The outer framework of the body corresponds to the signs of the Zodiac—that great, celestial circle within which all the planets and their moons have their orbits about the Sun. Thus the first sign, Aries, corresponds to the head of the body, with its physical features and psychological traits. The nature of an Aries individual is to leap head-first into life's opportunities. He is known to be quite headstrong and, when upset, is prone to pressure at the temples and to headaches. Pisces, the last sign of the Zodiac, rules the feet, and correspondingly, Pisces individuals absorb all the shocks of walking through life and are therefore extremely sensitive and universal

---

[1] Since most of Mankind is ignorant of the Law of Correspondences, it was erroneously thought that the biblical statement "Man was made in the image of God" was a literal description of Divinity. This belief has, of course, contributed to the continuation of the personification of the Absolute (in the West) as usually a man with a white beard sitting on a throne of gold and precious jewels. In the coming age, this view will be gradually clarified as Man's level of consciousness expands to a point at which he can conceptualize Divinity in less physical terms. The truth is that Man is really made in the image of his Universe, and the study of astrology allows the student to appreciate this statement in its actual context.

in their outlook. Diagram 4 will clarify the total relationship of the body to the signs.

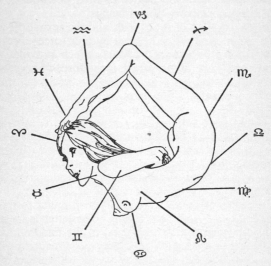

Diagram 4: The Signs and the Parts of the Body.

The internal organs and the circulatory systems of the body are ruled by the planets.[2] This seems logical because their orbits lie within the boundaries of the Zodiac of Signs. But there is another very important series of organs which, if judged by their size, would appear insignificant—the endocrine glands. In fact, they serve as the actual receptacles for the flow of planetary magnetism, rays, waves, or vibrations into the human organism. In short, *the endocrine glands are the physical connection between the planets and Man.* Chart 1 reveals the functional relationships existing between the glands and the planets.

Two glands deserve our special attention—the

---

[2] The terms *ruled* and *governed* are quite important. They signify that the planet, sign, or house mentioned is closely linked with a certain object, type of person, occupation, and so on. These sympathetic relationships are of the utmost importance to horoscope interpretation.

gonads and the pineal (corresponding to the planets Uranus and Neptune respectively). These two bodies operate to a very small degree of their potential in the consciousness of most human beings.

The functioning of the gonads and the sexual process seems to be primarily influenced by four forces: Venus, which stimulates sensuality; Mars, which provides the passion and drive; Pluto, which is the force of regeneration; and Uranus, which provides the creative inspiration. The creative urge manifests itself differently in each person. For some it can be expressed as pure lust (Mars). For others it can be felt as the desire to merge the Self with the infinitely loftier planes of creative consciousness, thus becoming an instrument for the resultant outpouring of energy. It is this latter principle which is at work in the lives of priests, nuns, religious hermits, and other consecrated persons.

The pineal gland should already be familiar to many under the name "The Third Eye." The latter is located within the brain, behind the eyes, in the middle of the forehead. The proper and complete development of this gland (in addition, of course, to the others) corresponds to a state of universal consciousness which can lead Man to total "perfection"—that is, the highest state of Being which can be manifested in human form. The pineal is associated with highly developed clairvoyance and is as yet a largely unrealized evolutionary potential. *It is the rate and quality of attunement of these two glands to their corresponding planetary force fields and their resultant activation and secretion which is directly related to the degree of personal consciousness (evolution) in each individual.*

By presenting the heavenly bodies in pairs (except for Mercury and Pluto), it will be seen that each planetary body in a given couple complements the nature of the other. The study of the planets (and the signs, for that matter) as they relate to each other in pairs will also bring the reader in touch with another of the cosmic Laws—Polarity. Polarity refers to the creative force field existing between all dualisms in life. Thus it can be seen that the nature of Polarity is omnipresent, for outside of the realm of the Absolute

Chart 1: The planets and the endocrine glands.[a]

Name of Gland	Biological function	Planet [b]	Significance in Horoscope	Organs ruled
thymus	general growth	Sun	integrates all parts of chart; indicator of general state of health, stamina, well-being.	heart
pancreas	digestion, assimilation of food	Moon	urge for self-preservation; regulator of instinctual behavior; storehouse of memory; emotional nature.	breasts, stomach
thyroid	respiration	Mercury	speech; communication; general mental agility and adaptability to circumstances.	lungs, larynx
parathyroid	regulator of metabolism of chemical balancing agents: lime and phosphorous; blood circulations; tissue and general body building	Venus	ability to harmonize self with others; artistic talents, i.e. the creation of form thru inspiration.	kidneys, physical magnetism
adrenals	stimulates blood pressure and production of blood sugar to prepare individual to fight or flee adverse circumstances	Mars	projector of personal desires; emotions of combat or challenge; nature of aggressive traits.	sex organs, eyes
posterior pituitary	body healing, reflexes, expansion of tissues	Jupiter	broadens mind; gives nobility in character; altruism; accentuates and enlarges any influence with which it is combined.	liver
anterior pituitary	skeletal system, reason, general mental processes	Saturn	gives sense of structure to life; gives limitations in order to strengthen; builds career objectives.	bones, teeth, skin
gonads	reproduction; creative activities; inspiration	Uranus[b]	intuitive mental processes; a type of consciousness not usually developed in ordinary Man; inventive abilities.	parts of nervous system
pineal	unknown	Neptune[c]	psychic abilities; perception in the invisible realms, highest aspects not usually developed in ordinary Man.	parts of nervous system

ONE, everything exists in a dualistic state: night-day, male-female, yin-yang, creation-destruction, right-left, up-down, positive-negative, and so on. In addition to the absolute "poles" of each Polarity, there are energies which embody the various in-between states of each pair. Thus we have twilight and dusk as well as late and early evening and late and early morning. These are only a few points existing between the absolute day of noon and the absolute night of midnight. Actually every instant constitutes a slight shift of this Polarity. The Chinese illustrate the nature of Polarity through the symbol of the yin-yang:

The statement here is that within the dualism of the manifested universe (the circle), there is always a relative amount of yang (male) force within yin (female) and vice-versa.

When we become deeply involved with another

---

a Pluto is not associated with any known endocrine gland. Its purpose is to regenerate the whole of human consciousness and raise it to increasingly finer and purer levels. It is also closely associated with the sexual processes and death.

b "(Sex) must be connected with the ultimate principle of two sexes, and their joint power of creation. And it will include all the deepest emotions which arise from this interaction, and which, besides children of the body, give rise to music, poetry, the arts, and the whole aspiration of man to create in emulation of his Maker." R. Collin, *The Theory of Celestial Influence*, p. 150.

c "The Neptune principle seems particularly associated with the *thalamus*, the spinal canal and the nervous and mental processes generally. The thalamus is a part of the brain from which optic and hearing nerves spring; it has nervous connections with the pituitary gland. In fact, the thalamus has been called the conductor of the pituitary (rhythms of growth) whereby the whole of the endocrine system is co-ordinated . . . Neptune's correspondence is with one of the subtlest and most 'refined' forces working within the mind and body of man." J. Mayo, *Astrology*, p. 41.

human being, we can see how polarity works in our
own lives. The more one interacts with another human
being, the more that person either repulses or har-
monizes with his or her partner. The force of the
polarization will either completely destroy the interchange or create a permanent third entity—the relationship itself. Even a temporary polarization between
a man and a woman on the physical level can result
in the creation of a third entity—a child.

To summarize: To conceptualize the meaning of the
planets, we shall say that they represent the WHAT of
astrology: *"What* type of celestial energy is manifesting itself through which particular heavenly body?"

QUESTIONS FOR CHAPTER 6.

1. What is meant by the word "energy"?
2. Show how the human body is a microcosm of the
   solar system.
3. What is the significance of Diagram 4?
4. What is meant by the term *ruled* in the astrological
   sense?
5. What is meant by the Law of Polarity? Give several
   examples of polarity not mentioned in the chapter.
6. What does the Chinese symbol of the yin-yang mean
   to you?
7. Explain the statement: " *'What'* is the function of
   the planets."
8. *(optional):* Contemplate the Law of Polarity for ten
   minutes and write down your impressions in your
   special notebook. In the same way, contemplate
   human sexuality.

A. The Sun and the Moon

1. The Sun: Source of Life.

a. SYMBOL.

The Sun's glyph consists of the circle with the dot
in its center. The solar disc shows the outpouring of
the force of Life (the circle) through the aperture of
the dot; thus the potential creative energy of the

Absolute emerges into manifestation. The dot also represents the creative spark of Divine Consciousness which is within each one of us, linking Man with the Source of Light and making him a co-creator in the Universal Plan.

b. PRINCIPLE: INDIVIDUALITY.

Your Individuality is the essence of your being. Most people, however, are not in true contact with their Source but are only conscious of passing thoughts and emotions. Because they do not relate these to a larger whole, they lead a life of separate moments. A person in tune with his inner Self—that is, what is symbolized by the Sun—is not fooled by a fleeting image or a passing sensation.

The Sun is also the focusing point for the integration and coordination of the many facets of one's being. In the natal horoscope, a poorly placed or weak Sun by House position or aspect often results in chronic illness and a lack of stamina as well as a general imbalance in the native's life.[3]

c. FUNCTION IN THE NATAL CHART.

The Sun is a person's Will to Be and thus the *generator* of all the energy of life. Tapping its potential gives to the person the ability to express the true Self in the exterior world and draw boundless strength from that unlimited Source. The purposes to which that strength is put is a vital determining factor of one's destiny.

The Sun is to a human as the nucleus is to the atom. Even though thoughts, emotions, and physical functions

---

[3] An understanding of the nature of planetary aspects—interrelationships—is vital to horoscope interpretation. The aspects are treated in detail in Part II.

are separate aspects of your total being, each draws energy from the *center* (Sun) in order to fulfill its particular life purpose. This center corresponds to the heart in the physical body. The Sun is also associated with the circulatory system, the spinal cord, and growth in general.

d. ASTROLOGICAL AFFINITIES AND BASIC CHARACTER TRAITS.

positive	*negative*
bountiful energy	lack of stamina
courage	lack of self-confidence
pride	ostentatiousness
generator of light	egocentricity

The Sun is also the ruler of the sign Leo and all affairs of the Fifth House. It relates to many positions of authority, such as those of magistrates, princes, and religious and spiritual leaders. In the horoscope of women, the Sun represents the men in their lives, the husband in particular. In the horoscope of both sexes, the Sun is often related to the father or father-image. The Sun is the male, activating, creative factor in everyone's chart; it is "the spark of life."

QUESTIONS.

1. In what respect is Man a "co-creator in the Universal Plan"?
2. How is the direction of one's energy directly connected to one's destiny?

OPTIONAL EXERCISES.

1. Contemplate the following statement: The Sun is to a human being as the nucleus is to the atom.
2. Meditate each day for a maximum of fifteen minutes on the phrase "the Source of your being."

2. *The Moon: Sustainer of Life.*

a. SYMBOL.

While the Sun represents the infinite creative energy available to an individual, the Moon's function is to give a *form* to that energy and to make the potential an actuality. The Moon's symbol is the crescent—the joining together of the two halves of the circle, which is now broken. One semicircle represents Divine Consciousness, while the other symbolizes human consciousness. The joining of these two forces gives rise to the *personality*. In effect, the Moon is related to all that is receptive in human nature: the behavioral instincts, feelings, the subconscious, and the storehouse of daily life experiences.

b. PRINCIPLE: PERSONALITY.

Just as the Moon goes through many phases as seen from Earth, in our daily life each one of us also goes through many phases in that we change our way of relating to outer circumstances of life depending on the stimulus. For example, we respond one way to our parents, another to a lover, another to an enemy, and so on. In short, each of us has myriad ways of self-expression. More often than not, the changes we undergo are either instinctual or socially conditioned. It is through the personality that Man's flexibility is achieved, but it also becomes necessary for the evolving being to be able to use the personality as a tool of essence (solar force) rather than identifying its transient phases as the source of the Self.

c. FUNCTION IN THE NATAL CHART.

In addition to the important significance of the lunar influence, the Moon represents domestic life and relationships with family. It stands for the mother, and in a man's chart it has a great deal to do with women in general and his wife in particular. The Moon also indicates rapport with the general public and serves to express the degree of attachment to ethnic origins and traditions.

The relative strength or weakness of the Moon in the natal chart has a direct bearing on the nature of the imagination, of sympathies, and of a sense of self-preservation. In the physical body the Moon rules the breasts, the sympathetic nervous system, and the flow of bodily secretions; it is closely associated with the female reproductive organs and cycles.

d. ASTROLOGICAL AFFINITIES AND BASIC
   CHARACTER TRAITS.

positive	*negative*
protectiveness and nurturing ability	selfishness and smothering attention
adaptability	diffusiveness
security and generosity	fear and possessiveness

The Moon is the ruler of the sign Cancer and all affairs of the Fourth House. She relates to all occupations dealing with land, food, and children and is closely connected with the ocean, its various flora and fauna, and its allied professions.

The Moon is the female, receptive factor in a person's chart—"the form of life."

QUESTIONS.

1. Why is control of the personality important to one's evolutionary development?
2. In your opinion, what are the signs in which the Moon would act most powerfully? Most poorly? Why?

OPTIONAL EXERCISES.

1. Contemplate: The Sun is the Father; the Moon, the Mother; and Man, the Child.
2. Observe the changes of your personality as you go through the next twenty-four hour period. Note these changes in your special book. Try to develop

an inner "witness" to your reactions to life around you. Try to develop an objectivity in respect to your personal feelings.

B. Mercury: Communicator of Life

a. SYMBOL.

Mercury's symbol represents the force of *active intelligence*. The circle represents the source of energy which gives life to the mind. The mind receives impulses from two directions, indicated by the cross below and the semicircle above. The former stands for Earth-bound activities and the relationship of the rational mind to its surroundings. The crescent is symbolic of the higher aspects of mind: Man's link to the truly original and inspirational. In this respect we can see how mercurial individuals fall into two broad categories—the imitator and the genius.

b. PRINCIPLE: THE RATIONAL MIND.

The rational mind is that special gift of Mankind separating him from the animal kingdom. Mercury's function is to allow Man to isolate his purely instinctual nature through the logical processes of reason. In addition, Mercury's position in the horoscope indicates a person's general ability to communicate ideas through the written or spoken word.

c. FUNCTION IN THE NATAL CHART.

Mercury stands alone, for it is dual in itself; in male signs its analytical nature predominates, while in female signs its ability to synthesize is the stronger force at work. Thus its natural rulership is over male Gemini (the idea) and female Virgo (the form the idea takes).

Mercury gives Man the need to know. It makes him ask questions and causes him to probe the external world of appearances. If Mercury is too influential a force, however, a tendency arises to prevent the higher aspects of one's being (the intuitional and psychic centers) from entering consciousness.

In the physical body Mercury is closely associated with the nervous system, the respiratory tract, and especially the lungs.

   d. ASTROLOGICAL AFFINITIES AND BASIC
      CHARACTER TRAITS.

positive	*negative*
intelligent reasoning	word traps
discrimination	nit-picking
alertness and level-headedness	nervousness and lack of sympathy

Mercury is the ruler of Gemini and Virgo and of all affairs dealing with the Third and Sixth Houses. It relates to those occupations dealing with education, travel, writing, clerical work, and all types of agents and agencies.

As the "Messenger of the (Planetary) Gods," Mercury is integrally linked to transmitting impulses from all aspects of Being to the conscious mind.

QUESTIONS.

1. Why is analysis considered a "male" function, while synthesis is a "female" one?
2. In your opinion, which are the signs in which Mercury would act most beneficially? With most difficulty? Why?

OPTIONAL EXERCISE.

1. Contemplate the symbol for Mercury until you feel that you are thoroughly familiar with the essence of its meaning.

C. Venus and Mars

1. Venus: Beauty of Life.

a. SYMBOL.

Venus' glyph is the cross surmounted by the circle. This combination of elements indicates that Spirit is inspiring matter to increasingly more perfect forms of expression. It is also representative of the predominance of higher aspirations over the material and sensual desires of Earth.

b. PRINCIPLE: ATTRACTION AND UNIFICATION.

Venus is that force within each human being which signifies the ability to attract other people as well as material possessions. It can be called *personal magnetism*. Venus attempts to "soften the edges" so that the experiences of life are made more beautiful. Venus is that aspect of the person which can be classified as the artist, the romantic, and the poet. Her vibrations work entirely through the feelings; in this respect Venus is the embodiment of love—the sentiments and the desire for union.

c. FUNCTION IN THE NATAL CHART.

Venus gives Man the need to grow both materially and spiritually, and her powers of attraction are those which lead one on a path toward continual increment. Thus a poorly placed Venus in the natal chart can give rise to difficulties in love and money. Quite often a challenging position of Venus demonstrates a need for the individual to learn the true meaning of sharing and giving.

The vibrations of Venus manifest themselves at their purest when in the sign of Pisces. It is then that selfishness is transmuted into selflessness and personal love becomes universal love.

In the physical body Venus rules the venous system, the kidneys, and the urinary tract and is associated with overall physical attractiveness.

d. ASTROLOGICAL AFFINITIES AND BASIC
   CHARACTER TRAITS.

positive	*negative*
sharing	acquisitiveness
beautification	self-indulgence
bringer of peace	laziness

Venus is the ruler of Taurus and Libra and of all affairs dealing with the Second and Seventh Houses. She relates to all occupations having to do with the arts and music as well as those fields which are associated with glamor, jewelry, and clothing design. In addition, her Taurean rulership brings Venus into close contact with plants and those occupations which relate to nature.

QUESTIONS.

1. What is the difference between personal love and universal love?
2. Why does Venus display her highest vibrations through Pisces?
3. What do you think the effects of Venus in Virgo would be like?

OPTIONAL EXERCISES.

1. Observe the type of people who are attracted to you over the course of the next week or so. What does this tell you about your own "personal magnetism"?
2. Observe the way you share material possessions (as well as your love) with others.
3. Compare the results from Exercises 1 and 2 with the position of Venus in your horoscope.

2. *Mars: Projector of Life.*

a. SYMBOL.

The glyph for Mars represents the polarity to Venus' symbol. The more ancient symbol (placed in parentheses above) reveals the cross of matter placed over the circle of Spirit, showing the tendency for the desires of the flesh to win out over higher aspirations. Thus the needs of the individual become more important than the needs of Mankind.

In its highest aspect, however, Mars represents the emergence of new forms of self-expression which result from the interplay of Spirit and matter. If wisely applied, these forms can be inspirational and point the way toward further advancement. More often than not, the influence of Mars on horoscopes in general indicates the desire to command and hold some form of power over others. In this respect the vibrations of the Red Planet can be summarized as *the active force of the ego expressing itself in the immediate environment.*

b. PRINCIPLE: PERSONAL DRIVE.

The two signs of Mars, Aries and Scorpio, are the polarities of the two signs of Venus, Libra and Taurus. Thus in a certain sense Mars is the "husband" of Venus.

Mars is the sexual drive, the urge to singularization as opposed to unification with another or with some greater cause. Mars is the need to stand out above the crowd and to make an impression on one's surroundings. Venus is the pacifist, and Mars is the war-monger. When these two bodies are harmoniously joined in the horoscope, the result is a balance of forces which, if well channeled, results in an inner understanding of when to be cooperative and when to be aggressive.

c. FUNCTION IN THE NATAL CHART.

Most people need a relatively strong (but not over-powering) Mars in their horoscopes; it gives the courage and stamina to endure the pressures of life. Mars is the urge to win and succeed. It confers the ability to strive for what one desires and, if it is especially well placed in the natal map, a facility for cutting through confusion and life's "red tape."

In its lower aspect Mars represents what is animal in Man—base emotional drives and instinctive aggression. In its higher aspect Mars is that part of the Self whose function it is to create new forms of creativity through the destruction of whatever is no longer useful.

In the physical body Mars rules the red corpuscles, the external male reproductive organs, the nose, the musculature tissues, and the excretory tract.

d. ASTROLOGICAL AFFINITIES AND BASIC
   CHARACTER TRAITS.

positive	*negative*
dynamic energy	manipulation
courage	cowardice
sexual drive	sexual abuse

Mars is the predominant ruler of Aries and the co-ruler of Scorpio; it also has a great deal to do with the affairs of the Eighth House and especially the First House. It relates to all occupations dealing with war and the use of sharp tools and weapons, as well as some forms of research and surgery.

QUESTIONS.

1. Compare the symbols of Mars and Venus. How are they antagonistic to each other? How do they complement each other?
2. Why is the direction of sexual energy so closely related to destiny?
3. Why is Mars the ruler of both the organs of generation and excretion?

MEDITATION EXERCISE (OPTIONAL).

1. Contemplate the relationship between the lower Self
and the higher Self and the process of the transmutation of energy needed to integrate the former into
the latter.

D. Jupiter and Saturn

1. Jupiter: The Wisdom of Life.

  a. SYMBOL.

The giant planet's glyph is composed of the semicircle of the Moon (=soul) rising above the cross of
matter. Jupiter represents that stage in Man's development in which the soul has triumphed over its experiences on Earth (the cross) and has obtained
through these experiences the wisdom which imparts
the understanding of Universal Law as it applies to
terrestrial life. Through the rays of Jupiter, Man is
liberated from personal and restrictive opinions so that
he can act impartially out of his understanding of
Truth.

  b. PRINCIPLE: EXPANSION.

The rays of Zeus-Jupiter manifest themselves through
the mind of Man and help to create the desire for
the expansion of the Self on two levels. As Man is
basically dualistic—that is, composed of an animal
self which binds him to Earth and an active Spirit
self that inspires him toward "the heavens"—Jupiter's
rays also work dually. They can therefore contribute

to someone's desire to explore the realms of the five senses and/or provide a person with the mind of a philosopher. They can contribute to unrestrained sensual activity or produce the teacher seeking to expand the faculties of understanding so that the Great Plan may be comprehended and taught to others.

c. FUNCTION IN THE NATAL CHART.

In addition to its ability to develop the higher mental attributes, Jupiter, like Venus, is a planet of general good fortune. If it is well placed in the horoscope, it can bestow great material abundance. If poorly placed, however, it can signify a wastrel and a completely self-indulgent individual. Jupiter's rays can create a philanthropist, but when these rays are perverted, greed and avarice result. Jupiter can bless its recipient with an understanding of the deeper significances of life, especially those gained through travel and higher education. If, however, such people do not have a cohesive or higher purpose for their studies or travels, Jupiter can help to produce wanderers and dilettantes.

In the physical body Jupiter is closely associated with the liver, the hip joints, and the posterior pituitary gland, as well as with cell nutrition in general.

d. ASTROLOGICAL AFFINITIES AND BASIC CHARACTER TRAITS.

positive	negative
expansion	waste
religiosity	hypocrisy
wisdom through understanding	opinionatedness

Jupiter is the ruler of Sagittarius and co-ruler of Pisces. It is also closely related to the affairs of the Ninth and Twelfth Houses (especially with the religious and altruistic aspects of the latter). Jupiter is connected with all occupations dealing with the law, religion, higher education, banking, and international finance.

QUESTIONS.

1. Compare the significance of Mercury with that of Jupiter. What are some of the differences between these two bodies in respect to their functions in the mental realm?
2. In your opinion, in which of the twelve signs would Jupiter be most beneficial? Least so?
3. The asteroid belt separates Jupiter from Mars, Earth, Moon, Venus, Mercury, and the Sun. What symbolic significance do you see in this separation?

EXERCISE (OPTIONAL).

1. After drawing the symbol for Jupiter on a blank index card (preferably in purple ink), contemplate it and write down your thoughts in your notebook.

2. *Saturn: Limitations of Life.*

   a. SYMBOL.

Saturn's glyph is composed of the same two elements as Jupiter's, but the two parts of the symbol are inverted. Thus it can be seen that it is through the lessons of Saturn that Man is taught how to harmonize his imagination (the semicircle) with the immediate circumstances of his life (the cross). Saturn's rays relate to the Earth. They demand that one pass through the tests of material existence before being allowed to enter into the realm of the Soul and the resultant exalted state of consciousness.

Saturn also serves Man in the role of Satan the

Tempter. When the vibrations of Saturn-Satan combine with an egocentric personality, people often trade (the state of being associated with) their Souls for material possessions and temporal powers. In this respect Saturn is symbolic of the structure of values which lead to evolutionary growth. Thus Saturn is the "bridge" between the forces of universal consciousness—the extra-Saturnian planets (Uranus, Neptune, and Pluto)—and the forces of material existence and the personal Self— the inter-Saturnian planets.

b. PRINCIPLE: STRUCTURE AND CONSOLIDATION.

Saturn is the Teacher who says: "Listen, my young friend. Before you can go on to the sixth step in your growth, you must grasp the essence of the fifth step. In order to expand your consciousness or material worth or social positions, you must first learn the structure of the Laws of the Universe, the principles of economics, and the patterns of the culture in which you live."

c. FUNCTION IN THE NATAL CHART.

Saturn has been much maligned through a misunderstanding of its purpose. It has been called the "greater malific" and, like Satan, has been made the scapegoat of Man's unregenerated energies. But Saturn and Satan are simply the forms projected by the temptations of the lower self. *It is by generating enough strength to overcome such temptations through self-discipline and the limitation and redirection of desire that the evolutionary progress occurs.*

This concentration on polarity—"God" versus "Satan," "good" versus "evil"—only strengthens disharmony. One of Man's tasks is to enter upon a plane of consciousness which is free of duality, so that he may see the unity and harmony in the structure of the Universal Plan. Then he will understand that the apparent dichotomy between so-called good and evil is just a tool which may lead to a state of perfect balance transcending both poles. In this respect Man must understand the function of Saturn in the horoscope.

In a more pragmatic sense, Saturn forces the fulfillment of obligations and responsibilities, so that personal growth may occur. Its position by sign, House, and aspect points the way to these necessary lessons and the degree and nature of self-discipline or its lack.

In the physical body Saturn rules the skin, knees, teeth, and bones and is closely connected with the organs of hearing.

d. ASTROLOGICAL AFFINITIES AND BASIC
CHARACTER TRAITS.

positive	negative
helpful limitations	needless restraints
understanding of structure	too much calculation
self-discipline	a certain "tightness"
common sense	a lack of human feelings

Saturn is the ruler of Capricorn and co-ruler of Aquarius. It is also associated with the affairs of the Tenth and Eleventh Houses. Saturn relates to all occupations dealing with the building trades and architecture, as well as with banking, finance, government workers, and supervisory personnel.

QUESTIONS.

1. What lessons would a person have to learn if, in the natal chart, Saturn were interchanging its rays with Venus? Mars? the Moon?
2. In your opinion, what are the best signs for Saturn? The worst placements?

EXERCISES (OPTIONAL).

1. Contemplate the differences between the symbols of Saturn and Jupiter, and enter your thoughts in your notebook.
2. Mediate upon the area(s) of your life which need additional self-discipline. Compare your thoughts in this matter with the position of Saturn in your natal horoscope.

E. Uranus and Neptune

Once we pass the orbit of Saturn, we come across the three planets of "the higher octave." Briefly stated, the energy contained within the vibrations of Uranus, Neptune, and Pluto represents those cosmic forces which affect the whole of Mankind in a general sense but which do not necessarily manifest themselves in a personal sense in the lives of each individual.[4]

1. Uranus: Awakener of Life.

a. SYMBOL.

The glyph for Uranus tells us that the planet's vibrations contain the link connecting the Soul of the individual (one semicircle) with the collective Soul of Mankind (the other semicircle). The two semicircles are placed on either side of the cross—signifying that the joining of the personal consciousness with that of the greater collective leads to development on Earth (the cross) which will aid in Man's higher evolution (the little circle of the Spirit).

b. PRINCIPLE: INTUITIONAL FACULTIES OF THE MIND.

Uranus shows the way the individual may become liberated from the bondage of the personality. In this respect personal enlightenment can be attained through the conscious incorporation of being into the consciousness of the entity called collectively Man. This connection ultimately leads to an even greater realm of consciousness, and so on without end.

c. FUNCTION IN THE NATAL CHART.

In addition to the intuitional principle, Uranus also functions in an individual's life to point the way to

[4] See *As Above, So Below*, chaps. 28–30.

THE PLANETARY ENERGIES 57

particular forms of original self-expression. People who are especially Uranian are the bohemians of society. In a generational sense, we can see the rays of Uranus strongly at work among the so-called New Age, post-World War II people. A great many people in this group consider the more unconventional the forms of one's self-expression, the more desirable.

The rise in the interest in the occult sciences among the general public of all ages, as well as the vast numbers of sincere students of these disciplines, are other Uranian manifestations. We could also list as Uranian the experiences gained through the collective life style of the many different communes which have recently sprung up across this and other countries. On a personal level, however, the vibrations of Uranus appear in very few nativities. When they do, they tend to produce the truly original inventor, artist, technician, and occultist—someone whose contribution stands out above the world's present "stand-out" crowd. In short, a real "superstar" is born.

In the physical body Uranus is associated with the electrical impulses of the nervous system.

  d. ASTROLOGICAL AFFINITIES AND BASIC
     CHARACTER TRAITS.

positive	negative
originality	eccentricity
inventiveness	erraticness
intuition	irrationality
social reform	anarchism

Uranus, the ruler of Aquarius, is closely associated with affairs of the Eleventh House. It relates to all occupations dealing with computers, broadcasting, rocket technology, social welfare, aviation, and many professions which have yet to be developed within the aforementioned areas.

QUESTIONS.

1. In your opinion, what would be the effects of the vibrations of Uranus if they were to interchange in

a positive sense with those of Venus? The Moon? The Sun?

2. What is the relationship between Mercury and Uranus? How are they alike? In what ways do they differ?

EXERCISE (OPTIONAL).

1. Contemplate the relationship between personal conciousness and collective consciousness.

2. *Neptune: Inspiration of Life.*

   a. SYMBOL.

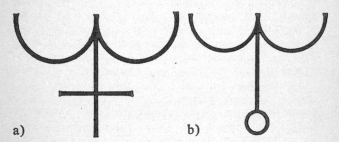

a)   b)

Glyph *a* depicts the trident of Father Neptune and is composed of the semicircle of the soul pierced by the cross of matter, resulting in the three-pronged fork. The prongs represent (1) the physical body and the five senses; (2) the astral or emotional body and its desires; and (3) the lower mental sphere and its egocentric thoughts.

The vibrations of Neptune allow these three areas to become more sensitized, so that one may elevate these spheres of one's being to a more refined level or run the risk of becoming inundated by the undertow of unregenerated energy.

In variation *b* of Neptune's trident, the semicircle is pierced by the staff of life so that personality is freed from egocentric motivations and allowed to work in cooperation with Spirit (the little circle). Thus we can see in this glyph the infusion of higher consciousness which produces the mystical visions (or hallucinations) associated with this planet.

b. PRINCIPLE: UNIVERSAL LOVE AND THE PERFECTION OF VALUES.

As the higher octave of Venus, Neptune also works on the emotional level. But unlike its more personal sister, Neptune loves for the sake of loving and not for the motivations of return (or shared experience), which are so much a part of the rays of Venus. Neptune teaches that it is through pure and unselfish love that Man is transformed into "The Christ." By "The Christ" we do not necessarily mean Lord Jesus the Christ, nor do we mean Lord Krishna the Christ, nor Lord Moses the Christ, nor Lord Buddha the Christ, nor any other specific Being of this Title. "The Christ" is the name given to an individual Soul which has achieved a state of Perfection—that is, *the highest form which the God Force can take when incarnated in the human form.*

c. FUNCTION IN THE NATAL CHART.

In most cases Neptune cannot show its highest vibrations in a personal sense. Its influence on the horoscopes of the vast majority of people is just to sensitize the area of the horoscope in which it is placed according to the nature of its position. If its placement is in disharmony with other planets, signs, or other important points in the natus, Neptune's vibration will invert and cause unnecessary secretiveness and deception. At its worst, Neptune is the embodiment of illusions, obsessions, and hallucinations. In this respect it is noteworthy that Neptune rules alcohol; tobacco; and drugs in general, especially marijuana, LSD, and the other hallucinogens.

When active in its positive polarity, Neptune raises and sensitizes everything it touches and makes it much more subtle. It inspires artistic and musical creativity, as well as adding vision to all aspects of film work. At its highest, Neptune produces the true mystics of the world as well as great clairvoyants, mediums, and other individuals who are in touch with the Masters and the Teachers. Edgar Cayce, for example, was strongly influenced by the rays of this planet (see chap. 26).

Neptune rules the pineal gland and those parts of the nervous system which respond to psychic impressions.

d. ASTROLOGICAL AFFINITIES AND BASIC CHARACTER TRAITS.

positive	*negative*
mystical visions	delusions
wide scope of perception	craftiness
artistic bent	self-dramatizations

Neptune is the ruler of Pisces and is closely connected with the affairs of the Twelfth House. It relates to all occupations dealing with film, dance, drugs, oils, cosmetics, and the ocean. It is also associated with smugglers, healers, black and white magicians, psychics, and psychiatric workers.

QUESTIONS.

1. What effect do you think Neptune would have on an individual if it were placed in close proximity to one's Moon? Sun? Mercury?
2. What is the relationship between Uranus and Neptune? How do they basically differ?

EXERCISES (OPTIONAL).

1. Meditate on the "Christ Principle."
2. Study the teachings of each of the Master Christs mentioned in this section. Try to relate Their lessons to the socioeconomic and historical situations in which They appeared.

F. Pluto: The Transformer of Life

a. SYMBOL.

Glyph *a* combines the first two letters in PLuto and the initials of the astronomer who is credited with having made the calculations leading to Pluto's discovery,

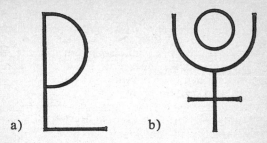

a)   b)

Percival Lowell. The glyph itself is simply a convenience.

Symbol *b* expresses the entire concept of the regenerative processes of involution and evolution. The circle of Spirit (during the involutionary process) emits its rays of life, which are then encased by the receptive nature of the soul (semicircle). The rays descend further, until they reach the plane of the Earth, where they manifest into a particular physical form (the cross). In the reverse evolutionary process the experiences of physical life cause an awakening in consciousness. These realizations are assimilated in the soul and then transmuted into the ethers of the Spirit, where they are integrated. Then they are sent back down again through involution to further energize and develop the Earth, Nature, and Man.

b. PRINCIPLE: REGENERATION.

The processes of involution and evolution are continuous and will not cease on this planet until all the kingdoms of life have achieved the perfection of consciousness of their particular form. Until that time, Man and all other creatures will die and be reborn. In this process the weak and unnecessary strains of life are transformed into the stronger and more ideal. Thus every generation of humanity is an experiment in consciousness, as is every individual. Man is able to alter his destiny by the direction he gives to the power he obtains through his consciousness. If he wishes to create mutations and pollutants, he may do so; but he must bear the weight of these created states by the return flow of Karma.

Mars, Pluto's lower octave, paves the way for

change, but Pluto is the force which transforms the atomic structure of life so that the various energy particles can regroup into their new form. Mars may represent the sexual desire of the couple, but it is the force of Pluto which unites the sperm and the egg at conception to produce the embryo.

c. FUNCTION IN THE NATAL CHART.

As with the other two trans-Saturnian planets, Pluto's vibrations are not consciously felt or used by the vast majority of individuals for personal reasons. Its purpose is to provide the energy which causes the breakdown of certain psychological blocks preventing evolutionary growth. For example, Pluto combined in a negative sense with the Moon can indicate that those relationships having to do with one's ethnic roots, mother, or women in general can be traumatic. The combination may also indicate a difficulty in breaking out of certain fears in the expression and integration of the Self in any given social environment.

On the other hand, when Pluto is working in a positive sense, it serves to bring about a regenerative force to the area in the horoscope in which it is placed or to the planets with which it is joined. For example, if Pluto is well situated with Jupiter, it can signify the ability to update or revitalize certain doctrines and philosophies. It can also mean that the person will experience some uplifting or even transcendental events through foreign journeys or higher studies.

Pluto's effects may seem to manifest themselves with sudden explosiveness, but like the volcano, the forces of the eruption have been gathering momentum for a long time before they culminate in a lava flow.

In the physical body Pluto seems linked to the general regenerative faculties of the cells and with the processes of the reproductive organs.

d. ASTROLOGICAL AFFINITIES AND BASIC
   CHARACTER TRAITS.

Pluto is the ruler of Scorpio and closely associated with the affairs of the Eighth House. It is also related to the First House and to Aries. It is involved with occupations having to do with all forms of underground work, such as work in mines, caves, and subways as

positive	*negative*
transformer	annihilator
tension eliminator	overforceful explosions
agent of evolutionary forces	destroyer of old forms

well as the activities of spies, detectives, and crime syndicates. Pluto's energy is also at work through the transforming abilities of psychic healers.

QUESTIONS.

1. What are the major differences and similarities between Pluto and Mars?
2. Why do you suppose Pluto is associated with both mining and the criminal underground?

EXERCISES (OPTIONAL).

1. Meditate on the processes of evolution and involution.
2. Contemplate the regenerative principle as it occurs in conception and death.

G. The Moon's Nodes

In addition to the positions of the ten planets, the astrologer usually considers many other sensitive points in a given horoscope in order to make a complete assessment of its factors. Two of these are the Northern and Southern Nodes of the Moon. The Nodes indicate the point in space where the Moon crosses the ecliptic (the Earth's orbit around the Sun) from north to south and vice versa. The Northern Node (☊), also called the Dragon's Head, is considered a point which brings about positive increments. It is associated with the nature of Venus and Jupiter. The Southern Node (☋), also called the Dragon's Tail, is thought of as a vibration which teaches some important restrictive lessons. It is more in keeping with the nature of Saturn. These two points travel backward through the Zodiac and are always exactly opposite one another in such a way that if the Northern Node were at 26° ♉ 30′, the Southern Node would be found at 26° ♏ 30′.

There is a great difference of opinion among astrologers as to the actual implications of the Nodes. This writer has found that they are *points of connection*. When interpreting the Nodes, the whole horoscope must be taken into consideration, but in general it can be said that if the Northern Node is rising, for example, an individual usually meets the right people at the right time and has a great deal of personal charisma (John Lennon has it exactly conjunct his Ascendant). The Southern Node shows connections or attitudes which have to be worked out, so that there is a flowing vibration to the area in the chart in which it is placed. In the Seventh House it indicates that one must not depend too much on one's partners nor on the ease with which one makes personal relationships. It indicates that special care must be taken not to abuse people and to rely on one's own efforts in life.

The Northern Node in the Second House and the Southern in the Eighth signify an ease in attracting wealth, but one should avoid abusing connections in this respect and not depend too much on other people's material resources.

The House position (see chap. 9) of the Nodes indicates the area in one's life in which their activities take place. The sign positions (see chap. 7) reveal the means or vehicles of expression through which the Nodes manifest their connection-making functions.

EXERCISE (OPTIONAL).

On a blank index card, place the symbol for the Sun and contemplate it. Do the same for each of the planets. Repeat as often as you wish. Observe how your comprehension of the planetary forces increases and deepens.

7.

THE ZODIACAL PRINCIPLES

As the various planetary energies represent "The WHAT of Astrology," the signs can be said to symbolize "The HOW of Astrology": *how* does the celestial energy of the planets manifest itself, and *how* is this energy modified as it travels through the zodiacal force field to Earth?

I. CATEGORIES

There are three basic categories from which all the signs draw their characteristics: elements (triplicity), qualities (quadriplicity), and gender.[1]

A. The Elements

1. Fire (Aries, Leo, Sagittarius). Fire expresses itself through dynamic creativity. It serves to stimulate and project the planetary energy made manifest through it.

2. Earth (Taurus, Virgo, Capricorn). Earth expresses itself through practicality, depth, and stability. It serves to stabilize, crystallize, and nurture the planetary energy manifested through it.

3. Air (Gemini, Libra, Aquarius). Air is the element of communication and human interaction. It serves to connect, disseminate, and spark intellectual movement

---

[1] A more detailed portrait of the categories can be found in *As Above, So Below*, chaps. 5 and 6.

in the planetary energy which manifests itself through it.

4. Water (Cancer, Scorpio, Pisces). Water is the element of the emotional plane of being. It tends to lend sensitivity (often about the unseen), resourcefulness, and inspiration to the planetary energies made manifest through it.

B. Qualities

1. Cardinal (Aries, Cancer, Libra, Capricorn). The Cardinal signs serve as *generators* of activity. They are usually self-motivated, ambitious, and precipitating activity.

2. Fixed (Taurus, Leo, Scorpio, Aquarius). The Fixed signs serve as *concentrators* of energy. All four of these zodiacal designations give determination of purpose and stability to the energy manifest through them.

3. Mutable (Gemini, Virgo, Sagittarius, Pisces). The Mutable or common signs serve to *transfer* energy. They lend changeability, versatility, and resourcefulness to the planetary energies working through them.

C. Gender

The law of duality permeates all of created life. Thus we have two sexes on Earth and in the Zodiac. In this respect all fire and air signs are said to be male—outgoing, self-expressive and centrifugal. All earth and water signs, on the other hand, are said to be female—indrawing, self-repressive, and centripetal in nature.

QUESTIONS.

1. What reaction do you think would result from mixing:
   a. fire and earth; fire and air; fire and water?

    b. earth and air; earth and water?
    c. air and water?

2. In what way are the seasonal changes of the year related to the Cardinal signs? the Fixed signs? the Mutable signs?

EXERCISES.

1. Take out several horoscope blanks and draw connecting lines between all the signs in the same element. Use a different color for each of the triplicities (red = fire; green = earth; yellow = air; blue = water). Study the resultant forms.

2. Do the same for the qualities (red = Cardinal; green = Fixed; yellow = Mutable; or choose colors you feel are appropriate). Study the resultant forms.

3. Connect all the positive signs; connect all the negative signs. Study the resultant forms and compare.

II. THE POLARITIES

The twelve signs can also be divided into two broad categories: those signs from Aries to Virgo, which represent the personal sphere of life's activities, and those from Libra through Pisces, which represent the social or universal sphere.

By presenting the signs in their pairs of polarities, I hope to demonstrate the relationship between these two primary directions.

Remember that this material concerns the nature of the signs and does not apply to individuals born under any of the twelve designations unless specifically stated.

A. Aries-Libra

1. Aries (Cardinal, Fire, Positive). The inspirational activity of fire works through a strong motivational outward force when it is manifested through Aries.

    a. SYMBOL (♈). All the symbols of the signs are formed pictographically and ideographically. The pictograph corresponds to the part of the human body to which each sign correlates, while the ideograph is the

emblem of the *principle of energy* embodied by the
sign. When we look at the symbol for Aries, we see that
the two semicircles represent the eyebrows, and the
line between them is the nose of the human face. Since
Aries is the sign ruling the head, Aries individuals like
to be at the head of all their undertakings (or anyone
else's, for that matter). In the same sense, a very apt
adjective for Aries or Aries energy would be "headstrong," and, of course, this glyph also represents the
Ram's head.

Ideographically this symbol is a fountain, representative of the tremendous outpouring of life force inherent in the first sign.

b. PRINCIPLE: BEGINNINGS. In the northern hemisphere the month of Aries coincides with the commence-
ment of spring; the buds are on the trees, but they
have not matured into leaves. Thus Aries is full of
potential creativity without the stability of completion.
In other words, Aries may embody a strong thrust but
a poor delivery.

c. THE ARIES INDIVIDUAL. An Aries is always seeking some form of activity that will allow some form of
self-projection upon the immediate environment. Aries
people are well liked because they stimulate others to
action and sow the seeds which other people may successfully cultivate. Those born under Aries like to stand
out in a crowd or even lead the crowd. They are eager
and ambitious to achieve their goals, though they often
lack the necessary patience when working with people.
They have a very poor sense of any method and
rhythm other than their own and can often find themselves in difficult straits as a result of pushing their
desires upon other individuals with little or no tact
or timing. "Now" is the Aries word, and it is said with
great urgency and emphasis.

d. HIGHER ASPIRATIONS. Aries is the pioneer who
paves the way for other people's growth. In so doing,
he may often be the sacrificial lamb who donates his
efforts and inspirational thoughts to the well-being of
the human race.

e. KEY PHRASE: I AM, THEREFORE I AM.

f. KEY WORDS:

positive	negative
courageous	rash and foolhardy
inspiring	overbearing
trailblazing	opportunistic
life-initiating	egotistical

2. *Libra (Cardinal, Air, Positive).* The connective intellectual aspects of air express themselves in Libra through personal activity and outward social aggressiveness.

a. SYMBOL (≏). As the midpoint of the Zodiac, Libra corresponds to the middle of the body—the diaphram (‿) and the navel (∿). Ideographically Libra is the scales of balance: the joining of forces between thought and the manifestation of that thought in a physical form. Thus the Libran is constantly at work trying to balance the ideal with the real.

b. PRINCIPLE: HARMONY OR SHARED ACTIVITIES. As Aries is the beginning of spring, so Libra represents the beginning of fall. This symbolizes a turning point in development, for if Aries is the entrance of the individual into the creation of a personal life structure, Libra shows the transition into a social structure. This is why Aries is most concerned with self-initiated activities, while Libra is most concerned with cooperative ventures. Thus, while Aries has no difficulty in making individual decisions, Libra has a tremendous indecisiveness in this respect. The motivating drive of Libran activities is *Perfection In Action.*

c. THE LIBRA INDIVIDUAL. The Libran is a sociable, well-liked, well-meaning person always eager to please. In this respect Librans often run into difficulty, since it is impossible to please everyone all the time. Libra has the ability to bring out talent in others and to coordinate these special characteristics for the greatest mutual satisfaction. In short, the individual born in Libra is the matchmaker of the Zodiac, whether he exercises this talent with people, places, or objects.

The Scales are ruled by Venus, the goddess of love, and as such Librans find it extremely difficult to make it through life without a partner. Libra has the tendency to put loved ones on an ethereal pedestal, idealizing

the "other half." This form of image-making is a result
of Librans' tendency to see themselves through their
partners. They are therefore deeply crushed when their
selected god or goddess turns out to be mortal like
themselves.

Librans must take care not to fall into a pattern of
dependency on other people's energies or ability to
make decisions. Libra can learn incisiveness from
Aries, while the latter can certainly benefit from
Libra's tact and cooperative nature.

d. HIGHER ASPIRATIONS. Librans can develop into
the most objective and impartial of individuals. They
can infuse peace and beauty into all people with whom
they come into contact and grace their environment
with the beautiful rays of Aphrodite.

e. KEY PHRASE: WE ARE, THEREFORE I AM.

f. KEY WORDS:

positive	*negative*
helpful and charming	manipulative and false
unifying	dependent
"how may we best work together?"	"be cooperative, do things my way!"
easy-going but aspiring	lazy and parasitical

B. Taurus-Scorpio

1. Taurus (Fixed, Earth, Negative). The stability and
practicality of Earth is expressed through Taurus with
great determination and depth of understanding.

a. SYMBOL (♉). The more stylized symbol for
Taurus (♉) clearly shows the shoulders and neck,
those parts of the anatomy associated with the second
sign. The more modern symbol (♉) reveals the idea
behind this glyph: as the circle represents the fullness
of life, so Taurus grows through its ability to take in
nourishment and material resources from its environment. Naturally all symbols for Taurus are representa-
tions of the head of a bull.

b. PRINCIPLE: STABILITY. Taurus represents the

natural urge to preserve and amass the wealth of Creation. It falls during the second month of spring, that period in which Nature is in full bloom. Taurus is therefore identified with the potential bounty of the land and the strong generative force inherent in springtime.

c. THE TAURUS INDIVIDUAL. If Aries is the pioneer out to discover new lands to conquer, Taurus is the settler. Aries sows the seeds, but Taurus makes sure that they are properly planted, watered, and protected. In this respect Taureans are very security-conscious and feel most comfortable when they know that what they have is truly theirs. They can become wholly subject to this natural tendency, putting all their energy into the amassing of wealth and material possessions. Taurus is also a child of Venus, but the difference between Libra and Taurus is that, while Libra dreams about beauty, Taurus works to obtain it. Both Libra and Taurus can be lazy; in Libra this is due to indecisiveness and the fear of hurting someone by any direct activity, while in Taurus this inertia stems from a fear of upsetting existing circumstances (the principle of Taurus, fixed-earth, being *stability*). Venus gives romantic rays to both of its signs. In Libra this results in a flirtatious manner, although the true desire is for the ideal partner. Taurus also seeks a prince(ss) charming, but with a much more realistic attitude about love; it will usually choose loyalty, devotion, and material security over the promise of a storybook romance.

d. HIGHER ASPIRATIONS. In its highest essence Taurus can be Mother Nature, bestowing bounty and beauty upon the children of the Earth. Through its stabilizing vibrations Taurus helps to bring roots to the rootless and love to the loveless.

e. KEY PHRASE: I HAVE, THEREFORE I AM.

f. KEY WORDS:

positive	*negative*
preserving	acquisitive
self-sustaining	greedy
nurturing	selfish
loyal	possessive

2. *Scorpio (Fixed, Water, Negative)*. The waters of
Scorpio emerge through its fixity like ice which melts
into creative expression through the release of its
regenerative forces. The emotional resourcefulness of
Scorpio works in surreptitious ways to bring about the
fulfillment of desire.

a. SYMBOL (♏). The symbol is a pictograph of the
erect male sexual organ. The coils in the first part of
the glyph represent the tension and potential force
prior to orgasm. It is also a picture of the scorpion and
its tail, ready to attack. Ideographically the Scorpio
symbol shows the regenerative nature of the life forces
available to Scorpio, just as sperm is constantly manu-
factured by the testes. The key to Scorpio's power
rests in the timing and degrees of intensity of the release of this potential.

b. PRINCIPLE: REGENERATION. The month of
Scorpio occurs with the complete defoliation of autumn.
It would seem that all is barren. The leaves have fallen
to the ground, but they will soon decompose to form
the nutrients which will seep back into the Earth and
provide the nourishment from which the tree will sustain its life. Trees, as all forms of Nature, are under
the general rulerships of Taurus. The external manifestation of the recycling of life in the tree will show
itself as the budding leaves of Aries (Mars' other
sign).

c. THE SCORPIO INDIVIDUAL. Taurus is representative of personal resources, usually meaning wealth in
terms of money, land, and possessions. Scorpio is connected with other people's resources. As Libra is the
turning point from *Personal Man* to *Man in Society*,
so Scorpio is concerned with the collective resources
of that society.

Scorpio is a water sign, and on an individual level
Scorpians draw from other people the vital life force
which they then use for their own purposes. There are
three basic Scorpio types: the Scorpion, the Eagle,
and the Dove. The Scorpion is the lowest of these.
Totally self-seeking, he uses his tremendous personal
magnetism, insight, and sensitivity to build his own
success, despite the cost to others.

The Eagle type possesses an objectivity which permits him to soar above the web of emotional entanglements so that he may peer into the heart of any matter. He can rekindle another person's potential creativity through subtle stimulation and cooperative efforts. The Eagle will use another person's resources for personal gain, but such use will also bring mutual benefits.

The Dove is a very rare type indeed. In the Catholic tradition the Dove is a symbol for the Holy Ghost—the invisible presence of the Holy Spirit. In this respect the Dove is a healer and metaphysician who is constantly at work draining negative energies from others, repolarizing that energy through his or her own force field, and infusing into other people their newly regenerated and healing strength.

    d. HIGHER ASPIRATIONS: THE DOVE.

    e. KEY PHRASE: I DESIRE, THEREFORE I AM

    f. KEY WORDS:

positive	negative
loyal	possessive
urge to (re)create	destructive
intricate	scheming
responsible	power-hungry

C. Gemini-Sagittarius

1. Gemini (Mutable, Air, Positive). The communicativeness of air is expressed through Gemini in a multitude of ways with versatility and change.

    a. SYMBOL (♊). The pictograph shows the lungs as well as the two arms and the thorax, those parts of the body associated with this sign. The lungs and vocal cords are the physical means through which Man is able to speak (Gemini is also associated with the nervous system in general). The two arms are the instruments Man uses to write and to gesticulate in emphasizing his words. Ideographically, this symbol represents duality, i.e. the function of the rational mind to differentiate between the object and the viewer.

Gemini's glyph also represents the path between two poles, the message-giver.

b. PRINCIPLE: COMMUNICATION. Gemini stands for the way Man formulates concepts and ideas of personal behavior which allow him to communicate with his fellow Man. Gemini represents the youthful mind, ever eager to assimilate data and store accumulated knowledge. As a Mutable or changeable sign (the month of Gemini is the connecting period between spring and summer), Gemini is always busily jumping from one thought, idea, or subject to another. He is more the compiler of the encyclopedia than the contributing scholar writing about his particular interest.

c. THE GEMINI INDIVIDUAL. Gemini is like a bee who, presented with a field of flowers, buzzes from one beautiful blossom to the next, gathering a little bit of nectar from each without apparent pattern. Gemini is so eager to explore all the avenues of expression life has to offer that he often loses himself in the effort to match physical momentum with mental imagery. In order for Gemini to be truly successful, he must learn when to merge his versatility and beautiful sense of rhythm with stability of purpose (planets in the Fixed signs will help Gemini in this respect). Gemini is naturally competitive. He is very aware of the differences dividing people and becomes easily bored with stable conditions. In addition, he enjoys the game of competition—or any game, for that matter. Gemini must learn not to dissipate his energies through superficial entanglements. Instead he must try to hear all the individual instruments in the symphony of life, at the same time integrating its various elements into a perfectly integrated whole.

d. HIGHER ASPIRATIONS. Gemini's greatest gift to humanity resides in his ability to communicate ideas. Thus Gemini finds a tremendous purpose as a writer or educator.

e. KEY PHRASE: I THINK, THEREFORE I AM. We must see that Gemini is represented by human figures (the Twins) and not by an animal such as the Bull, Ram or Scorpion. Gemini's special human characteristic is the rational mind, that part of Man's being which allows him to separate and modify his emotional responses and impulses from his outward activities.

f. KEY WORDS:

positive	negative
diverse	superficial
intellectual	intuition blocked by verbal amplification
original	imitative

2. *Sagittarius (Mutable, Fire, Positive).* The creative activity of Sagittarius manifests itself in an outgoing and ever-changing way.

a. SYMBOL (♐). Pictographically this symbol represents the thighs and the upper portion of the leg to the knee. This is the part of the anatomy ruled by the Archer. As an ideograph it represents the arrow, symbolizing the ever-searching mind. Sagittarius, however, is most concerned with sending out ideological arrows and with soaring through the air on expansive journeys rather than with either finding the target or reaching the destination.

b. PRINCIPLE: THE PHILOSOPHICAL MIND. Gemini is preoccupied with individual methods of communication and thought formation. Sagittarius, on the other hand, is more concerned with social laws, mores, and customs. For example, Sagittarius would be the motivating force behind the Constitution of the United States, while Gemini's influence would be in finding words to match the philosophical concept of such a document. While Sagittarius would be most interested in Man's evolution through the experience of living under a certain political or philosophical system, Gemini would be more concerned with the logic of the law.

c. THE SAGITTARIUS INDIVIDUAL. Although Sagittarius as a sign is concerned with social order and philosophy, not all Sagittarians can be philosophers or legislators (although many of them often think of themselves as such). Sagittarius feels most comfortable in a teaching role and, as a result, prefers lending his opinion to a certain situation than being told how to act in a given set of circumstances. Sagittarius has to be wary of thinking that his personal philosophy and opinions about social order are proper concepts for everyone. In this respect Sagittarius can be the most liberal or the most bigoted of thinkers.

We call Sagittarius a dual sign, and if we look at the mythical creature representing Sagittarius—the Centaur—we will see the exact form of this dualism. As the Centaur is half man and half horse, so Sagittarius usually finds an inner division between the exploration of the highest human values and the indulgence of the lowest sensual desires.

d. HIGHER ASPIRATIONS. Sagittarius tends to embody wisdom and the ability to teach lofty understandings of human existence to others. In this respect the Sagittarian will often have to transmute the energies of the lower self into the perfection of the higher.

e. KEY PHRASE: I SEEK, THEREFORE I AM.

f. KEY WORDS:

positive	*negative*
generous	wasteful
truthful	dogmatic
direct	tactless
knowledgeable	opinionated

D. Cancer-Capricorn

1. Cancer (Cardinal, Water, Negative). The emotional and sensitive nature of water emerges in Cancer in a highly personal and often self-preserving manner.

a. SYMBOL (♋). Pictographically we see a stylization of the breasts, the part of the anatomy ruled by this sign. Ideographically we see two cups, one turned upward and the other turned down. This symbol exemplifies the gathering of resources on the one hand, so that on the other they can be given out in times of need to Cancer's loved ones. Thus collection, preservation, and selective sharing of resources are quite typical of this sign.

b. PRINCIPLE: FOUNDATIONS. We have seen the beginning of an individual's development in Aries, his stabilization in Taurus, and his ability to communicate through Gemini. The synthesis of these elements occurs in Cancer, the sign connected with home and basic psychological foundation. It is in Cancer that Man awakens to the fact of his interdependence with people. Cancer is the sign of the tribe (while Capricorn, its polarity, is the sign of the civilization). As a tribal member, Cancer is forced into making some contribution to the society in which he lives, but the extent of this obligation is not clear. He is thus overly concerned with his own preservation and with that of his family. In this respect we can say that a Cancer individual finds it difficult to sacrifice ethnic roots or traditions for personal growth.

c. THE CANCER INDIVIDUAL. The Cancerian is very maternal and seeks to protect and nurture, although at times this concern turns into undue worry. Cancer is extremely sensitive to her or his environment and to others' feelings. She or he will often be extremely intuitive about other people's relationships, especially if there is personal involvement. Like the Moon, Cancer has many phases or moods, ranging from the most fear-filled (the dark side of the Moon) to the most joyful (the Full Moon).

Cancer is extremely impressionable and has an almost photographic memory, which is especially acute if the thought is a sentimental one. Cancer has a love of the old and antique but must learn to constantly "clean house." This refers not only to the periodic sweeping out of useless objects in order to make way for new collections, but also to the release of old thoughts, grudges, and sentiments no longer viable in the present. Cancer can clutter her heart with visions of childhood or lost loves. Such thoughts preoccupy her life to such an extent that they leave little room for the appearance of today's new loves. Cancer can take from the past well-learned lessons but should seek to apply these to the present.

d. HIGHER ASPIRATIONS. Individuals born under this sign can help others to grow through their beautifully sensitive and protective nature. In order to realize their own sense of security and be as truly giving as they desire, they must overcome their fear of lack. Once this is accomplished, they may become the receptacle through which the creative abundance of life flows freely.

e. KEY PHRASE: I FEEL, THEREFORE I AM.

f. KEY WORDS:

positive	*negative*
providing	possessive
sensitive	over-emotional
mediumistic	given to hallucinations
dependable	flighty
motherly	smothering

2. *Capricorn (Cardinal, Earth, Negative)*. The practical and stabilizing tendency of Earth is activated by the cardinality of Capricorn based on an inner idea of the structure of matter.

a. SYMBOL (ϑ). Pictographically this is the symbol for the knee and shin, the parts of the body ruled by Capricorn. Ideographically it is the hieroglyph of the mountain goat, the animal which represents this sign. The goat is sure-footed and cautious as it climbs the mountain in search of nourishment. In the same way Capricorn utilizes all possible resources to reach the pinnacle of success.

b. PRINCIPLE: STRUCTURE. As Cancer represents the tribal unit, Capricorn represents civilization, i.e. a conglomerate social structure based on the interchanges and developments of various associated tribes. When a planet is manifesting itself through Capricorn, its energy will consolidate and most probably be released in a concise and often restricted form. The nature of the Capricorn vibration is to provide the structure upon which a larger form will be created. For example, the mechanisms of the bureaucracy of government are Capricornian in that they are the skeletal basis upon which society will construct its various activities.

c. THE CAPRICORN INDIVIDUAL. This is the builder, the architect of the Zodiac, who is constantly at work not only climbing the mountain, but also creating the mountain he climbs. In this respect it is often very difficult for a Capricorn to undo what he has already done. In other words, Capricorns are habit-makers who find it extremely difficult to break existing patterns of behavior. In the same way they take on responsibilities that can be extremely burdensome, and they often feel guilty when forced to relinquish such onerous relationships.

Capricorns feel the need to take care of others, but their generosity is usually not bestowed without some mutually beneficial factor. These individuals are extremely careful in the handling of material resources and invariably make the most out of the least.

d. HIGHER ASPIRATIONS. Capricorn is extremely aware of Man's need to make some contribution to society. He can in this respect impose severe restrictions and limitations upon his personal life, so that he may provide some service which will benefit the larger society. Capricorn can have a vision of utopia but will strive to make sure that the dream becomes a working reality.

e. KEY PHRASE: I BUILD, THEREFORE I AM.

f. KEY WORDS:

positive	negative
ambitious	self-seeking
realistic	depressive
constructive	unimaginative
hard-working	sticking to routine

E. Leo-Aquarius

1. *Leo (Fixed, Fire, Positive).* The inspirational nature of fire works through Leo in a determined and self-expressive manner.

a. SYMBOL (♌). The pictographic aspect of this glyph is the human heart, the part of the body ruled by the Lion. The heart is the center from which blood is pumped into the rest of the organism as well as the point to which it returns after making its long journey.

Leo can therefore stimulate activity by giving forth the energy of life through a process of the organization and centralized diversification of authority.

b. PRINCIPLE: INTEGRATION. The blood travels to every cell in the body, giving life and removing waste products. Thus Leo represents the process of the continual interchange between self-expression and the collection of resultant experiences. The wise Leo is constantly at work purifying the "blood" of these experiences, crystallizing knowledge into wisdom, and sending out new rays of energy from his ever-expanding center.

c. THE LEO INDIVIDUAL. It is no coincidence that the expression "the heart of a lion" indicates a courageous, bountiful, noble, and proud nature. It is an apt description of the positive side of Leo, with one modification—Leo "turns himself on" only to those individuals with whom he or she is personally involved. All others must learn to keep their respectful distance from this, the king of the Zodiac. Leos are very fussy about whom they bestow their favors upon and periodically vacillate. They enjoy being the center of attention and having a loyal entourage to surround them with supportive vibrations. Leos appreciate a good time, are admirers of the beautiful and artistic, but can be extraordinarily self-indulgent.

d. HIGHER ASPIRATIONS. If Leo depersonalizes his love, he will find that the intensity of his light will shine upon *all* people with equal brightness. The greatest Master is the greatest Servant. Leo will find his or her place in the Universe through selflessly providing others with his or her magnanimous and sustaining strengths.

e. KEY PHRASE: I CREATE, THEREFORE I AM.

f. KEY WORDS:

positive	*negative*
noble	snob
generous	egocentric
praiseworthy	boastful
warm	overpowering

2. Aquarius (Fixed, Air, Positive). The intellectual qualities of air become stabilized thought processes which are expanded through Aquarius in an ever-widening circle of social relationships.

a. SYMBOL (♒). The ankles are ruled by this sign, whose symbol depicts the movement of the feet while walking. It is also a picture of waves, symbolizing the dissemination of information, a major characteristic of this sign. Aquarius is called the Water Bearer. The significance of this appellation will further reveal the nature of the sign. Man is carrying the water of the collective consciousness of the human race: the totality of Man's shared experiences on Earth. The Water Bearer is Man perfected by this wisdom, which he pours out in the hope that all of humanity may become enlightened.

b. PRINCIPLE: HUMANITARIANISM. Capricorn provides a structure upon which civilization has been established; Aquarius represents the outgrowth of that civilization—the new ideas which arise from the development of society. In this respect Aquarians are revolutionaries, constantly envisioning the progress of society and attempting to alter present-day circumstances to meet the future needs.

c. THE AQUARIUS INDIVIDUAL. It is essential that Aquarians learn to balance their flashes of intuitive perception with the reality of surrounding circumstances. Leo represents the heart, but Aquarius rules the circulatory system. Leo is therefore concerned with the personal use of authority, while Aquarius is much more involved with the population which must live under a given governmental system. In this respect an Aquarian often rebels, in his unabating eagerness to change the established order. For this reason, as well as for the great intuitive faculties with which many Aquarians are endowed, Aquarius is called the sign of the inventor.

Aquarius is especially interested in assuring for all Mankind equal participation in the bounty of the Earth and wishes all people to be free of oppressive circumstances. Aquarians are always on the lookout for fellow bohemians and for anything which strays from the norm. They enjoy unorthodox and unconventional relationships and usually respect other people's beliefs. They must take care, however, not to assert their personal ideologies in such a dogmatic fashion that they lose objectivity.

d. HIGHER ASPIRATIONS. Aquarians seek to build a better world today for tomorrow. In this respect they constantly seek a way to serve the whole of humanity by making an active contribution to society.

e. KEY PHRASE: I ENVISION, THEREFORE I AM.

f. KEY WORDS:

positive	negative
unusual	eccentric
inventive	destructive
intuitive	scatterbrained
concerned	frigid

F. Virgo-Pisces

1. Virgo (Mutable, Earth, Negative). The potential resources of Earth are used in a diversified manner by Virgo in order to find a practical means of self-expression.

a. SYMBOL (♍). The coils of this glyph represent the convolutions of the intestines, that part of the digestive tract specifically ascribed to Virgo. We may also derive from it the multifaceted nature and resourcefulness of individuals born under this sign. The final closed loop can also be said to represent the untouched vagina, thus revealing Virgo as a sign with a tremendous potential for creative self-expression, without a precise or specific direction for its release.

b. PRINCIPLE: DISCRIMINATION AND SYNTHESIS. Virgo, coming after Leo and before Libra, is therefore the last of the zodiacal segments in the "personal hemisphere." Leo is prone to ostentatious and often overly sensual behavior, while Libra is that path through which Man makes his "debut" in society. Virgo's function is to prepare Man for his social role by carefully weeding out what is too personal and self-centered. Virgo is called the sign of service; it utilizes what one has learned from the previous five signs and endeavors (still in the personal sense) to bring this information to others. It is also known as the sign of health, because it attempts to purify itself before entering society through the gates of Libra.

c. THE VIRGO INDIVIDUAL. A Virgo is especially interested in performing some sort of service rather than taking supreme control over a corporation or a group of people, as are Leo and Capricorn. Virgos are extremely critical because they can see their own foibles in the activities of others; wishing to divest themselves of these character flaws, they become extremely annoyed when such defects are expressed by those around them. Virgo is also called the sign of the ulcer, since Virgos are apt to worry excessively while they attempt to go through life exactly categorizing everything they touch. Virgos should be easier on themselves and should concentrate their energies on those areas of service and practical know-how which come most naturally to them.

d. HIGHER ASPIRATIONS. If Virgos can serve without manipulating those whom they serve, they will find tremendous gratification in the understanding of true selfless assistance.

e. KEY PHRASE: I SELECT, THEREFORE I AM.

f. KEY WORDS:

positive	negative
detailed	nit-picking
organized	messy
helpful	critical
efficient	worrisome
loyal	fickle

2. Pisces (Mutable, Water, Negative). The ever-changing waters of Pisces give rise to a multifaceted way of self-expression based on a complex and highly impressionable nature.

a. SYMBOL (♓). The glyph for Pisces is a highly stylized depiction of the heels of the feet placed back to back. Each foot is going in a different direction, but they are connected by a silver cord. The two directions in which the feet are walking (or in which the fish are swimming) represent Aquarius on the one hand and Aries on the other. In other words, the constant Piscean struggle is between participation in the collectivity of humanity as a whole and in individualizing the Self as a separate agent outside this human ocean. Hamlet's phrase "to be or not to be" could very much describe the Piscean dilemma.

b. PRINCIPLE: SACRIFICE. Like Virgo, Pisces feels compelled to serve humanity in some way. But while Virgo seems to find his or her identity through service itself, Pisces finds gratification through the loss of personal identity through service. Virgo is the stage before Man's entering into society, but Pisces is that area of the Zodiac which is completely responsive to social need. It represents the sum total of the collective experiences of all the other signs.

c. THE PISCES INDIVIDUAL. Just as the ocean has many depths and undercurrents, so the Piscean embodies the complexity of the many levels of life simultaneously existing in the vastness of the sea. It is no wonder, therefore, that Pisceans are the least understood of all individuals. In their attempt to seek a rapport with the totality of all experience, Pisceans often lose footing and must periodically withdraw from society in order to reestablish individual identity. Pisceans are so impressionable that it becomes mandatory for them to seek out carefully selected environments, friends, and interests, so that individual growth may proceed without the many disastrous ups and downs which all too often characterize their lives.

Pisces has a tremendous ability to tap into the realms of imagination and is therefore exceptionally creative in the arts. Just as a fish floats effortlessly through water, Pisceans find an equal freedom in music and dance. Pisceans, who must feel unrestricted at all times, too often find life filled with the very limitations they find so difficult to bear. They therefore seek the otherworldly and are very prone to mysticism, occultism, and religion on the one hand and drugs, alcohol, and sensual self-indulgence on the other.

d. HIGHER ASPIRATIONS. Pisces has the ability to transcend personal love, attaining universal love, thus inspiring others with their great faith and tremendous understanding. This sign is especially given to producing religious figures and outstanding humanitarians.

e. KEY PHRASE: I BELIEVE, THEREFORE I AM.

f. KEY WORDS:

positive	negative
resourceful	manipulative
inspirational	nebulous and misty
imaginative	fanciful
self-sacrificing	lacking cohesive identity

After the experiences of life have been collected, dissolved, and assimilated by the universal solvent contained in the waters of Pisces, Man is ready to utilize his previous discoveries and the efforts of humanity by stepping out once more into consciousness through the onrushing life force of Aries.

EXERCISES.

1. Take six 3″ x 5″ blank index cards. Draw the symbols of one pair of signs on each, writing the following concepts underneath:
    a. Aries-Libra: Personal vs. Social Projection of Energy.
    b. Taurus-Scorpio: Personal vs. Social Collection of Energy.
    c. Gemini-Sagittarius: Personal vs. Social Mental Concepts.
    d. Cancer-Capricorn: Personal vs. Social Security.
    e. Leo-Aquarius: Personal vs. Social Creativity.
    f. Virgo-Pisces: Personal vs. Social Service.
2. Contemplate each card for a few minutes. Repeat as often as you wish. Observe how your comprehension of the signs and their principles grows.

8.

THE PLANETS IN THE SIGNS

All planets modify each other through a complex system of interrelationships called Aspects (see Part II, chaps. 14–16). In other words, in the practical sense no planet will express itself purely by its sign position. The key to accurate horoscope interpretation resides in the ability to synthesize the various modifying factors at work in every phase of the delineation.

Each sign has a planetary ruler: Mars is the ruler of Aries, Venus of Taurus, Mercury of Gemini, and so on. The energy of the ruling planet is therefore most easily, naturally, and powerfully manifested when it is posited in its own sign. A person born with Jupiter in Sagittarius will most easily express the purest and highest vibrations of this planet—subject, of course, to the state of the individual's consciousness as well as to the "tone" of the horoscope as a whole.

In any evaluation of predominant planetary strengths, however, the energy of a celestial body in the sign of its rulership must be considered as a dominant force in the person's life. When a planet is in such a position it is said to be in *dignity* or *honor*. Thus the energy the planet embodies is most free when it is not inhibited by the vibrations of a sign uncongenial to its nature.

When a planet is in the sign opposite the one it naturally rules, it is said to be in *detriment* or *dishonor*. Mars in Libra, Venus in Scorpio, Mercury in Sagittarius, and so on, are position of detriment (see Table of Planetary Honors and Dishonors at the end of this chapter). In such a situation the energy of the specific planet is repressed from harmonious release; as a result, its effects are either weak or negative, depending on the nature of the entire map.

In addition to its dignity, each planet has another complimentary sign through which its energy is positively expressed. This is called the sign of its *exaltation*. In this placement a planet is not only strong in its operational effectiveness but is also in a position to be most actively creative.

When a planet is in the sign opposite its exaltation, it is said to be in its *fall*. When so posited, its nature and potential positivity is severely restricted, and one's response to the specific planetary vibration becomes quite limited. If a native's ruling planet is so placed and afflicted by challenging aspects from other bodies, the result can be the total negation or inhibition of the mode of self-expression.

The honor or dishonor of the planets apply in their most important sense to the bodies within the orbit of Saturn and Saturn itself. The extra-Saturnian bodies— Uranus, Neptune, and Pluto—remain so long in each sign that their position becomes much more important in a generational rather than a personal sense.

I. THE SWIFT-MOVING PLANETS

1. Sun in the Signs.   The life-generating creative potential of the solar force will manifest itself through:

a. ARIES as an ever-searching desire to find those avenues and opportunities for constant self-projecting activity as well as the tendency toward impulsive forms of self-expression (exaltation).

b. TAURUS as a desire to express the Self through cautious and established patterns of behavior which will lead to increases of material security.

c. GEMINI as a desire to express the Self through constant variations in life style and the pursuit of intellectual stimulation and growth.

d. CANCER as a desire for self-expression through the consistent action of collecting material resources in order to establish emotional security and firm roots.

e. LEO as a desire to constantly express the Self through the organization and direction of one's own and other people's activities by a constant interchange of affection or power with those close (dignity).

f. VIRGO as a form of self-expression which centers on bringing order into one's surroundings as well as a type of existence which is very dependent on being needed.

g. LIBRA as a form of self-expression seeking perfection in social relationships as well as an urge to bring harmony into one's surroundings (fall).

h. SCORPIO as a desire to transform the environment, oneself and others often with an eye on the opportunity to use other people's energies in order to further one's growth and self-expression.

i. SAGITTARIUS as an ever-seeking desire to expand the Self through consistent but ever-changing activities as well as through the gathering of information based on sensual and intellectual experiences.

j. CAPRICORN as a need to structure one's surroundings so that nothing is left to chance, as well as the deep desire to build an ever-growing participation in one's social sphere.

k. AQUARIUS as the need to disseminate information and to participate in ever-widening circles of social relationships as well as in the alteration of conventional modes of thinking and behavior (detriment).

l. PISCES as an urge to express the Self through an ever-deepening understanding of others, as well as the desire to be of service to those in need.

2. Moon in the Signs. The receptive, form-giving, emotional aspect of the lunar force is manifested in:

a. ARIES as a feeling for security in one's own actions, as well as sudden surges of emotions which can lead to impulsive relationships.

b. TAURUS as a feeling of security through material and emotional attachments as well as a strong tendency toward a deep appreciation of the fundamental values of life (exaltation).

c. GEMINI as a feeling of security in one's ability to adapt to any given set of cricumstances, as well as ever-changing environmental and social interactions.

d. CANCER as a feeling of security in one's own particular environment, as well as the need to make every place in which one lives a "home" and to nurture those with whom one comes in contact (dignity).

e. LEO as a feeling of security when in the center or "limelight" of activity, as well as the tendency to dramatize all emotional situations.

f. VIRGO as a feeling of security through personal intervention in an advisory capacity in the service of other people, as well as a sometimes overly critical assessment of personal relationships.

g. LIBRA as a feeling of security through other people's reactions to one's own actions, as well as an ever-present need to bring harmony into one's own and other people's relationships.

h. SCORPIO as a feeling of security through possessiveness in personal relationships, as well as a drive to control the environment and the ability to sever relationships with great finality (fall).

i. SAGITTARIUS as a feeling of security through a lack of responsibilities and an ever-present need to be completely free to relate to an ever-changing environment.

j. CAPRICORN as a feeling of security through the structure and control of the immediate environment, as well as the tendency to use an instinctual understanding of people for self-aggrandizement (detriment).

k. AQUARIUS as a feeling of security through social connections and the ability to relate to all types of people intuitively, as well as a desire to take part in social movements and group activities.

l. PISCES as a feeling of security through the ability to adjust personal feelings to the constant bombardment of vibrations and impressions in the environment, thus creating the need for periodic seclusion. An often inspirational and compassionate placement for the Moon.

3. Mercury in the Signs. The logical processes of the rational mind and the ability to communicate orally and through the written word is expressed through:

a. ARIES as a tendency to make snap judgments, decisions, and opinions as well as an ability to perceive the nature of the relationships in one's environment with alacrity and intuition. *Immediate action stimulated by thought processes.*

b. TAURUS cautiously and deliberately, with a tendency to greater depth than precision, as well as an instinctive awareness of the nature of the practical aspects of relationships. *Deliberate action stimulated by thought processes.*

c. GEMINI with great versatility, adaptability, and speed, as well as a natural talent with words and an ease of perceiving the structure of relationships. *Consistently changing activity stimulated by thought processes* (dignity).

d. CANCER as an impressionable mind which creates its forms of communication through the actualization of imagination as well as the tendency to retain thoughts for sentimental reasons. *Imaginative behavior stimulated by thought processes.*

e. LEO as the need to put a personal "stamp" on the methods of self-expression. This position can contribute to great personal creative expression, but it is a rather difficult placement for objectivity and spiritual development unless the person is functioning in a wider and more impersonal sense than is usually indicated by Leo. *Self-centered creative activity stimulated by thought processes* (fall).

f. VIRGO with great precision and attention to detail as well as a tendency toward overconcern in relation to seemingly minor issues. *Orderly and meticulous activity stimulated by thought processes* (dignity).

g. LIBRA as a need to establish perfect judgment and a balanced mind, especially in the realm of personal relationships. *Harmonious activity stimulated by thought processes.*

h. SCORPIO as an instinctual understanding of the nature of human relationships, as well as a tendency to comprehend the causal nature of outer activity. *Secret and subtle activities stimulated by thought processes.*

i. SAGITTARIUS in a manner which often has little to do with the practical reality at hand, as well as a tendency to exaggerate the importance of personal opinion so that issues become matters of principle rather than actualities. *Philosophical activities stimulated by thought processes* (detriment).

j. CAPRICORN as a desire to structure the mind in such a way that a cohesive mental pattern is established, often at the cost of the imagination. This placement also results in a serious mind which tends toward skepticism as well as the ability to profit the most from the least. *Constructive activity stimulated by thought processes.*

k. AQUARIUS with great originality as well as the tendency toward the development of intuitional faculties of the mind. In addition, it allows for communication with all types of people. *Inventive activities stimulated by thought processes* (exaltation).

l. PISCES with some difficulty, since the ability to be precise in thinking patterns is beclouded by the watery nature of this sign. It does, however, give an extreme sensitivity, which can result in a highly developed psychic and/or artistic nature (compare the horoscope of Edgar Cayce Part III, chap. 26). *Compassionate activity stimulated by thought processes* (detriment).

4. Venus in the Signs. The personal magnetism, sense of social harmony, and artistic nature of an individual embodied by Venus is expressed through:

a. ARIES as the making of personal relationships as a reflection of one's own romantic ideals, as well as the tendency to be self-centered in personal relationships. Lust often overcomes love in the impulsive relationships stimulated by this position of Venus (detriment).

b. TAURUS in a very strongly pronounced manner, often giving rise to deeply involved and long-lasting romantic relationships, as well as the tendency to attract material resources and to be artistically self-expressive (dignity).

c. GEMINI with great changeability and versatility. There is a tendency for many short-lived relationships, which can occur simultaneously, as well as a certain ease and grace in one's social life.

d. CANCER with great sentimentality. There is a tendency to become extremely attached to others, with the resultant inability to release relationships. Family relationships are usually strong and can be instrumental in helping an individual achieve a sense of rapport with others.

e. LEO with a great sense of the dramatic, as well as the tendency to remain extremely loyal to one's loved ones. Venus in Leo has a tendency to try to make close relationships an extension of the Self. There may be a strong desire to self-expression through the arts.

f. VIRGO with great precision. The personal relationships are often scrutinized too closely, with an overly critical eye on the partner. There is dissatisfaction with anything less than perfection in one's social relationships and in one's artistic self-expression (fall).

g. LIBRA with an instinctive desire to achieve a perfect state of coexistence in one's personal relationships. There is a tendency toward match-making and a certain artistic ability which seeks to bring a state of harmony and beauty into the environment (dignity).

h. SCORPIO with a keen awareness of the manner in which personal relationships can be used to further growth and material abundance. There is a tendency to constantly reconstruct relationships so that they become more refined, but an equally strong tendency to annihilate relationships once they no longer serve any useful purpose (detriment).

i. SAGITTARIUS with great expansiveness. There is a tendency to know many people in many places and to avoid relationships which involve any deep sense of committal. The artistry is usually in the life style, since there is a great "bon vivant" quality when Venus is in this position.

j. CAPRICORN with an eye toward material and/or prestigious objectives. There is often a seriousness about personal attachments, and the frivolity natural to Venus is somewhat subdued in this position. Artistic sentiments are expressed with a consideration for creations that show a practical purpose.

k. AQUARIUS with great originality. There is an openness in social relationships which brings the native into contact with people of varying backgrounds, as well as an attraction to those forms of artistic expression which are unconventional and seem different in the era in which one lives.

l. PISCES with compassion and universality of outlook. There is a tendency for overindulgence in continually changing forms of sensual self-expression as well as the ability to be sympathetic and completely understanding of all people. The appreciation for art is often highly sensitized, especially in the realm of music and dance (exaltation).

5. *Mars in the Signs.* The drive toward the aggressive outward expression of the desire for personal achievement as well as the nature of the sexual drive embodied in the energy of Mars are expressed through:

a. ARIES directly, often without consideration for other people's rhythms or wishes. There is an ability to handle life courageously and to cut through obstacles with ease. The sexual nature can often be too self-gratifying, without due consideration for the partner (dignity).

b. TAURUS persistently. There is a tendency to be overly self-seeking in material ambition and to thwart oneself through inertia and lack of direct action. The sexual nature tends to be strong but is usually expressed with passivity and sensuality (detriment).

c. GEMINI with versatility. There is a tendency to fluctuate in one's drives and to dissipate one's energies through the handling of too many projects simultaneously. The sexual nature requires ever-changing stimuli.

d. CANCER insecurely. There is a tendency to approach one's aims indirectly and often surreptitiously. The sexual drive is closely linked with emotional possessiveness and may express itself with great indolence.

e. LEO passionately. There is a tendency to be very consistent in one's approach to the fulfillment of one's desires and a great need to be appreciated for one's prowess both as an individual and as a lover.

f. VIRGO analytically. There is a tendency to constantly question one's own purposes and activities, as well as the ability to dissipate one's energy through a lack of cohesion. Mars in Virgo can also give a certain degree of covert behavior. The sexual nature can be either very disoriented or cool and moralistic.

g. LIBRA indecisively. The nature of Mars is somewhat softened in this position, so that a lack of personal aggressiveness is noteworthy. However, this influence does give the tendency to be argumentative; Martian qualities are often expressed through conflicts in personal relationships (detriment).

h. SCORPIO intensely and covertly. There is a tendency to be very secretive about personal projects and sexual self-expression. The drive for power is usually strong and can be accomplished through the careful manipulation of other individuals (dignity).

i. SAGITTARIUS restlessly. There is a tendency to expand goals beyond what the present circumstances warrant. At the same time there is a desire to place the responsibilities of personal actions on other people's shoulders, so that a continual shifting of objectives occurs. The sexual nature is either lusty and noncommittal or highly moralistic.

j. CAPRICORN constructively. There is a tendency to act with circumspection and a preconceived plan in structuring of ambitions. The sexual drive can be divorced from sentiment and is usually either restrained, aloof, and purposeful or indulgent, with a great lust for power and control (exaltation).

k. AQUARIUS erratically and unconventionally. There is a tendency to incorporate personal goals into a larger social superstructure. This position of Mars may give alterations of extreme activity or laziness. The sexual nature also tends to work in this way and with an openness toward experimentation.

l. PISCES inconsistently and indiscriminately. There is either a tendency toward a lack of cohesive direction in personal goals or an ability to bring together many facets of a situation, so that one is in a controlling if somewhat clandestine position. Mars in Pisces can therefore make a great strategist or an incompetent. The sexual nature is strongly linked to the emotional nature and in some cases can be self-indulgent or unfocused.

6. Jupiter in the Signs. The urge to expand one's understanding of life through pursuits which enlarge one's scope of experience or material situation, embodied by the planet Jupiter, is expressed through:

a. ARIES as a need to experience growth in an immediate and personal sense. Thus an individual is apt to pursue those travels and studies which further philosophical growth.

b. TAURUS with an eye toward the practical expression of such experiences in the material sphere of life. It also gives the ability to apply philosophical concepts into the context of the reality at hand.

c. GEMINI through the personal intellect. There is a tendency to fit all idealism and experiences gained through higher studies and travel into personal concepts of life. Thus there is a widening of the mind through added facts rather than a deepening through a crystallization of these facts into wisdom (detriment).

d. CANCER emotionally through a compassionate understanding of human life. There is a tendency to merge philosophical concepts with personal experiences and an ability to share what is assimilated through intimate relationships (exaltation).

e. LEO ostentatiously or magnanimously. There is the tendency to personify, project, and teach the understandings which have been acquired through experiences and studies. Usually this position lends nobility to the character, but it can also be a contributing factor toward inordinate pride.

f. VIRGO critically. There is a tendency to scrutinize very carefully all matters which are not immediately pragmatic and to analyze quite carefully philosophical concepts and religious suppositions (detriment).

g. LIBRA socially. There is a tendency to travel and engage in higher studies, accompanied by at least one convivial companion. In addition, this position endows the native with a cooperative spirit, so that he would wish to share understandings and abundance with others.

h. SCORPIO intensely. There is the tendency to take one's desire to know very seriously, with an ability to probe into the meaning behind religious and philosophic dogma in the search for truth. On the other hand, this position of Jupiter can greatly intensify the desire to amass power and control others.

i. SAGITTARIUS zealously and with great enthusiasm. This is Jupiter's own sign and will give an individual with this placement a great need for self-exploration in the realms of life characterized by this planet. Care has to be taken that restlessness and lack of patience do not result in scattered experiences (dignity).

j. CAPRICORN with an eye toward self-aggrandizement. This position gives a strong desire for the amassing of wealth and influence. There is the tendency to attempt to structure one's philosophy so that it "fits" into one's life style and serves as a springboard for the attainment of one's ambitions. "An executive position" (fall).

k. AQUARIUS idealistically. This position tends to make one very open to experimenting with new ideas, religions, and philosophies, as well as giving the desire to participate in those groups which propagate various new dogmas.

l. PISCES sincerely or indiscriminately, depending on the "tone" of the entire horoscope. This position of Jupiter allows the person to be open and interested in all forms of religious and philosophical studies, especially if the latter are emotionally oriented rather than scientific or intellectual. The drawback to this placement of Jupiter is a lack of consistence or structure in the search for higher values. A significator or great faith in the universe (dignity).

7. *Saturn in the Signs.* The formative, limiting, and structuring aspects of Saturn manifest themselves through:

a. ARIES as a tendency to place personal idea of law and order on others. In addition, a certain degree of self-righteousness and a desire for control is associated with this position (fall).

b. TAURUS with great strength and determination of purpose. There is a tendency toward restricting immediate activities and self-indulgent experiences for the sake of future rewards resulting from such careful planning and limitations. A strong note of materialism is usually present.

c. GEMINI intellectually. There is usually a substantial ability to use the mind and various types of mental pursuits for general growth and the fulfillment of ambitions. The sense of timing and understanding of the structuring of thought for successful self-expression is usually very keen.

d. CANCER with difficulty. People with this position are usually very sensitive to external forces which try to restrict them or structure them in any way. There is a lack of understanding of the meaning of self-discipline as the emotional waters of Cancer are always trying to seep through the strong disciplinary barriers of Saturn (detriment).

e. LEO autocratically. The person has a desire to be a law unto himself and often a difficult time adjusting his own usually strong ambitions to cooperative ventures or mutual needs (detriment).

f. VIRGO meticulously. This position increases Virgo's natural sense of order to a point at which undue details can be quite obsessive. The task is to be able to separate the essential from the unessential.

g. LIBRA with a great sense of balance. This position imparts the opportunity to develop a perfect sense of timing and objectivity in regards to social relationships and also provides a means to achieve goals through cooperative efforts (exaltation).

h. SCORPIO ruthlessly. There is a very strong desire to control all available resources, so that they fall into a pattern whereby they may be used by the individual for his or her own purposes. This position also gives the ability to probe very deeply into the nature of existing circumstances, so that opportunities may be seized for personal advancement.

i. SAGITTARIUS with an eye toward the careful incorporation of the understanding gained through general life experiences into the fulfillment of ambitions. A fine ability to make expansive ideas into practical realities.

j. CAPRICORN with a tendency toward incorporating the surrounding opportunities for material gain and/or social position into long-range plans for success. This position of Saturn lends powers of endurance, foresight, and organization (dignity).

k. AQUARIUS with the ability to merge on a practical level one's idealism with the social conditions of one's era. On the other hand, it can represent a fixity of ideas which does not allow for easy adjustment to the changing opinions of society. Thus, one can build one's social outlook upon a set of principles which can be very limiting in their application (dignity).

l. PISCES either fearfully or indiscriminately. There is a tendency for the individual to avoid the self-discipline necessary to channel his energies in a steady direction. On the other hand, there is a great resourcefulness, for a person with this position of Saturn is not easily pigeonholed.

II. THE TRANS-SATURNIAN PLANETS

Uranus, Neptune, and Pluto spend such a long time (seven, fourteen, and between twenty-one and thirty years respectively) in each sign that whole generations of individuals are born with these outer planets in the same zodiacal positions. We can readily understand, therefore, that the nature of the slower-moving planets by sign is more effective in a collective than in an individual sense.

It is through the study of these three bodies *by House position* that the astrologer will be able to ascertain their significance in the individual life structure. In this respect the next chapter will be much more revealing. We can, however, briefly describe the general influence of these three planets by sign as follows:

1. Uranus. The erratic activities and sudden flashes of intuition as well as the urge to break away from convention, which are characteristics of this planet, are modified according to the sign in which Uranus is placed. For example, Uranus entered Libra in late 1968 and does not leave this sign until September 1975. So far during this seven-year cycle we have seen a tremendous rise in the Women's Liberation movement which has greatly affected the nature of marriage and male-female relationships in general. In addition, such previously unconventional relationships as menages-à-trois, as well as homosexual and communal marriages, have become commonplace among the younger generations, as has otherwise "taboo" experimentation on many levels of society. It can be seen therefore that those individuals *born* with Uranus in Libra will embody these tendencies toward experimentation in human relationships.

2. Neptune. The urge toward mystical experiences and the desire to explore the unseen, characteristics of Neptune's influence on Man, will be modified according to its sign position. For example, since early 1970 and until 1984 (when Neptune enters Capricorn, the sign of government control) Neptune has been in Sagittarius. This has given rise to an ever-increasing universal urge to travel. In addition, new religions and increased participation in all forms of philosophical pursuits and occult studies have been on the increase and will continue to be so. The other side of Sagittarius —the beast—has become manifest in the rise of pornographic movies (film being under the rulership of Neptune). We have also witnessed an increase in gambling, such as the legalization of off-track betting in New York state and the growth of local and state lotteries. People born with Neptune in Sagittarius will tend to embody the great Sagittarian restlessness for the seeking of experiences which expand both the senses and the Spirit.

3. Pluto. The annihilating, transforming, and regenerating characteristics of Pluto are modified in their effects upon humanity according to the sign in which this planet is placed. Pluto entered Libra for the first time in October of 1971 and is due to remain in this sign until the last decade of this century. Although it is too early to forecast the complete significance of this planet-sign relationship on the world and on those individuals in whose charts this configuration occurs, we can note the following tendencies.

a. THERE WILL BE a complete restructuring of the idea of justice as it is practiced in today's courts of law. Libra is the ideal of perfect justice and rules lawyers in general. (Neptune in Sagittarius will also contribute to this transformation, since Sagittarius is the sign of the actual courts and codes of justice, while Neptune is the planet of prisons.)

b. CHINA IS RULED BY LIBRA. Pluto's passage through this sign suddenly brought this nation into the public eye after more than two decades of silent and hidden (at least to the general public) development of its socioeconomic structure. The role of China will be seen to increase in world politics during the period of Pluto's passage through its sign.

c. MARRIAGE (and all social relationships, for that matter) will undergo a reappraisal of the ideas prompting its present form in society. People will tend to question the value of their relationships as hidden motivations come to the surface through social interactions. This trend is extremely noteworthy at the present time as Uranus is also passing through the sign of partnerships.

d. NEW AVENUES FOR PEACE can be developed, with a restructuring and shifting of the balance of world power and the use to which nuclear energy is applied.

EXERCISES.

1. On blank index cards place the symbols for each of the planet-sign combinations and contemplate these as often as you can.
2. Memorize the meanings of the planets in the signs. This can be done through the outright retention of what has been written.
3. It will also be helpful to list the symbols of the various sign-planet combinations and then, in your own words, write in the meaning alongside each.
4. Be patient. Time and experience are very helpful and necessary teachers.

Table 1: *Planetary Honors and Dishonors*

Planet	Dignity	Detriment	Exaltation	Fall
Sun	Leo	Aquarius	Aries	Libra
Moon	Cancer	Capricorn	Taurus	Scorpio
Mercury	Gemini, Virgo	Sagittarius, Pisces	Aquarius	Leo
Venus	Taurus, Libra	Scorpio, Aries	Pisces	Virgo
Mars	Aries, Scorpio	Libra, Taurus	Capricorn	Cancer
Jupiter	Sagittarius, Pisces	Gemini, Virgo	Cancer	Capricorn
Saturn	Capricorn, Aquarius	Cancer, Leo	Libra	Aries
Uranus	Aquarius	Leo	Scorpio	Taurus
Neptune	Pisces	Virgo	Cancer	Capricorn
Pluto	Scorpio	Taurus	Aquarius	Leo

9.

THE PATTERN OF THE HOUSES
AND THE ASCENDANT

If the planets are the WHAT of astrology and the signs the HOW, the Houses are considered the WHERE. *Where* in the person's life, in which area of earthly existence, does the energy indicated by the planet-sign configurations manifest itself with the greatest intensity?

No matter what your choice of House division (See chapters 11–13), the natal horoscope consists of twelve Houses. Each of these celestial domiciles corresponds to a number of activities gathered together under a collective title, such as the "House of Self" or the "House of Partnerships." They represent the major concept underlying the particular influence of each House.

Just as there are several basic divisions into which the signs are categorized, there are three major divisions into which the Houses are classified. These are *angular, succedent*, and *cadent*.

A. The Angular Houses (Ascendant-First, Descendant-Seventh, Midheaven-Tenth, and Nadir-Fourth).

When planets are placed at the angles, the various energies they embody become the most active and important influences in the chart. Briefly stated, planets located in the First House represent a constant source of potential energy which is ever present in a person's relationship to his immediate environment. Planets in the Tenth House represent those energies which will be used to promote either a person's success in the professional sphere of life or the forces which prevent such achievement. Planets in the Seventh House repre-

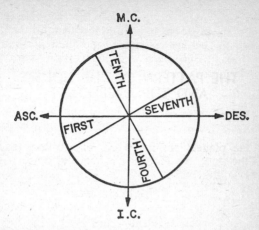

sent the energies at work in marriage and all close partnerships; they also have a great deal to do with the type of person we encounter and the nature of the circumstances surrounding their entrance into our lives. Planets in the Fourth House which indicate the basic motivational drives behind our outer activities, take on a tremendous psychological significance. They also indicate the nature of one's home and domestic affairs in general, as well as the events which surround the last twenty-odd years of a person's life.

1. First House: Ascendant. The Ascendant—or, as it is also called, the First House cusp or Rising Sign— is the projected image, the door through which we express and activate our inner motivations and psychological needs in the immediate environment. It characterizes our body types as well as the way other people receive their first impressions of us.

For example, if you were to spend your life in a room with only one window and that window were tinted blue, no matter what the inside of your room looked like to you, people on the outside would only see you and the contents of your room through this blue tint. In the same way, you would see others and the world outside your room through this same blue tint.

Therefore, in order to achieve an objective understanding of one's Self and of life in general, it becomes
essential that natives understand the difference between
their *essence* (Sun Sign) and *image* (the Ascendant).
The relationship between the two is signified by the
Moon, which stands for the nature of individual receptivity. It is the constant adjustment of personality
(Moon) which takes the energy from the Sun, modi-
fies it according to feelings, and transmits it to the
Ascendant, which then projects it in the form of an
image onto the immediate environment. This process
is representative of the triad: Father Sun = generator
of life; Mother Moon = sustainer of life; and Child
Ascendant = physical manifestation of life.

When the characteristics of each of the twelve signs
are applied to the Ascendant, they are modified so that
they are more closely related to one's external approach
to life than to one's inner motivations—which are, of
course, characterized by the Sun Sign. In this respect,
the following twelve paragraphs will give some indication of the nature of each of the signs when rising.

A person's initial approach to life is modified
through:

a. ARIES as an urgent need to express oneself
through a constant projection of one's energy upon
the immediate environment. The individual can often
react to given stimuli with over-enthusiasm or unnecessary haste. Aries rising is indicative of an eager but
often short-sighted individual. This placement usually
indicates a great need (and ability) to succeed at everything one undertakes, with immediate returns as a primary goal.

b. TAURUS as a need to achieve some form of concrete success through the projection of oneself upon
the environment. Therefore, no matter what the inner
motivations, one's drives will be externally expressed
with caution and circumspection. There is, in addition,
an awareness of possibilities of material reward for all
expended energy. Taurus rising can endow the person
with great physical magnetism and an appreciation of
the arts; alternately, it can indicate a rather fearful
and restrained form of self-expression.

c. GEMINI with a desire to express oneself in many ways through a great sense of versatility and a need for a constantly changing environment. An individual with this constellation is usually light-footed, enjoys changing his or her appearance, and is often active in an attempt to gain as much experience in as many areas as possible. This life style can result in a shallow and superficial expenditure of energy or in keen awareness of the many differences existing in society.

d. CANCER by a keen awareness for self-preservation. Cancer rising lends an extremely sympathetic and sensitive approach to life but with an overriding tendency to take all initial impressions personally. Unless conditioned by other modifying factors, this Ascendant can give an extremely subjective approach to life. The initial drive is to secure a foundation or "home base," from which all outer activities can proceed. With this in mind as a conscious goal, a Cancer Ascendant can either give great creativity or a great sense of insecurity to his or her form of self-expression.

e. LEO in a grandiose manner. There is a tendency to dramatize and to be keenly aware of life as a stage upon which one plays out one's "personal drama." A Leo Ascendant gives the ability to organize oneself and others quite efficiently, as well as a great creative potential, an understanding of children, and a need for personal appreciation. Leo rising usually imparts a proud and handsome appearance and a love of clothes and beautiful surroundings.

f. VIRGO as great attention to the minor details in one's manner of self-expression. A Virgo Ascendant can indicate a person who is extremely fastidious in his or her image and surroundings or one who is at a loss as to how to organize himself. A certain tightness or controlled image is present in an effort at self-presentation according to a personal concept of "proper" appearance. A Virgo Ascendant gives the ability to learn about oneself through an eagerness to be of help to others as well as a multifaceted resourcefulness.

g. LIBRA in a continual search for social relationships. A Libra Ascendant gives the need for a great many contacts; the person tends to see himself through the eyes and reactions of others. There is a talent for bringing harmony and beauty into one's surroundings through a natural "match-making" approach to life. This Ascendant is said to produce the most perfectly formed physical bodies, and it definitely lends charm and attractiveness. Very often there is a strong indecisiveness when it comes to self-expression.

h. SCORPIO with a certain degree of self-control and the need to express oneself a little at a time. A Scorpio Ascendant gives the ability to see all the various levels of activity and interactions occuring simultaneously around one, but it also introduces some difficulty or resistance to entering upon a field of activity in a personal, or at least extroverted, sense. Very often this intensity is "felt" but not mentally "understood" because of the watery nature of this sign. Awareness of the sexual energy in the environment is strong as well, as is the ability to drastically alter the surrounding circumstances.

i. SAGITTARIUS with great expansiveness of self-expression. A Sagittarius Ascendant imparts a need to cover a tremendous amount of territory; such an individual can be seen to be in a constant hurry. There is a generally brave and optimistic approach to life and a very friendly and outspoken nature. The individual tries to avoid all circumstances which tend to bind or limit spontaneous actions. This trait can make a person into an opportunist.

j. CAPRICORN in a very self-restrained manner. A Capricorn Ascendant imparts constraints on any form of impulsive activity because there is a tremendous need to project a "good" self-image and to maintain that created image in the face of all changes in relationships. It can thus become a very static influence. It is, however, a fine contributing factor toward personal success and long-range plans for the fulfillment of ambitions. Capricorn rising can view a situation from many angles, assessing the total structure of a better set of circumstances before any commitment. This is very important, for this Ascendant makes one true to one's word through a binding realization of duty.

k. AQUARIUS in a desire to express oneself in highly original ways. Aquarius on the Ascendant contributes to the making of a truly original individual insofar as one feels the need to act in some way contrary to the established order. This influence can lead to either highly inspirational contributions to society or to a desire to be self-willed and contrary just for the sake of being different. There is also the need to participate in group efforts, to the extent that one can best express oneself through such interactions.

l. PISCES by an extremely impressionable approach to life which can manifest itself either through the various arts or through a highly introverted and withdrawn nature. In any case, Pisces on the Ascendant tends to a surreptitious form of self-expression and makes for a strategist. Those individuals with Pisces rising will be drawn to environments which provide constantly changing emotional stimuli, so that they may express themselves through the many avenues which they feel open to them. There is usually an alteration between periods of great extroversion and equally strong introversion.

The First House is the natural domicile of Aries and its natural ruler, Mars.[1]

2. Fourth House.   The Fourth House is the foundation of life insofar as it reveals the nature of one's domestic situation. It is also a contributing factor which reveals the way events in life often terminate.

The Fourth House is the natural domicile of Cancer and its ruler, the Moon.

3. Seventh House.   The nature of the First House can be characterized as the "House of Self." The Seventh House, its polarity, can be called the "House of Others." It concerns itself with marriage and the marriage partner as well as with business partnerships. It is the House of open enemies and opponents as well as of those circumstances in which one has to develop

---

[1] The student would do well to study the nature of the sign and planet naturally associated with each of the Houses.

a sense of cooperation in order to successfully achieve one's goals.

The Seventh House is the natural domicile of Libra and its ruler, Venus.

4. Tenth House. This domicile is extremely involved with one's social position and the career through which one makes one's social contribution. It is the House of the most dominant parent in one's life while the Fourth House represents the other, less influential parent.

The Tenth is the natural House of Capricorn and its ruler, Saturn.

B. The Succedent Houses

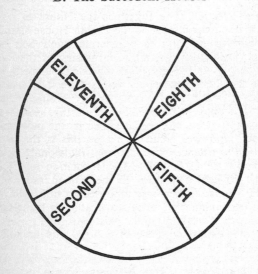

The Second, Fifth, Eighth, and Eleventh Houses are concerned with resources and the collectivization of energy in the following ways.

1. Second House. The Second House deals with rewards coming from personal efforts as indicated by the First House. The Second is also affiliated with property and individual financial security in general.

This is the natural domicile of Taurus and its ruler, Venus.

2. Fifth House.   The Fifth House is concerned with family resources, in the form of children, and the expression of personal creative ability in the arts which come about as the result of a firm establishment of oneself as an individual as expressed through the Fourth House. The Fifth House is also extremely important in regard to one's romantic life to the extent that one's love nature is very much an expression of the state of emotional development (Fourth House).

The Fifth House is the natural domicile of Leo and its ruler, the Sun.

3. Eighth House.   The Eighth is the House of other people's resources insofar as the Eighth House signifies the ability or inability to regenerate one's Self and material possessions through a harnessing of the energies available to the individual through partners and general social relationships. This is especially true in regard to legacies and other benefits brought either through marriage, business, and partnerships or in ways in which money is not directly earned by the individual. It is the "House of Death" because this is the phase of human existence wherein the individual passes through a state of complete transformation and joins with the collective energies of the human race. It is also the "House of Sex" (as opposed to the Fifth, the "House of Romance"), since sex is another transforming principle at work in human existence.

It is the natural domicile of Scorpio and its rulers, Mars and Pluto.

4. Eleventh House.   The Eleventh House concerns social connections obtained through one's career or position. This is the sphere of activity where personal ideas for self-expression become broadened through the assimilation of new data and the application of intellectual growth toward the larger collective of humanity.

The Eleventh, the "House of Friends and Associates," is the natural domicile of Aquarius and its rulers, Uranus and Saturn.

C. The Cadent Houses

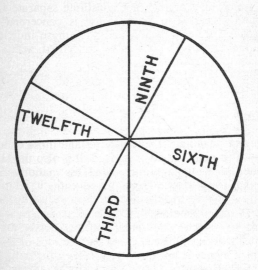

The Third, Sixth, Ninth and Twelfth Houses are concerned with human relationships and transitional states of being. These areas of life manifest themselves as follows.

1. Third House. The Third House concerns short-distance travel (those lasting one day or less, or a series of such short journeys which may collectively last longer). Its primary function is to describe the nature of *relationship* to the immediate environment (as opposed to the First House, which shows self-projection upon the immediate environment). A study of the Third House is often instrumental in determining the general mental structure of a given individual. It is also the "House of Immediate Family" (excluding parents and including neighbors and fraternal-type friends) and the sphere of the horoscope devoted to high school.

The Third House is the natural domicile of Gemini and its ruler, Mercury.

2. Sixth House. The Sixth House controls various jobs which may or may not constitute separate facets of one's career. The Sixth House is concerned with the general state of health and with those individuals who are employees. It is also concerned with small animals, especially household pets.

This is the natural domicile of Virgo and its ruler, Mercury.

3. Ninth House. The Ninth House has special regard to long-distance travel, higher education, and the personal understanding of social mores and those concepts from which national law is derived. It is also the House of one's religious aspirations and associations. Since it is the Third House from the Seventh, it relates to a partner's relatives, just as the Third House from the First signifies kin.

This is the natural domicile of Sagittarius and its ruler, Jupiter.

4. Twelfth House. The Twelfth House affects clandestine relationships and hidden enemies. In this respect the Twelfth House may also indicate those internal factors which can contribute to one's undoing. The Twelfth is called the "House of Karma" and for good reason. The situations described through a study of this domicile, its ruler in a given nativity (as opposed to its natural rulers), and those planetary bodies located within its boundaries describe the circumstances an individual must overcome in order to be free of firm bindings and destructive restrictions as well as negative patterns of recurrent relationships. Such institutions as prisons, asylums, and monasteries and other forms of secluded places of residence or confinement are also associated with the Twelfth.

This is the natural domicile of Pisces and its rulers, Jupiter and Neptune.

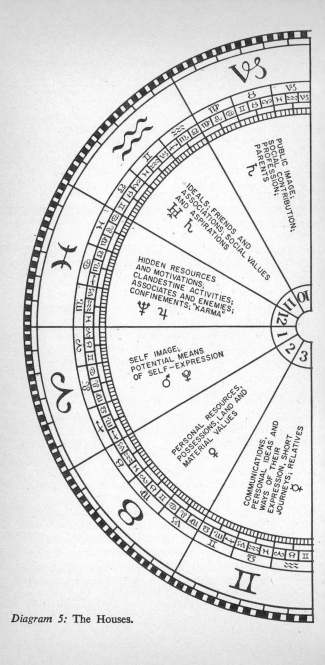

Diagram 5: The Houses.

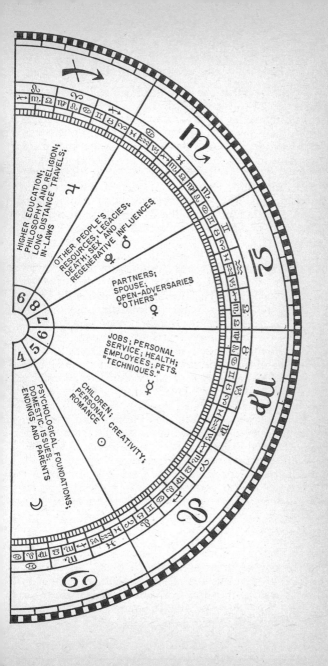

HIGHER EDUCATION;
PHILOSOPHY AND RELIGION;
LONG DISTANCE TRAVELS;
IN-LAWS
♃

OTHER PEOPLE'S
RESOURCES; LEGACIES;
DEATH; SEX AND
REGENERATIVE INFLUENCES.
♂ ♀

PARTNERS;
SPOUSE;
OPEN-ADVERSARIES
"OTHERS"
♀

JOBS; PERSONAL
SERVICE; HEALTH;
EMPLOYEES; PETS.
"TECHNIQUES."
☿

CHILDREN;
PERSONAL CREATIVITY;
ROMANCE
☉

PSYCHOLOGICAL FOUNDATIONS;
DOMESTIC ISSUES;
ENDINGS, AND PARENTS
☽

SUMMARY

We can see that the first three Houses are specifically oriented to the expression of oneself, as the First is one's immediate approach to life, the Second constitutes one's personal wealth, and the Third one's personal way of relating to those people in the immediate environment. The next three Houses involve relationships based on the family as signified by the Fourth House. The Fifth House is the fruit of the family or the children as well as the creative ability coming from a firm foundation, while the Sixth House represents those jobs necessary to support a family as well as those social connections directly related to the family such as servants and household pets. The next group of three is based on social inter-relationships with its foundation in marriage or business as designated by the Seventh House. The Eighth House shares the fruits of those relationships and reveals the potential for greater gain. The Ninth House reveals one's understanding of the underlying concepts upon which a social structure is based and the future aspirations resulting from that understanding. The last three Houses are the most impersonal of all insofar as they involve the merging of the individual's efforts into the collective of humanity. This is based in the Tenth House which signifies one's social contribution and position, while the Eleventh House represents the fruits of endeavors based on group involvements (as contrasted with the Eighth House which is most concerned with one's immediate partners). The Twelfth House signifies those areas of the personal life which have to be refined so that the energy contained therein may be purified for use by the Forces of Creativity.

EXERCISE.

Take out or draw a horoscope blank. In each of the twelve segments, write in the natural, planetary ruler as well as the affairs of each of the Houses.

Check your answers with Diagram 5. Try to do all work from memory.

10.

THE PLANETS IN THE HOUSES

Now that we have discussed the nature of the Houses, we can examine how the effect of the planets is manifested by their presence in each of the twelve cosmic domiciles:

1. The Sun. An individual's sense of self-integration and the structure of one's inner motivations as characterized by the Sun appear as follows.

a. IN THE FIRST HOUSE as the need to project oneself and be a dominating force at all times in any environment in which the individual finds himself or herself. There is a tendency toward general optimism and a "sunny" disposition, although care has to be taken that the drive to be the center of attention does not become overwhelming.

b. IN THE SECOND HOUSE as a need to focus oneself in circumstances which provide material security, stability of purpose, and a great deal of determination toward self-establishment.

c. IN THE THIRD HOUSE as a need for the continual self-expression through a variation in one's surroundings and social interchange as well as the drive toward the exploration of Self through the intellectual processes.

d. IN THE FOURTH HOUSE as a need to firmly establish roots; this need may appear as a driving force toward establishing the Self in society through a highly personalized environment. This position can give a strong attachment to the family, the nature of which would be determined by planetary aspects to the Sun.

e. IN THE FIFTH HOUSE as a strong need continually to express one's creative drive in accordance with the

115

sign in which the Sun is placed. This position gives great desire for a good time, party–going, and convivial relationships.

f. IN THE SIXTH HOUSE with great concern for one's own place in the scheme of things and the desire to establish that place through some sort of service to others. There is also a tendency to be concerned with matters of health, but this planet is not an indication of ill-health unless other factors in the horoscope so indicate.

g. IN THE SEVENTH HOUSE through a complete dependence on personal relationships and the interactions between one's own motivations and other people's reactions to this expression. This position is indicative of someone constantly involved with the making of social ties complimentary to self-expression.

h. IN THE EIGHTH HOUSE through an ability to transform one's environment as one attempts to fulfill lunar drives. There is an instinctual awareness of the resources available from personal contacts.

i. IN THE NINTH HOUSE as a need to explore oneself through those experiences in life which tend to be broadening in either an educational or a sensual manner. There is a tendency toward developing one's potential but an avoidance of binding circumstances which are often necessary for self-discipline.

j. IN THE TENTH HOUSE as a need to achieve social position or at least to engage in work which comes before the public. There is a tendency to be extremely self-driven and ambitious as there is a constant striving toward some form of influence over others. This position gives the need for power but not always the ability to handle it.

k. IN THE ELEVENTH HOUSE as a need to integrate oneself with a larger collective. This position imparts an interest in public work and participation in organizations and group activities. It gives a certain idealism and an approach to life which is often innovative and wide in scope.

l. IN THE TWELFTH HOUSE through activities that are behind the scenes rather than in the public eye. This position gives a strong need for seclusion, but it is also a contributing factor to a person's degree of resourcefulness. Some individuals with a Twelfth House Sun do not become aware of their potential for self-expression until later on in life, for there is the tendency to feel either inhibited on inferior in some way when the solar force inhabits the domicile of Neptune's ocean. The inner life is often much more profound and important to such an individual than is the outer.

2. *The Moon.* The receptive, emotional, and impressionable nature of an individual as characterized by the Moon will manifest itself as follows.

a. IN THE FIRST HOUSE as a strong need to be appreciated by everyone with whom the individual comes into contact, as well as a great sensitivity to the slightest change in the environment. The Moon in this position usually makes for an unsteady individual, one who is always "going through phases."

b. IN THE SECOND HOUSE as a need to establish a permanent set of values. This is a stabilizing position for the Moon and can constitute a great deal of common sense. It allows one to make the best with what one has. There is a further tendency for personal finances to "go through phases" when the Moon is in this domicile.

c. IN THE THIRD HOUSE through an awareness of the needs of the immediate family as well as a tendency toward involvement with education and travel, the success of which depends upon other planets in relation to the Moon. With the Moon in this position, opinions about life and the application of those opinions to daily existence are constantly "going through phases."

d. IN THE FOURTH HOUSE with great strength. There is a tendency to be exceedingly dependent upon family and roots. The relative usefulness of such connections is very dependent on the aspects the Moon receives from the other planets. The Moon's position in her own domicile strengthens sensitivities to others, but faith in oneself and home life often "goes through phases."

e. IN THE FIFTH HOUSE through a strong romantic nature and the desire to become closely associated with people in a highly personal and intimate sense. Love life and general relationship with women often "go through phases."

f. IN THE SIXTH HOUSE as a need to help people through an occupation which involves some form of close association with the general public, as well as the desire to put one's own life in order through every change of fate. Matters of health and/or job "go through phases" when the Moon is in this position.

g. IN THE SEVENTH HOUSE with a keen awareness and subsequent personal adjustment to the emotional states of others with whom one has direct dealings. There is a tendency to early marriage as well as close interdependence with a partner. In general, such partnerships often "go through phases" when the Moon is in this position.

h. IN THE EIGHTH HOUSE as great sensitivity to the resources available to the individual through his or her social affiliations and partnerships. Such a position gives an instinctual understanding of the fluctuations in other people's emotional states and the ability to transfer such states for personal good or ill, depending upon the nature of the whole map. Intimate and economic relationships "go through phases" when the Moon is in this position.

i. IN THE NINTH HOUSE through great sensitivity to the experiences gained from traveling, study, or general social interchange. This position gives a great need for an ever-widening and changing environment. Personal direction and goals often "go through phases" with the Moon in this position.

j. IN THE TENTH HOUSE as a drive toward self-fulfillment through some form of public view. There is an instinctual ability to feel the pulse of the general public and to capitalize on such feelings when the Moon is in the Tenth House, but success and social position often "go through phases" when the Moon is in this position.

k. IN THE ELEVENTH HOUSE as a need to experience life through an ever-changing and widening social sphere wherein an individual may develop those ideals which may lead to personal growth. There is a strong tendency for friendships and associations as well as opinions to "go through phases" when the Moon is in this position.

l. IN THE TWELFTH HOUSE with hidden emotions and clandestine relationships. There is the tendency to be extremely impressionable to the environment and to take advantage of opportunities offered, but in ways which are not overtly apparent. With the Moon in this position, general feelings about life are constantly fluctuating and "going through phases."

3. Mercury.   Thought processes are modified by Mercury's position as follows.

a. IN THE FIRST HOUSE as a strong intellectual approach to life and a need to translate activities into logical thought patterns. This position also indicates someone who is always "on the go."

b. IN THE SECOND HOUSE as a means of converting experience into ideas which will produce material rewards and a state of financial security.

c. IN THE THIRD HOUSE as an ever-searching mind eager for intellectual experimentation and learning. In addition there can be a great deal of travel in the life when Mercury is in its own domicile.

d. IN THE FOURTH HOUSE with concern for personal security and a tendency to frequently change residences.

e. IN THE FIFTH HOUSE as a need to express thoughts with a "personal stamp" as well as a mind given to artistic creativity and sensitivity. A fluctuation in romances and an instant communication with children is also noticeable.

f. IN THE SIXTH HOUSE as a practical approach to life through accomplishment. This position of Mercury can indicate a mind geared to detail. It keeps one extremely busy as there is a great deal of general movement in one's life with Mercury in this position.

g. IN THE SEVENTH HOUSE as a need to adjust opinions to the thoughts of others as well as the ability to be extremely sociable and at ease with people in general.

h. IN THE EIGHTH HOUSE by holding opinions which can impart a transforming quality to the minds of others. This position of Mercury gives a highly curious and probing mind.

i. IN THE NINTH HOUSE by a need to expand one's opinions in ever-widening circles. This position of Mercury can be highly impractical or it can give the mind of the philosopher. There is a need for travel and/or higher studies, the relative success or failure of which is shown by Mercury's interplanetary relationships.

j. IN THE TENTH HOUSE as a way to achieve one's ambitions through writing, speaking, or some other form of communication. This position can indicate a natural talent for speaking before the public.

k. IN THE ELEVENTH HOUSE through interchanges with groups of people and through the ability to study those areas of knowledge, such as the natural and occult sciences, which serve to broaden the mind.

l. IN THE TWELFTH HOUSE by uncertainty about one's own opinions, because the scope of vision is wide but neither sharp nor personal. This position is excellent for work of a mediumistic or artistic nature.

4. Venus. The nature of personal magnetism and social nature as well as the ability to attract wealth is modified as follows.

a. IN THE FIRST HOUSE with a great deal of intensity, charm, and general attractiveness. Venus in this position can often give a highly artistic and/or sensual nature. An individual with this position can tend to extreme laziness in self-expression or can be extremely active and highly artistic. As with all discussions of planets in the Houses, the sign position of the heavenly bodies is a modifying factor.

b. IN THE SECOND HOUSE with a great deal of strength. Venus is extremely comfortable here and can bestow its blessings quite freely, especially in the financial sense, unless other planets and aspects alter the nature of Venus' beneficence.

c. IN THE THIRD HOUSE with an ease of communication and a general ability to bring harmony and abundance to close associates and family, as well as lending an artistic and balanced overtone to the mental faculties.

d. IN THE FOURTH HOUSE with an inner need to express oneself in a harmonious and artistic sense and not to be the cause of any disruptions. The latter part of life tends to be surrounded by comfortable circumstances.

e. IN THE FIFTH HOUSE with an ease for attracting romantic involvements. This position can give success with children as well as artistic ability. A highly sensual and romantic nature is often noted.

f. IN THE SIXTH HOUSE through success at various jobs and the ability to bring harmony and order into other people's lives through personal intervention. There is usually a strong cooperative sense in relations with coworkers and employees.

g. IN THE SEVENTH HOUSE by the success or failure of close partnerships. There is a need to be socially active and a certain grace and poise in dealing with others.

h. IN THE EIGHTH HOUSE by other people's financial states. If Venus is well-aspected here, legacies and benefits may accrue from relatives or business partnerships. This position also gives a transforming ability within the structure of personal relationships, the nature of which depends, of course, on the entire horoscope.

i. IN THE NINTH HOUSE by fortunate circumstances surrounding travels and the ability to profit from higher education and adventure. Since the Ninth House is the third from the Seventh, it becomes the sphere of the partner's relatives. Thus a well-aspected Venus in this position tends to give benefits from in-laws.

j. IN THE TENTH HOUSE by social condition and career. This position gives the ability to use personal magnetism and charisma to attract benefits in the professional sphere. In addition, Venus' position in this domicile characterizes the type of business with which one is involved. (The sign in which Venus is placed will be most helpful in pinpointing the specific nature of this involvement.)

k. IN THE ELEVENTH HOUSE by gains through associates and friends, as well as a general interest in social values. Goals and ideas can be thwarted or attained through friendships and will be indicated by the aspects to Venus.

l. IN THE TWELFTH HOUSE by clandestine relationships. There is a tendency to secrecy in expressing romantic involvements. On the other hand, Venus in this house denotes a tendency to be of service to all types of individuals and can be a very unselfish placement. Great compassion is indicated, but there is a tendency for a lack of discrimination when it comes to personal relationships.

5. *Mars.*   The aggressive, assertive, and dynamic projection of desires is manifested as follows.

a. IN THE FIRST HOUSE as fearlessness and a constant source of energy which can be most beneficial in self-assertion but which also leads to a need to dominate immediate surroundings. This position gives great recuperative abilities, strength, and determination.

b. IN THE SECOND HOUSE through material aims which are diligently pursued. If Mars is poorly aspected in this position, troubles with finances, especially in holding on to resources, are indicated.

c. IN THE THIRD HOUSE by a constant fount of mental activity which, if not properly directed, can lead to nervousness and can cause quarrels with the people in the immediate environment.

d. IN THE FOURTH HOUSE as a constant undertone of high-strung emotions, irritability, or the urge to dominate. A poorly aspected Mars in this position can often indicate strife in the domestic sphere, an overly dominant parent, or certain difficulties surrounding the changing of residences.

e. IN THE FIFTH HOUSE through a great sense of personal creativity which is often asserted egotistically but which can also be extremely stimulating to others. This position often reveals a very strong sensual nature and can, if poorly aspected, indicate strife and breaks in romantic relationships.

f. IN THE SIXTH HOUSE by an ability to create a tremendous amount of activity through work. This position of Mars can show mechanical ability (especially if it is involved with Mercury or Uranus), but it can bring strife with coworkers if a sense of cooperation and a respect for other people's methodologies are not realized.

g. IN THE SEVENTH HOUSE by partnerships. This position can bring relationships that cause strife and disharmony because of the impulsive way in which they were begun. There is often a need to dominate partners and/or spouses. On the other hand, if this energy is well-directed, it can be a great source of inspiration for partnerships and can engender a strong cooperative spirit.

h. IN THE EIGHTH HOUSE through dependence on other people's financial and/or emotional resources to fulfill personal goals. This position can be a most helpful tool in helping other people to rearrange the structures of their lives, but it can also allow one to live off other people inordinately. The sexual and potential creative nature is usually quite strong but needs the proper motivation and channels.

i. IN THE NINTH HOUSE with strong opinions, with a need for adventure and travel, and, if well-placed, with fervent religious feeling. There is a great restlessness when Mars is in this position because of a continual search for excitement.

j. IN THE TENTH HOUSE with a great desire to be successful in a chosen profession and, if other factors in the horoscope concur, with the potential know-how necessary to obtain those goals. Cooperation with people in authority as well as with one's father or mother is a lesson which usually has to be learned.

k. IN THE ELEVENTH HOUSE through using the positions of friends and associates to fulfill personal goals. Mars in this domicile gives an inventive nature and a strong sense of idealization, but other factors in the chart would have to point the way to the practical realization of ambitions.

l. IN THE TWELFTH HOUSE surreptitiously. This position makes for a very good strategist, since inner plans are not revealed easily when Mars is in this House. There are apt to be secret enemies or certain skeletons lurking in the closet. People with this position have to learn constantly to express themselves creatively, so that their energies do not backfire into self-destruction.

6. Jupiter. The expansive, noble, and philosophical vibrations of Jupiter will express themselves as follows.

a. IN THE FIRST HOUSE as an extremely generous and buoyant approach to life. Such individuals must do things in a big way and are often very exhilarating people to know. On the other hand, if Jupiter is poorly aspected or in a sign not harmonious with its own nature, it can be a very selfish, self-indulgent, and wasteful influence. In either case, travel and a desire for adventure are noted.

b. IN THE SECOND HOUSE as an indicator of wealth and material good fortune. This is especially true if Jupiter is well-aspected by Saturn, Venus, or the Moon. On the other hand, it can show a tendency to gamble resources and to spend beyond one's means.

c. IN THE THIRD HOUSE with a great tendency toward constant travel and the desire to express oneself in the intellectual sphere. There can be some very fine relationships with close relatives and neighbors as well as with associates. This position indicates a tendency to seek out learning experiences in every aspect of life.

d. IN THE FOURTH HOUSE with a generally wide and compassionate understanding of other people's feelings, especially in relation to oneself. This position of Jupiter, if well-placed, gives a large and often well-to-do family and can indicate the making of a home in a foreign country. Such people never have any difficulty in finding a place to live unless Jupiter is poorly placed, in which case more money may be spent for a residence than is practical.

e. IN THE FIFTH HOUSE through a love of adventure, sports, and gambling. These individuals enjoy taking chances with life, and if Jupiter is well-aspected, they usually receive an abundance of "luck." There is often joy and great reward in love and with children as well as a general uplifting and positive feeling about life.

f. IN THE SIXTH HOUSE through an ability to bring

optimistic, expansive, and creative feelings to work and fellow employees. If Jupiter is afflicted, however, it can indicate someone who is overindulgent in food or drink and whose health suffers accordingly. This position of Jupiter can either make one successful through service to others or result in extreme criticism of other people's activities.

g. IN THE SEVENTH HOUSE through a strongly cooperative and helpful nature. There is a tendency to benefit both financially and philosophically from partnerships, but if Jupiter is poorly placed in this House, there may be great selfishness and a tendency to expect too much from relationships.

h. IN THE EIGHTH HOUSE through economic or philosophical benefits resulting from inheritances. This position of Jupiter can result in a strong leaning toward the mystic or occult, but it can also expand the sexual nature to such an extent that it becomes a dominant force in relationships. If well-placed, Jupiter in this position can be greatly uplifting to others in very subtle ways, but if poorly aspected, it can make the native very exploitative.

i. IN THE NINTH HOUSE through good judgment and a keen interest in philosophy and religion. If poorly placed, however, Jupiter in this House leads to exaggerations of all kinds and a confused philosophy of life. In either case, travel and a love of adventure is indicated when Jupiter is in its own domicile.

j. IN THE TENTH HOUSE as a tendency to be quite successful in one's chosen career, the nature of which is characterized by Jupiter's sign. It gives the ability to bring additional wealth and broad vision in any field.

k. IN THE ELEVENTH HOUSE through a great love of social life and an ability to achieve goals and realize ideals through friendships and associations. If well-aspected, this position is an excellent indication of a constant source of help from friends. If it is poorly placed, an overindulgence in social life can lead to a dissipation of energy and a lack of cohesive direction.

l. IN THE TWELFTH HOUSE as a very compassionate nature always ready to help other people. This position shows unexpected benefits in times of need. On the other hand, if Jupiter is poorly placed, this position gives a tendency toward making decisions which can prove to be self-deceptive, overemotional, and wasteful. One can give too much away, both emotionally and physically.

7. *Saturn.* The consolidating, limiting, and conserving tendencies which are embodied by Saturn are manifested as follows.

a. IN THE FIRST HOUSE as a highly self-repressed nature, which can lead to a generally melancholy approach to life. If well-placed, Saturn in the First House leads to a type of caution and circumspection which can eventually bring success. A First House Saturn imparts a need to deal with the realities of life at a very early age.

b. IN THE SECOND HOUSE through lessons in the proper handling of personal resources. A well-placed Saturn in this domicile indicates someone who can profit most from investing the least, but a poorly placed Saturn can deprive a person of wealth or at least bring certain fears concerning the use of money.

c. IN THE THIRD HOUSE as an ability to engage in intensive study and intellectual self-discipline. On the other hand, this aspect can limit one's understanding and bring a general depression to relationships. Saturn in the Third can contribute to a student's success, but it can also cause the halt of an education before its completion. Naturally the whole horoscope will have to be examined before a final judgment can be given in this respect.

d. IN THE FOURTH HOUSE as lessons in responsibilities or duties to one's family. It can mean that the individual has to carry on the family tradition, either for his own benefit or in ways that restrict individual freedom.

e. IN THE FIFTH HOUSE through lessons in creative self-expression. Saturn in the Fifth can limit the number of children or bring responsibilities where children are involved. It can indicate a person who can become a teacher butt whose attitude might be somewhat authoritarian.

f. IN THE SIXTH HOUSE as a strong sense of responsibility or an inordinate number of burdens attached to jobs. This position also indicates a very practical nature insofar as the individual will gear his approach to work with a consideration of the conservation of energy. If well-placed, Saturn in this position gives a strong constitution, which can endure all types of illnesses; but if poorly placed, it leads to chronic diseases.

g. IN THE SEVENTH HOUSE through lessons of cooperation and in duties to the marriage partner and to partnerships in general. Saturn in this position can align one with mature individuals and attract one to an older spouse. It is also an indication of someone who might marry late in life, but a study of Venus and the Moon is necessary to judge the situation properly.

h. IN THE EIGHTH HOUSE through lessons involving other people's resources. This position can be quite useful in showing people how to make the most of their assets, but it can also be a tool for taking advantage of other people's bounty. Quite often there is a desire to control the environment and a need to wield power, often at others' expense. There may either be a blockage in sexual expression or the desire to use sex to gain control over others. Experiences related to death can prove very educational or deepen an appreciation of the life cycle.

i. IN THE NINTH HOUSE through structuring the mental faculties, possibly leading to the establishment of a practical philosophy of life. If used properly, this position of Saturn can strengthen the mind and make it more concrete. Experiences gained through travel are often quite beneficial in this respect.

j. IN THE TENTH HOUSE as lessons learned through the striving for personal attainment in the professional sphere. One of two major tendencies is noted: success becomes greater with age, through a gradual process of increased influence; or success is denied through constant stumbling blocks, so that one repeatedly comes back to the starting point.

k. IN THE ELEVENTH HOUSE through lessons learned through friends. There is a tendency to seek out older people with whom one has some very beneficial (or, if

Saturn is poorly aspected, difficult) relationships. This is a good position for Saturn because it allows for a structuring of ideas and practical avenues for their expression.

l. IN THE TWELFTH HOUSE through certain feelings of self-repression which thwart the fulfillment of ambitions. It also leads to an irrational approach to self-discipline or any form of limitations, since there is a deeply rooted fear of such circumstances. On the other hand, this position can give many benefits through those occupations or pursuits involving seclusion or isolation and is a perfect location for Saturn for someone involved in research projects or metaphysical studies.

8. Uranus. The erratic and unconventional though often inventive and intuitional nature of Uranus manifests itself as follows.

a. IN THE FIRST HOUSE as the tendency to be extremely individualistic. This is the type of person whose life is always filled with surprises leading to sudden realizations and drastic changes. These work for good or ill, depending on the aspects this planet receives from other points in the chart. It usually indicates a very nervous and restless individual, who must work out his or her personal direction in life through some activity which deals with large groups of people.

b. IN THE SECOND HOUSE as sudden circumstances which change personal finances. This can take the form of ideas leading to increase or to such drastic circumstances that one's finances are constantly "wiped out."

c. IN THE THIRD HOUSE through mental faculties. This can be an exceptionally good placement for Uranus (as well as for the individual) because the higher intuitional aspects of the mind are given free rein to creatively express themselves in the House of Mercury. On the other hand, such a person can have unconventional attitudes about school which lead to abrupt changes in education. This placement can also lead to certain ideas without the proper structure for their implementation in the immediate environment.

d. IN THE FOURTH HOUSE as drastic changes in one's

domestic situation which cause frequent change of residences. It can also produce someone who is at odds with his social, economic, or ethnic background and the need to project very individualistically in the domestic sphere.

e. IN THE FIFTH HOUSE as a need or an ability to project dealings with children, romantic adventures, and creative self-expression.

f. IN THE SIXTH HOUSE in work and health. There is a tendency to change jobs frequently because of dissatisfaction with routine. An undisciplined nervous system can play havoc with health.

g. IN THE SEVENTH HOUSE as sudden changes in partnerships and a highly unconventional type of marriage. People with this placement are attracted to unusual people with whom they seek to form sudden and unusual relationships.

h. IN THE EIGHTH HOUSE through strong psychic feelings which, if not well-disciplined, can lead to erratic and uncontrollable harmful impulses. This tendency is often manifested in the sexual realm, leading to extremely unconventional desires, especially if Uranus is aspected with Venus, Mars, or the Moon. A well-aspected Uranus in the Eighth can bring sudden inheritances and financial benefits through unexpected windfalls.

i. IN THE NINTH HOUSE through unorthodox ideas concerning religion or philosophy. If well-placed, this position can give a gifted mind and contribute to those experiences obtained through travel or higher education which serve to enrich and broaden an individual's approach to life.

j. IN THE TENTH HOUSE through an occupation which involves the whole populace in some way. This is an excellent position for a politician or someone involved with mass-marketing and even points the way toward an inherent faculty for the occult sciences. Uranus in this position is not conducive to holding a "conventional job," for an individual with this placement needs plenty of room in which to be inventive.

k. IN THE ELEVENTH HOUSE as interchanges with a great many individuals and their respective opinions and ideas. This position can contribute to a personality that is constantly changing friends because of a great need to experiment with social life. This position of Uranus allows all the inherent qualities of the planet to surface quite easily.

l. IN THE TWELFTH HOUSE as a strong sense of intuition but with difficulty in listening to the Self in this respect; such people can be their own worst enemies. On the other hand, if the energy of Uranus is well-disciplined, this position is an excellent placement for all types of research work as well as for studies in the occult and mystic sciences.

9. Neptune. The imaginative though sometimes hallucinatory nature of Neptune will act as follows.

a. IN THE FIRST HOUSE as a veil of mystery surrounding an individual such that there is a strong allure. Neptune in this position confers great resourcefulness, and such a person can project in any number of ways, depending on the impressions received from the stimuli in the immediate environment. Care must, however, be taken not to become lost in glamor, as there is a tendency to insecurity, and a certain self-deceptiveness may result. There is also a tendency to "let things slide" and a general lackadaisical feeling when Neptune is so strong in a chart.

b. IN THE SECOND HOUSE as either a tendency to be extremely resourceful in ways of accumulating financial resources or a tendency to extreme wastefulness or underhandedness in financial dealings.

c. IN THE THIRD HOUSE through the mental faculties. There is a tendency to become lost in dreams and to lack a rational approach to life or, if Neptune is well-placed, a highly receptive mind which can see all sides of an issue before arriving at a final judgment. This is an excellent position for artists, poets, film makers, and mystics.

d. IN THE FOURTH HOUSE as a very strongly emotional factor leading to a highly receptive nature. If Neptune is well-placed, there is a great desire to examine hidden mysteries which may concern the origins of Man and each person's personal place in that large panorama. If poorly placed, however, it can result in delusions about family, a very unstable home life, or a parent who tends to embody the negative qualities of Neptune. There is often a certain element of self-sacrifice in regard to domestic life when Neptune is placed in this domicile.

e. IN THE FIFTH HOUSE with the tendency to dramatize life. This position is very good for the professions mentioned under Neptune in the Third House. It also means that there is often some form of self-sacrifice in romantic relationships. In this respect it can bring attachments to underdogs. If poorly aspected, Neptune can indicate clandestine and often illicit relationships.

f. IN THE SIXTH HOUSE as a tendency to be highly resourceful in an approach to a task and to be very helpful to those in less fortunate positions. Any illnesses signified by Neptune in this position have a strong emotional component and are often indicative of psychosomatic conditions.

g. IN THE SEVENTH HOUSE as an attraction toward people and relationships which can show up as a desire to be either truly giving and self-sacrificing or deceptive and clandestine. There is also a tendency to glamorize partners rather than view them realistically.

h. IN THE EIGHTH HOUSE very strongly with a psychic nature. If well-aspected and well-controlled, this position can be an exceptionally good tool for all types of work dealing with the mystic or occult. On a more material level, however, it can bring deception and difficulties in those areas dealing with other people's resources. Certain unforeseen complications can surround legacies. With this position of Neptune, death often comes during sleep.

i. IN THE NINTH HOUSE in a way which can highly refine the philosophical and religious feelings or can bring delusionary opinions in these areas. A great deal, of course, depends upon the aspects received by Neptune from the other planets. Another manifestation of Neptune in this position is a tendency to daydream and becloud true judgment with wishful thinking.

j. IN THE TENTH HOUSE as influence over career, since this is an excellent position for those occupations involving service and/or the arts. On the other hand, this placement can bring tremendous difficulties in finding one's position in society by a constant fluctuation in career objectives, or through a general lack of ambition. Care must be taken to protect a public image especially from public scandal if Neptune is poorly placed at the Midheaven.

k. IN THE ELEVENTH HOUSE in the sphere of social activities. Neptune here means that an individual may need discrimination in the selection of friends because there is a certain susceptibility to other people's suggestions and opinions. On the other hand, if these vibrations are well-directed and under the individual's control, they can lead to humanitarian services and abilities in the psychic sciences. There is a need to separate ideals from the means at hand to turn dreams into practical realities.

l. IN THE TWELFTH HOUSE with great strength. There can be an undue fear of confinement or a tendency toward confinement. On the other hand, if the vibrations of this planet are expertly channeled, this position is a fantastic tool for the development of psychic abilities. In this position Neptune gives great resourcefulness, but unless it is well-aspected by other planets, there can be disturbing fears surrounding the expression of feelings and sometimes an overly active imagination.

10. *Pluto.* The regenerating, transforming, or completely annihilating tendencies of Pluto manifest themselves as follows.

a. IN THE FIRST HOUSE as a great need for solitude on the part of the individual with such a placement. Pluto rising marks a loner, someone who is constantly undergoing a process of transformation which is tested through sporadic attempts at social interactions. This is an extremely powerful position, for it adds a certain intensity which allows the individual to transform his or her environment and to have a certain amount of control over others. The life is filled with drastic endings and constant new beginnings directly related to inner growth.

b. IN THE SECOND HOUSE in financial circumstances. When it is well-aspected, Pluto in this position can act as a "never-ending fountain of gold." But when it is afflicted, it can suddenly withdraw rewards worked for over a long period of time. Pluto's action is always swift, but it is not impulsive like Mars', for Pluto works for long periods underneath the surface of apparent activities before its manifestation appears in the physical world.

c. IN THE THIRD HOUSE as an ever-changing opinion of the Self and the world. When well placed, this position can lead to a constant renewal of thoughts which give great mental insights. However, Pluto destroys the structure of thought and in extreme cases can lead to mental breakdowns (especially if malefically configurated with Neptune and Mercury.

d. IN THE FOURTH HOUSE through a need to overcome traditional roots which can provide the stumbling block to growth. On the other hand, if Pluto is well placed herein, it can give a need to explore family tradition, so that one can draw from one's heritage a sense of personal identity and a continual renewal of psychological foundations. If Pluto is poorly placed here, it can lead to feelings of homelessness which may result in a constant change of residences.

e. IN THE FIFTH HOUSE as a need to transform the nature of romantic proclivities and to refine artistic or creative self-expression. Children can be the means through which great growth can take place, but a poorly aspected Pluto in the Fifth can be a contributing factor toward the denial of children.

f. IN THE SIXTH HOUSE as an ability to bring new life into various jobs or to lack consistency in the completion of any given task. In this respect one can inspire others through application to work, or one can bring about great chaos through an abuse of responsibility. Pluto in the Sixth can give great recuperative strength, but if it is poorly aspected, it can be a cause of a continual energy drain.

g. IN THE SEVENTH HOUSE as an intensity in personal relationships. This position can bring a partner who functions as a great source of renewal and strength or, if Pluto is poorly placed, it can cause break-ups and sudden endings of relationships after long disputes.

h. IN THE EIGHTH HOUSE very strongly. When Pluto is in this position, it can act very surreptitiously either as an agent of renewal or as a complete drain of other people's emotional or financial energy. In a highly developed person this is a helpful tool for healing or working psychically.

i. IN THE NINTH HOUSE through religious or philosophical beliefs. Pluto in this position can bring new life into established doctrines, and there is a great ability to evolve through the pursuits of the Ninth House. The experiences gained in travel often serve as transforming agents.

j. IN THE TENTH HOUSE as an ability to breathe new life into the chosen career or into a business which is seemingly dead or dying. If other positions in the horoscope concur, Pluto in the Tenth adds to the ability to make long-range and highly technical plans as well as laying the foundation for resources accumulated through repetitive cycles of return.

k. IN THE ELEVENTH HOUSE as a tendency for friends to suddenly leave and not be heard from for long periods, if ever again. The transforming principle is closely associated with social life, since friends are often the agents through which evolutionary growth or blocks to that growth appear.

l. IN THE TWELFTH HOUSE when least expected. If it is well-aspected, Pluto acts as a sort of "guardian angel" which annihilates harm that might otherwise occur. There is an ability to find some inner resources of strength when they are needed to make the next step in plans. When it is poorly aspected, however, negative forces are always at work trying to destroy ideas, projects, relationships, and in extreme cases, one's very being. Planetary aspects to Pluto in the Twelfth will certainly help to pinpoint these destructive energies. In a highly developed person, this position allows constant amassing of new energy from the collective bounty of humanity.

EXERCISE.

This may be a long exercise to do but it is essential:

1. Select a section in your notebook.
2. Title each page with a planet in this order: ☉, ☽, ☿, ♀, ♂, ♃, ♄, ♅, ♆, ♇.
3. Number 1–12 down the page, leaving several lines between each number.
4. Fill in the basic effects of the planet appearing on top of the page when it appears in each of the Houses corresponding to the number in the margin of the page.
5. Check answers with text.

PART II

The Road: Chart Erection And Interpretation

NOTE

Now you have the astrological alphabet at your fingertips. The next task is to use it to formulate words and sentences. This means that we must first erect the natal chart and then proceed to interpret it. The mathematical processes necessary to erect and to calculate the chart are very simple. The astronomical and physical laws on which these calculations are based are somewhat more complicated. An accurate and comprehensive picture of the astronomy and physics involved in astrological work would require an entire volume. More than one such work is already extant in order to serve this need. The most outstanding of these texts to my knowledge are: *The Astrologer's Astronomical Handbook* by Jeff Mayo and *Simplified Astronomy for Astrologers* by David Williams.

Though a highly technical appreciation of astronomy is well worth the students' effort, however, it is not essential. Serious students will become increasingly familiar with the physical basis for their chosen field as their studies progress.

In this volume I intend to pass on to the reader the method of chart erection and interpretation which has served me best during the years, as well as many short cuts and hints developed through the erection of thousands of charts. I know that many readers are already well versed in the various methods of setting up a wheel; nevertheless, these tips will be of definite use to both the beginner and the advanced student, helping them to accomplish the work with the greatest ease and accuracy.

II.

TIME: THE UNIVERSAL FACTOR

Time is inherent in the manifested universe. The measurements of time and the various kinds of existing time are based on Man's interpretation of the life cycles he sees around him. It is quite simple to understand how Man came to measure the year—one revolution of the Earth about the Sun—and the day—one revolution of the Earth about its own axis. These movements are founded in natural phenomena. But what about that bane of astrologers—Daylight Savings Time and such other artificial time factors as War Time (more light for the manifestation of more darkness)? What are Summer and Double Summer Time all about? These designations and divisions of time which are Man-made mutations, are by necessity of prime importance to the astrologer. Two primary steps are required in order to set up the wheel of the horoscope. Natal chart erection entails the correct placement of the Midheaven, Ascendant, and the other House cusps around the wheel. The calculation of these factors is based on the true local time of birth (or Local Mean Time). There must also be exact positioning of the planets, nodes, and parts within the wheel. The calculation for this procedure is based on the relationship between the given time of birth and Greenwich Mean Time. The reason for this step is that the planets in the various ephemerides are listed according to either their noon or midnight positions, GMT. Thus the planetary positions for any birth occuring at any other time but noon or midnight GMT (depending on the ephemeris) must be adjusted.

A. Time Standards and the Importance of Greenwich Mean Time

The advent of the Industrial Revolution and the commercial expansionism of the world powers brought the need for a consistent and universal time system. In the United States, for example, a Standard Time system was begun in 1883. The definite geographical boundaries for these Time Zones was not firmly established, however, until 1918. Up to that time, and especially before 1883, each community in each state and territory used a different time standard, resulting in delays in railway transportation, lost revenue, and general confusion.

Shortly after the United States decided to inaugurate definite Time Zones within its boundaries, the leading nations of the world, meeting at the International Meridian Conference in 1884, agreed to consider the Greenwich Observatory in England as the Zero degree

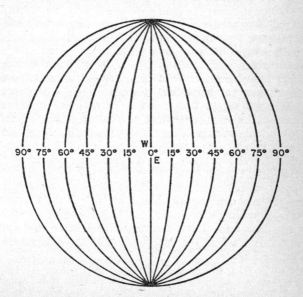

Diagram 6: Earth's Longitudinal Divisions.

of longitude on all maps (the equator, of course, is 0 degrees of latitude). If the number of degrees in the circumference of the Earth (360°) is divided by 24 (hours of the day), 15 degrees of terrestrial longitude equals one hour of time. These pole-to-pole segments of the Earth's major meridional divisions give the Earth a tangerinelike appearance. In other words, the surface of the Earth turns 15 degrees or one-twenty-fourth of its daily motion around its axis in one hour. If we further divide 60 (minutes in an hour) by 15 (degrees of longitude), we realize that the Earth moves one degree about its axis in four minutes.[1] We can therefore erect the following table:

Table 2: Longitude and time

$$
\begin{aligned}
360° \text{ of motion (longitude)} &= 24 \text{ hours} \\
15° \text{ of motion (longitude)} &= 1 \text{ hour} \\
1° \text{ of motion (longitude)} &= 4 \text{ minutes} \\
15 \text{ minutes of motion (longitude)} &= 1 \text{ minute} \\
1 \text{ minute of motion (longitude)} &= 4 \text{ seconds}
\end{aligned}
$$

The student should take great care that hours, minutes, and seconds of clock time are never confused with degrees, minutes, and seconds of arc (motion).

We refer to Greenwich (0°) as the *Prime Meridian*; each degree East or West of Greenwich is also called a *meridian* (of longitude). Each 15 degrees of terrestrial longitude is known as a *Time Zone* or *Time Standard*. For the Western astrologer, some of the most important of these Time Standards are as follows.[2]

1. Greenwich Mean Time (GMT = 0E/W) is used throughout the British Isles as well as in Algeria, Belgium, France, Holland, Luxembourg, Morocco, Portugal, and Spain.

---

[1] This is actually an approximation; in reality the Earth's diurnal axial speed is closer to 23 hours and 56 minutes. The missing four minutes is not forgotten by astrologers. We will discuss this accumulation of the "spare" time when we discuss Sidereal Time.

[2] All the Time Standards and Zones of all the countries of the world can be found in *Time Changes in the World; Time Changes in The United States; and Time Changes in Canada and Mexico,* all of which are compiled by Doris Chase Doane.

2. Time East of Greenwich

a. MIDDLE OR CENTRAL EUROPEAN TIME (MET OR CET = 15E) is used in Austria, Czechoslovakia, Denmark, Germany, Hungary, Italy, Norway, Poland, Sweden, Switzerland, and Yugoslavia.

b. EASTERN EUROPEAN TIME (EET = 30E) is used in Bulgaria, Egypt, Greece, Finland, Israel, and Rumania, among other countries. Russia and China are so vast that the former country covers eleven Time Zones (from 30E to 180E), while China's territory is divided into five Time Zones whose Standard Time Meridians begin at 82E30 and end at 127E30.

3. Time West of Greenwich

a. ATLANTIC STANDARD TIME (AST = 60W) is used in Nova Scotia, Puerto Rico, Chile, Paraguay, Argentina, and parts of Brazil.

b. EASTERN STANDARD TIME (EST = 75W) is used along the entire eastern coast of the United States, in eastern Canada, and in parts of Central and South America. This meridian passes almost exactly through Philadelphia.

c. CENTRAL STANDARD TIME (CST = 90W) is used throughout the American Midwest and in parts of Central America and Canada.

d. MOUNTAIN STANDARD TIME (MST = 105W) is used in the Rocky Mountain states of this country as well as in parts of Canada and Mexico. This meridian passes through Denver, Colorado.

e. PACIFIC STANDARD TIME (PST = 120W) is the Time Zone for the entire western coast of the United States and Canada.

f. ALASKA STANDARD TIME is standardized on 150W; in reality Time Zones of 120W, 135W, and 165W are also used in various parts of this state.

Once the nature of Time Zones is understood, it becomes a simple task to ascertain the time in any place in the world relative to Greenwich Mean Time; the only prerequisite is the longitude and Time Standard of that place. The rule is quite explicit: *If the location in question lies* WEST *of Greenwich, the standard time of that location will be* EARLIER *than GMT. Conversely, if the location lies* EAST *of Greenwich, the standard time is* LATER *than GMT.*

For example, New York City is standardized by EST = 75W (75 = 15 × 5). Thus, when it is noon in England, it is 7:00 A.M. in New York (or at any place in the EST Zone). By the same calculation, when it is 9:00 A.M. in England, it is 10:00 A.M. in Sweden (standardized at 15E). Since the Earth turns on its axis from West to East, when the Sun is overhead at any point on the Earth's surface, any point farther East has already passed the Sun's rays and hence is later in time. Any point farther West, on the other hand, has yet to pass under the Sun and is thus earlier in time. Noon in Chicago is 11:00 A.M. in Denver and 1:00 P.M. in New York. Table 3 clarifies these time differences.

SUMMARY.

To determine the equivalent Greenwich Mean Time from the given *Standard Time* (ST) of birth, you proceed as follows.

First, determine the Standard Time Zone in which the birth in question occurred.

Then *add* one hour to the ST for every 15 degrees of longitude that the Zone is *west* of Greenwich:

180W + 12 hours	90W + 6 hours
165W + 11 hours	75W + 5 hours
150W + 10 hours	60W + 4 hours
135W + 9 hours	45W + 3 hours
120W + 8 hours	30W + 2 hours
105W + 7 hours	15W + 1 hour

Subtract one hour from the Standard Time for every 15 degrees of longitude that the Zone is *east* of Greenwich:

180E — 12 hours	90E — 6 hours
165E — 11 hours	75E — 5 hours
150E — 10 hours	60E — 4 hours
135E — 9 hours	45E — 3 hours

Table 3: World Time Zones

150W	135W	120W	105W	90W	75W	60W	45W	30W	15W	0W/E	15E	30E	45E	60E
		PST	MST	CST	EST	AST				GMT	MET	EET		
MIDNT	1 a.m.	2 a.m.	3 a.m.	4 a.m.	5 a.m.	6 a.m.	7 a.m.	8 a.m.	9 a.m.	10 a.m.	11 a.m.	NOON	1 p.m.	2 p.m.
1 a.m.	2 a.m.	3 a.m.	4 a.m.	5 a.m.	6 a.m.	7 a.m.	8 a.m.	9 a.m.	10 a.m.	11 a.m.	NOON	1 p.m.	2 p.m.	3 p.m.
2 a.m.	3 a.m.	4 a.m.	5 a.m.	6 a.m.	7 a.m.	8 a.m.	9 a.m.	10 a.m.	11 a.m.	NOON	1 p.m.	2 p.m.	3 p.m.	4 p.m.
3 a.m.	4 a.m.	5 a.m.	6 a.m.	7 a.m.	8 a.m.	9 a.m.	10 a.m.	11 a.m.	NOON	1 p.m.	2 p.m.	3 p.m.	4 p.m.	5 p.m.
4 a.m.	5 a.m.	6 a.m.	7 a.m.	8 a.m.	9 a.m.	10 a.m.	11 a.m.	NOON	1 p.m.	2 p.m.	3 p.m.	4 p.m.	5 p.m.	6 p.m.
5 a.m.	6 a.m.	7 a.m.	8 a.m.	9 a.m.	10 a.m.	11 a.m.	NOON	1 p.m.	2 p.m.	3 p.m.	4 p.m.	5 p.m.	6 p.m.	7 p.m.
6 a.m.	7 a.m.	8 a.m.	9 a.m.	10 a.m.	11 a.m.	NOON	1 p.m.	2 p.m.	3 p.m.	4 p.m.	5 p.m.	6 p.m.	7 p.m.	8 p.m.
7 a.m.	8 a.m.	9 a.m.	10 a.m.	11 a.m.	NOON	1 p.m.	2 p.m.	3 p.m.	4 p.m.	5 p.m.	6 p.m.	7 p.m.	8 p.m.	9 p.m.
8 a.m.	9 a.m.	10 a.m.	11 a.m.	NOON	1 p.m.	2 p.m.	3 p.m.	4 p.m.	5 p.m.	6 p.m.	7 p.m.	8 p.m.	9 p.m.	10 p.m.
9 a.m.	10 a.m.	11 a.m.	NOON	1 p.m.	2 p.m.	3 p.m.	4 p.m.	5 p.m.	6 p.m.	7 p.m.	8 p.m.	9 p.m.	10 p.m.	11 p.m.
10 a.m.	11 a.m.	NOON	1 p.m.	2 p.m.	3 p.m.	4 p.m.	5 p.m.	6 p.m.	7 p.m.	8 p.m.	9 p.m.	10 p.m.	11 p.m.	MIDNT
11 a.m.	NOON	1 p.m.	2 p.m.	3 p.m.	4 p.m.	5 p.m.	6 p.m.	7 p.m.	8 p.m.	9 p.m.	10 p.m.	11 p.m.	MIDNT	1 a.m.
NOON	1 p.m.	2 p.m.	3 p.m.	4 p.m.	5 p.m.	6 p.m.	7 p.m.	8 p.m.	9 p.m.	10 p.m.	11 p.m.	MIDNT	1 a.m.	2 a.m.

This table lists those Time Zones which the Western astrologer is likely to encounter most frequently. For other World Time Zones, the student can easily extend this table.

120E — 8 hours   30E — 2 hours
105E — 7 hours   15E — 1 hour

The result is the GMT.

EXAMPLES.

A. 1. Birth at 4:34 A.M. EST (75W) on September 2, 1930;
   2. 75W = + 5 hours;
   3. 4:34 A.M. + 5 hours = GMT;
   4. GMT = 9:34 A.M., September 2, 1930.
B. 1. Birth at 12:34 P.M. CET (15E) on September 2, 1930;
   2. 15E = — 1 hour;
   3. 12:34 P.M. — 1 hour = GMT;
   4. GMT = 11:34 A.M., September 2, 1930.
C. 1. Birth at 11:14 P.M. CST (90W) on September 2, 1930;
   2. 90W = + 6 hours;
   3. 11:14 P.M. + 6 hours = GMT;
   4. GMT = 5:14 A.M., *September 3, 1930.*
D. 1. Birth at 1:19 A.M. EET (30E) on September 2, 1930;
   2. 30E = — 2 hours;
   3. 1:19 A.M. — 2 hours = GMT;
   4. GMT = 11:19 P.M., *September 1, 1930.*

EXERCISES.

A. Using an atlas, determine the Standard Time Zone for each of the following cities: New York, Los Angeles, Paris, Rome, Amsterdam, London, Madrid.
B. If it is 1 A.M. in Paris, what time is it in London? in New York? in Rome? in Los Angeles?
C. If it is 2:15 P.M. in Chicago, what time is it in Denver? in San Francisco? in Geneva? in Philadelphia?
D. Give the equivalent GMT and date for the following:
   1. March 1, 3:07 A.M. EST
   2. March 1, 10:19 A.M. MST
   3. March 1, 7:01 P.M. PST

4. March 1, 1:40 P.M. EET
5. March 1, 12:14 A.M. CET

B. The Conversion of Standard Time to Local Mean Time

If Greenwich Mean Time is needed in order to properly calculate the planetary positions for the longitude of birth, Local Mean Time (or True Local Time, as it is also called) is required to determine the true Ascendant, Midheaven, and other House cusps of the natal horoscope. The importance of the Ascendant and the other angles of the chart has already been discussed. No matter which one of the systems of House division is employed, it is vital that the four points— Ascendant, Descendant, Midheaven, and Nadir—be accurate. In order to approach this accuracy, we must establish the Local Mean Time (LMT) of birth. It is *not* the same as the Standard (clock) Time.

Let us erect a horoscope for a fictitious person. We will assume that Joy, as we will call her, was born at the exact moment these words are being written— 5:06 P.M. EST, New York City, Longitude 74W, Latitude 40N43, November 21, 1972.

Since New York uses Eastern Standard Time, the equivalent Greenwich Mean Time for 5:06 P.M. is 10:06 P.M. New York City is not situated exactly on the EST Meridian (75W) but occupies a geographical location 1 degree *east* of that position—74W. Since 1 degree of longitude equals 4 minutes of clock time, we must *add 4 minutes to EST. Thus the LMT for New York City at 5:06 P.M. EST is 5:10 P.M.* (If Joy had been born in Buffalo, New York—longitude 79W)— we would have to *subtract 16 minutes from the EST,* since Buffalo lies 4 degrees to the West of the Eastern Standard Time Meridian. *Thus the LMT for Buffalo at 5:06 P.M. EST is 4:50 P.M.*)

SUMMARY.

In order to convert Standard Time to Local Mean Time, proceed as follows:

1. Write down the Standard Time of birth.
2. Determine the number of degrees East or West of the ST meridian where the place of birth is located.
3. Multiply this number by 4 (minutes).
4. *Add* this sum to the ST if the birthplace is *east* of the meridian. *Subtract* this sum from the ST if the birthplace is *west* of the Meridian.
5. The result is the LMT.

EXAMPLES.

A. 1. Birth at 2:09 P.M. EST (75W) in Lancaster, Pa. (76W15);
   2. Lancaster = 1°15′ West of 75W;
   3. 1°15′W × 4 = − 5 (minutes of time);
   4. 2:09 P.M. − 5 = LMT;
   5. LMT = 2:04 P.M.

B. 1. Birth at 1:19 A.M. PST (120W) in Los Angeles, Calif. (118W15);
   2. Los Angeles = 1°45′ East of 120W;
   3. 1°45′E × 4 = + 7 (minutes of time);
   4. 1:19 A.M. + 7 = LMT;
   5. LMT = 1:26 A.M.

C. 1. Birth at 6:29 P.M. MET (15E) in Copenhagen, Denmark (12E30);
   2. Copenhagen = 2°30′ West of 15E;
   3. 2°30′W × 4 = − 10 (minutes of time)
   4. 6:29 P.M. − 10 = LMT
   5. LMT = 6:19 P.M.

D. 1. Birth at 4:34 A.M. EET (30E) in Tel Aviv, Israel (34E45)
   2. Tel Aviv = 4°45′ East of 30E
   3. 4°45′ E × 4 = + 19 (minutes of time)
   4. 4:34 A.M. + 19 = LMT
   5. LMT = 4:53 A.M.

E. 1. Birth at 9:06 P.M. GMT (0W/E) in Glasgow, Scotland (4W15)
   2. Glasgow = 4°15′ West of 0W/E
   3. 4°15′W × 4 = − 17 (minutes of time)
   4. 9:06 P.M. − 17 = LMT
   5. LMT = 8:49 P.M.

EXERCISES.

Convert the following Standard Time births to LMT:

1. 10:14 P.M. GMT, Paris, France (2E15)
2. 9:19 A.M. EST, New York City (74W)
3. 4:09 P.M. CST, Chicago, Illinois (87W30)
4. 2:00 A.M. PST, San Francisco, Calif. (122W30)

C. Daylight Savings and War Time

Although as early as 1784 the great statesman Benjamin Franklin proposed that all clocks be put ahead one hour during the summer months, it was not until World War I that the first systematization of Daylight Savings Time was put into effect. This was in Germany, and the year was 1916. Soon after, the United States, Canada, Britain, and western Europe also incorporated DST into their year for the duration of the War. In 1920 DST was ordered discontinued by the United States Congress, but various local communities began to pass legislation to continue the practice. Thus one of the most aggravating and error-causing aspects of astrological work was brought into existence.

Daylight Savings Time was not universally or uniformly adopted. The dates of its starting and ending vary considerably from state to state and from year to year. Some communities in the same state use or have used it, while others do or did not. Some states and counties have banned it, only to return to it a few years later, while others have used it regularly since its inception. The differences are almost infinite and decidedly confusing.

Fortunately the modern astrologer need not be concerned with these problems, because the research for all time changes in this and in all other countries has been accomplished by Doris Chase Doane, whose works have already been mentioned. A good phrase to remember in order to know what to do with that elusive hour is "spring ahead and fall behind." In other words, from the last Sunday in April until the last

Sunday in October (for recent years only), the clocks are put ahead one hour where DST is observed. The clocks are then put back an hour to place the rest of the year on Standard Time.

What has been officially known as War Time was invented during World War II. The period covered by United States War Time is February 7, 1942, to September 30, 1945. During this period (as well as in 1918–1919), Daylight Savings Time was in constant use through the entire year. In England and in certain European countries this general period (the dates differ with each country) is known as Double Summer Time; that is, DST was observed for the entire year, but during the summer months the clocks were put ahead an additional hour.

If the given birth time for an individual is in Daylight Savings or War Time, the astrologer must *subtract an hour* to obtain the Standard Time. If the birth occurred in Europe during Double Summer Time, *two hours* must be deducted. *This calculation must be made before proceeding on to any other step.*

SUMMARY.

1. Daylight Savings Time and War Time are artificial time changes instituted to provide additional daylight hours.
2. In order to obtain the Standard Time of a birth occurring during a DST or WT period, one hour must be subtracted from the given birth time (two hours during Double Summer Time).

EXAMPLES.

1. A birth recorded in New York at 2:46 P.M. EDST would actually have taken place at 1:46 P.M. EST.
2. A birth recorded in Chicago at 9:29 A.M. WT actually occurred at 8:29 A.M. CST.
3. A birth occurring in London at 8:34 P.M. Double Summer Time took place at the GMT equivalent of 6:34 P.M.

EXERCISES.

Convert DST or WT into ST for the meridian of birth:
1. 9:19 A.M. DST in Chicago
2. 4:48 P.M. DST in Denver
3. 6:17 A.M. DST in London
4. 1:21 P.M. WT in New York

D. Sidereal Time

It is difficult to explain Sidereal Time, because it is necessary to understand a good deal of celestial dynamics to comprehend it fully. Nevertheless, it must be mentioned and briefly discussed, for its use is essential to the erection of the horoscope. Briefly stated, Sidereal Time measures the exact rotation of the Earth and registers the difference between the actual time of the daily axial rotation and the twenty-four-hour day of clock time. The difference between a Sidereal day and a Standard one is approximately four minutes. This accumulation of time begins on Sidereal clocks when 0 degrees of Aries culminates over the meridian of the observer. We say that the Sidereal time at noon on any day of the year corresponds to a specific culminating degree of the ecliptic (Zodiac of the Signs). It is from this degree of culmination that the degree of the Ascendant is determined.

The ephemeris gives the Sidereal Time for noon (or midnight) at the Greenwich Observatory. In order to ascertain which degrees of the ecliptic are rising and culminating for a birth occurring at a location other than at the Greenwich meridian, *the astrologer must convert Greenwich Sidereal Time into Local Sidereal Time*; this final process will be demonstrated in the following chapter.

Sidereal Time for noon (or midnight) of any given day is found in every ephemeris. In tables printed in English, Sidereal Time will be found under the heading *S.T.* or *Sid.T.* German ephemerides use *S.Z.* or *Sternzeit*, meaning "star time."

To erect the natal horoscope of Joy, who was born

on November 21, 1972, we must check on November
in the ephemeris for the year in question. The Sidereal
Times listed for Noon, Greenwich Mean Time for
November 20, 21, and 22 read as follows:

D	S.T.		
	H	M	S
20	15	58	23
21	16	02	20
22	16	06	16

With this Greenwich Sidereal Time for noon, we can
actually proceed to set up the natal chart.

SUMMARY.

To erect a natal horoscope, the following information must be obtained. The specifics given here apply
to the fictitious Joy.

a. Name: Joy
b. Place of Birth: New York City
c. Long.: 74W; Lat.: 40N43
d. Date of Birth: November 21, 1972
e. Given Time of Birth: 5:06 P.M. EST
f. Source of Time: Birth Certificate
g. Local Mean Time: 5:10 P.M.
h. Greenwich Mean Time: 10:06 P.M.
i. Greenwich Sidereal Time: 16:02:20

EXERCISES.

1. Open your ephemeris, look it over carefully. You
   will see that some of the symbols and numbers are
   making a great deal of sense to you. Before too
   long the entire ephemeris will be clear to you.
2. In the ephemeris, turn to the year of your birth.
   Inspect the symbols and numbers which appear after
   the day of your birth. Look at the positions of the
   planets and note the degree and sign for each. Note
   your Greenwich Sidereal Time of Birth. Follow the
   same procedure with two or three other birth dates.

12.

THE WHEEL OF LIFE

The next step in setting up a horoscope is to determine the House cusps of the particular natal chart. This information will be found in the Table of Houses and obtained as a result of the Local Sidereal Time of birth. While I use the Placidean system of House division, I would also like to include the Equal House method of chart erection because this system is finding favor with a great many students and is quite a simple technique to master.

A. Local Sidereal Time

In order to find the Ascendant, Midheaven, and the other House cusps, Greenwich Sideral Time must be converted to Local Sidereal Time. This process takes four steps:

First, determine the Sidereal Time at Greenwich for the previous (or coming) noon on the day of birth. In the example of Joy, this is *16:02:20.*

Then determine the *interval* between the *Local Mean Time* of birth and the previous (or coming) noon.

For example, Joy's LMT of birth is 5:10 P.M. The interval between this time and noon is + 5 hours, 10 minutes. If the birth had occurred at 5:10 A.M., the interval would be −6 hours, 50 minutes. *Add the interval* to the Noon Sidereal Time if the LMT of birth occurred in the P.M. hours; *subtract the interval* from the Noon Sid.T. if the LMT of birth occurred in the A.M. hours.

In Joy's case, we would proceed thus:

p.m. birth	a.m. birth
16:02:20	16:02:20
+05:10	−06:50

The next step is called *Acceleration on the Interval*. Since clock time is somewhat slower than Sidereal Time (24 hours of clock time = 24 hours, 4 minutes of S.T.), a clock hour must be equated with a Sidereal one so that the correct time factor can be determined. To do so, *lengthen each clock hour of the interval by 10 seconds*. These 10 seconds per hour (1 second per 6 minutes) is the *acceleration*.

In the example, Joy was born 5 hours and 10 minutes after noon. Thus *the acceleration on the interval of birth is 52 seconds* (5 hours = 50 seconds; 10 minutes = 1.8 seconds, rounded off to 2 seconds). This sum must also be *added to the Noon Sidereal Time*. Had the birth occurred *before noon*—say at 5:10 A.M. —the equivalent acceleration would have to be *subtracted from the Noon Sid.T.* This calculation would amount to an acceleration of −68 seconds, as the interval is −6 hours, 50 minutes.

Thus our calculations so far read:

p.m. birth		a.m. birth
H. M. S.		H. M. S.
16:02:20	(Greenwich Noon Sidereal Time	16:02:20
+05:10	(Interval between Noon and LMT)	−06:50
+ :52	(Acceleration on the Interval)	− 1:08

One final adjustment remains to be made. Just as the acceleration on the interval is an adjustment for time, another must be made for space. This rectification is called the *Correction for Longitude*. The formula for this slight measure is quite simple: one *adds* 10 seconds of time for every 15 degrees of longitude that the place of birth lies *west* of Greenwich and conversely *subtracts* 10 seconds of time for every Time Zone (= 15 degrees of longitude) that the place of birth lies *east* of Greenwich. *This is done regardless of the* A.M. *or* P.M. *factor of the LMT.*

In the example, Joy was born in EST (or five Time Zones *west* of Greenwich). Thus *the longitudinal correction is +50 seconds.*[1] This we will now add to our growing list of figures:

p.m. birth		a.m. birth
H. M. S.		H. M. S.
16:02:20	(G.noon Sid. T.)	16:02:20
+05:10	(interval)	−06:50
+ 52	(acceleration)	− 1:08
		9:11:12
+ 50	(long. corr.)	+ 50
21:12:122		9:11:62
21:14:02	(Local Sidereal Time)	9:12:02

or
(Calculated Sidereal Time)

The Local Sidereal Time will correspond to the degree of the ecliptic (Zodiac of Signs) culminating at the meridian and time of birth. The Table of Houses will show the Local Sidereal Time for the *latitude of the place of birth* and thus reveal exactly the degree of this as well as of the other House cusps.

To check out Joy's P.M. birth, we open the A/P (or Raphael's) Table of Houses for the latitude of New York (40N43) and look down the column headed *Sidereal Time.* The *nearest Sidereal Time* to our calculated figure is *21:13:52.* The entire column of figures is shown in Table 4.

Fill in a horoscope blank exactly as shown in Diagram 7.

At the line "*21:13:52*", we place the degree and sign listed under column 10 in the Table of Houses on the Tenth House Cusp (Midheaven): 16.♒. We do the

---

[1] The mathematical purist will note that the correction should be 49.25 seconds, as New York is located at 74W longitude, and 1° long. = .75 sec. of correction. This difference and those of other horoscopes the student is likely to calculate during his or her work is so slight that it makes no appreciable change in the resultant House cusps. For this reason, we can safely assume that one Time Zone = 10 secs. and proceed as indicated.

Table 4: Houses for Latitude 40N43.

Sidereal Time H.	M.	S.	10 ♒ °	11 ♒ °	12 ♈ °	Ascen ♉ °	Ascen ′	2 ♊ °	3 ♋ °	
20	08	45	0	26	3	20	52	17	9	
20	12	54	1	27	5	22	14	18	9	
20	17	03	2	29	6	23	35	19	10	
20	21	11	3	♓ 1	8	24	55	20	11	*Note change of sign*
20	25	19	4	2	9	26	14	21	12	
20	29	26	5	3	11	27	32	22	13	
20	33	31	6	5	12	28	46	23	14	
20	37	37	7	6	14	♊ 0	03	24	15	*Note change of sign*
20	41	41	8	7	15	1	17	25	16	
20	45	45	9	8	16	2	29	26	17	
20	49	48	10	10	18	3	41	27	18	
20	53	51	11	11	19	4	51	28	19	
20	57	52	12	12	21	6	01	29	20	
21	01	53	13	13	22	7	09	⊙ 1	20	*Note change of sign*
21	05	53	14	14	24	8	16	2	21	
21	09	53	15	15	25	9	23	3	22	
21	13	52	16	16	26	10	30	3	23	*Nearest Sidereal Time to 21:14:02*
21	17	50	17	17	28	11	33	4	24	

21	21	47	18	18	29	12	37	5	25	
21	25	44	19	19	♉	13	41	6	26	
21	29	40	20	21	2	14	43	6	27	
21	33	35	21	22	3	15	44	7	28	Note change of sign
21	37	29	22	23	4	16	45	8	28	
21	41	23	23	24	6	17	45	9	29	
21	45	16	24	25	7	18	44	10	♌	
21	49	09	25	27	8	19	42	11	1	Note change of sign
21	53	01	26	28	9	20	40	12	2	
21	56	52	27	29	11	21	37	12	3	Note change of sign
22	00	43	28	♈	12	22	33	13	4	
22	04	33	29	1	13	23	30	14	5	Note change of sign
22	08	23	♓	3	14	24	45	15	5	

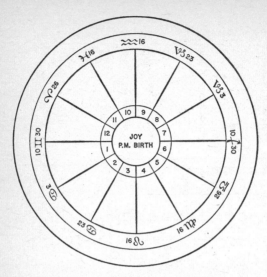

Diagram 7: Wheel for P.M. Birth.

same for the Eleventh and Twelfth House cusps; 16♓
and 26♈ respectively. On the First House Cusp (Ascendant), we place 10♊30²; on the Second House
cusp, we place 3♋, and on the Third House cusp we
place 23♋. What is done on one side of the Wheel
must be done on the other. Thus we keep the same
degree of the Zodiac, but we change the sign to its
polarity. The Fourth House cusp then becomes 16♌;
the Fifth, 16♍; the Sixth, 26♎; the Seventh, 10♐30;
the Eighth, 3♑; and the Ninth, 23♑.

Applying the same method to the example of an
A.M. birth, the nearest Sidereal Time to *9:12:02* is given
as 9:13:52. The resulting horoscope House cusps appear in Diagram 8.

The Table of Houses has served its need for the
present. Going back to Joy's map for a P.M. birth, we

---

² The calculation of the exact Ascendant (and other cusps) resulting from the slight difference between the calculated S.T. and
the nearest S.T. may be accomplished through a rather complex
mathematical formula. The process, called *interpolation*, need not
concern the beginning student.

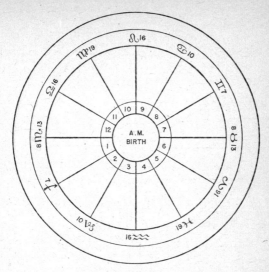

Diagram 8: Wheel for A.M. Birth.

see that we have Cancer and Capricorn on the cusps of two Houses each and Taurus and Scorpio on none. Actually we say that these two signs have been *intercepted.* This occurrence, common in birth charts of individuals born in the higher southern or northern latitudes, is based on the curvature of the Earth and the tilt of the planet's axis.

Such intercepted signs must be placed in the chart in their proper sequence. Thus Taurus is posited between Aries and Gemini in the Twelfth House, and Scorpio is placed between Libra and Sagittarius in the Sixth. The corrected wheel is shown in Diagram 9.

The interpretive value of intercepted signs seems to vary among astrologers, depending on their own experience. I believe that the affairs pertaining to the signs and Houses in question receive additional prominence, since they seem to permeate most aspects of life. Since the signs involved are not "fixed" in place by attachment to a specific House cusp, the energy these signs represent becomes more noticeable in the

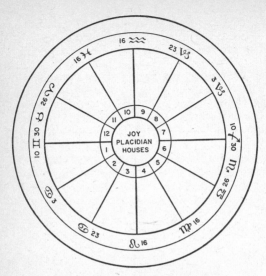

Diagram 9: Placidian Houses.

whole "character" of the chart. This would be especially pertinent when planets are placed in intercepted signs. I do not believe, as many other astrologers
have asserted, that these planets are weakened. Rather,
it seems to me that the planetary energy though dif-
fused by such a position, does not necessarily lose
strength. Because the energy embodied by the intercepted planet is somewhat more difficult to bring under
the conscious control of the individual, it can result in
the need to focus more attention on the activities of the
planet so intercepted, so that a more cohesive individuality may result (see chaps. 16 and 17).

B. The Equal House System

The Equal House System serves to eliminate any
discussion of interception by the modifications it introduces on the more traditional, Placidean method.

In order to erect the horoscope through the use of

the equal Houses, one performs all the calculations demonstrated so far. It is only after the Local Sidereal Time is established that the differences between the Placidian and the Equal House methods become evident.

After ascertaining the degree of the Ascendant from the Table of Houses, all the other degrees of the remaining House cusps are replaced *with this same degree*. The Midheaven as well as the Nadir are used as they appear in the Table of Houses but are given a special place in the wheel, while the Tenth and Fourth House cusps remain at the same degree of their respective signs as the Ascendant. Diagram 10 of Joy's horoscope drawn up in the Equal House fashion should make all this quite clear.[3]

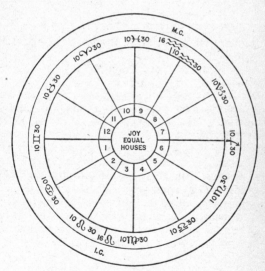

Diagram 10: Equal Houses.

---

[3] The student may obtain more information about the Equal House System by writing to The Faculty of Astrological Studies, c/o The English Universities Press, Ltd., St. Paul's House, Warwick Lane, London, E.C. 4. The remainder of all the astrological material and example horoscopes calculated in this text will be presented according to Placidus.

SUMMARY.

Local Sidereal Time is established as follows:
1. Find the Sid.T. for noon of the previous (or coming) day of birth.
2. Find the interval between the LMT of birth and noon. Add the interval to the noon Sid.T. if the LMT of birth is P.M.; subtract the interval from the noon Sid.T. if the LMT is A.M.
3. Find the acceleration on the interval: 10 seconds per hour, 1 second per 6 minutes. Add if P.M., subtract if A.M. birth.
4. Find the correction for longitude: 10 seconds per 15 degrees of longitude of the birthplace East or West of Greenwich. Add if west; subtract if east.

EXAMPLES.

1. January 16, 1951; Paris, France; 2:35 P.M. LMT; Long. 2E.
   - a.   19:40:27   (G. noon Sid.T.)
   - b. +02:35   (interval)
   - c. +   26   (acceleration)
   - d. −   02   (long. corr.; 2 deg. E = +1.5 or 2 seconds)[4]

   _____
   21:75:53
   _____
   22:15:53   (Local Sid.T.)

2. April 27, 1952; Denver, Colorado; 10:55 A.M. LMT; Long. 105W.
   - a.   02:21:39
   - b. −01:05
   - c. −   11
   - d. +   1:10
   _____
   01:17:38

EXERCISES.

Find the Local Sidereal Time for the following (show all the calculations):

[4] For births occurring in the Greenwich Time Zone, the correction for longitude may be safely omitted from the calculations.

1. September 23, 1953; Cleveland, Ohio; 3:56 P.M. LMT; Long. 82W.
2. October 12, 1954; San Francisco, Calif; 9:18 A.M. LMT; Long. 122W30.
3. November 29, 1955; Chicago, Ill.; 2:38 A.M. LMT; Long. 87W30.

C. Factors of Additional Importance

Three further questions should be answered in this chapter, for they involve certain mathematical problems which frequently arise when calculating the House cusps.

What happens when the Calculated Sidereal Time (Local Sid.T.) exceeds 24 hours? *Answer: Subtract 24 hours from the total.*

EXAMPLE.

Let us say that a birth occurred on December 4, 1932, at 10:14 P.M. PST in Los Angeles, California (Long. 118W15; Lat. 34N03). The LMT for this nativity is 10:07 P.M., and the Sid.T. for noon, GMT, prior to birth is 16:52:21. With this data, we set up the following list of figures:

$$
\begin{array}{ll}
16:52:21 = & \text{(Sid. T. noon, GMT)} \\
+\ 10:07 = & \text{(Interval)} \\
+\ \quad 1:41 = & \text{(Acc. on Int.: } 10\,h = \\
& 100 \text{ sec.; } 7\,m = 1 \text{ sec.)} \\
+\ \quad 1:20 = & \text{(Long. corr.: 8 Time} \\
& \text{Zones x 10 sec.} = 80 \\
& \text{sec.} = 1\,m\ 20 \text{ sec.)} \\
\hline
26:61:82 & \\
\end{array}
$$

when reduced = 27:02:22
minus 24 hrs. = − 24:00:00
─────────────
[03:02:22] = (Local Sidereal Time)

The next step would, of course, require finding the Nearest Sidereal Time in the Table of Houses and copying the House cusps onto the chart.

What happens if the birth occurs before noon and the Sidereal Time at Greenwich is less than the interval? *Answer: Add 24 hours to the Greenwich Noon Sidereal Time.*

EXAMPLE.

Let us say that a birth occurred on May 16, 1943, at 2:05 A.M. CWT in Chicago, Illinois (Long. 87W45; Lat. 41N52). The LMT for this nativity is 12:56 A.M. (1 hour having to be deducted for War Time), and the Sidereal Time for the coming Greenwich Noon is 03:33:19. In order to obtain the Local Sidereal Time, we proceed as follows:

```
   03:33:19    (G. Noon Sid. T.)
 + 24:00:00
   ─────────
   27:33:19
 − 11:04       (Interval to coming Noon)
 −     1:51    (Acc. on Int.: 11 h = 110 sec.; 4 m = 1
   ─────────      sec; 111 sec. = 1 m 51 sec.)
   16:27:28
 +     1:00    (Long. corr.: 6 Time Zones = 60 sec. =
   ─────────      1 min.)
   16:28:28    (Local Sidereal Time)
   ═════════
```

Now you are ready to consult the Table of Houses for the House cusps.

How does one calculate the Local Sidereal Time for a birth occurring in the Southern Hemisphere? *Answer:* Proceed as follows: Add 12 hours to the (calculated) Local Sidereal Time of birth. Should the sum exceed 24 hours, *subtract 24 from the total* after adding the 12 hours. Then reverse the signs as listed in the Table of Houses for the equivalent northern latitude.

EXAMPLE.

In order to obtain the House cusps for a birth occurring on November 19, 1932 at 7:00 A.M. in Melbourne, Australia (Long. 145E; Lat. 37S45), you would calculate as follows:

```
       1 12
   15:5♂:♉3    (G. Noon Sid. T.)
 — 05:00:00    (Interval)
 —       50    (Acc. on Int.)
 —     2:30    (Long. corr.: 15 Time Zones x 10 sec. =
                  150 sec. = 2 m 30 sec.)
   10:49:43
 + 12          (Southern Hemisphere correction)
   22:49:43    (Local Sidereal Time)
```

When we look up 22:49:43 in the Table of Houses for Latitude 37N45, we find that the Nearest Sidereal Time is 22:29:53. For this figure the Tenth House cusp is listed as 11♓, and the Ascendant is 2♋04. We must now alter these positions so that the Tenth House cusp will read 11♍ and the Ascendant will be 2♑04. The other House cusps would be similarly reversed.

It should be noted that the signs in which the planets are placed *should not be reversed*. Their positions relative to the Zodiac of the Signs is not altered by the fact that an individual is born in the southern or the northern hemisphere of the Earth. All required differences in calculation are limited to the locations of the House cusps.

D. The Horoscope Calculation Sheet, Part I.

The data sheet for horoscope calculation will provide the student with a complete summary and guide to all the calculations done up to the present. The student should copy out the sheet, have copies made of it, and use it in his or her work. On the sample sheet we shall fill in the blanks with the figures obtained to set up Joy's horoscope.

EXERCISES.

1. Find the House cusps for the following nativities. Show all calculations.
   a. May 22, 1947 at 3 p.m., New York City.
   b. December 12, 1958 at 3 a.m., Denver, Colorado.
2. Find the House cusps for three people who are close to you (yourself included, if you like) for whom you know the exact birth time.

Horoscope calculation sheet

PART I: Finding the House cusps of the natal chart

Name: _____ Joy _____ Date of Birth: _____ November 21, 1972 _____

Birthplace: _____ New York City _____

Birth Time: _____ 5:06 _____ [a.m. / **p.m.**] Long. _____ 74W _____ Lat. _____ 40N43 _____

Source of Birth Time: _____ Certificate _____

Kind of Time (Circle): <u>EST</u> CST MST PST W.T. EDST CDST MDST PDST Other

Local Mean Time: _____ 5:10 _____ [a.m. / **p.m.**] Greenwich Mean Time: _____ 10:06 _____ [**a.m.** / p.m.]

Local Sidereal Time: _____ 21:14:05 _____ Nearest Sidereal Time: _____ 21:14:25 _____

Adjusted Calculation Date:[a] _____

A. Conversion of Birth Time to Greenwich Mean Time

	H	M	S
1. No. of degrees of Standard Time Meridian	75 West		
2. Standard Time of Birth	5	06	00 p.m.
3. Time equivalent in hours (15° = 1 hour)			
a. Add if Meridian is West	+ 5	00	00
OR—b. Subtract if Meridian is East			
4. Greenwich Mean Time equivalent	[10	06	00 p.m.]

B. Conversion of Standard Time to Local Mean Time

		5	06	00 p.m.
1. Standard Time of Birth				
2. No. of degrees birth E/W of Standard		1 deg. East		
3. No. of degrees x 4 minutes				
a. Add if birthplace is E of Meridian	+00		04	00
OR—b. Subtract if birthplace is W of Meridian				
4. Local Mean Time equivalent	[5		10	00 p.m.]

C. Conversion of Greenwich Sidereal Time to Local Sidereal Time

		16	02	20
1. G. Sid. T. for Noon of day of birth				
a. Add 24 hrs. if necessary				
2. Interval between LMT and Noon	+05		10	00
a. Add if birth after noon				
b. Subtract if birth before noon				
3. Acceleration on Interval (10 sec. = 1 hr.)				
a. Add if birth after noon	+			52
b. Subtract if birth before noon				
a. Add if birth is West Long.				
4. Longitudinal Correction (10 sec. = 1 T Zone) ..	+			50
b. Subtract if birth is East Long.				
5. Local Sidereal Time equivalent	[21		14	02]
a. Subtract 24 hrs. if necessary				
6. Nearest Sidereal Time in Table of Houses	[21		14	25]

[a] Used as the basis for the Progressed Horoscope. See chap. 8.

13.

THE PLANETARY BLUEPRINT

The time has come to move on to the second major stage in chart erection: the proper calculation of the planets and the correct placement of the heavenly bodies within the wheel.

If you have not fully understood the first half of the calculation procedures, you should go back and review the previous two chapters. You may find it helpful to sit down with an atlas and look at the map of the world. Think about some of the trips you have made to different parts of the United States or travels abroad, and reflect upon the differences in time you encountered in each of these locations. Review the exercises and examples given in the previous pages. Do not rush or hurry through the material; take your time and absorb these lessons.

I. WORKING WITH DIURNAL MOTION TABLES

We have related the longitude and latitude of the place of birth to the Zodiac of Signs. Now we must learn to relate the celestial longitude and declination of the planets to this same position on the Earth.[1] In other words, we are graphically producing a clear relationship between the microcosm of the individual nativity and the macrocosm of the solar system. "As

---

[1] The declination of a planet is its distance north or south of the celestial equator—that is, the equator of the Earth extended infinitely out into space. The declination is the second physical coordinate which determines the planet's position and influence in relation to terrestrial life.

above, so below; as it is in the Heavens, so it is on the Earth."

A. Calculating the Planets for a P.M. Birth

In order to adjust the planetary positions to one specific life, we must begin our calculations with the planets' positions at noon of the day of birth, GMT. (For the sample horoscopes we are using an ephemeris calculated for noon, GMT. A student with a midnight, GMT, emphemeris can easily adapt the methods outlined in this volume to suit his or her needs.) We must copy out these figures from the ephemeris for the day of Joy's birth. For reasons which will soon become evident, we shall also copy out the positions for the noon following her birth:

DATE	☉	☽	☿
Nov. 21:	29♐17	6♊58	9♐43ᴿ
Nov. 22:	00♏17	22♊10	8♐40ᴿ

♀	♂	♃	♄
26♎15	3♏40	8♑51	18♊31ᴿ
27♎28	4♏18	9♑03	18♊26ᴿ

DATE	♅	♆	♇	☊
Nov. 21:	21♎08	4♐46	3♎51	19♑23ᵃ
Nov. 22:	21♎11	4♐48	3♎52	19♑20

ᵃ The North Node of the Moon—that is, the position of the Moon when she intersects with the ecliptic. This position changes at the approximate rate of 3 min. of arc, retrograde, daily. The point in space directly opposite the Northern Node (also called the Dragon's Head) is the Southern Node (Dragon's Tail). The significance of these points will be discussed in the following chapter.

The Horoscope Calculation Sheet shows that the equivalent GMT for Joy's birth is 10:06 P.M. This means that, in order to accurately determine the positions of the planets at the exact time of Joy's birth, we will have to find out how far the heavenly bodies moved from noon of the day of her birth to 10:06 P.M. This requires two stages. First, determine how far the planets moved within the 24 hours between the noon prior to birth and the coming noon, GMT.

Next, determine the proportion of movement equal to the hours and minutes beyond noon that the birth occurred (in this case, 10 hours, 6 minutes). Add this sum to the noon positions of the planets.

The first step is relatively easy, for the positions of the planets have already been established by the emphemeris. All that has to be done to calculate how far a planet has moved in the heavens between noon on November 21 and noon of November 22 is to subtract the position of the former from that of the latter. In other words, to obtain the diurnal movement of the Moon, simply subtract:

    Moon Nov. 22 = 22Ⅱ10
    Moon Nov. 21 = 06Ⅱ58
    _____
    Travel in 24 hrs. = 15° 12′ of arc

Repeating this process, this time using the positions for the Sun, Venus, and Mars, comes out as follows. In all calculations we must remember that a sign = 30 degrees; one degree = 60 minutes (of arc); and one minute = 60 seconds (of arc).

    Sun Nov. 22 = 0♐17
    Sun Nov. 22 = 29♏17
    _____
                1°   00′ = travel in 24 hours

By changing 0°17′ to 30°17′, we can perform the above subtraction.

    Mars Nov. 22 = 4 ♏ 18 (= 3 ♏ 78)
    Mars Nov. 21 = 3 ♏ 40
    _____
                   38′ = travel in 24 hours

    Venus Nov. 22 = 27 ♎ 28
    Venus Nov. 21 = 26 ♎ 15
    _____
                1°   13′ = travel in 24 hours

The second step is a bit more complicated. To facilitate the necessary computations, either the Table of Diurnal Planetary Motion or the Table of Proportional Logarithms must be used. I prefer the method involving the Diurnal Table. The use of this tabulation helps to eliminate the possibility of simple arithmetic errors and definitely saves time. Any ephemeris contains a logarithmic table, however. Its use, as well as that of the Diurnal Table, is explained below. Used correctly, both tables yield exactly the same results.[2]

A. The Diurnal Table Method

The Table of Diurnal Planetary Motion is in two segments. The first is used to chart the position of the Sun *only*. The second part is used to calculate the positions of the Moon and the other planets and nodes. The introduction to the table provides the student with a very simple explanation as to its use. For our purposes, just a small portion will make the examples more comprehensive.

Let us compute the position of the Moon in Joy's chart. We know that the Moon traveled 15°12′ of arc between noon of November 21 and noon of November 22. We must know how much of 15°12′ is covered in 10 hours, 6 minutes (the GMT of birth).

When we consult the Table of Diurnal Planetary Motion, we find that at the rate of 15°12′ per day (top of the column), the Moon traveled 6°20′ in 10 hours and 3′48″ (or 4′) in 6 minutes (of time).

When we add these two figures together we find that: *10 hours and 6 minutes of time = 6°24′ of arc (motion).*

We must now add 6°24′ to the position of the Moon at noon on November 21:

```
    6♊58   (= noon)
+   6  24   (= 10 hrs. 6 min.)
= 13♊22   (= position of Moon at time of Joy's birth)
```

In the same way, we shall now compute the positions of the Sun, Venus, and Mars. All figures are reduced to the nearest minute of arc.

---

[2] The Table of Diurnal Planetary Motion will prove itself to be extremely valuable to those advanced students who make use of solar and lunar returns in their work.

Chart 2.
Diurnal Table of Planetary Motion (Segment)

Time	RATE OF 24-HOUR MOTION							
Mins.	15°11′			15°12′			15°13′	
	°	′	″	°	′	″	°	′	″
1		0	38		0	38		0	38
2		1	16		1	16		1	16
3		1	54		1	54		1	54
4		2	32		2	32		2	32
5		3	10		3	10		3	10
6		3	48		3	48		3	48
7		4	26		4	26		4	26
8		5	04		5	04		5	04
9		5	42		5	42		5	42
10		6	20		6	20		6	20
11		6	58		6	58		6	58
12		7	35		7	36		7	36

Time	RATE OF 24-HOUR MOTION							
Hours	15°11′			15°12′			15°13′	
	°	′	″	°	′	″	°	′	″
1		37	57		38	00		38	02
2	1	15	55	1	16	00	1	16	05
3	1	53	52	1	54	00	1	54	07
4	2	31	50	2	32	00	2	32	10
5	3	09	47	3	10	00	3	10	12
6	3	47	45	3	48	00	3	48	15
7	4	25	42	4	26	00	4	26	17
8	5	03	40	5	04	00	5	04	20
9	5	41	37	5	42	00	5	42	22
10	6	19	35	6	20	00	6	20	25
11	6	57	32	6	58	00	6	58	27
12	7	35	30	7	36	00	7	36	30

Source: *Tables of Diurnal Planetary Motion*, National Astrological Library, pp. 156–157.

Sun:	a. rate of travel in 24 hours	=	1° 00′
	b. travel in 10 hours	=	25′
	c. travel in 6 minutes	=	15″
	d. travel in 10 hrs., 6 min.	=	25′

If we add this interval of 25′ to the Sun's noon position of 29♏︎17, we have the location of the Sun at Joy's birth:

29 ♏ 17
+   25
= 29 ♏ 42

Venus: a. rate of travel in 24 hours = 1° 13′
       b. travel in 10 hours   =   30′ 25″
       c. travel in 6 minutes   =   18″
       d. travel in 10 hrs., 6 min. =   30′ 43″ or 31′

When we calculate as above, we find that:

26 ♎ 15 (noon position)
+   31 (Interval)
= 26 ♎ 46 (Venus at birth)

Mars: a. rate of travel in 24 hours = 0° 38′
      b. travel in 10 hours   =   15′ 50″
      c. travel in 6 minutes   =   09″
      d. travel in 10 hrs., 6 min. =   15′ 59″ or 16′

Thus:

3 ♏ 40 (noon position)
+   16 (Interval)
= 3 ♏ 56 (Mars at birth)

B. Retrogradation and the Position of Mercury at Birth

Mercury must be treated somewhat differently from the previous examples, because this planet is traveling "retrograde." This means that the planet, as seen from the Earth, appears to be moving backward along the ecliptic (Zodiac of Signs). This is not actually happening, for all the heavenly bodies only move forward. What we are seeing is an optical illusion.

You have probably experienced this feeling of retrogradation yourself. Whenever you are traveling in a slower-moving train and a faster one overtakes you, you get the sensation that while the faster train is passing, you are going backward along the tracks.

In actuality you are still going forward, but at a slower rate. The reasons for planetary retrogradation are a bit more complicated than the matter of train speeds, for we must also consider the angular relationships existing between the Earth and the planets in retrograde. The example of the trains will give you some idea, however, of the principles at work. (The significance of retrograde planets in the interpretation of the natal horoscope, is discussed in its proper sequence in the chapters on interpretation.)

If, we examine Mercury's position on the day which concerns us, we note that on November 21 Mercury was placed in $9 \nearrow 43_R$ but that on November 22 its position shifted to $8 \nearrow 40_R$. This is a difference of *1°03′ of retrograde motion* in the 24-hour period. In order to find out how much Mercury traveled in 10 hours, 6 minutes, we must perform the same process as we did with those planets which were traveling in *direct* motion.

Travel in 10 hours =	26′ 15″$_R$
Travel in 6 minutes =	16″$_R$
Total travel =	26′ 31″ or 27′$_R$

Instead of adding 27′ to Mercury's position at noon on November 21, one *subtracts* it:

Mercury position on Nov. 21 =	$9 \nearrow 43_R$
minus the interval of travel =	27
= Mercury's position at birth =	$9 \nearrow 16_R$

The daily motion of Jupiter, Saturn, Uranus, Neptune, and Pluto are so slight that they can be easily calculated. For example, 10 hours, 6 minutes is just slightly less than half a day. Since Jupiter's motion for the 24-hour period in question is 12′, we add 5′ to its placement at noon on November 21 to arrive at its position at the time of Joy's birth (Jupiter = $8 \text{♑} 51$ at noon + 5′ = $8 \text{♑} 56$ at birth). Since Saturn is moving retrograde at the rate of 5′ for the day, we subtract 2′ from its position at noon on November 21

$(18\text{♊}31_R - 2' = 18\text{♊}29_R$ at birth). In the same fashion we can determine the positions of the slowest-moving planets and arrive at the following placements at birth:

Uranus $= 21 \text{♎} 12$
Neptune $= 4 \text{♐} 49$
Pluto $= 3 \text{♎} 52$

Part IIa of the Horoscope Calculation Sheet gives a step-by-step summary of just this process; in addition, it leaves spaces where the calculated positions of the planets may be listed. It is most important that the latter be accurately determined and easily found among your calculations, so that when they are actually placed within the wheel, all possible errors are avoided.

B. Calculating the Planets for an A.M. Birth

We have just found the positions of the heavenly bodies for a birth occurring at 10:06 P.M. GMT. How would we go about finding the locations of the planets if the birth were at 10:06 A.M. GMT (5:06 A.M. EST)? The necessary procedure is quite similar to the one we have already learned. We must first determine how far the planets moved within the twenty-four hours between the noon prior to birth and the coming noon, GMT. Next we must determine the proportion of movement equal to the hours and minutes that the birth occurred before noon. (In this case, 1 hour, 54 minutes.) This sum will be subtracted from the coming noon positions of the planets.

For the first step, the planets for November 20 and 21 must be found in the ephemeris. We will list only the positions of the faster-moving planets. Since 1 hour, 54 minutes equals only about one-twelfth of the day's movement, it is possible to take the noon positions of the slower-moving planets as they are given in the ephemeris for the day of birth and to place them accordingly in the horoscope. The swifter planets will be placed as follows:

Horoscope calculation sheet

PART IIa: Calculation of the planetary positions (Diurnal Motion Table)

GMT of Birth: 10:06 [P.M.] (A.M.)   Interval before (or after) noon, GMT: +10   H +10 M 6

Date of Birth: Nov. 21, 1972

	☉	☽	☿	♀	♂
a. Coming noon position	0♐17	22♊10	9♐43ᴿ	27♎28	4♏18
b. Previous noon position	29♏17	6♊58	8♐40ᴿ	26♎15	3♏40
c. Movement in 24 hours	1°00'	15°12'	1°03'	1°13'	38'
d. Movement in Interval					
1. hours	25'	6°20'	26'15"	30'25"	15'50"
2. minutes	15"	4'	16"	18"	9"
3. total	=25'	=6°24'	=27ᴿ'	=31'	=16'
e. Add to previous noon (if P.M. birth)	29♏17	6♊58		26♎15	3♏40
f. Sub. from previous noon (if A.M. birth)			9♐43ᴿ		
g. Positions at birth	29♏42	13♊22	9♐16ᴿ	26♎46	3♏56

Further positions:

- ♃ 8♑56
- ♄ 18♎29ᴿ
- ♅ 21♎12
- ♆ 4♐49
- ♇ 3♎52
- ☊ 19♑
- ☋ 19♎
- ⊕ᵃ 6♎

ᵃ The symbol for the Part of Fortune. Its significance and method of calculation appears later on in the present chapter.

DATE	☉	☽	☿
Nov. 21:	29♏︎17	6♊︎58	9♐︎43$_R$
Nov. 20:	28♏︎16	21♉︎38	10♐︎36$_R$

♀	♂
26♎︎15	3♏︎40
25♎︎01	3♏︎01

Performing the necessary subtractions, we find that the 24-hour rate of motion for each of these planets is as follows:

Sun:
$$29 ♏︎ 17$$
$$- 28 ♏︎ 16$$
$$1° \quad 01'$$

Moon:
$$6 ♊︎ 58 \ (= 36° \ 58')$$
$$- 21 ♉︎ 38$$
$$15° \quad 20'$$

Mercury:
$$10 ♐︎ 36_R$$
$$- 9 ♐︎ 43_R$$
$$53_R$$

Venus:
$$26 ♎︎ 15$$
$$- 25 ♎︎ 01$$
$$1° \quad 14'$$

Mars:
$$3 ♏︎ 40$$
$$- 3 ♏︎ 01$$
$$39'$$

Turning once again to the Diurnal Table, we ascertain how much of this movement occurred during the hour and 54 minutes between birth and noon, GMT. We arrive at the following figures:

Sun:

Travel in 1 hour	= 2' 31"
Travel in 54 min.	= 2' 17"
Total travel	= 4' 48" = 5'

Moon:

> Travel in 1 hour = 38′ 20″
> Travel in 54 min. = 34′ 30″
>
> Total travel   = 72′ 50″
> When reduced = 1° 13′ 00″

Mercury:

> Travel in 1 hour = 2′ 12″$_R$
> Travel in 54 min. = 1′ 59″$_R$
>
> Total travel   = 3′ 71″$_R$ = 4′$_R$

Venus:

> Travel in 1 hour = 3′ 05″
> Travel in 54 min. = 2′ 46″
>
> Total travel   = 5′ 51″ = 6′

Mars:

> Travel in 1 hour = 1′ 37″
> Travel in 54 min. = 1′ 28″
>
> Total travel   = 2′ 65″ = 3′

We may now proceed to subtract each of these sums from the coming noon positions (all except that of Mercury, of course, which we must add as it is traveling retrograde):

Sun: 29 ♏ 17
     −   05
     ‾‾‾‾‾‾‾‾‾‾
     29 ♏ 12 (position at birth)

Moon: 6 ♊ 58
     − 1 13
     ‾‾‾‾‾‾‾‾‾‾
     5 ♊ 45 (position at birth)

Mercury: 9 ♐ 43$_R$
      +   4$_R$
      ‾‾‾‾‾‾‾‾‾‾
      9 ♐ 47$_R$ (position at birth)

Venus: 26 ♎ 15
     −   06
     ‾‾‾‾‾‾‾‾‾‾
     26 ♎ 09 (position at birth)

Mars: 3 ♏ 40
       —   03
       3 ♏ 37 (position at birth)

EXERCISE.

Copy the Horoscope Calculation Sheet, Part IIa and replace the figures listed for Joy's birth with the ones you have obtained for the above A.M. birth.

II. THE PROPORTIONAL LOGARITHM METHOD FOR CALCULATING THE PLANETS

If the reader has obtained a Table of Diurnal Planetary Motion, he or she can skip the next few pages devoted to logarithms. After completely mastering the diurnal-motion system, the student may proceed to examine logarithms without risk of confusion.

It should also be stated that, unless exact and detailed work is required (usually associated with the many aspects of prognosticatory work), the planets may be calculated to the nearest full degree. Thus beginning students can extend their mental computations of the proportional movements of the slower-planets to the faster-moving ones. It is a good idea, however, to master one of these two techniques, especially when it comes to determining the position of a planet on the cusp of a sign (such as the Sun in Joy's horoscope) or the position of the Moon because of the tremendous distance it covers (relative to the other planets) in one twenty-four-hour period.

The advanced student will find many uses for logarithms and should be completely fluent in their operation.

Despite its formidable appearance, the Table of Proportional Logarithms is quite simple. The student is already familiar with the process of equating time with movement (arc) through the use of the Diurnal Table of Planetary Motion. The logarithmic table fills the same function; only the method of calculation is different.

Table 5: Proportional Logarithms

Hours or Degrees

Min.	0	1	2	3	4	5	6	7	8	9	10	11	12	13	14	15	16	17	18	19	20	21	22	23
0	3.1584	1.3802	1.0792	9031	7781	6812	6021	5351	4771	4260	3802	3388	3010	2663	2341	2041	1761	1498	1249	1015	0792	0580	0378	0185
1	3.1584	1.3730	1.0756	07	63	6798	09	41	62	52	3795	82	04	57	36	36	56	93	45	11	88	77	75	82
2	2.8573	1.3660	1.0720	8983	45	84	85	30	53	44	80	75	2998	52	30	32	52	89	41	07	85	73	71	79
3	2.6812	1.3590	1.0685	59	28	69	73	20	44	36	80	68	92	46	25	27	47	85	37	03	81	70	68	75
4	2.5563	1.3522	1.0649	8935	10	55	73	10	35	28	73	62	86	41	20	22	43	81	33	0999	77	66	64	72
5	2.4594	1.3454	1.0614	8912	7692	6741	5961	5300	4726	4220	3766	3355	2980	2635	2315	2017	1738	1476	1229	0996	0774	0563	0361	0169
6	.3802	1.3388	1.0580	8888	74	26	49	89	17	12	59	49	74	29	10	12	34	72	25	92	70	59	58	66
7	.3133	1.3323	1.0546	65	57	12	37	79	08	04	52	42	62	24	05	08	29	68	21	88	66	56	55	63
8	.2553	1.3258	1.0511	42	39	6698	25	69	4699	4196	45	36	56	18	00	03	25	64	17	84	63	52	52	60
9	.2041	1.3195	1.0478	19	22	84	13	59	90	88	38	29	2950	13	2295	1998	20	60	13	80	59	49	48	57
10	2.1584	1.3133	1.0444	8796	7604	6670	5902	5249	4682	4180	3730	3323	45	2607	89	93	1716	1455	1209	0977	0756	0546	0345	0153
11	.1170	1.3071	1.0411	73	7587	56	5890	39	73	72	23	16	38	02	84	89	11	51	05	73	52	42	42	50
12	.0792	1.3010	1.0378	51	70	42	78	29	64	64	16	10	33	2596	79	84	07	47	01	69	49	39	39	47
13	.0444	1.2950	1.0345	28	52	28	66	19	55	09	09	03	91	91	74	74	02	43	1197	65	45	35	35	44
14	.0122	1.2891	1.0313	06	35	14	55	09	46	49	02	3297	27	85	69	74	1698	38	93	62	42	32	32	41
15	1.9823	1.2833	1.0280	8683	7518	6600	5843	5199	4638	4141	3695	3291	2921	2580	2264	1969	1694	1434	1189	0958	0738	0529	0329	0138
16	.9542	1.2775	1.0248	61	01	6587	32	89	33	15	88	84	15	75	59	65	89	30	85	54	34	26	26	35
17	.9279	1.2719	1.0216	39	7484	73	20	79	25	12	81	78	09	69	54	60	85	26	82	50	31	22	22	32
18	.9031	1.2663	1.0185	17	67	59	09	69	17	11	74	71	2897	64	49	55	80	22	78	47	27	18	19	29
19	.8796	1.2607	1.0153	8595	51	46	5797	59	09	09	67	65	91	58	44	50	76	17	74	43	24	15	16	25
20	1.8573	1.2553	1.0122	8573	7434	6532	5786	5149	4594	4102	3660	3258	2891	2553	2239	1946	1671	1413	1170	0939	0720	0511	0313	0122
21	.8361	1.2499	1.0091	52	17	19	74	39	85	94	53	52	85	47	34	41	67	09	66	35	17	08	09	19
22	.8159	1.2445	1.0061	30	01	05	63	29	77	86	46	46	80	42	29	36	63	05	62	32	13	05	06	16
23	.7966	1.2393	1.0030	09	7384	6492	52	20	68	79	39	39	74	36	23	32	58	01	58	28	09	03	03	13
24	.7781	1.2341	1.0000	8487	68	78	40	10	59	71	32	33	68	31	18	27	54	1397	54	24	06	00	00	10
25	1.7604	1.2289	0.9970	8466	7351	6465	5729	5100	4551	4063	3625	3227	2862	2526	2213	1922	1649	1393	1150	0920	0702	0495	0296	0107
26	.7434	1.2239	0.9940	45	35	51	18	90	42	55	18	20	56	20	08	17	45	88	46	17	99	91	92	04
27	.7270	1.2188	0.9910	24	18	38	06	81	34	48	11	14	50	15	03	13	40	84	42	13	95	88	90	01

28	0098	87	85	92	09	38	80	36	08	2198	09	45	08	04	40	25	71	5695	25	02	03	.9881	.2139	.7112
29	94	83	81	88	05	34	76	32	03	93	04	39	01	00	32	16	61	84	12	7286	8382	.9852	.2090	.6960
30	0091	0280	0478	0685	0902	1130	1372	1627	1899	2188	2499	2833	3195	3597	4025	4508	5051	5673	6398	7270	8361	0.9823	1.2041	1.6812
31	88	77	75	81	98	26	68	23	94	83	88	27	89	90	17	99	42	62	85	54	39	.9794	.1993	.6670
32	85	74	71	78	94	23	63	19	90	78	83	21	83	83	10	91	32	51	72	38	19	.9765	.1946	.6532
33	82	71	68	74	91	19	59	14	85	73	77	16	76	76	02	82	23	40	59	22	59	.9737	.1899	.6398
34	79	67	64	70	87	15	55	10	80	68	72	10	70	70	3995	74	13	29	46	06	06	.9708	.1852	.6269
35	0076	0264	0461	0667	0883	1111	1351	1605	1875	2164	2472	2804	3164	3556	3987	4466	5003	5618	6333	7190	8279	0.9680	1.1806	1.6143
36	73	61	58	64	80	07	47	01	71	59	67	2798	57	49	79	57	94	07	20	74	8259	.9652	.1761	.6021
37	70	58	54	60	76	03	43	1597	66	54	61	93	51	42	72	49	84	5596	07	59	74	.9625	.1716	.5902
38	67	55	51	56	72	1099	39	92	62	49	56	87	45	35	64	40	75	85	6294	43	59	.9597	.1671	.5786
39	64	51	48	53	68	95	35	88	57	44	51	81	39	28	57	32	65	74	82	28	43	.9570	.1627	.5673
40	0061	0248	0444	0649	0865	1092	1331	1584	1852	2139	2445	2775	3133	3522	3949	4424	4956	5563	6269	7112	8159	0.9542	1.1584	1.5563
41	58	45	41	46	61	88	27	79	48	34	40	70	26	15	42	15	47	52	56	97	20	.9515	.1540	.5456
42	55	42	37	42	57	84	22	75	43	29	35	64	20	08	34	07	37	41	43	81	81	.9488	.1498	.5351
43	52	39	34	39	54	81	18	71	38	24	29	58	14	01	27	4399	28	31	31	66	66	.9462	.1455	.5249
44	48	35	31	35	50	76	14	66	34	19	24	53	08	95	19	90	18	20	18	50	50	.9435	.1413	.5149
45	0045	0232	0428	0632	0846	1072	1310	1562	1829	2114	2419	2747	3102	3488	3912	4382	4909	5509	6205	7035	8081	0.9409	1.1372	1.5051
46	42	29	24	29	43	68	06	58	25	09	14	41	96	81	05	74	00	98	93	20	43	.9383	.1331	.4956
47	39	26	21	25	39	64	02	53	20	04	09	36	89	75	3897	65	4890	88	80	05	23	.9356	.1290	.4863
48	36	23	18	21	35	61	1298	49	16	2099	04	30	83	68	90	57	81	77	68	6990	05	.9330	.1249	.4771
49	33	20	14	18	32	57	94	45	11	95	2398	24	77	61	82	49	72	66	55	75	04	.9305	.1209	.4682
50	0030	0216	0411	0614	0828	1053	1290	1540	1806	2090	2393	2719	3071	3455	3875	4341	4863	5456	6143	6960	7985	0.9279	1.1170	1.4594
51	27	13	08	11	24	49	86	36	02	85	88	13	65	48	68	33	53	45	31	45	75	.9254	.1130	.4508
52	24	10	04	08	21	45	82	32	1797	80	82	07	59	41	60	24	44	35	18	30	66	.9228	.1091	.4424
53	21	07	01	04	17	41	78	28	93	75	77	02	53	35	53	16	35	24	06	15	47	.9203	.1053	.4341
54	18	04	0398	01	14	37	74	23	88	70	72	2696	47	28	46	08	26	14	6094	00	29	.9178	.1015	.4260
55	0015	0201	0394	0597	0810	1034	1270	1519	1784	2065	2367	2691	3041	3421	3838	4300	4817	5403	81	6885	29	0.9153	1.0977	1.4180
56	12	97	91	94	06	30	66	15	79	61	62	85	35	15	31	92	08	93	69	71	10	.9128	.0939	.4102
57	09	94	88	90	03	26	61	10	74	56	56	79	28	08	24	84	4799	82	57	56	00	.9104	.0902	.4025
58	06	91	84	87	0799	22	57	06	70	51	51	74	22	01	17	76	89	72	45	41	7891	.9079	.0865	.3949
59	03	88	81	83	95	18	53	02	65	46	46	68	16	3395	09	68	80	61	33	27	7873	.9055	.0828	.3875

If you examine the logarithmic table, you will see that down the left-hand side is a column headed *Min.*, followed by the numbers 0 through 59. Along the top are the numbers from 0 through 23. These digits stand for minutes of time or minutes of arc and hours of time or degrees of arc respectively. Thus we have a complete conversion table. To calculate the positions of the planets through the use of logarithms, we must proceed as follows.

Step 1. Determine the distance the planets traveled in the 24-hour period between the noon prior to birth and the coming noon, GMT. Find the corresponding logarithm for this amount of *movement*.

Step 2. Determine the interval between noon and the time of birth and find the equivalent logarithm for this amount of *time*. The logarithm of the interval is a constant throughout all the calculations in one horoscope. It is thus referred to as the *permanent logarithm*.

Step 3. *Add* the log found in the second step to the log found in the first step, *regardless of whether the birth is* A.M. *or* P.M.

Step 4. Check the resulting sum of the logs with the Table of Proportional Logarithms to find the equivalent in degrees and/or minutes of arc.

Step 5. Add this figure to the noon position of the planet if the birth time, GMT, was in the P.M. hours. Alternately, subtract this figure from the noon position of the planet if the birth time, GMT, was in the A.M. hours.

The result is the position of the planet for the time of birth.

A. Calculating the Positions of the Planets for a P.M. Birth

Let us practice by computing the locations of the heavenly bodies for Joy's natal chart through the use of logarithms. (In this and in the coming example of an A.M. birth, we shall only compute the positions of the faster-moving planets. The positions of the slower-moving bodies can always be calculated mentally.)

The log of the interval (10h6m) equals .3759 (permanent log).

1. Sun.

```
daily motion   = 1° 00′ = log   1.3802
+ permanent log =                 .3759
─────────────────────────────────────
log of motion  =                1.7561 = 1.7604
               (nearest log in table) = 25′
```

We now add this amount (25′ of arc) to the Sun's position at noon, GMT.

```
  29 ♍ 17
+       25
───────────
= 29 ♍ 42  (Sun's position at birth)
```

Checking this result with our calculations from the Table of Diurnal Planetary Motion, we see that the sums are the same.

Let us continue this process with the Moon, Mars, Venus, and Mercury.

2. Moon.

```
daily motion   = 15° 12′ = log   .1984
+ permanent log =                .3759
────────────────────────────────────
log of motion  =                 .5743 = .5740
                 (nearest log) = 6° 24′
```

We obtained this figure by determining that the sum of the two logs was .5743. We then searched the Table for the number which comes closest to .5743. Under the heading *6* we found the figure .5740, which corresponds to *24* on the left-hand side under the heading *Min.* We can thus conclude that log 5740 is equal to 6°24′ of arc.

We now add this amount to the Moon's position at noon, GMT:

```
  6 ♊ 58
+ 6    24
───────────
= 12 ♊ 82 or 13 ♊ 22 (position at birth)
```

3. Venus.

    daily motion $= 1°$ 13′ $=$ log 1.2950
+ permanent log $=$ .3759
    log of motion $=$ 1.6709 $=$ 1.6670
                           (nearest log) $=$ 31′

We now add this amount to Venus' position at noon, GMT.

    26 ♎ 15
+   31
$=$ 26 ♎ 46 (position at birth)

4. Mars.

    daily motion $=$ 38′ $=$ log 1.5786
+ permanent log $=$ .3759
    log of motion $=$ 1.9545 $=$ 1.9542
                           (nearest log) $=$ 16′

We now add this amount to Mars' position at noon, GMT.

    3 ♏ 40
+   16
$=$ 3 ♏ 56 (position at birth)

5. Mercury.

Since this planet is traveling retrograde, we must reverse the process and subtract the equivalent movement in minutes of arc from its noon, GMT, position:

    daily motion $= 1°$ 03′$_R =$ log 1.3590
+ permanent log $=$ .3759
    log of motion $=$ 1.7349 $=$ 1.7270
                         (nearest log) $=$ 27′

Thus:

    9 ♐ 43$_R$
−   27
$=$ 9 ♐ 16$_R$ (position at birth)

B. Calculating the Positions of the Planets
for an A.M. Birth

There is only one important difference between calculating an A.M. and calculating a P.M. birth through logarithms. The equivalent motion in degrees and/or minutes of arc is to be *subtracted* from the noon, GMT, position of the planet. The result is, of course, the location of the planet at birth. We must *add* the equivalent motion to the noon, GMT, position of an A.M. birth only when the planet is retrograde.

In order to clearly illustrate the above, we have drawn up the Horoscope Calculation Sheet, Part IIb. and filled in the blanks with the correct figures for the sample birth at 10:06 A.M. GMT.

EXERCISE.

Copy the Horoscope Calculation Sheet Part IIb and replace the figures listed for the A.M. birth with the ones you have obtained for Joy's P.M. birth.

C. Calculating the Part of Fortune

The Part of Fortune (also called the "Pars Fortunae" or "Fortuna") is one of many such "Parts" in the horoscope contributed by Arabian astrology.[3] It found its way into Western astrology through the infusion of Moslem thought during the Middle Ages.

The Part of Fortune is falling into obsolescence in the work of many astrologers, but it is still commonly used. Along with quite a number of my colleagues and contemporaries, I believe that it is a valid contribution to the judgment of the whole nature of a given horoscope. You may wish to experiment with it to see its effects on your own chart and others'. A very simple and sure method of checking the significance of the Part of Fortune is to note what transpires when other planets form conjunctions or oppositions to its posi-

---

[3] Some of these are The Part of Spirit, The Part of Marriage, The Part of Divorce, and The Part of Commerce.

Horoscope calculation sheet

Part IIb: Calculation of the planetary positions (proportional logarithms)

GMT of Birth: 10:06 [P.M.] A.M. — Interval before (or after) noon, GMT: H −1 M 54

Date of Birth: Nov. 21, 1972 — Permanent Logarithm: 1.1015

	☉	☽	☿	♀	♂	
a. Coming noon position	29♏17	6♊58	10♐36ᴿ	26♎15	3♏40	♃ 8♑51
b. Previous noon position	28♏16	21♉38	9♐43ᴿ	25♎01	3♏01	♄ 18♊31ᴿ
c. Movement in 24 hours	1°01'	15°20'	53'ᴿ	1°14'	39'	♅ 21♎08
d. Log. of movement	1.3730	0.1946	1.4341	1.2891	1.5673	♆ 4♐46
e. Permanent log.	1.1015	1.1015	1.1015	1.1015	1.1015	☿ 3♎51
f. Sum of d. and e.	2.4745	1.2961	2.5356	2.3706	2.6688	☊ 19♑23
g. Nearest log.	2.4594	1.2950	2.5563	2.3802	2.6812	☋ 19♎23
h. Travel in Interval	5'	1°13'	4'ᴿ	6'	3'	⊕ 22♉
i. Add to P.M. birth; Sub. from A.M. birth; Reverse if retrograde	29♏17 / −5	6♊58 / −1 13	9♐43ᴿ / +4ᴿ	26♎15 / −6	3♏40 / −3	
j. Positions at birth	29♏12	5♊45	9♐47ᴿ	26♎09	3♏37	

tion by *transit*. (This will be fully explained in chap. 8.)

The symbol for Fortuna is the cross within the circle: ⊕. According to DeVore, in his *Encyclopedia of Astrology* (p. 187), this is also the modern symbol for the Earth, the ancient Chinese glyph for "a field," and the Egyptian hieroglyph for "territory." The interpretive value of this Part is implied in its name, for the House position in which it is found is an indication of a special area of life which may contain or contribute to material benefits for the individual concerned.

The Part of Fortune bears the same mathematical relationship to the Ascendant of the chart as does the Moon to the Sun. This means that if you were to add up the degrees separating the Ascendant from the Part of Fortune, you would arrive at the same sum as you would if you were to add up the number of degrees separating the Moon from the Sun. This is expressed in the formula $\text{☽} : \odot :: \oplus : \text{Asc.}$ This relationship is symbolic of Fortuna's material sphere of influence because the Ascendant is the point of contact between the individual and his or her physical environment. Thus the Part of Fortune further serves to support the individual's efforts to relate to the world in which he lives in a material sense, just as the Moon helps the individual to relate to the environment through the receptive nature of the emotions.

In order to calculate the Part of Fortune we follow the formula $\text{☽} + \text{Asc.} - \odot = \oplus$. In other words, the position (by degrees of the ecliptic) of the Moon plus the position of the Ascendant minus the position of the Sun will give the position of the Part of Fortune. Let us illustrate this formula by determining the location of Fortuna in each of our two sample horoscopes. We must first change the zodiacal positions of the Sun, Moon, and Ascendant to degrees of the circle. This is quite a simple task, for each degree of the Zodiac of Signs has a name as well as a number. Thus 2 Taurus is the 32nd degree of the ecliptic (30 degrees of Aries plus 2 degrees of Taurus); 19 Leo is the 139th degree of the ecliptic (30 degrees each of Aries, Taurus, Gemini, and Cancer = 120 degrees, plus 19 degrees

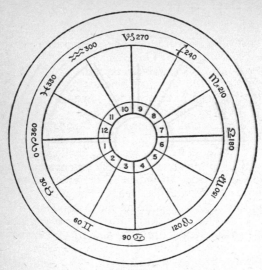

Diagram 11: The Part of Fortune.

of Leo = 139 degrees). Diagram 11 should make this quite clear.

Thus, equating the positions of Joy's Sun, Moon, and Ascendant, we come up with the following figures:

Sun = 29 ♏ 42 = 239° 42'
Moon = 13 ♊ 22 = 73° 22'
Asc. = 10 ♊ 30 = 70° 30'

Returning to the formula: Moon plus Asc. minus Sun = Fortuna,

Moon = 73° 22'
+ Asc. = 70   30
          143° 52'

We note that the Sun's position is 239°42'. To complete this subtraction, we simply add a whole circle of 360° to the sum of the Moon and Ascendant and then subtract the Sun's position:

```
   143° 52'
+ 360  00
  ─────────
  503  52
─ 239  42
  ─────────
= 264° 10', or 24 ♐ 10 (Part of Fortune)
```

If this is unclear, refer back to the previous diagram. Note that 0° ♐ = 240°. The sum we reached from completing our formula was 264° 10', resulting in the position of 24 ♐10 for Fortuna.

What do we do if the position for Fortuna works out to be more than 360 degrees? We subtract a whole circle of 360° from the total.

EXAMPLE.

Ascendant 19 ♓20; Moon 24 ♐17; Sun 10 ♉17.

FORMULA.

Moon plus Ascendant minus Sun equals Fortuna.

PROCEDURE.

```
   24 ♐ 17 =      264° 17'
+ 19 ♓ 20 =      349  20
=               ─────────
                 613  37
─ 10 ♉ 14 = ─     40  14
=               ─────────
                 573  23
                ─ 360  00
─────────────────────────
Fortuna    =     213° 23', or 3 ♏ 23.
```

Computing the Part of Fortune for the sample A.M. birth, the positions of the Sun, Moon and Ascendant are as follows:

```
  Moon =  5 ♊ 45 =     65° 45'
+  Asc. =  8 ♏ 13 =    218  13
=                    ─────────
                       283  58
─   Sun = 29 ♏ 12 = ─  239  12
──────────────────────────────
  Fortuna         =    44° 46' or 45° = 15 Taurus
```

EXERCISES.

1. Find the Part of Fortune for the following coordinates:
   a. Asc. 10 ♉ 14; Moon 24 ♐ 17; Sun 19 ♓ 20.
   b. Asc. 24 ♐ 17; Moon 19 ♓ 20; Sun 10 ♉ 14.
   c. Asc. 10 ♉ 14; Moon 19 ♓ 20; Sun 24 ♐ 17.
2. Find the Part of Fortune in your own chart.
3. If the horoscopes of friends are available to you,
   make a study of the positions of Fortuna in each
   of their charts and note what significance, if any,
   this Part plays in the lives of the individuals in
   question. Record the results of this survey in your
   notebook.

D. Inserting the Planets within the Wheel

Let us list once again the positions of the planets,
nodes, and Fortuna as we have calculated them for
Joy's birth chart. Putting them in their zodiacal order
(from earliest position to latest) will allow us to clearly
see their locations and avoid error.

☽ 13 ♊ 22	♂ 3 ♏ 56
♄ 18 ♊ 29ᴿ	☉ 29 ♏ 42
☋ 19 ♋	♆ 4 ♐ 52
♀ 3 ♎ 52	☿ 9 ♐ 16ᴿ
♅ 21 ♎ 12	⊕ 24 ♐
♀ 26 ♎ 46	♃ 8 ♑ 56
	☊ 19 ♑

Placing these positions in the wheel erected in chapter
11 reveals Joy's horoscope as shown in Diagram 12.

SUMMARY.

1. We have placed the nodes and Fortuna (preferably using a different color of pen than the one
   used for marking the planets) closer to the center
   of the horoscope so as not to confuse these points
   with the more important positions of the planets.
2. The planets are arranged in such a way as to appear

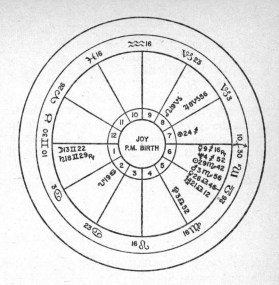

Diagram 12: Joy's Horoscope (P.M. Birth).

as close to their actual position in relation to the House cusps as possible. Thus the Moon is seen very near to the Ascendant and not somewhere in the middle of the First House.

3. The planets are placed so that they are always viewed right-side up. This facilitates the recognition of their position.

Now let us place the planets within the wheel of our sample horoscope for an A.M. birth (shown in Diagram 13).

☽	5 ♊ 45	♂	3 ♏ 37
♄	18 ♊ 31ʀ	☉	29 ♏ 12
☊	19 ♋	♆	4 ♐ 46
♀	3 ♎ 51	☿	9 ♐ 47ʀ
♅	21 ♎ 08	♃	8 ♑ 51
♀	26 ♎ 09	☋	19 ♑
⊕	3 ♏		

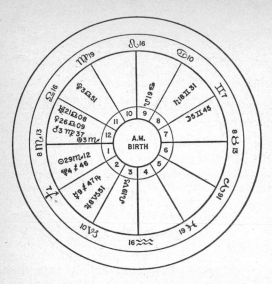

Diagram 13: Joy's Horoscope (A.M. Birth).

EXERCISE.

Erect complete horoscopes for the following birth data:
a. March 9, 1947, Philadelphia, Pa., 6:06 A.M.
b. September 22, 1961, Los Angeles, Calif., 7:17 P.M.

14.

THE GEOMETRY OF THE SPHERES

The Sun is the center of the solar system and is the force which gives life to all the planets. The planets, in turn, rechannel this energy back to the Sun through the nature of their own reflected light. They also share the Sun's energy by means of the planetary rays which extend in all directions into space. Thus the vibrations of all the heavenly bodies have an influence upon the Sun and upon one another. The geometric angle at which these electromagnetic rays strike each planet is very important in determining the nature and effect of these planetary emanations on terrestrial life. These angles of relationship are termed *aspects,* and each one carries its own characteristics.

All the "major" (or more powerful) aspects and many of the "minor" (or less powerful) aspects are formed by the natural divisions of the circle. Thus, if we divide the 360 degrees of the ecliptic by two, we arrive at two angles of 180°; by three, three angles of 120°; by four, four angles of 90°; and so on. If we arrange the aspects in terms of these divisions, we arrive at the listing that follows.[1]

In addition, several other aspects are worth noting, the most important of them being the *inconjunction* (or quincunx), which is an angle of 150 degrees. Another aspect, though of lesser interpretive value, is the *sesquiquadrate* (or sesqui-square) which measures

[1] Although it is vitally important to the horoscope, we are not listing the "conjunction" in this table, for it is not formed by any division of the circle, being in reality a *position* and not an angle. It is formed by the presence of two or more planets at the same degree of the ecliptic. This is, of course, quite possible, as all the planets have widely separating orbits but travel within the circle of the zodiacal signs.

Dividing the circle by:	equals an angle of:	termed:
2	180 degrees	the opposition
3	120 "	the trine
4	90 "	the square
5	72 "	the quintile
6	60 "	the sextile
7	51½ "	the septile
8	45 "	the semi-square
9	40 "	the novile
10	36 "	the semi-quintile
11	32½ "	unclassified[a]
12	30 "	the semi-sextile

[a] In this writer's experience, this angle has no interpretive value per se. If planets are 32½ degrees apart, they should be considered as being in semi-sextile.

135 degrees. All these aspects are formed by measuring their relative distances along the ecliptic; for example, Venus at 14 Aries is 60 degrees (sextile) from Mars at 14 Gemini.[2]

In our present study of geocentric astrology, the Earth is considered the focal point for all planetary influences. Thus an angle between two planets also creates a triangular relationship to the Earth. If, for example, Saturn and Jupiter are 90 degrees apart, the Earth's position is considered as being at the midpoint of these two bodies and receptive to the nature of the type of energy indicated by the square of these two planets.

In addition to major and minor, the aspects may be placed in two other categories: those angles indicating an easy outpouring of creative energy and those aspects indicating blockages and tensions. We may call this first group the aspects of *flow* and the second the aspects of *challenge*.

The equilateral triangle is a form representing total creative harmony. Its structure is symbolic of the work-

[2] There are many other minor aspects but, along with the septile, novile, and semi-quintile, they have little relevance to the chart as a whole. The sesqui-square, used by some astrologers, indicates a point of stress between the energies of the planets in such a configuration.

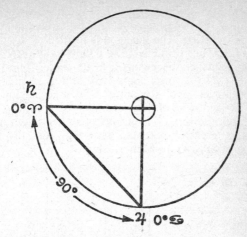

ings of Life (Spirit-Sun) through Form (Soul-Moon) in order to produce the Manifested Universe (Matter-Ascendant). It will be seen that the aspects of flow are based on the 120-degree angle and its division by two (60°) and four (30°). When we examine the hexagon, we see that it is also a beautifully harmonious structure.

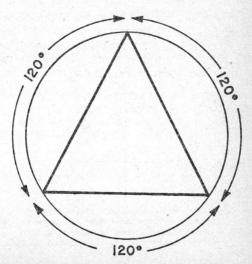

Its nature is such that when it is illuminated by a ray of light, all parts of its form receive the illumination in equal proportion. The hexagon is formed by six 60-degree angles, but if one were to connect any three alternating points of the hexagon to its center, one would form a *cube*, a form comprised of three inner 120-degree angles and six outer 60-degree angles. The latter is symbolic of the fecundity of creativity as it represents the three dimensions of organic life and the unending creative potential resulting from the interchange of Spirit-Soul-Matter. Thus:

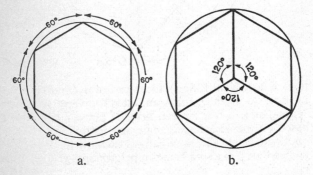

a.   b.

When, on the other hand, we divide the circle into two equal parts, we have two angles of 180 degrees, representing duality or the separation of the Absolute into the Finite. When it is further divided by two, it yields four 90-degree angles—the square. Thus:

c.

The square is symbolic of matter which has reached a state of total crystallization. In other words, no further growth or creative potential is possible. Furthermore, the release of the energy locked in by the square is inimicable to life and is destructive when released. *In our transcendental approach to astrology, we shall see, however, how very vital, helpful, and beneficial such squares (and oppositions) can be to individual evolutionary progress.*

When two planets are in an aspect, there are a minimum of three forces simultaneously at work (this is increased if more than two planets are involved in a configuration, as shown in the following chapter): the energy of each of the two and the nature of the angle which joins them.

The result of an aspect is rather like a chemical reaction. Mixing one part of oxygen with two parts of hydrogen results in the compound water, a substance expressing the properties of both its components but also possessing its own nature. If enough heat is applied to the water, it vaporizes into gas. If the water is chilled sufficiently, it naturally freezes into ice. In astrological (al)chemistry, the angles represent the different external forces conditioning the response of the elements (planets).

This same concept can be applied to the nature of a child—a being who embodies the various traits of both his parents but also exhibits his own personality and genetic characteristics. Depending upon the external stimuli, the child will at times act more like the mother, at other times he will express more of the paternal heritage, and at other times he will act and think like neither of the parents.

This is also true of the vibrations contained within the aspects—which are, of course, the offspring of planetary intercourse. Thus the forces embodied by Venus and Mars, for example, will produce effects which vary widely depending on their angle of relationship. Let us say that Venus will stand for oxygen and Mars will symbolize hydrogen. If we have a square between Venus in Cancer and Mars in Aries, we could express this aspect as H_3O, or "heavy water." This is because the original balance of regular water (the Venus-Mars relationship) has been altered by the addition of another atom of hydrogen (the strength of the position of Mars in its own sign). This influence will outweigh the strength of Venus in Cancer, a sign which is good for Venus, but not an especially powerful one for her.

Thus the key to the interpretation of an aspect lies in your understanding of the nature of each of the planets and their relative strength by sign and House position. This, of course, is in addition to an understanding of the influences which the specific angular relationships hold in themselves.[3]

A. The Major Aspects

No one aspect should be taken by itself without first seeing its relationship to all other aspects in a given chart. This very important point in interpretive synthesis is discussed in greater detail in chap. 8. Probably the most complex individual aspect is the *conjunction,* especially when more than two bodies are involved.

1. Conjunction. This aspect is formed when two or more planets lie within such close proximity that their energies completely interpenetrate. We call the conjunction an aspect of *intensity* and *power,* as the forces contained within each planet are compounded by the intimacy of their relationship. We can symbolize the conjunction by "O ♈," for this is the point of initial release of energy into manifestation. Thus people with a conjunction of Mars and Venus in their natal charts are very concerned with the release of those energies involved in personal, sexual, romantic, and social relationships.

We refer to the conjunction as neither an aspect of flow nor challenge; we call it a *variable* aspect. This

---

[3] This is a very opportune time to go back to Part I of this text and review the meanings of the planets, the signs and the Houses. The more profound one's understanding of these basics is, the more comprehensive will be one's application of the following.

is because the conjunction is not formed by an angular relationship possessed of its own attributes. The nature of the conjunction depends on the resultant interchange between the planets so placed. If you were to take two expensive perfumes and mix them together in one vial, you might get a smell resembling "Chanel Five and Dime"; on the other hand, you might get a fragrance even more beautiful than each of the scents separately. The outcome depends on the chemical compositions of the component fragrances and their relative strengths.

We know, for example, that the natures of Mars and Saturn are inimical to each other. Mars likes to race ahead on the slightest provocation, while Saturn prefers to take a long, hard look at a situation before commitment. Thus a conjunction of these two bodies is like driving a car with the brakes on—not only do you not get very far, but you also strain the mechanisms of your vehicle. If, however, you had a conjunction of Venus and the Moon in your natal chart, you would have a beautiful blend of planetary energies. The sensitivity of the lunar force would work quite well with the love of beauty embodied by Venus.

Another factor to be considered in determining the effects of a conjunction is the place of the planets involved by sign and House. Let us continue to use our examples of Mars-Saturn and Moon-Venus. If the Mars-Saturn conjunction occurred in Aries in the Eighth House, the force of Mars would definitely overcome that of Saturn, and the control and sense of proper restrictions symbolized by Saturn would serve to underline the aggressive Mars in Aries vibration. The net result of this configuration would be a great drive to be a law unto oneself, the setting up of one's own sense of restrictions, and the imposition of these values on others. Unless mitigated by other, softening qualities in the chart, this particular conjunction can trigger quite a ruthless, selfish drive for power. If the Venus-Moon conjunction were in Libra, Venus would be the stronger influence; an individual with such a placement would be more sensitive to the harmony existing within the structure of most areas of human relationships. If the conjunction took place in the Moon's sign, Cancer, the results would be much more subjective, the individual leaning more toward a striving for harmony and perfection of relationships within the family circle. The Moon-Venus in Cancer would be quite a bit more sentimental and attached to loved ones than the Moon-Venus in Libra.

Conjunctions can be said to be in effect when the planets lie within 8 degrees of each other. This *orb of influence* can be expanded to 10 degrees if either of the planets is the Sun or the Moon, and as much as 17 degrees if the conjunction is between the Sun and the Moon.

2. *Opposition*.   When two planets are so placed as to form an angle of 180 degrees, they are said to be in opposition. In most cases, this means that the planets are in signs of their natural polarity. Just as signs directly across from each other can be a cause for either grave conflict or great growth, the same holds true of the opposition aspect; its main purpose in the horoscope is to bring about an *awareness* or *objectivity* on the part of the individual concerned. Though opposing signs are in complementary elements, they are in the same quality. Taurus-Scorpio, for example, is earth and water, but both are fixed signs. Thus in an opposition in which these two signs are involved, there is room for creative harmony if *values* (the fixed quality) are allowed to merge by *a greater awareness of cooperative efforts* (the opposition), so that growth may be achieved through a *deeper understanding* of the planetary energies (earth and water).[4]

We may symbolize the opposition by the polarity of Aries-Libra—that is, Self versus Other. In other words, an opposition brings about a certain conflict of

---

[4] Sometimes, because of the 8-degree orb of influence of an opposition, planets can oppose each other and be neither in complementary elements nor in the same quality (Saturn at 28 Taurus opposing Venus at 2 Sagittarius, for example). In such a case, I feel that the opposition is weakened, as the direct confrontation, which is the result of such an angle, is made somewhat more indirect or even nebulous by this "crossing of the line." This is an area open to research, and I invite the comments and opinions of other students and astrologers.

interests because of some external activity in the environment. Supposing a chart shows an opposition between Mars and Venus. An individual with such a placement could find himself interested in another person platonically (Venus), while the other person's feelings are much more passionate (Mars). Conversely, the individual wishes a physical relationship with another while the latter desires to remain "good friends." In another sense, Venus opposing Mars could indicate that a person tends to be assertive (Mars), when in reality cooperation (Venus) is needed to improve a situation; or the reverse may be true—the person vacillates (Venus) when direct action is required (Mars).

Learning the lessons indicated by the planets in an opposition aspect imparts a sense of balance in respect to the energies embodied by the heavenly bodies in the configuration. Any planets which are *trine* or *sextile* to either end of the opposition will be instrumental in the resolution of the difficulty. The opposition is an aspect of challenge, but the situation is usually accompained by less tension than one indicated by the square.

3. *Square.* When two or more planets are so placed as to form an angle of 90 degrees, they are said to be in square. In most cases, this means that the planets are in signs of their own quality—cardinal, fixed, or mutable—but in conflicting elements (fire-water, earth-fire, air-earth, and water-air). (Because of the 8-degrees-allowable orb for a square, we often find planets technically in this aspect with positions in differing qualities and the same element. Venus at 28 Aries, for example, is square to the Moon at 2 Leo. This particular class of square is easier to handle than ordinary ones, as the similarity of element will aid in the release of the planets' energies. Such a square would bring fewer problems to bear in the area of the life indicated than if the Moon were at 28 Cancer.)

The square indicates a conflict of interests, but, unlike the opposition, it will be expressed *subjectively* and *internally* and become a definite problem area in a given life if not properly resolved. It is a seat of inner tensions brought about through an inability to restructure and transmute the energies indicated by the planets. *The attempt on the part of the individual to transcend his or her squares provides the necessary energy for personal evolution. Thus we term squares "dynamic aspects," since without them there is little drive to succeed.*

We can symbolize the square by the relationship existing in Aries-Cancer or in Aries-Capricorn. In the case of the former, we have the individual desires (Aries) working in a completely subjective milieu (Cancer), allowing little room for outside aid and advice. This results in a blockage of further growth and a great resistance to change. In the case of the latter, we have the individual desires (Aries) working in a completely routine and tradition-bound milieu (Capricorn). This results not only in a fear of alteration of procedure, but also in a compulsion to perpetuate and further crystallize these self-restraining habits.

In order to give an example of the square in operation, let us continue to examine the Mars-Venus relationships. When these two bodies are at a 90-degree angle, an individual is sure to encounter some confusion in his ability to differentiate between love and lust. Such a person would also have a problem distinguishing among purely egocentric goals in personal relationships, mutual goals, and truly selfless goals. Selfishness can easily result from such a configuration; there are, most certainly, frequent conflicts with friends and associates.

The square aspect does not let one rest until the problem indicated is either accepted or solved. Thus the square can be the key to either an adjustment to life's circumstances and limitations or the driving force to reshape oneself in order to be free of such restrictions. A horoscope with none or few squares (or oppositions) is said to be a weak chart, for it often indicates a lazy, "put off to tomorrow" type of person. If one has a problem, one wants to solve it so that the pain disappears. In so doing, many lessons are learned about oneself and about life which contribute to further self-realization and understanding. We should thus be as thankful for our squares (and oppositions) as we are for our trines and sextiles, those aspects which provide the help and flow of energy necessary to over-come our challenges.

4. Trine. When two planets are so placed as to form an angle of 120 degrees, they are said to be in trine. In most cases this means that the planets are in signs of their own element—fire, earth, air, or water—but in different qualities (cardinal-fixed, fixed-mutable and mutable-cardinal). Trines also have an orb of 8 degrees (10 if one of the aspecting planets is either the Sun or Moon), which means that two bodies could be trine even if placed in conflicting elements (Mars in 2 Taurus trine Uranus in 26 Leo, for example). This condition will weaken the trine, however, making it much less effective and positive an influence than if Mars were at 26 Aries and Uranus at the same degree in Leo. Thus we can expect an easy and creative energy flow to take place, since signs in the same triplicity and signs adjoining quadruplicities are in sympathy with one another.

We can symbolize the trine by the relationship existing in either Aries-Leo or Aries-Sagittarius. In the former, we have a centralization (Leo) of individual desires (Aries), which are then organized, refined, and made into productive plans of activity (Leo). In the latter, we have an expansion (Sagittarius) of individual desire (Aries) to a point whereby they are broadened and made workable for a large number of people (Sagittarius).

A trine between Venus and Mars usually indicates (if the rest of the chart concurs) that an individual has great charm with people of both sexes and has great tact, knowing just when to be receptive and when to assert himself or herself. This trine comes with the need for a wise head to make the best of, and not abuse the personal magnetism indicated by, this configuration.

Too many trines (and sextiles) in a chart can definitely retard an individual's self-discovery by failing to provide enough challenges. We can call such a chart one belonging to a "Lotus Eater," for such a person will be content to glide through life, untouched by cares and also untouched by the need to evolve.

5. *Sextile.* When two planets are so placed as to form an angle of 60 degrees, they are said to be in sextile. In most cases this will mean that the planets are in complementary elements and in alternating qualities. The orb of a sextile is 4 degrees (5-6 if one planet is either the Sun or Moon), thus making it possible to have two planets in a technical sextile but in adjoining elements and qualities (Mars in 3 Capricorn sextile to Uranus at 29 Aquarius, for example). This is not an indication of disharmony, but it does weaken the effect of the aspect in the chart, although in this case Mars and Uranus will still act as a force for positivity in the native's life. Thus we can state that the sextile is an aspect indicating a *working cooperative effort which can lead to productive growth.* An individual with an abundance of sextiles in his or her natal chart is usually quite a helpmate. Sextiles confer ease in making situations flow harmoniously, but unlike the trine (about which the individual need not concern himself too much in order to reap the benefits indicated in that configuration), sextiles demand a little push from the Will. In effect, the sextile can be said to be quite a *safe* aspect, for the energy of the bodies so placed lend themselves quite readily to *conscious control.* This is quite important for the seeker, as the process of evolution entails a conscious direction to the release of energy. Thus a sextile between Venus and Mars imparts the opportunity to enjoy other people's company through harmonious social relationships. If such a person wishes to make use of this aspect of his being within the totality of his personality structure, he may do so. But he does not feel compelled to be the social butterfly, which is more often the case when these two planets are in trine.

We can symbolize the sextile by the relationships existing in Aries-Gemini and Aries-Aquarius. In the former, we have a diversification (Gemini) of individual ideas and desires (Aries), so that more avenues of self-expression may be explored (Gemini). In the latter, the original idea (Aries) has been raised to a conceptual state whereby it can be a viable instrument of inspiration for many others (Aquarius).

Before going on to a discussion of the minor aspects, let us pause and reflect on what we have already covered in the first part of this chapter.

QUESTIONS.

a. What is an aspect?
b. What are some of the differences between aspects of flow and aspects of challenge?
c. What makes the conjunction a variable aspect?
d. In your opinion, what effects would a conjunction between the Moon and Uranus produce? How would this be modified in Scorpio? in Aquarius? in Cancer? How would these same bodies react in square? in trine? in sextile?
e. How can squares and oppositions help personal growth?
f. How may an excess of trines retard personal growth?

EXERCISES.

a. Quietly contemplate the forms of the triangle, the square, and the hexagon. Write down your impressions in your notebook.
b. You will find it helpful to (re)read those chapters in *As Above, So Below* which deal in greater detail with the elements, the qualities, and their interrelationships.
c. List all the major aspects from memory and note the number of degrees in each angle and the orb of influence allowable.

B. The Minor Aspects

We have just studied the five major aspects used by practically all astrological workers. Their mastery is vital to the student's competence and interpretive skills. The minor aspects represent a series of lesser angles, some of which have been listed earlier.

Each astrologer has his or her own preferences and experiences in regard to the minors. Some astrologers only utilize the major aspects, while others employ them all, even the very eclectic "vigintile" (18°) or the "tredecile" (108°). I have decided to take a middle path and to list those aspects which the student will come in contact with most frequently. I would, however, like to share some opinions concerning the relative value of those aspects which have assumed a certain degree of importance in my work. I have found it valid to consider, in order of strength, the inconjunction (or quincunx), the semi-square, the semi-sextile, and in the horoscopes of conscious seekers of Light, the quintile.

6. Inconjunction (or Quincunx). When two planets are so placed as to form an angle of 150 degrees, they are said to be inconjunct. This aspect falls exactly midway between the trine and the opposition and describes a condition of energy which is neither entirely flowing harmoniously in a person's life nor exactly challenging one's resources. Thus we can say that this angle causes some confusion and stress in the areas of life indicated by its placement in the natal chart.

The late "astrological Patriarch" of San Francisco, Gavin Arthur, put a tremendous emphasis upon this aspect in his work and even allowed it an orb of 7 degrees. I have found that orbs up to 4 degrees are operable, but after careful reflection, I must agree with Arthur in respect to the importance due this often misunderstood and ignored aspect.[5] Too many inconjunctions in a chart can result in a rather unsteady individual, one who works at getting things done but who often leaves tasks either incomplete or with much to be desired. It is a "seesaw" type of aspect, sometimes working most harmoniously for an individual and then, quite suddenly, reversing its effects. Gavin Arthur categorized some traits of this angle by calling it "the neurotic aspect."

We can symbolize the inconjunction by the relationships existing in Aries-Virgo and Aries-Scorpio. In the

---

[5] The strength of the quincunx is greatly increased when it is part of a larger configuration in which two planets are inconjunct a third and sextile to each other. This is called "The Finger of Fate" and is discussed in the following chapter.

former, the initial release of energy of the planets in question (Aries) must be carefully shaped and purified through use in the service of others (Virgo). In the latter, this release of energy (Aries) must be transformed into a higher level of manifestation (Scorpio) so that further development can take place.

7. *Semi-square*. When planets are so placed as to form an angle of 45 degrees, they are said to be in semi-square. This is a point midway between the semi-sextile (30°) and the sextile (60°). The energy embodied by the planets in the configuration has been activated into working together through the semi-sextile but has not reached a greater state of maturation (power), as indicated by the 60-degree angle.

We can symbolize this aspect by noting the relationship between 0° Aries and 15° Taurus (that is, the forty-fifth degree of the ecliptic). It is here that the initial release of energy (Aries) becomes fixed in its place in an individual's total structure. At this point the energy can be said to be in its adolescence, for the individual, although aware of the planets in the semi-square, is not quite certain how to properly channel this energy interchange to his or her best advantage. We can therefore say that semi-squares can result in misplaced judgments in the areas of life indicated in the natal chart. This is a minor aspect, however, and its influence can easily be modified by more positive and powerful angles elsewhere in the chart. On the other hand, the semi-square can add to certain challenging situations through relationships with squares and oppositions. Once again, the entire horoscope must be carefully scrutinized before final judgments are made.

8. *Semi-sextile*. The semi-sextile is an aspect of 30 degrees and indicates the first ray of cooperative effort between two planetary energies. It can be symbolized by the relationship existing in Aries-Taurus. The seed (Aries) is planted in the earth (Taurus), where it will ripen and grow. It is thus an aspect of *promise*.

9. Quintile. The quintile aspect is formed when planets are placed at a 72-degree angle to each other. It is an aspect which will only have meaning in a chart of a spiritually progressing individual, for it indicates the ability to harmonize the energies of the planets involved on an inner plane of understanding. It is an aspect of *evolutionary potential.*

C. Parallels and Counter Parallels

The term *declination* refers to the distance a planet is placed either north or south of the celestial equator. These positions are easily found in any ephemeris. Should two or more planets lie within 1 degree of each other, either both north or both south, they are said to be in *parallel of declination* and are considered to be in a mild form of conjunction. Should one of the planets lie to the north and the other to the south (also within 1 degree), they are considered as being in counterparallel, a mild form of opposition.

Both these aspects are really modifiers. In other words, if Venus and Mars are conjunct in a horoscope as well as parallel, their conjunction and consequent effects on the horoscope are strengthened. A conjunction of Mars and Uranus is not, for the most part, a harmonious configuration; if a parallel also exists between these two, their effects would be even more discordant, while a counterparallel would make their vibrations more challenging to an individual's resources and equilibrium.

A trine between the Sun and Jupiter is quite a blessing; a parallel between the two would slightly enhance the good fortune indicated, while a counterparallel would slightly detract from its beneficent rays. In effect, we can categorize these two aspects of declination as Minor Variables, and they should always be judged in relation to the actual longitudinal aspects existing between the planets—that is, their positions along the ecliptic. Parallels and counterparallels carry some weight in the judgment of future tendencies in a given life.

D. Some Other Important Factors

1. Applying and Separating Aspects. Aspects are formed by the planetary motions, and some of the planets move faster than others. Unless the heavenly bodies are moving into or out of a retrograde position, they can be listed (from the swiftest to the slowest) as follows: Moon, Mercury, Venus, Sun, Mars, Jupiter, Saturn, Uranus, Neptune, and Pluto.

The effects of aspects are always stronger when they are applying and weaken considerably as they separate. It is up to the astrologer to determine this factor in his delineation of a given chart. If, for example, the Moon is at 6 Aquarius and Mars at 9 Taurus in a chart, the Moon is said to be in an applying square to Mars. In other words, the Moon will eventually overtake Mars' position. If, on the other hand, the Moon is at 9 Aquarius and Mars at 6 Taurus, the Moon is said to be in a separating square, since she has already passed the point of exactitude (6 Aquarius). It should be remembered that a planet applying at a distance of, let us say, 7 degrees to a major aspect will be much stronger in its effects than one separating by 7 degrees.

2. How to Measure the Aspects. Beginning students always spend too much time computing planetary distances. Initially it is not a bad idea to spend ten or twelve hours on a chart; in reality, one has to! But with progress, it should take no more than three-quarters of an hour to calculate the Ascendant, the planets, and the aspects as well as to complete the initial analysis as indicated by the Horoscope Calculation Sheet, Part III (see chap. 8). One way of shortening the calculating time and still maintain full accuracy in determining the aspects is to follow these simple instructions. These formula and rules are for finding exact aspects and, as the experienced student knows, very few angles are so placed. Actually, these are ways of pinpointing the focal points of the aspects so that the student will be able to quickly identify any planet, node, part, or House cusp which is placed within allowable orbs of these points of exactitude.

a. Always measure aspects by signs, not by Houses, for in the Placidean system of House division, a House may contain degrees of three signs: the sign on the cusp; an intercepted sign; and the sign on the following cusp.

b. Always look for aspects on both sides of the planet in question.

c. CONJUNCTIONS are clearly visible.

d. SEMI-SEXTILES are found by noting planets placed at the same degree, *one sign apart*.

e. SEXTILES are found by noting planets at the same degree in complementary elements, *two signs apart*.

f. SQUARES are found by noting planets at the same degree in the same quality, *three signs apart*.

g. TRINES are found by noting planets at the same degree in the same element, *four signs apart*.

h. INCONJUNCTIONS are found by noting planets at the same degree, *five signs apart*.

i. OPPOSITIONS are found by noting planets at the same degree in complementary elements and in the same quality, *six signs apart*.

j. SEMI-SQUARES are found by noting the following:

If a planet's position ends in the number:	the position of a planet semi-square to it ends in:
1	6
2	7
3	8
4	9
5	0
6	1
7	2
8	3
9	4
0	5

For example:

a. ♄ 1 ♈ ∟ (semi-square) ♅ 16 ♉
b. ♄ 17 ♈ ∟ ♅ 2 ♊
c. ♄ 28 ♈ ∟ ♅ 13 ♋

We are now using astrological shorthand, for you should begin to get used to it and to write it yourself to express astrological terms and concepts.

k. QUINTILES are somewhat more difficult to locate, but you can find them if you search for planets farther away from a given point than a sextile but nearer than a square. Or you can add (or subtract) 12 degrees to the sextile position of a point and see if any other body falls into that position. For example, to see if any planet is quintile the Moon at 18 ♉, you would: ⚹ (sextile) 18 ♉ = 18 ♓ or 18 ♋; position of Q = 6 ♓ or 30 ♋ (0 ♑).

3. Extending the Planetary Orbs.   The orbs of all the aspects used in this text are found in Table 6. These numerical designations are rather flexible, and like most astrologers, the student will probably develop his or her own variations on the limits of orbal influences. It is important to mention, however, that orbs may be extended under the following conditions: when either of the luminaries is one of the aspecting planets; when the only planets involved in an aspect are the Sun and Moon; when more than two planets are in mutual aspect. This last factor is called "the transition of the light" and may be illustrated as follows:

Venus and Saturn are 10° apart, out of technical orb for a conjunction, but as Uranus is within a proper orb of an opposition to both bodies, it brings about a conjunctile effect between them.

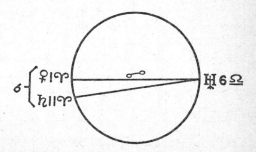

Here we have a "planetary picture" known as a

Table 6: The Aspects

Name	Degrees	Orb[a]	Symbol	Meaning of Symbol	Meaning of Aspect	Key Phrase[b]
conjunction	0	8-10-12	☌	a single body—that is, any planets in ☌ can be said to be as one, possessing all the qualities indicated by the specific combination	power and intensity; a variable aspect	is united with
opposition	180	8-10-12	☍	two bodies confronting each other, held tightly together by bands of polarized energy	awareness and objectivity; challenges	versus
square	90	8-10-12	□	square, indicates the boxed-in condition of the energies contained within the configuration	dynamic tension; challenges	challenges
trine	120	8-10-12	△	triangle, indicates harmonious interchange of energy leading to growth	ease and abundance; aspect of flow	flows well with
sextile	60	4-5-6	*	six-pointed star, indicates the six positive signs (fire and air)	cooperative activity; aspect of flow	works well with
inconjunction	150	2-3-4	⚼[a]	cusps of Houses 1, 6, and 8, indicates affinity of aspect with ♍ and ♏ and spatial factor of 150°	uncertainty and fluctuation; challenges	stressful
semisquare	45	2-3-4	∟	right angle, indicates the joining of two verging and dissimilar forces	mishandling of energy; challenges	misalliance
semisextile	30	2-3-4	⎵[c]	cusps of Houses 1 and 2, indicates affinity with ♈ and ♉ and spatial factor of 30°	permits ease, initial harmony; aspect of flow	is sympathetic with
quintile	72	2-3-4	☆[c]	symbol of evolving Man, the pentagram with point turned upwards	permits fruitful internalization of energy for deeper understanding	elevates

T-Square. Jupiter is within orbs of the square to Venus, and the latter is square Mars. If taken alone, Jupiter and Mars would not be in aspect, but because of the mutual rays of Venus, they are brought into a (wide) opposition.

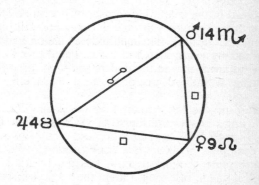

There is another condition in which orbs may be extended, based on the level of consciousness of the native. The more self-realized (individualized) a person becomes, the more he or she is aware of the total structure of his or her being. Such people are conscious of the more subtle elements within their component energies and are readily able to identify these factors. The more evolved the consciousness of a native, the greater is the ability to direct and utilize all the energy at his or her disposal. Thus a highly developed person is more likely to make use of a semi-sextile or a wide

---

[a] The first digit indicates orb between planets; the second, between planet and Sun or Moon; the third, between Sun and Moon.

[b] See chap. 5.

[c] These are my own symbols for these aspects, since I believe them to be much more descriptive of the significance of these minors than their traditional emblems. These are: inconjunction ⊼ semi-sextile ⊻, and quintile Q. The student may note that the traditional symbol for the sesqui-quadrate is ⬚ and represents a square plus a semi-square (= 135°); it is an aspect of minor challenge. The parallel (‖) and the counterparallel (‖) are modifiers of existing longitudinal aspects. The parallel is conjunctile in its effects while the counterparallel is oppositional. Both have an orb of 1-1½ degrees.

trine than is a person of ordinary consciousness, who most probably is not aware of the specifics indicated by the minor or less exact major aspects in the chart.

No numbers or scales are readily available for measuring consciousness. The degree of consciousness of a fellow being is *felt* by the sensitive workers, for it is not shown in the chart. This aspect of interpretation is part of the astrologer's art and is developed with time, after he has dealt with a multitude of charts and has spent many years in search of Light. The degree of this special attunement and the understanding of its proper use comes with the degree of personal dedication.

Before proceeding further, I would like to illustrate the finding of aspects through an example chart. Diagram 14 uses John Lennon's, because it contains some fine examples of planetary configurations. We will measure some of the aspects at this point without interpreting them, reserving a more thorough delineation of this map as the text progresses.

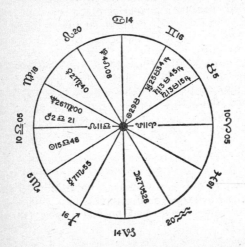

Diagram 14: Aspects in John Lennon's Chart.

a. CONJUNCTION. The most obvious conjunction exists between Jupiter and Saturn in Taurus in the

Eighth House. It can be considered exact, for the two bodies are only 30′ apart. Stated in astrological shorthand: ♃ ♂̷ ♄ ♉ 8

b. OPPOSITION. Mercury in Scorpio is applying to the opposition of Jupiter and Saturn: ☿ ♏ ☍ ♃ ♄ ♉

c. TRINE. The Moon in Capricorn is separating from a close trine to Neptune in Virgo but applying to the trine of Mars in Libra: ☽ ♑ △ ♆ ♍ △ ♂ ♎

d. SQUARE. Venus in Virgo is in a wide, separating square from Uranus in Taurus: ♀ ♍ □ ♅ ♉

e. SEXTILE. Mars is applying to the sextile of Pluto in Leo: ♂ ♎ ✶ ♇ ♌

f. INCONJUNCTION. The Sun in Libra is separating from the quincunx of Saturn and Jupiter:

☉ ♎ –< (or ⊼) ♄ ♃ ♉

g. SEMI-SQUARE. Venus is separating from the semi-square of the Sun: ♀ ♍ ∟ ☉ ♎

h. SEMI-SEXTILE. Venus is separating from the semi-sextile of Mars: ♀ ♍ > (or ⌄) ♂ ♎

i. QUINTILE. The Sun is applying to the exact quintile of Pluto: ☉ ♎ ☆ (or Q) ♇ ♌

QUESTIONS.

1. What is the difference between an applying and a separating aspect?
2. In the following examples, which of the planets applies, which separates?

   1. ☽ 10 ♈ □ ♀ 15 ♋
   2. ♃ 14 ♉ △ ♀ 10 ♍
   3. ♄ 19 ♊ ☍ ☉ 16 ♐

3. How can you easily find an opposition? a square? a trine? a sextile? a quincunx?
4. When may you extend planetary orbs (three reasons)?

EXERCISES.

1. Find two degrees of the Zodiac which are semi-square to the following positions:

   1. ♂ 24 ♋   3. ☉ 6 ♍
   2. ♆ 21 ♌   4. ☿ 19 ♎

2. Find two degrees of the Zodiac which are quincunx
   to the following positions:

   1. ♅ 1 ♏   3. ☽ 27 ♑
   2. ☉ 12 ♐   4. ♀ 0 ♒

3. Make sure you are completely familiar with the
   Summary Table of Aspects.

OPTIONAL THEMES FOR CONTEMPLATION
AND MEDITATION.

1. "The Measurement of Consciousness"
2. "The Path of Self-Dedication"

15.

INTERPLANETARY RELATIONSHIPS

At this point in our study, we have covered the nature of the planets and the various angles in which they may be configurated in the natal chart. Let us tabulate and synthesize the results of this material by presenting a brief synopsis of what the planets indicate when they are joined together by major aspects. To fully appreciate this chapter and place its contents in the proper perspective, several points should preface this list.

1. Aspects are *always* modified by other aspects; therefore all aspects must be carefully weighed and correlated before final judgment is passed. The ability to do this takes time, experience, and patience.

2. Aspects are *always* modified by the signs in which the planets are placed.

3. Aspects are *always* modified by the Houses in which the planets are placed.

4. Our approach to astrology places more emphasis upon the planets involved in a configuration than on the angle connecting them. Any configuration of the Sun and Jupiter, for example, will bring a certain amount of excess into the life. We know that the trine of these two bodies may lead to creative productivity through the proper channeling of such excess, while the square of these planets usually results in wastefulness. A person with the square, who has achieved a level of awareness in which he or she is at work rechanneling the energy represented by this challenging aspect, can conceivably transmute such an angle into a more flowing one through *conscious control. The purpose of knowing one's horoscope is the ability to transcend it.*

An encyclopedia with a compendium of example

charts could be compiled about all the facets of all the aspects. What I am presenting is some insight into the nature of the interplanetary relationships gleaned from personal study and experience. I have, where possible, included a "name" for many of the aspects in order to facilitate the conceptualization of their significance. I would also recommend that the student consult the following texts in order to gain the additional opinions of these wise teachers concerning the interplanetary relationships: *Astrology: The Cosmic Science* by Isabel Hickey; *The Astrological Aspects* by Charles E. O. Carter; and *Astrology* by Jeff Mayo.

I. ASPECTS OF THE SWIFTER-MOVING PLANETS

A. The Aspects of the Sun

1. Sun-Moon   Key words: Will-Feelings.

a. ☉ ☌ ☽   WILL UNITES WITH FEELINGS. This might appear to be a harmonious configuration, but on the whole it does not allow for an objective approach to life, since goals are usually too personally oriented. In short, it becomes extremely difficult to get a good perspective on oneself and see oneself as others do. *"Me-Me."*

b. ☉ ✳ ☽   WILL WORKS WELL WITH FEELINGS. This aspect leads to cooperative efforts between the individual's external environment and his inner drives. People usually want to help such a person achieve his goals, while the individual with such a configuration often seeks to be helpful to others. *"Me and thee."*

c. ☉ △ ☽   WILL FLOWS WITH FEELINGS. This aspect denotes an easy adjustment to life and, unless other indications are to the contrary, indicates a smooth life. A good relationship between the creative drive and receptivity to the environment appear to successfully express this drive. It can, however, contribute to laziness unless ♂ and/or ♄ are strong. *"Me for thee and thee for me."*

d. ⊙ □ ☽ WILL CHALLENGES FEELINGS. This configuration denotes a restless life, always in search of endless experiences, with an inner conflict between what one wants and the means of achieving one's goals. This is one indication of tension in childhood or general difficulty with the opposite sex. This aspect asks the individual to focus on life's purposes. *"Me against thee."*

e. ⊙ ☍ ☽ WILL VERSUS FEELINGS. This aspect provides a tremendous sense of objectivity, as the person must always be aware of others. In this respect the individual can feel that the nature of the environment and associates can serve as a detriment to achieving goals. Obstacles are presented externally, thereby demanding consistency and strength. *"Me or thee."*

f. ⊙ NOT IN ASPECT WITH ☽. This configuration indicates the possibility for wasting a great deal of energy on nonessentials. The individual must constantly align his or her forces and consolidate approaches to life in order to avoid dissipation. *"Me or thee?"* or *"Beating about the bush."*

2. Sun-Mercury Key words: Will-Communication.

As Mercury can only be a maximum of 28 degrees away from the Sun, no aspect other than the conjunction or semi-sextile can be formed. One rule to remember when judging the relationship between these two bodies is: the further Mercury is from the Sun, the better. If Mercury is closer than 8 degrees to the Sun, the individual has a difficult time depersonalizing his thoughts so that a wider spectrum of understanding can be made possible. Mercury is really at its best when in a sign other than the Sun, since it then gives an individual a much wider and more comprehensive approach to life.

3. Sun-Venus Key words: Will-Personal Magnetism.

At the most, Venus can be 48 degrees away from the Sun. This means that only the conjunction and semi-square aspects can be formed between these two bodies.

a. ⊙ ☌ ♀   WILL UNITES WITH PERSONAL MAGNE-
TISM. This aspect gives a desire for complete inner
peace and harmony; it denotes an artistic nature, a
romanticist, a lover of beauty, a poet. It can lead to
an overly sensual nature if energy is not properly
channeled. Attracts people, wealth, and good times.
"Femme Fatale" or *"the Embodiment of Peace."* (The
semi-square indicates stress in the areas mentioned
above).

4. Sun-Mars Key words: Will-Personal Drive. A
very volatile combination.

a. ⊙ ☌ ♂   WILL UNITES WITH PERSONAL DRIVE.
Watch out for an individual with this configuration,
especially if it occurs in fire, ♏︎, or ♑︎. Such a person
is very ambitious, must be on top, and has a tremendous sexual drive unless it is otherwise channeled. The
individual seeks challenge (or always feels challenged);
he or she is a daredevil who acts with no holds barred.
"The Fighter."

b. ⊙ □ ♂   WILL CHALLENGES PERSONAL DRIVE.
This configuration leads to a very restless, often self-
seeking, individual who can take too much on him
or herself in order to prove his or her own abilities.
Such an aspect often contributes to instability, gives
strong sexual urges, is never satisfied with personal
accomplishments, and is therefore the aspect of one
who strives. It can lead to success if used properly.
"The Cosmic Itch."

c. ⊙ ☍ ♂   WILL VERSUS PERSONAL DRIVE. Outside forces are continually bringing challenges which
force the person to overcome the situation and better
his or her worldly position. Like the square, this aspect
can indicate a certain amount of violence in the life
as well as a bad temper. *"The Challenger."*

d. ⊙ △ or ✶ ♂   WILL FLOWS OR WORKS WELL
WITH PERSONAL DRIVE. The individual can easily
gather his forces in order to accomplish his goals in
both of these angles. In the trine, it takes a slighter
effort to succeed at one's aims. *"The Door-Opener."*

Note: All aspects between ⊙ and ♂ impart a certain

degree of self-sufficiency. The ☍, □, and ☌ can express this trait with somewhat more egotism than when these two bodies are connected by △ or ✶

5. Sun-Jupiter   Key words: Will-(Mental/Physical) Expansion.

a. ☉ ☌ ♃ WILL UNITES WITH EXPANSION. This configuration widens horizons and gives an optimistic, bouyant, generous, and philosophical nature. It brings foreign travel, for the native is usually quite restless, always looking to broaden his personal arena of experience. Physically, it can indicate a large and sometimes corpulent individual. *"The Seeker."*

b. ☉ □ ♃ WILL CHALLENGES EXPANSION. The square can produce the same wanderlust as the ☌, but there seems to be much greater waste of energy in the pursuit of knowledge and/or sensual experience. The square can indicate gluttony and greed. *"The Squanderer."*

c. ☉ ☍ ♃ WILL VERSUS EXPANSION. This aspect represents much of the qualities of the □, but the ☍ should bring about more physical travel. The individual will have many opportunities, which can often lead him far afield from his starting point. Such an individual may have a "grass is always greener" complex and frequently goes unsatisfied. All challenging aspects between the ☉ and ♃ can lead to religious difficulties. *"The Wanderer."*

d. ☉ △ or ✶ ♃ WILL FLOWS OR WORKS WELL WITH EXPANSION. These are the aspects of "Luck." They signify many pleasant journeys which contain important and uplifting experiences. These aspects denote a philosophical nature, a generous and cheerful person, and a certain degree of material comfort and ease, as well as a thirst for knowledge. *"The Cosmic Blessing."*

6. Sun-Saturn   Key words: Will-Consolidation

a. ☉ ☌ ♄ WILL UNITES WITH CONSOLIDATION. This configuration can inspire an individual to achieve prominence in the world, or it can be a strong depressive factor. A great deal depends on other planets in aspect to the conjunction. It does denote people who take life seriously, who should cultivate "light" and cheerful friends, and who should always seek to express themselves through some creative medium. *"The Builder."*

b. ☉ □ ♄ . WILL CHALLENGES CONSOLIDATION. This angle is an aspect of test, requiring an individual to work very hard in order to achieve goals. Very often an inner sense of underachievement or restraint can prevent successful self-expression. Such persons always want to make sure that their positions in life are permanent, as they are often internally insecure. *"The Struggle for Success."*

c. ☉ ☌ ♄   WILL VERSUS CONSOLIDATION. This opposition can indicate a person who refuses to accept the many obstacles put before him or one who constantly bows down underneath them. In order to make this aspect work for the good, such people must learn how to work within the structure of their limitations, reshaping themselves to conform to a pattern which is quite difficult to change. This aspect teaches acceptance and can give great strength and powers of endurance if handled wisely. With all challenging aspects of Saturn and the Sun, the individual has to take care not to create habits which become difficult to break, or take on too many odious responsibilities. *"Obstacles in the Path."*

h. ☉ △ or ✳ ♄   WILL FLOWS OR WORKS WELL WITH CONSOLIDATION. These aspects allow the person to live up to his or her commitments and joyfully accept duties and responsibilities which help him or her to grow and succeed in life. Help comes from older friends and figures. The flowing aspects of Saturn impart sound common sense and self-confidence. *"The Architect."*

7. Sun-Uranus   Key words: Will-Intuition.

a. ☉ ☌ ♅   WILL UNITES WITH INTUITION. This very powerful aspect denotes a life full of surprises and sudden flashes of insight. A person with such a configuration can be a genuis even as he is among the most erratic and unpredictable people. If poorly aspected, the ♂ can often act with many of the traits exhibited by the □ and ☍. *"The Non-Conformist."*

b. ☉ □ ♅ WILL CHALLENGES INTUITION. This aspect gives many of the same traits as the conjunction, but it can lead to much more violence and irresponsibility. A strong independent streak runs through such a person, so that great stubbornness and dogmatism can result. This gives a very erratic individual, often stepping way ahead of himself. *"Jumping-Jack Flash."*

c. ☉ ☍ ♅ WILL VERSUS INTUITION. This aspect can result in someone's becoming involved with an adverse group of people or engaging in a dangerous course or foolish activity in spite of one's better judgment. Much of the restlessness, independence, and surprises of the square and the conjunction are also present, but the opposition brings an especially consistent barrage of unusual experiences. The □, ☍, or ♂ can indicate compulsive antisocial behavior.

d. ☉ △ or ⚹ ♅ WILL FLOWS OR WORKS WELL WITH INTUITION. These angles indicate an individual who is very inventive and progressive in his or her attitudes. Such a person is usually filled with inspiration and ideas which, if well directed, work for the betterment of humanity; he or she is original and creative but not necessarily erratic. A flowing aspect or positively oriented ♂ of the ☉ and ♅ are excellent for astrological and other occult studies. *"The Inventor"* or *"The Occultist."*

8. Sun-Neptune   Key words: Will-Illumination.

a. ☉ ♂ ♆ WILL UNITES WITH ILLUMINATION. Individuals with this configuration usually have an aura of some mystery about them. If they are highly developed, this angle brings true mystic visions. If not, it enshrouds one in glamorous and self-deluding images. This aspect denotes one who likes to travel the paths of the invisible and otherworldly. We could call this aspect *"The Dreamer"* for the many or *"The Mystic"* for the very few.

b. ☉ □ ♆ WILL CHALLENGES ILLUMINATION. This is a very difficult aspect to overcome, for its effects are particularly nebulous. Like all Neptunian configurations, it usually becomes manifest as a liking for the mystic, occult, and illusionary but with a strong tendency to get lost along the path. More often it represents a deceptive individual, one who presents the most advantageous side of himself or herself while hiding his or her true nature and motivations. It shows a person who has a difficult time connecting with his "center." *"The Deceiver."* (A strong and positive Saturn can be most helpful in balancing this configuration.)

c. ☉ ☌ ♆   WILL VERSUS ILLUMINATION. Like the ☌, this aspect is very nebulous in its effects. It indicates a person who can be too sensitive to his or her environment, one who is easily swept away from his or her inner purpose by outside vibrations. These people are usually much stronger when they are by themselves than when they are in the company of others. They have to learn how to use their powers of perception wisely, depersonalizing what they feel by stressing a more universal awareness. *"The Chamelion"* or, if properly used, *"The Psychic."*

d. ☉ △ or ✶ ♆   WILL FLOWS OR WORKS WELL WITH ILLUMINATION. This individual gets along well with everyone and can easily move around on all levels of society. Such a person is very charming and artistic, with some leanings toward the mystical and the arts. A strong Mercury along with this aspect can make for a very fine occultist. All affairs of Neptune can be made to serve the interests of the native in a very harmonious way. *"The Inspirer."*

9. Sun-Pluto   Key words: Will-Regeneration.

a. ☉ ☌ ♇   WILL UNITES WITH REGENERATION. The potential creative ability of a person with this conjunction is quite vast. It is an aspect which can bring great evolutionary growth, as the individual has to undergo continual metamorphoses. Depending on the nature of the soul, this can be an aspect for great self-discovery or equally vast self-annihilation. It makes for a magnetic and intense individual who is very much a loner. *"The Evolutionary"* for some, *"The Devilutionary"* for others.

b. ☉ □ ♀ WILL CHALLENGES REGENERATION. Whatever Pluto touches has to undergo a change in its essential structure in order to become more highly developed. When Pluto is square the Sun, it makes the necessary metamorphosis of inner drives very difficult. Such transformations do occur, but not without tensions and breakdowns. This presents a real challenge when striving for evolutionary achievement. *"Breakdown-Buildup."*

c. ☉ ☌ ♀ WILL VERSUS REGENERATION. Two, often simultaneous, effects are possible: the person can act as an agent for other people's transformations and/or become transformed through the challenges presented by the environment. These difficulties force one to undergo changes in order to adjust to life, resulting in personal metamorphosis. Both types of reaction to this opposition come with some difficulty. If this occurs in Leo-Aquarius, there is an ideological breakdown; if in Cancer-Capricorn, an emotional and structural collapse occurs.

d. ☉ △ or ⚹ ♀ WILL FLOWS OR WORKS WELL WITH REGENERATION. An individual fortunate enough to have either of these aspects will undergo the deep transformations indicated in the above but with greater ease. In addition, this aspect gives renewal of strength so that illness can be more readily overcome or even prevented during one's lifetime. It is an aspect of physical as well as psychic recuperation. *"The Underground Spring of the Life Force."*

B. The Aspects of the Moon

1. Moon-Mercury Key words: Feelings and Communication (Rational Mind)

a. ☽ ☌ ☿ FEELINGS UNITE WITH COMMUNICATION. The effects of this conjunction depend to a large extent on the sign in which the configuration is found. If the sign is one of water or Taurus, then the Moon will be the stronger; if in air or in Capricorn, Virgo, or Aries, Mercury will be the predominent influence. The conjunction gives a witty, curious, quick, and easily adjustable individual, one who is always on the go. *"The Busybody."*

b. ☽ □ ☿ FEELINGS CHALLENGE COMMUNICA-TION. This is an aspect of nervous activity and self-doubt. The individual questions and is never sure of his or her feelings about people and ideas. The heart and the head seem to be in constant conflict. One is constantly trying to rationalize one's activities and sentiments. A great restlessness and frequent changes of residence also categorize this influence. *"Where to go and Why?"*

c. ☽ ☍ ☿ FEELINGS VERSUS COMMUNICATION. This aspect, although expressing much of the influence of the square, is also a challenge to be true to oneself in regards to one's personal relationships, one's reactions to one's environment and one's means of self-expression. It can contribute to one who tends to alter the facts to suit his mood. The □ and ☍ also signify one who often talks too much and says too little.

d. ☽ △ or ⚹ ☿ FEELINGS FLOW OR WORK WELL WITH COMMUNICATION. An individual with one of these aspects is able to communicate his or her ideas and feelings to others quite successfully. There is still the same sort of restlessness in all connections between these two bodies, but any movement is much more purposeful than the type of travel indicated by the challenging aspects. If used negatively, even these aspects can result in deception, as the person can easily paint beautiful verbal pictures to suit his or her needs. *Remember: a fine aspect does not (necessarily) make a fine person. "The Charming Speaker."*

2. *Moon-Venus Key words: Feelings-Personal Magnetism.*

a. ☽ ☌ ♀ FEELINGS UNITE WITH PERSONAL MAGNETISM. This is a most graceful, charming, artistic, and often sensual combination. It is an indication of wonderful relationships with women and an indicator (if other factors in the map concur) of a successful home life and material gains (this is especially true if it is placed in Taurus). It gives a very sociable and, if in Pisces or Cancer, very compassionate nature. Care must be taken to avoid self-indulgence. *"Tea and Sympathy."*

b. ☽ □ ♀ FEELINGS CHALLENGE PERSONAL MAGNETISM. The person with this aspect has great difficulty in achieving success in the social sphere. There are often problems with women, and such people find that they attract all the "wrong" people (or are attracted to such maligned individuals). There is often a lack of self-control in and an overreaction to social situations. The individual may be overly solicitous or overbearing. In general the aspect denotes excessively emotional persons, with poor control over their feelings. It can also indicate sensuality and self-indulgence.

c. ☽ ☌ ♀ FEELINGS VERSUS PERSONAL MAGNETISM. Even the challenging aspects of the Moon and Venus do not deny one friends or invitations. What occurs, especially in the opposition, is an uncomfortable feeling in social situations. This is especially true if a challenging Saturn is also configured. Very often one accepts invitations to gatherings which are completely contrary to one's nature, and there is difficulty in meeting the "right" people. *"Social Ineptitude."*

d. ☽ △ or ⚹ ♀ FEELINGS FLOW OR WORK WELL WITH PERSONAL MAGNETISM. Just the reverse occurs with the flowing aspects. The individual is sought after by many and is constantly invited to the best gatherings in his or her level of society. There is opportunity for social advancement as well, especially if Saturn is well placed in the map. This gives a person who knows instinctively how to be charming and who may also possess some artistic and poetic leanings. *"Popularity."*

3. Moon-Mars   Key Words: Feelings-Personal Drive.

a. ☽ ☌ ♂ FEELINGS UNITE WITH PERSONAL DRIVE. This is not an especially good conjunction, as the nature of the two bodies are quite antithetical. It is often indicative of someone with poor control over his or her emotions. Such a person frequently gives way to anger, jealousy, envy, and a whole assortment of unregenerated feelings. Most certainly a dynamic aspect, it helps an individual succeed but often at the expense of others. *"Selfishness."*

b. ☽ □ ♂ FEELINGS CHALLENGE PERSONAL DRIVE. This aspect also indicates a selfish person who must have his or her own way at all costs. It reveals a nitpicker, a harpie, a shrew, someone who takes offense at the slightest provocation. In the horoscope of women it can reveal trouble with giving birth or show that their mothers had difficult pregnancies and deliveries. I have found that if Pluto is also involved with either the square or opposition of the Moon and Mars, a woman may have lost a child through miscarriage, abortion, or death, or that she is barren. In a man's chart it gives poor understanding of women and a general lack of sympathy. It may also reveal that the man has fathered a child which has been lost through one of the ways indicated above. *"Offence-Defence."*

c. ☽ ☍ ♂ FEELINGS VERSUS PERSONAL DRIVE. Many of the indications of the square are also present here, but the person has less inner tension and agitation. An individual with this configuration may often seek to release pent-up negative and violent emotions through social intercourse. Thus such people often engage in arguments with the people around them. This is a configuration which leads to a "what can I dig up here" type of attitude. There can be trouble or even scandal with women (especially if Neptune is involved and receiving challenging aspects). *"Don't tred on me."*

d. ☽ △ or ⚹ ♂ FEELINGS FLOW OR WORK WELL WITH PERSONAL DRIVE. These aspects indicate someone who can make the best of any situation, for it gives an inner sense of courage and self-confidence. Opportunity is easily recognized, and initiative can match any challenge. This is a "lucky" aspect in someone's chart, for it usually endows the person with a great deal of sex appeal. *"The Stout-Hearted Man."*

4. *Moon-Jupiter Key words: Feelings-(Physical or Mental) Expansion.*

a. ☽ ☌ ♃ FEELINGS UNITE WITH EXPANSION. All aspects between these two bodies are basically harmonious. The only possible difficulty lies in overdoing. The conjunction shows happy-go-lucky individuals, very generous and supportive to all people with whom they come in contact. Travel, abundance, and worldly women are likely to come into the life. If, however, there are challenging aspects to this conjunction, especially from the Sun, Mercury, or Mars, there can be great restlessness and an exaggeration of feelings, which tend to go overboard in response to any sensual stimulus.

b. ☽ ☐ ♃ FEELINGS CHALLENGE EXPANSION. Persons with this aspect are likely to exaggerate their feelings about people. There is a tendency to be overly optimistic and to lose sight of reality. There may also be difficulty in formulating or controlling religious feelings for *if the rest of the map concurs*, this can give rise to a zealot. It is also an indication of a person who likes to take life easy and not work too hard. *"Always put off until tomorrow what you can do today."*

c. ☽ ☍ ♃ FEELINGS VERSUS EXPANSION. Restlessness is also a key word in this configuration. There is much of the wanderlust found in ☉ ☍ ♃, but here the emphasis is located more in the realm of people and relationships with them. Such people may therefore put their trust or finances in the wrong hands. False pride and extravagance are other attributes of the challenging aspects between these two bodies. *"Maybe this time. . . ."*

d. ☽ △ or ✶ ♃ FEELINGS FLOW OR WORK WELL WITH EXPANSION. This person is given a helping hand throughout life as people (especially women) are always ready to assist the native in both good and difficult times. Self-exploration in human relationships, higher knowledge, and travel really pay off. This aspect can give a true sense of altruism and a nobility of character. No matter what other configurations are in the chart, this aspect is *"The Ray of Hope."*

5. Moon-Saturn Key words: Feelings-Consolidation.

a. ☽ ☌ ♄ FEELINGS UNITE WITH CONSOLIDATION. All aspects between these two bodies are basically inharmonious, although the flowing aspects can be most helpful if they are properly channeled. The conjunction tends to give a self-restrained, ultra-conservative viewpoint. A person with such a configuration needs to be encouraged even while he or she shuns a helping hand or a warm arm around the shoulders. This conjunction can also strip one of vitality and is not good for general health. It does give endurance and common sense, but selfishness has to be overcome if the individual wishes to transcend this configuration. If this conjunction is trine or sextile to the Sun or Jupiter, it makes for a great business executive. Emotional self-expression is difficult; we can call this aspect *"Melancholia."*

b. ☽ □ ♄ FEELINGS CHALLENGE CONSOLIDATION. Like the conjunction, this aspect leads to brooding and a general inability to express one's love nature. There is a certain coldness, and unless the aspect is modified by other angles, there is a tendency toward a crafty and calculating personality. Saturn's rays are those of the teacher, showing us what we must overcome. In this instance it is difficulties with one's own mother or one's own childhood, which are indicated by a challenging Saturn. *"The Cold Heart."*

c. ☽ ☍ ♄ FEELINGS VERSUS CONSOLIDATION. Other people or life's general circumstances can put so many burdens on a person with this opposition that individual freedom seems severely limited. There is generally less selfishness than in the above two aspects, but the lessons to be learned deal with the proper execution of responsibility. A difficult childhood and/or a stern parent may also be indicated. As with all aspects of Saturn, both challenging and flowing, there is a tendency for aloneness (though not necessarily loneliness). At its most challenging, this can be called the aspect of *"The Oppressor"*; at least it is *"The Call to Duty."*

d. ☽ △ or ⚹ ♄ FEELINGS FLOW OR WORK WELL WITH CONSOLIDATION. Much of the saturnine qualities of the emotions is toned down with the flowing aspects. We do find attention to duty and very often a harmonious, though tradition-bound, attachment to the family. This aspect makes for excellent insight and business acumen, as the individual is well aware of the possibilities for growth and gain present in everyday experiences. This aspect gives patience and depth and allows one to understand the structuring of human relationships. *"Common Sense."*

6. Moon-Uranus   Key words: Feelings-Intuition.

a. ☽ ☌ ♅ FEELINGS UNITE WITH INTUITION. This can be a very helpful aspect for someone interested in the occult and metaphysical. There is an inner understanding of human nature and an instant rapport with all races and nationalities. As such, the individual is very likely to come into contact with all types of people. This conjunction can, however, lead the native into wrong company, as there is also a certain antisocial attitude which becomes more pronounced in the square. In more highly developed people, this aspect can lead to a personal humanitarian doctrine, but one which is often at variance with the prevailing socioeconomic structure. Interesting women are constantly entering the life, and there is the likelihood of an unusual childhood. The domestic situation and life style are generally unconventional.

b. ☽ □ ♅ FEELINGS CHALLENGE INTUITION. This denotes a person who often does not listen to himself or herself—a very erratic individual who is always changing social groups and friends. Such a person has a difficult time staying in one place, and, if other aspects support the tendency, can come from a broken home or be the cause of one. This configuration may indicate a tremendous nervousness and violent emotional outbreaks (especially if Mars is involved through some challenging aspect or is conjunct).

c. ☽ ☍ ♅ FEELINGS VERSUS INTUITION. Unusual people may come into the life, bringing assorted difficulties. The person misjudges his or her friends and associates. There can be strong antisocial feelings, as this type of person will step on the grass just because there is a sign to the contrary. This individual craves excitement and may be the type who is drawn to the scenes of accidents and/or fires. In more highly evolved individuals, the aspect does show some interest in the occult, but often this is expressed under conditions adverse for true progress.

d. ☽ △ or ✳ ♅ FEELINGS FLOW OR WORK WELL WITH INTUITION. As with all the aspects of ☽ and ♅, there is a love for the bizarre and for unconventional living habits. The square between these two bodies leads to compulsion in this respect, a type of "I've got to be different" attitude. The flowing aspects usually permit such sentiments to be expressed through healthy and creative outlets. Thus a person with the △ or ✳ may become involved in some form of social work or public relations. The more mystically oriented people will find comfort and inspiration through some form of occult work, as this configuration contributes to a highly developed sixth sense.

6. Moon-Neptune   Key words: Feeling-Illumination.

a. ☽ ☌ ♆ FEELINGS UNITE WITH ILLUMINATION. This aspect gives an openness to life. Individuals in whose horoscope this configuration is found do not like to be restrained in their way of relating to the environment and feel that they should be allowed to explore any avenue of self-expression. In this respect they may feel or actually find themselves persecuted by existing moral codes. This is a highly artistic and inspirational combination for many while for the few this configuration leads to mystic experiences. *"The Visionary"* or *"The Escapist."*

b. ☽ □ ♆ FEELINGS CHALLENGE ILLUMINATION. As in all connections between the Moon and Neptune, a certain element of discrimination must be exercised to carefully separate the real from the unreal. A person with the square has many moods and is never really sure about feelings for others or the way others feel about him. This is decidedly a deceiving influence, and care must be taken in personal relationships, especially those involving women. Drugs, alcohol, and most aspects of mysticism should be carefully avoided unless this aspect is modified by others (a strong and positive ♄ and ☉ would be most helpful). *"The Hallucinator."*

c. ☽ ☍ ♆ FEELINGS VERSUS ILLUMINATION. The

opposition holds many of the same qualities as the square, with the important difference that the native can be more easily driven into a deceptive social environment. The square is a more self-deceiving aspect. In the opposition, therefore, associates can contribute to one's undoing. Friendships must be thoroughly scrutinized. *"The Deceived."*

d. ☽ △ or ✶ ♆ FEELINGS FLOW OR WORK WELL WITH ILLUMINATION. This aspect is found in the horoscopes of many creative people, especially those involved in film, art, or dance. It is an uplifting, inspiring, and versatile aspect, allowing the native to bring beauty into his or her surroundings. For some it is an indication of positive contact with forces existing in the invisible realms.

7. Moon-Pluto   Key words: Feelings-Regeneration.

a. ☽ ☌ ♀ FEELINGS UNITE WITH REGENERATION. This is a very versatile and intense aspect, which can give rise to sudden emotional outbursts or panic. If the conjunction is receiving other challenging aspects and/or is in the horoscope of one who has not learned to transcend the great infusion of feelings this configuration signifies, hysteria from ungrounded fears may result. This conjunction may indicate broken homes or illegitimate children. On the other hand, the Moon conjunct Pluto in the horoscope of a more highly evolved person gives tremendous insight into the psychology and psyche of all people with whom one comes into contact. This aspect shows the constant changing of the form of creative self-expression as directly related to the emotional state.

b. ☽ □ ♀ FEELINGS CHALLENGE REGENERATION. People with this configuration find it extremely difficult to transcend the lower emotions such as jealousy, envy, hate, and vengeance to reach higher forms of expression such as generosity, universal love, and spiritual aspiration. All configurations involving Pluto allow for the transmutation of energy embodied by the planet which is configurated with it. In the horoscope of consciously evolving souls, ☽ □ ♀ gives a great desire to purify the baser feelings listed above. The inner tension engendered by this intense emotional energy *forces* the transference of any negativity into a more positive channel. *"The Need to Purify."*

c. ☽ ☍ ♀ FEELINGS VERSUS REGENERATION. The circumstances of one's personal relationships cause one to rechannel one's negative emotional energy. This aspect tends to make one seek to gain control over the environment and over associates. This is often done in an extremely subtle and underhanded way, eventually resulting in outbursts, which destroy other people's relationships as well as one's own. *"The Devastator."*

d. ☽ △ or ✶ ♀ FEELINGS FLOW OR WORK WELL WITH REGENERATION. These aspects signify an easier path toward the purification of emotions and feelings. It brings into the life those experiences which awaken within ourselves higher emotional qualities and aspirations. It is a strong contributing factor to growth in conciousness. The trine and sextile also contribute to the native's understanding of the human psyche, but without the often troubling intensity of the conjunction.

C. Aspects of Mercury

1. Mercury-Venus   Key words: Communication (Rational Mind)-Personal Magnetism.

Mercury and Venus can never be more than 72 degrees away from each other; therefore the only major aspects they can form are the conjunction and the sextile.

a. ☿ ☌ ♀ COMMUNICATION UNITES WITH PERSONAL MAGNETISM. This aspect is characterized by the phrase, *"The charm of self-expression."* If other factors in the chart coincide, it contributes to graceful oratory and general ease in the use of the written word. It denotes a sociable, affable, light-hearted, and usually optimistic person, but unless the general "tone" of the nativity proves otherwise, such a native is not especially profound.

b. ☿ ⚹ ♀ COMMUNICATION WORKS WELL WITH PERSONAL MAGNETISM. These are people with unusually good taste in everything they do. They are especially fond of literature, the arts, and people involved with these pursuits. ☿ is melody, ♀ is harmony; the net result is someone who is liked by all.

2. Mercury-Mars Key words: Communication-Personal Drive.

a. ☿ ☌ ♂ COMMUNICATION UNITES WITH PERSONAL DRIVE. Quick-minded, acting immediately upon what he thinks, this type of person talks his way to success. The native is a thinker whose modus operandi is often devastating in its speed and suddenness. The configuration gives a good mind for engaging in technical, mechanical, or scientific research, especially if there are good saturnine aspects. A sarcastic tone often accompanies this *"Quick Tongue."*

b. ☿ □ ♂ COMMUNICATION CHALLENGES PERSONAL DRIVE. This square gives the compulsion to speak one's mind. Such natives may talk so much that it is easy to lose track of what has been said, so that constant repetition results. This aspect often characterizes a nervous and unstable mind with a sharp tongue. *"The Chatterbox."*

c. ☿ ☍ ♂ COMMUNICATION VERSUS PERSONAL DRIVE. Natives with this configuration often say the wrong thing at the wrong time. Even more than people with the square (who really just like to hear themselves talk), ☿ ☍ ♂ people love a good argument. *"The Debater."*

d. ☿ △ or ⚹ ♂ COMMUNICATION FLOWS OR WORKS WELL WITH PERSONAL DRIVE. Natives in this configuration are very clever in writing and speaking, seeing the point and going right to it. They possess a certain sense of tact and diplomacy yet maintain a clear direction of purpose. Usually we find this aspect in the charts of precise thinkers and organizers (unless a befuddling, challenging aspect of Jupiter or Neptune is involved). *"The Technician."*

3. Mercury-Jupiter   Key words: Communication-Expansion.

a. ☿ ☌ ♃ COMMUNICATION UNITES WITH EXPANSION. This conjunction functions at its best when neither of the two bodies is in detriment (see Table 1 of Honors and Dishonors). If such is the case, there is apt to be some form of misjudgment, having to do with the sign in which they are placed; for example, ☿ ☌ ♃ in ♍ can lead to excessive pettiness. If, however, the conjunction occurs in mutually beneficial signs, such as Aries, Aquarius, Cancer, Scorpio, or Libra, we may find an individual with great intellectual potential or compassionate insight. This aspect definitely characterizes the mind of someone who can see the larger issues at work in humanity as well as the smaller; care should be taken that the two are kept in their proper perspective. *"The Philosopher."*

b. ☿ □ ♃ COMMUNICATION CHALLENGES EXPANSION. Individuals with this configuration usually draw incorrect conclusions, since judgment tends to become impaired through general misunderstanding of facts. Problems often have to do with travel; extreme restlessness is prevalent, and language arts may be impaired. The loquacious mind never stops creating a barrage of ideas, blocking greater understanding. *"The Exaggerator."*

c. ☿ ☍ ♃ COMMUNICATION VERSUS EXPANSION. The individual with this configuration may express many of the difficulties indicated by the square. The opposition focuses attention on the large versus the small. In other words, a person can often make a mountain out of a grain of sand or vice-versa—and usually both. Sometimes there is a conflict between the intellect and religious aspirations (faith). *"The Pseudo-Intellectual."*

d. ☿ △ or ✶ ♃ COMMUNICATION FLOWS OR WORKS WELL WITH EXPANSION. This is an aspect of a clear thinker, one who can coordinate the differences existing between universal concepts and their application to everyday life. It also indicates a (successful) traveler and linguist, someone who can make the transitions among the various levels of thought, as well as among the differences between languages. We therefore call this configuration *"The Translator."*

4. Mercury-Saturn   Key words: Communication-Consolidation.

a. ☿ ☌ ♄   COMMUNICATION UNITES WITH CONSOLIDATION. This conjunction may manifest itself in two basic ways. It can show a slow thinker with a dull mind, or it can give a deep thinker with a serious mind. A great deal depends on the chart as a whole, especially on the sign in which this configuration is placed; the best position for it would be in air. Thus we can call this aspect either *"Depth of Mind"* or *"Dullness of Mind."*

b. ☿ □ ♄   COMMUNICATION CHALLENGES CONSOLIDATION. Individuals with this aspect usually tend to get stuck in certain thinking habits. To make matters worse, they often do not hear very clearly what other people say, without necessarily implying an organic hearing deficiency. These individuals close their ears to opinions which differ from their own. The mind tends to be depressive, and such individuals should cultivate a more hopeful framework. A good ♃ would certainly help! *"The Worrier."*

c. ☿ ☍ ♄   COMMUNICATION VERSUS CONSOLIDATION. This configuration usually implies many of the difficulties indicated by the square, although to a lesser degree. Usually external circumstances are filled with obstacles which stand in the way of travel. Plans have to be delayed quite frequently in order to compromise with existing circumstances. There can be feelings of inferiority, to the effect that "the world is against me," for example. In its most positive light, this aspect can teach mental discipline, responsibility, and the necessity for precision.

d. ☿ △ or ✳ ♄   COMMUNICATION FLOWS OR WORKS WELL WITH CONSOLIDATION. This configuration imparts common sense and a fine head for business. It allows one to make the most out of the least. Those fortunate enough to have such a flowing aspect in their charts have a way of achieving goals through careful planning and an awakened sense of existing opportunities. The △ or ✳ of ☿ and ♄ allows for consistent mental work and fine organizational ability.

5. Mercury-Uranus   Key words: Communication-Intuition.

a. ☿ ☌ ♅   COMMUNICATION UNITES WITH INTUITION. Obviously the result of such a configuration is some form of genius. The individual is inventive, original, and very quick to arrive at a correct conclusion without necessarily having to analyze all the data. There is a tendency, however, to be quite opinionated, and one is always eager to express oneself in new and unusually unconventional ways. Thought may come in "flashes," and there is an uncanny ability to come up with immediate solutions for complicated situations. *"A Lightning Mind."*

b. ☿ □ ♅   COMMUNICATION CHALLENGES INTUITION. Although this aspect also permits one to experience "flashes" of ideas and concepts, individuals with this placement often have an extremely difficult time relating such ideas to the everyday world. The mind often jumps ahead of itself, and there is usually a considerable degree of nervousness and verbosity. An extremely restless configuration indeed; the mind needs to be disciplined. A strong, positive Saturn can be of great help here. *"The Scattered Mind."*

c. ☿ ☍ ♅   COMMUNICATION VERSUS INTUITION. This is similar to the square, but as oppositions work through external circumstances, individuals with this configuration usually jump to erroneous conclusions about the people they know. The wrong type of friends and associates may often result from this particular configuration. There is also a tendency to pick up on other people's ideas and twist them to suit one's own purposes. This aspect can indicate a person who forces his way of thinking on others. *"The Rabble-Rouser."*

d. ☿ △ or ✳ ♅   COMMUNICATION FLOWS OR WORKS WELL WITH INTUITION. Individuals with this configuration are the inventors, innovators, occultists, political theorists, and dynamic thinkers of society. This is a fine aspect for all types of scientific, metaphysical research. *"The Progressive Thinker."*

6. Mercury-Neptune   Key words: Communication (Rational Mind)-Illumination.

a. ☿ ☌ ♆ COMMUNICATION UNITES WITH ILLUMINATION. There are two ways in which the conjunction may manifest itself in the majority of cases. It can indicate an artistic mind with great imagination and a strong appreciation for music and dance, or it can be the source of great nebulousness and an excessive and uncontrolled imagination. The real and unreal often merge into each other and rest in an undifferentiated state of confusion. In the horoscope of a very few this aspect can give revelations and mystic communication with the unseen. *"The Illusionist."*

b. ☿ □ ♆ COMMUNICATION CHALLENGES ILLUMINATION. This aspect is found in the horoscope of those individuals who often create their own version of the truth. It is a highly deceptive influence, to say the least. One should always scrutinize with great care all documents and legal proceedings (as is also true for challenging aspects between Mercury and Jupiter). *"The Sneaky Mind."* Note: It must always be remembered that aspects can be transcended. The positive rays of Pluto as well as a conscious redirection of energy on the part of the individual can result in a realignment of this or any other challenging aspect.

c. ☿ ☍ ♆ COMMUNICATION VERSUS ILLUMINATION. Many of the same qualities exhibited by the square are present in the opposition. This aspect is especially indicative of someone who can deceive or be deceived by those with whom he or she comes into contact. Such people believe that anything is possible and have quite a difficult time in staying on the Earth. A strong tendency to fantasize and daydream is present in both the major challenging aspects between these two bodies.

d. ☿ △ or ✳ ♆ COMMUNICATION FLOWS OR WORKS WELL WITH ILLUMINATION. This aspect is often found in the horoscope of successful writers, novelists, and other media people. It allows the native to see many sides of a situation and broadens his perspective on life. It helps to make a good psychiatrist or psychiatric worker, for there is often a highly developed degree of empathy with other people's thoughts and feelings (reinforced by good aspects with the Moon and/or Mars). This aspect is of help for those engaged in psychic and metaphysical work. *"The Inspirational Thinker."*

7. *Mercury-Pluto　Key words: Communication-Regeneration.*

a. ☿ ☌ ♇　COMMUNICATION UNITES WITH REGENERATION. This aspect can lead to extremely deep thinking. There seems to be an understanding on the part of the individual who has this configuration that there are many untapped levels of perception. These individuals seek to resolve the mysteries of life, and it is very difficult to keep a secret from such a probing mind. Very often the person's way of perceiving his or her immediate surroundings undergoes an extraordinary and complete metamorphosis. Opinions may change drastically and suddenly. *"The Detective"* or *"The Spy."*

b. ☿ □ ♇　COMMUNICATION CHALLENGES REGENERATION. This aspect can give rise to many disturbing thoughts and deep-rooted neuroses. Although there is a desire to transcend these negative thoughts, the attempt is accomplished with a great deal of tension. This aspect can also indicate a highly perceptive and sarcastic native, acutely aware of his own and other people's weaknesses and points of vulnerability. *"The Obsessed Mind."*

c. ☿ ☍ ♇　COMMUNICATION VERSUS REGENERATION. This aspect, along with the square, indicates a certain degree of disintegration of thought patterns, so that the mind is always busily at work trying to consolidate and crystallize the many ideas which constantly appear and disappear from one's frame of reference. The opposition is especially suggestive of someone who is extremely curious about people's secrets and ways of thinking. It can also indicate a person who engages in some sort of corruption to undermine existing circumstances (especially if Saturn or the Moon is also involved). It denotes a penetrating, incisive, and often highly complex mind; thought patterns have to be regenerated through proper interactions with others.

d. ☿ △ or ✳ ♇ COMMUNICATION FLOWS OR WORKS WELL WITH REGENERATION. These aspects give a natural ability to transcend certain set ways of thinking by viewing many levels of perception simultaneously. This is, therefore, an aspect found in someone engaged in education, advertising, or other areas geared toward the molding of the mass mind. For persons seeking higher levels of consciousness, the △ or ✳ between these two is a very helpful tool. *"The Transcendental Mind."*

D. Aspects of Venus

1. Venus-Mars   Key words: Personal Magnetism-Personal Drive.

a. ♀ ☌ ♂ PERSONAL MAGNETISM UNITES WITH PERSONAL DRIVE. The intensity of this conjunction becomes manifest in the individual's emphasis on his or her emotional-sexual involvements, which are usually passionate, intense, and frequent. In judging the effects of this conjunction, we understand that the sign in which the aspect is placed will decide which of the two is stronger. *"The Sensualist."*

b. ♀ □ ♂ PERSONAL MAGNETISM CHALLENGES PERSONAL DRIVE. This aspect shows up as an impetuous entering into relationships, with an inability to sustain the initial passion and enthusiasm. Such individuals usually blow hot one day and cold the next. There is also a tendency to be confused as to when to be cooperative with associates and when to be assertive. *"He loves me, he loves me not."*

c. ♀ ☍ ♂ PERSONAL MAGNETISM VERSUS PERSONAL DRIVE. Individuals in this sign find themselves in Platonic relationships when passion is called for and passionate when friendship is offered. As with the conjunction and the square, there is a great deal of sensuality, but the opposition usually leads to some form of dissatisfaction in the pursuit of personal relationships. Cooperation with other people's desires is being tested. *"Friend or lover, not both."*

d. ♀ △ or ✳ ♂ PERSONAL MAGNETISM FLOWS OR
WORKS WELL WITH PERSONAL DRIVE. Individuals in
this aspect have no trouble with members of the opposite sex unless other contrasting factors predominate.
There is an inner understanding of how to work best
with people so that one's own as well as the common
goal is achieved. There is a fine sense of putting into
order the many details found in daily life. A fine
aspect for social success: *"A Natural-Born Lover."*

2. *Venus-Jupiter Key words: Personal Magnetism-
Expansion.*

a. ♀ ☌ ♃ PERSONAL MAGNETISM UNITES WITH
EXPANSION. Individuals of this configuration are not the
type to sit quietly in the corner while the world spins
around them. They usually love a good time, make
enjoyable companions, are generally quite attractive
and find themselves in either comfortable material
circumstances and/or surrounded by people of substance. *"A Gift from Heaven."*

b. ♀ □ ♃ PERSONAL MAGNETISM CHALLENGES
EXPANSION. Although these individuals could find
themselves in the same happy circumstances as those
who have the conjunction, they are wastrels, super-
extravagant, and all too often ostentatious. *"The
Squanderer."*

c. ♀ ☍ ♃ PERSONAL MAGNETISM VERSUS EXPAN-
SION. A good piece of advice to individuals with such
a placement was stated by Capricorn Benjamin Franklin: "Waste not, want not." Here again we find the
extravagance of the square as well as many of the other
aforementioned characteristics. The opposition, however, serves to make an individual into a social butterfly in the never-ending pursuit of the "right crowd."
"The Social Climber."

d. ♀ △ or ✳ ♃ PERSONAL MAGNETISM FLOWS
OR WORKS WELL WITH EXPANSION. This aspect needs
few words to describe its function: wealth, popularity,
the social graces, an inner sense of beauty, and a
propensity to share blessings with others. *"The Golden
Horseshoe."*

3. *Venus-Saturn   Key words: Personal Magnetism-Consolidation.*

a. ♀ ☌ ♄ PERSONAL MAGNETISM UNITES WITH CONSOLIDATION. Although connections between these two planets do not often result in great social popularity, they can give a very long-lasting and loyal marriage or partnership. If well aspected by other planets, such as the Moon or the Sun, this aspect can embody the most positive side of Venus-Saturn. One can, however, feel duty-bound to close associates, and there is often a very serious attitude about finances and social life in general. There can be an attraction to older people when young and younger people when old. *"The Dutiful Partner."*

b. ♀ □ ♄ PERSONAL MAGNETISM CHALLENGES CONSOLIDATION. The lesson to be learned from this aspect is *sharing*. Very often people with this configuration hold back from a loved one the very emotion the latter needs most. In the same way, other people may hold back their love and/or material substance from a person with this aspect in his or her chart. There can be periodic lapses of funds, as well as separations from loved ones if this aspect is unmitigated by other favorable angles. *"The Love-Tester."*

c. ♀ ☍ ♄ PERSONAL MAGNETISM VERSUS CONSOLIDATION. One of the most positive features of the opposition and square between these two bodies is the eventual development of patience and compassion in dealing with others. If this lesson is not learned, suffering continues. Until it is transcended, the opposition can manifest as a manipulative tendency when handling other people's material resources. Some scheming is often involved, as well as a certain coldness in personal relationships. Because of the laws of karma, however, the manipulator should expect to be manipulated. Another important facet of this aspect is that one can work tremendously hard establishing oneself either materially or emotionally, but the rewards of such efforts are often negligible. For this reason we can call the opposition of Saturn and Venus *"Love's Labours Lost."*

d. ♀ △ or ✳ ♄   PERSONAL MAGNETISM FLOWS OR WORKS WELL WITH CONSOLIDATION. People with this configuration often receive the help of a loving partner and/or success in the business world later on in life. Sometimes there is assistance from older and more established individuals, and there is very definitely a great deal of respect for the latter. This aspect reveals a profound sense of duty which brings rewards with the passage of time. *"The Mature Partner."*

4. Venus-Uranus   Key words: Personal Magnetism-Intuition. In true Uranian fashion, we are going to depart from our format at this point to present a general picture of the type of energy which results from a linkage of these two planets. Two areas predominate; the first is the world of arts, the second is the arena of human relationships.

Venus-Uranus people are generally quite innovative in the medium through which they choose to express themselves. A good example of this is the chart of Yoko Ono Lennon, who is an Aquarius with Libra rising. One only has to examine her various projects, such as the filming of 300 or so famous French buttocks or some of her films, such as *Fly*, to get an understanding of the genre which can come from the original mind of a Venus-Uranus person. We can thus characterize these connections by calling them the *"Different Drummers."* In terms of social relationships, people with Venus-Uranus configurations have a great drive toward the unconventional. As a matter of fact, they tend to run away from establishment-oriented, socially acceptable partnerships and/or associations. They attract that segment of society which can be broadly designated as "bohemian," or "underground." Interracial and interfaith marriages are quite common among people with Venus-Uranus connections and, as we shall soon see, with Venus-Neptune configurations.

a. ♀ ☌ ♅   PERSONAL MAGNETISM UNITES WITH INTUITION. The typical tendencies manifest themselves with great intensity of expression.

b. ♀ □ ♅   PERSONAL MAGNETISM CHALLENGES INTUITION. These are the most rebellious of the Venus-

Uranus type. Felissa Rose, my assistant, who is quite familiar with Venus-Uranus people, feels that this aspect is prominent in the horoscopes of divorced people and of individuals who tend to break their relationships easily. She has found that such people seek conventional relationships to suppress their true desire for unconventional ones. I have found that Venus-Uranus (as well as Mars-Uranus) squares and oppositions give rise to "unusual" sexual behavior.

c. ♀ ☌ ♅ PERSONAL MAGNETISM VERSUS INTUITION. This aspect is similar to the square. These individuals consciously seek out unconventional relationships, which often result in problematic situations.

d. ♀ △ or ⚹ ♅ PERSONAL MAGNETISM FLOWS OR WORKS WELL WITH INTUITION. These aspects lead to the acquaintance of people of all proclivities. It gives social popularity and the desire to bring harmony and beauty to many people through some form of social or artistic work.

5. Venus-Neptune Key words: Personal Magnetism and Illumination.

a. ♀ ☌ ♆ PERSONAL MAGNETISM UNITES WITH ILLUMINATION. This conjunction can indicate someone who either lives a completely impractical, dreamlike existence or one who has taken the imagination and channelled it into some beautiful creative outlet. As with all conjunctions, other aspecting planets, as well as the general "tone" of the horoscope, have to be considered before final judgment is passed. Nevertheless, this configuration can be called the aspect of "Artistic Imagination" or of "Idle Imagination."

b. ♀ □ ♆ PERSONAL MAGNETISM CHALLENGES ILLUMINATION. This aspect indicates a great deal of self-deception in relationships in general and in romantic involvements in particular. People with this aspect have great difficulty in seeing the difference between the illusionary aspect of love—that is, "someday my prince(ss) will come"—and the reality at hand. The square is especially suggestive of someone who compulsively enters into relationships which ultimately prove disastrous. However, this configuration does not preclude the possibility of interest and talent in the creative arts. *"Fooled by Love."*

c. ♀ ☍ ♆ PERSONAL MAGNETISM VERSUS ILLU-MINATION. Both the square and the opposition indicate deception in romantic involvements, usually through extramarital and/or clandestine love affairs. The opposition is easier to handle than the square in this respect, as a greater sense of objective choice is involved. Both these challenging aspects indicate a need to sacrifice personal interests for the welfare of others. *"Personal versus Universal Love."*

d. ♀ △ or ✶ ♆ PERSONAL MAGNETISM FLOWS OR WORKS WELL WITH ILLUMINATION. These aspects indicate tremendous creative potential, artistic imagination, and an ability to get along with all people, regardless of ethnic or social background. This aspect also gives compassion and understanding in human relationships. *"The Lover of the Universe."*

6. Venus-Pluto   Key words: Personal Magnetism and Regeneration.

a. ♀ ☌ ♀ PERSONAL MAGNETISM UNITES WITH REGENERATION. The conjunction, square, and opposition of these two planets call for a transcendence of the way in which people relate to others. The conjunction is indicative of someone who has intense personal relationships, which may result in the total annihilation of partnerships. There is a tendency to totally dominate the person with whom one is involved. On a more positive level, this aspect can result in a continual renewal of strength and energy within personal relationships. It can be a force of great healing or one of total destruction.

b. ♀ ☐ ♀ PERSONAL MAGNETISM CHALLENGES REGENERATION. The desire for total dominance in one's relationships is pronounced in the square. The individual in whose chart such an aspect is found may consistently work (consciously or unconsciously) to undermine his or her partners or associates. Another facet of this aspect is the tendency to be very destructive and wasteful in handling material possessions. There is often great difficulty in coordinating creative efforts. Sexuality is also intensified by such a configuration.

c. ♀ ☌ ♀ PERSONAL MAGNETISM VERSUS REGENERATION. The opposition can give very violent relationships which end suddenly and with great finality. Jealousy and envy can be very prevalent in the relationships of someone with this aspect in the natal chart.

d. ♀ △ or ⚹ ♀ PERSONAL MAGNETISM FLOWS OR WORKS WELL WITH REGENERATION. This aspect can be a fount of tremendous artistic expression. Such individuals are always busy refining and changing their environment and their relationships. There is an inner urge to bring out a more intense sense of beauty and a finer sense of interaction in all close ties.

E. Aspects of Mars

1. Mars-Jupiter Key words: Personal Drive-Expansion.

a. ♂ ☌ ♃ PERSONAL DRIVE UNITES WITH EXPANSION. This conjunction gives the tendency toward excess and overindulgence in sensual pursuits. There is the tendency to spread oneself out too diffusely and to exaggerate the importance of one's opinions. The individual with this conjunction usually enjoys life, likes to speculate and gamble, and is quite adventuresome.

b. ♂ □ ♃ PERSONAL DRIVE CHALLENGES EXPANSION. Individuals with this configuration are too restless for their own good. The extravagance and self-indulgence exhibited in the conjunction is emphasized in the square. There is a great need for sensual self-expression and for large-scale projects which the individual may find too great a load to handle. *"Biting off more than you can chew."*

c. ♂ ☌ ♃ PERSONAL DRIVE VERSUS REGENERATION. One result of this opposition is conflict in religious or philosophical matters. While the same can be true of the square, the opposition tends to bring the tendency out into public view. This configuration gives the objectivity needed to resolve the situation and is yet another reason why the opposition between these two planets is easier to handle than the square: the tension is less, and there is greater perspective on the issue. Another facet of the challenging aspects is an alternation between a tremendous output of energy and complete laziness.

d. ☌ △ or ⚹ ♃ PERSONAL DRIVE FLOWS OR WORKS WELL WITH EXPANSION. These aspects result in someone who can build quite easily upon his or her ideas. It is a dynamic configuration, exhibiting a practical interest in religious and philosophical matters. *"The True Believer."*

2. Mars-Saturn   Key words: Personal Drive-Consolidation.

a. ☌ ☌ ♄ PERSONAL DRIVE UNITES WITH CONSOLIDATION. This is not an easy aspect to handle, for it gives a tremendous sense of personal ambition, which can often be quite frustrating in its realization. This aspect can be characterized as *"Driving a car with the brakes on"*—it gives a great deal of power but accompanies it by fear and tension. Felissa Rose feels that the conjunction manifests a certain sense of incertitude about one's goals and ambitions, thus resulting in an inability to make a move in one direction or another.

b. ☌ □ ♄ PERSONAL DRIVE CHALLENGES CONSOLIDATION. We can compare the square to hot- and cold-water faucets. Sometimes there is great striving, at other times great tension. The native seems to find it extremely difficult to find a form into which he may place his energy. *"Frustration."*

c. ☌ ☍ ♄ PERSONAL DRIVE VERSUS CONSOLIDATION. The opposition is characterized by obstacles in the path of ambition; on the other hand, the native may rush headlong into projects before the moment is right. Timing is usually off; the native acts too quickly on some occasions and too slowly on others. *"The Stop-Go."*

c. ☌ △ or ⚹ ♄ PERSONAL DRIVE FLOWS OR WORKS WELL WITH CONSOLIDATION. These individuals are fitted with the dynamic energy needed to actualize their projects. There is a fine working relationship between the set of surrounding circumstances and goals. Opportunities for growth seem to come at the right time, and these persons grow stronger as they grow older. *"The Master Builder."*

3. Mars-Uranus   Key words: Personal Drive and Intuition.

a. ♂ ☌ ♅ PERSONAL DRIVE UNITES WITH INTUITION. This is a highly volatile and unstable configuration, especially when placed in fire and/or the mutable signs. It denotes erratic activity, ebbs and flows of energy, and sudden, often explosive conditions in the areas of life indicated by its House position. Some individuals with this configuration, especially if in air, can have revolutionary or anarchistic concepts. (See the horoscope of Angela Davis in chapter 33.) *"The Revolutionary."*

b. ♂ ☐ ♅ PERSONAL DRIVE CHALLENGES INTUITION. If other configurations concur, this aspect is indicative of someone who is accident-prone or who has been involved in some form of violence. At the very least, the square indicates nervousness and irritability. It is extremely difficult for a person with the square or the opposition to finish his projects; the square gives an attraction for the bizarre and unusual methods of self-expression. *"A Lightning Bolt."*

c. ♂ ☍ ♅ PERSONAL DRIVE VERSUS INTUITION. The opposition is significant of someone who is always challenging. It signifies a person who stands apart from the crowd. On the other hand, it also may indicate a person drawn to revolutionary or at least reactionary political movements or even the criminal element in society. In any case, the opposition signifies one who opposes authority and the status quo.

d. ♂ △ or ⚹ ♅ PERSONAL DRIVE FLOWS OR WORKS WELL WITH INTUITION. These configurations are indicative of one who is both inventive and progressive. Original both in ideas but most certainly in methods, these people are usually at the forefront of any group involvement. *"The Leader of the Pack."*

4. Mars-Neptune   Key words: Personal Drive-Illumination.

a. ♂ ☌ ♆ PERSONAL DRIVE UNITES WITH ILLUMINATION. This aspect lends a certain amount of confusion about goals. Such individuals can see many possibilities, but they are often unable to make a decision and remain consistent in their efforts. *"Here, there, everywhere and nowhere."*

b. ♂ ☐ ♆ PERSONAL DRIVE CHALLENGES ILLUMINATION. This aspect is usually quite difficult to handle, as there are often self-destructive as well as cruel and generally "strange" impulses which enter into the imagination and have to be controlled. Such people are very sensitive to the negative elements in their surroundings. Drugs and most forms of mysticism should be avoided, and the nature of sexual drives must become more refined. *"The Obsessive Impulse."*

c. ♂ ☍ ♆ PERSONAL DRIVE VERSUS ILLUMINATION. This aspect can occur in the horoscope of people who find themselves doing what they really do not want to do. There is a tendency to drift and to be inconsistent in the output and direction of energy. Often one encounters people who can be extremely adverse to one's evolutionary growth. The sensual nature needs refining. The square and opposition of these two bodies give a tendency for unusual sexual experiences.

d. ♂ △ or ⚹ ♆ PERSONAL DRIVE FLOWS OR WORKS WELL WITH ILLUMINATION. Isabel Hickey calls this aspect "the practical idealist," as this combination of energies usually allows natives to successfully accomplish their envisioned goals. There is a great plasticity to the nature, which allows these people to make the most of any situation. This aspect puts the imagination to work and is often found in the charts of extremely creative individuals.

5. Mars-Pluto   Key words: Personal Drive-Regeneration.

a. ♂ ☌ ♇ PERSONAL DRIVE UNITES WITH REGENERATION. This aspect signifies a person who seeks to win at all costs. There is a great drive toward dominance and power and a never-ending supply of energy. As a result, this aspect is indicative of someone with tremendous creative potential toward either continual self-refinement or self-destruction. *"The Atomic Stockpile."*

b. ♂ □ ♀ PERSONAL DRIVE CHALLENGES REGENERATION. People with the square are known to have extremely violent tempers. They let nothing stand in their way and can be devastating enemies. In a sense this aspect acts like a bomb, constantly clearing the way by wiping out what has already been established. It therefore becomes rather difficult for a continuum of growth to take place, as projects, ideas, and energies are usually aborted before reaching fulfillment. On the positive side, this aspect can be used as a clearing house for personality traits and life circumstances which are no longer desirable, providing the individual can modify the intensity with which he releases himself. *"The Annihilator."*

c. ♂ ♂ ♀ PERSONAL DRIVE VERSUS REGENERATION. There is a tendency to use more power than necessary to accomplish goals. One can be too heavy-handed when a lighter touch is called for. Often there is brusqueness and ill temper in dealings with others. In the square, the opposition, and the conjunction, the sexual nature is very strong and constantly seeks release. Sexual energy is of course creative energy which, when properly channelled, can be the vehicle for great evolutionary growth. Thus Pluto-Mars people are capable of tremendous development and are filled with creative potential achieved through the constant transmutation of the lower nature into the higher. *"To win at any cost."*

d. ♂ △ or ⚹ ♀ PERSONAL DRIVE FLOWS OR WORKS WELL WITH REGENERATION. The processes described above are indicative of the trine or sextile in respect to the creativity which results from the transcendence of sexual and vital energies. With the flowing aspects, this transformation is achieved with greater ease. In addition, many opportunities become available for successfully accomplishing this important phase of personal development.

II. ASPECTS OF THE SLOWER-MOVING PLANETS

All aspects existing among Jupiter, Saturn, Uranus, Neptune, and Pluto are of such long duration that they affect literally millions and—in the case of Uranus, Neptune, and Pluto—tens of millions of people in the same way at the same time. Thus, in the horoscopes of the vast majority of people, aspects between these slower-moving bodies work in a generalized, generational sense (that is, through the collective unconscious of the human race) rather than individually. There are, however, certain exceptions.

If these slower-moving or "outer" planets have mutual aspects in the angular house and/or are configurated with the luminaries or the ruler of the chart, they take on a more personalized effect.

In the horoscopes of highly evolved individuals they take on an individualized effect directly related to the degree to which the native can respond to the vibrations symbolized by the outer planets.

As a corollary to the above, let it be said that as individuals evolve in consciousness, they will gradually be in a position in which the vibrations of the slower-moving bodies become manifest in a growing, personal sense.

F. Aspects of Jupiter

1. Jupiter-Saturn   Key words: Expansion-Consolidation.

a. ♃ ☌ ♄ EXPANSION UNITES WITH CONSOLIDATION. Jupiter is the planet signifying the desire to expand in search of new experiences. Saturn, on the other hand, represents the drive to consolidate and glean the wisdom from past experiences. I have found that many individuals with this configuration in their natal charts are greatly concerned with the moral issues of society at large. They are usually deep thinkers who have managed to balance these two contrasting energies in such a way that their view of life is very concerned with the ideological and economic basis of civilization (Jupiter the philosopher, Saturn the architect). On the other hand, these two planetary energies can neutralize each other in such a way that inertia and a general lack of concern with political-moral issues can result. A great deal depends on other aspects of the conjunction and, naturally, on the "tone" of the entire map. This conjunction occurs roughly every twenty-one years.

b. ♃ □ ♄ EXPANSION CHALLENGES CONSOLIDATION. This aspect causes a great restlessness, for the native may set forth on a venture or begin a project without bringing a previous situation to completion. There is a great fluctuation between the consolidation of previous achievements and the expansion of energy into new areas. On the intellectual plane, this aspect serves as a source of inner conflicts in one's moral outlook on life.

c. ♃ ☍ ♄ EXPANSION VERSUS CONSOLIDATION. The opposition can often divide a life into two parts or at the very least give periods of fluctuation. One part or one period is very expansive, while the other half or period entails a great many responsibilities and restrictive circumstances. In addition, many of the qualities mentioned in the square seem to be a constant undertone.

d. ♃ △ or ⚹ ♄ EXPANSION FLOWS OR WORKS WELL WITH CONSOLIDATION. These aspects are most fortunate, as they contribute to common sense and a good sense of timing. Such people have an understanding of their limitations and the foresight to balance their efforts with the situation at hand. Religious aspiration can be balanced with practical application of philosophical principles. This aspect is frequently found in the horoscope of individuals who are successful in the material sphere. *"The Banker."*

2. Jupiter-Uranus   Key words: Expansion-Intuition.

a. ♃ ☌ ♅ EXPANSION UNITES WITH INTUITION. This conjunction reveals a very strong thirst for knowledge and a love of adventure. Unexpected and often successful travels occur. The person often has original ideas and concepts which he or she enjoys sharing with others. This conjunction occurs every fourteen years. *"The Quest for Knowledge."*

b. ♃ □ ♅ EXPANSION CHALLENGES INTUITION. The square of these two bodies may indicate persons who are unsure of their beliefs or people who are extremely dogmatic about them. Surprising travel experiences also enter into the life, as well as interesting and varied groups of people. However, there is frequently a lack of judgment about how to handle oneself while traveling and/or among various ethnic or philosophical groups. Such persons can be too blunt in speech and action. *"The Dogmatist."*

c. ♃ ☍ ♅ EXPANSION VERSUS INTUITION. This aspect is similar to the square but easier to handle. The urge to travel and explore new avenues of knowledge remains a great part of this person's life experience. Such people, however, often find themselves dissatisfied with people and/or the knowledge acquired. There is, therefore, a certain degree of erratic and impulsive moving about in search of true values. *"The Unsatisfied Seeker."*

d. ♃ △ or ⚹ ♅ EXPANSION FLOWS OR WORKS WELL WITH INTUITION. This aspect introduces an element of genius into any horoscope. The person's judgment is keen, and he knows how to apply the wisdom he gains through his intuition. Many of the more positive facets of the conjunction of these two bodies are exhibited by the sextile and trine, as these traits are expressed with greater ease. These individuals come across those fortunate experiences in life which can awaken their appreciation of and commitment to truth. *"The Well-Traveled Soul."*

3. Jupiter-Neptune   Key words: Expansion-Illumination.

a. ♃ ☌ ♆ EXPANSION UNITES WITH ILLUMINATION. This conjunction gives a very strong imagination which, if not properly channeled, can lead to tremendous disillusionment as a result of frequent misjudgments about the reality of one's surrounding circumstances. This is an aspect which, when placed in the horoscope of a highly evolved person, can be very instrumental in obtaining psychic and healing powers. In most individuals, however, it simply signifies a tendency toward escapism and the constant pursuit of bizarre experiences. In any map in which this conjunction appears there is a yearning for the unseen. This conjunction occurs every thirteen years.

b. ♃ □ ♆ EXPANSION CHALLENGES ILLUMINA-TION. This angle brings into the open many of the negative qualities expressed in the conjunction. There is a certain gullibility and wooliness when dealing with harsh realities. These individuals often find themselves in a dream world which all too often results in rude awakenings. *"The Seeker of the Dream."*

c. ♃ ☍ ♆ EXPANSION VERSUS ILLUMINATION. Individuals who have the challenging aspects of Jupiter and Neptune in their charts often become involved in social work. This is especially true of the opposition. They can, however, lose the necessary objectivity in their efforts and fall prey to an inordinate amount of sentimentality and misplaced altruism.

d. ♃ △ or ⚹ ♆ EXPANSION FLOWS OR WORKS WELL WITH ILLUMINATION. These aspects contribute to a very kind and compassionate nature which is comfortably integrated into the totality of one's being (unless, of course, there are other challenging aspects to one or both of these bodies). This configuration is very good for all mystical, religious, and occult work. However, in the charts of the ordinary individual the results of this aspect are not especially significant unless placed in the angular houses.

4. Jupiter-Pluto   Key words: Expansion and Regeneration.

a. ♃ ☌ ♇ EXPANSION UNITES WITH REGENERA-TION. This conjunction indicates a tremendous desire for power over others, the nature and purpose of which depend upon the total structure of the being. There is an intense longing for exciting and/or religious experiences and, if placed in Leo, a special desire for self-aggrandizement. Such individuals are not easily limited by life, and if other factors in the chart agree, they can make tremendous strides toward understanding profound truths. This aspect also indicates someone who can take existing concepts and ideas and breathe new life into them. This conjunction occurs every thirteen years. *"The Magician."*

b. ♃ □ ♀ EXPANSION CHALLENGES REGENERATION. This aspect leads to a certain degree of difficulty in eliminating existing concepts and their replacement by more refined ones. We can also say that the aspect denotes an often frustrating drive for power. These individuals are rarely satisfied with their place in life and consistently try to better themselves, often at the expense of others. The square is also indicative of the misuse of knowledge. *"The False Prophet."*

c. ♃ ☍ ♀ EXPANSION VERSUS REGENERATION. Similarly to the square, the opposition may bring those challenging circumstances through which individuals are forced to refine their philosophical concepts. Once again the playing for power is in evidence. The challenging aspects of Jupiter and Pluto and the conjunction can indicate some form of mass religious or philosophical persecution.

d. ♃ △ or ✶ ♀ EXPANSION FLOWS OR WORKS WELL WITH REGENERATION. This is an excellent aspect for the type of philosophical mind which is constantly turning over the various contributions of the teachers of the ages and coming up with personal understandings. It indicates a very lively mind, ever eager to dig deeply for truth. *"The Seer."*

G. Aspects of Saturn

1. Saturn-Uranus Key words: Consolidation-Intuition.

a. ♄ ☌ ♅ CONSOLIDATION UNITES WITH INTUITION. This aspect is usually quite difficult to handle, for it is much like nitroglycerine—it can blow up at the slightest pressure. Saturn represents structure and form, Uranus represents revolutions and sudden explosions. People with this conjunction are therefore often very nervous, seemingly sitting on a powder keg, waiting for it to ignite. There is, however, a tremendous latent power which can be used for progressive social movements if the ability is present to work progressive ideas into the existing established order. This conjunction occurs every ninety-one years.

b. ♄ □ ♅ CONSOLIDATION CHALLENGES INTUITION. This is the type of individual who rebels against all forms of established law and is usually quite resistant to the pressure of authority. Like the conjunction, it is an extremely "touchy" aspect and can even be violent, especially when also under the challenging rays of Mars, Pluto, or the Sun. *"A law unto myself."*

c. ♄ ☍ ♅ CONSOLIDATION VERSUS INTUITION. These are the activists, constantly challenging the prevailing social conditions under which they live. As a result, such people can find themselves at odds with those in power. They can, however, make a contribution to society's welfare through the proper channeling of their reformatory drives. Those individuals who have the conjunction, the square, or the opposition of Saturn and Uranus insist on being their own bosses.

d. ♄ △ or ✳ ♅ CONSOLIDATION FLOWS OR WORKS WELL WITH INTUITION. This aspect causes the native to act as a bridge between generations. Individuals with this configuration tend to be relatively ageless, and they are quick to appreciate both the values of the present and those of the past. They are able to blend these two elements so that there is a joining of historical perspective within the context of the actual moment. This aspect leads to a successful coupling of inventiveness and common sense, of structure and ideas. *"The Progressive."*

2. *Saturn-Neptune Key words: Consolidation and Illumination.*

a. ♄ ☌ ♆ CONSOLIDATION UNITES WITH ILLUMINATION. In some cases this aspect contributes to great confusion in the proper understanding of personal limitations. There is a desire to break through existing circumstances and manifest one's dreams in the physical world; disillusionment may come through false hopes. On the other hand, this aspect allows the imagination to successfully merge with the framework of life's circumstances, so that the forces of inspiration are allowed to crystallize through the person to the Earth. I have found that this aspect gives an extraordinary ear for music and, in a very few, can bring true clairaudience. This conjunction occurs every thirty-six years.

b. ♄ □ ♆   CONSOLIDATION CHALLENGES ILLUMINATION. This aspect can cause great suffering, for there is dissatisfaction and confusion between what one has attained and what one wishes to attain. Very often there is an inability to coordinate and consolidate one's efforts. Just at the time when an increase of applied energy is required to realize a goal or ambition, the individual pulls the rug out from under his own feet. *"The Self-Defeatist."*

c. ♄ ☍ ♆   CONSOLIDATION VERSUS ILLUMINATION. Oppositions work in the world of the external, while squares take the form of more internal compulsions. The opposition between Saturn and Neptune indicates "swimming with leaden boots." In other words, the individual tries to glide through life without "paying his dues," yet the dues are always demanded. This individual has to learn to become more responsible in his or her interactions with society. The aspect can indicate criminal tendencies and/or confinement in institutions and prisons. Naturally, the entire horoscope has to be considered in this respect before final judgment is passed. *"Subterfuge."*

d. ♄ △ or ⚹ ♆   CONSOLIDATION FLOWS OR WORKS WELL WITH ILLUMINATION. This aspect can lead to the creation of a great architect, film producer, commercial artist, or practitioner of the mystical arts. Imagination is joined with common sense, resulting in concrete manifestations of inspirational thinking. The otherworldly (Neptune) and the mundane (Saturn) are happily configured. In order to handle any aspect of Neptune and Saturn well, it is important that the Sun and Moon be either well-aspected with them or strongly and positively placed in their own right.

3. Saturn-Pluto Key words: Consolidation and Re-generation.

a. ♄ ☌ ♀ CONSOLIDATION UNITES WITH RE-GENERATION. This is an aspect of great frustration. There is a strong urge to rid oneself of both an internal sense of limitation and any form of restrictive hold which may be placed upon one by society. Thus, this aspect appears in the horoscopes of people who are continually striving to be "free" in their methods of self-expression. A great tension is often produced, resulting in sudden and tremendous explosions which can have adverse effects on health and standing in society. On a positive level, this conjunction can be used to consistently refine the framework by which one relates to society's laws as well as giving one profound strength and power of endurance. This conjunction occurs every thirty-two years.[1]

b. ♄ ☐ ♀ CONSOLIDATION CHALLENGES REGEN-ERATION. Unless otherwise modified, this aspect can produce a cruel and harsh nature. It is very destructive to the established order and, if configurated with a challenging aspect from Mars or Uranus, can produce violent and self-destructive tendencies. There is a great dissatisfaction with life and a deep desire to annihilate existing forms.

c. ♄ ☍ ♀ CONSOLIDATION VERSUS REGENERA-TION. In my experience, there is a great similarity between the opposition and the square. The last opposition between these two planets occurred in 1931, at the height of the Great Depression and the rise of fascism in Europe and Asia. The force of the opposition, in effect, caused the uprooting of the economic structures of government so that new forms could take their place. *"De-structure or Re-structure."*

---

[1] Pluto was discovered at 18° Cancer. In August 1945 Saturn passed through this degree of the ecliptic, thus forming a conjunction "by transit." It was at this time that the atomic bomb was dropped on Hiroshima. Pluto rules atomic energy (actually the transmutation of the energy released by the smashing of the atoms), and Saturn, of course, rules world government. This joining of planetary energies ushered in the atomic age and unleashed a force which changed the structure of world power (see chap. 9).

d. ♄ △ or ⚹ ♀ CONSOLIDATION FLOWS OR WORKS WELL WITH REGENERATION. The trine gives the ability to make the most out of life. The potential for economic growth is enormous, and there is the ability to refine existing forms of authoritarian institutions. *"The Magnate."*

H. Aspects of Uranus

1. Uranus-Neptune Key words: Intuition-Illumination.

a. ♅ ☌ ♆ INTUITION UNITES WITH ILLUMINATION. The conjunction of these two planets in the horoscope of an individual who can respond to their vibrations results in the raising of consciousness to another level. It gives great abilities in the mystic and the occult. The conjunction occurs, however, approximately once in 171 years.

b. ♅ □ ♆ INTUITION CHALLENGES ILLUMINATION. This square is present in a majority of horoscopes of people born in the early 1950s. It signifies a difficulty in understanding the different levels of consciousness in daily life, resulting in muddled thinking, confusion, and ill-fated social movements. Individuals with this configuration should examine carefully their participation in various political or mystic organizations. Drugs should be scrupulously avoided.

c. ♅ ☍ ♆ INTUITION VERSUS ILLUMINATION. The opposition tends to give rise to much of the same circumstances as the square. Since it also occurs as infrequently as the conjunction, the astrologer has very few extant horoscopes from which to judge its effects on the individual. On a mass level it could lead to "delusions of the crowd."

d. ♅ △ or ⚹ ♆ INTUITION FLOWS OR WORKS WELL WITH ILLUMINATION. The trine of these two bodies last occurred in the horoscope of many individuals born in the 1937–1947 period. On an individual level the result would give the ability to properly handle higher levels of consciousness and a profound interest in the occult and mystic. On a mass level it contributes to a generalized expansion of consciousness and an awakening to new uses of heretofore untapped energy sources.

2. Uranus-Pluto   Key words: Intuition-Regeneration.

a. ♅ ☌ ♇   INTUITION UNITES WITH REGENERA-TION. Such a configuration can give rise to a tremendous elevation of consciousness, to inventiveness, to an exploration of untapped potentials of energy, or to extremely violent destructiveness, anarchy, and revolution. It last occurred in the mid-1960s in Virgo, and we shall wait to see how this configuration will manifest itself when this generation comes of age. I assume that it will give rise to a tremendous mechanical genius and will create a vast number of new occupations dealing with the increasingly technological tendencies of our age. This conjunction occurs once every 115 years.

b. ♅ □ or ☍ ♇   INTUITION CHALLENGES REGEN-ERATION. This aspect tends to manifest the more nega-tive qualities outlined above.

c. ♅ △ or ⚹ ♇   INTUITION FLOWS OR WORKS WELL WITH REGENERATION. These aspects are definitely instrumental in bringing out more positive aspects mentioned under the heading of the conjunction.

I. Aspects of Neptune

1. Neptune-Pluto   Key words: Illumination and Re-generation.

a. ♆ ☌ ♇   ILLUMINATION UNITES WITH REGEN-ERATION. Only in extremely evolved individuals can a personal response to these highest of planetary vibra-tions be experienced. The configuration allows for consistent refinement of spiritual understandings and a widening sense of communication with the "forces of nature" and the psychic roots of Man. All the major aspects existing between Neptune and Pluto would open the door to a great deal of controversy, confusion, and conflict in regard to religious matters. New forms of appreciating and viewing the Deity and associate

Powers would challenge existing forms of religious thought.

b. ♆ □ or ☍ ♀ ILLUMINATION CHALLENGES RE-GENERATION. These aspects can cause the native to be responsive to the negative polarity of the invisible realms and may lead to all types of obsessions, compulsions, and hallucinations.

c. ♆ △ or ✶ ♀ ILLUMINATION FLOWS OR WORKS WELL WITH REGENERATION. These aspects allow the person to respond to the more positive aspects of the invisible realms, which could lead, on the personal level, to an involvement with mystic or psychic schools of thought. Once again, only a very few can respond to such vibrations in an individualized way. The sextile appears in the vast majority of births between the early 1940s and the early 1970s. It tends to awaken various levels of spiritual consciousness to the masses and lends the desire to know more about the heretofore invisible and causal factors at work in the universe.

III. UNASPECTED PLANETS

Occasionally an isolated planet, unrelated to the rest of the horoscope by aspect, will appear in a chart. Such a planet represents certain energies which have not been integrated into the totality of being. The task for such a person is to incorporate the forces embodied by the unaspected body into the total life structure.

If the unaspected body is the Sun, for example, the individual would usually find it extremely difficult to create a cohesive life pattern. One is almost always in the "hands of the winds," for one can easily be blown about on the currents of life. Without any aspects, there is no connection between the solar force and those instruments—the planets—which project individual solar energy out into the environment and then return it in the form of crystallized experiences for reprocessing and personal growth. If the Sun is so debilitated, the astrologer will do well to study the position of the Moon, as this body would then take on especial prominence. A careful study of the principles the planets represent will result in a clear understanding of the nature of the energy which needs to be assimilated into the life pattern when an unaspected planet is found in a nativity.[2]

Transits and progressions (see chap. 19) to unaspected bodies should be judged with care. The nature of the specific heavenly body and the angle of relationship will directly affect the latent potential of any unaspected planet.

IV. ASPECTS TO THE ASCENDANT AND THE MIDHEAVEN

Since the degrees of the Zodiac which stand on the First and Tenth House cusps are based directly on the time of birth, the accuracy of the exact moment of the nativity is all-important in interpreting aspects to these sensitive points with any degree of certitude. If the birth time has been determined to within a very few minutes, aspects to the Ascendant and Midheaven are very important. If there is any doubt about the birth time, the astrologer should not stress the indications of planetary aspects to these significators. In any case, narrower orbs should be used with these important House cusps than with interplanetary relationships, and only the major aspects (including the inconjunction) should be used.

Planets which are aspecting the Ascendant modify physical appearance, initial approach to the immediate environment, and the way in which the native's actions are perceived by others. Planets aspecting the Midheaven are integrally involved with the type and choice of profession (if any), public standing (or lack of it), and the ability (or inability) to make a contribution to society.

The Sun conjunct the Midheaven, for example, indi-

___

[2] The term "unaspected" usually refers to planets not connected by one of the five major aspects. Minor aspects to otherwise unrelated bodies modify such planets and make them "loosely connected" but still in need of greater integration into the whole of the being.

cates an ambitious person or at least one who would
want to integrate his or her inner motivations with some
form of public work and/or the attainment of high
social position. The Moon in opposition to the Ascendant—that is, conjunct the Seventh House cusp—
may indicate that such people must constantly consider
their relationships with others and their activities when
entering on a course of action requiring individual initiative and decision-making. As with all aspects, the
whole horoscope must be studied before passing a final
judgment based on any one aspect.

QUESTIONS.

1. What would be the effects of a Moon-Jupiter conjunction in Aries? How would this differ from a
   Moon-Jupiter conjunction in Libra?
2. What is the difference between a Sun-Saturn trine
   in Aquarius-Gemini and the same configuration in
   Capricorn-Virgo?
3. How would you interpret an opposition between
   Mars and Venus in Taurus-Scorpio and this same
   aspect in Cancer-Capricorn?
4. What is the difference between Jupiter square Saturn
   in Gemini-Virgo and Jupiter square Saturn in Sagit-
   tarius-Pisces?
5. What are the basic differences between aspects
   among the inner planets and aspects between the
   outer bodies?

OPTIONAL EXERCISE.

1. After answering the first four questions, take each
   of the planetary aspects and see if you can judge
   how they are modified by sign position. For example, consider the conjunction of the Sun and
   Saturn and see how its effects become altered by
   each of the twelve signs. This is a long exercise;
   do not expect to finish it in one day. Your answers
   should be written out, so that you can concretize
   your understanding.

16.

PLANETARY PICTURES

Complex aspect patterns result when *three or more* of the heavenly bodies which we term the "planetary pictures" are involved.

Although there are at least a dozen of these "pictures" we will discuss the seven most commonly found in natal work. The great majority of horoscopes will usually contain at least one planetary picture, the most common of which are the T-Square, the Grand Trine, and the "Easy Opposition." Next to each description of a particular planetary picture, I have inserted a horoscope which serves as a fine example of the configuration in question. The planets comprising each picture are connected by lines, so that there will be no difficulty in locating these complex angles of relationship.

A. The Stellium or Stellitium: The Horoscope of Charles Baudelaire

The meaning of *stellium* is "a cluster of stars" and therefore can be seen to represent a multiple conjunction. This configuration should involve no less than four planets posited either within the same sign or within a 10-degree orb in adjacent signs. No matter what the Sun sign may be, the influence of the sign in which the stellium is found will have a considerable influence on the total structure of the natus in question. In addition, the House or Houses in which this stellium is found will be an important area of life. The multiple conjunction gives a tremendous intensity to the energies represented by the planetary bodies contained within

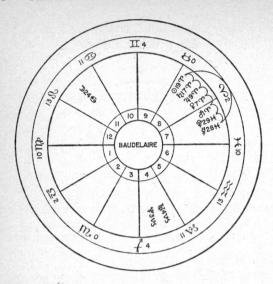

Diagram 15: Charles Baudelaire's Chart.

the configuration. This is perhaps one of, if not *the*, most difficult planetary pictures to interpret, as careful judgment (through weighing the relative strengths and weaknesses of the planets) becomes a very delicate matter. There are, however, several points which can be considered as an aid in delineation: Are any of the planets in dignity, detriment, exaltation, or fall by sign and/or House position? Are there any other planets in the horoscope which are aspecting some of the planets in the stellium and not others? What is the nature of the aspecting planet and that of the angle itself? How do the above strengthen or weaken any element in the stellium?

The horoscope of the poet Charles Baudelaire reveals an incredible seven-planet stellium in the Seventh and Eighth Houses; five of the bodies are in Aries, while Pluto and Mercury are in very late Pisces. An extraordinarily difficult and complex chart to delineate, it is a challenge to any astrologer—not to mention to M. Baudelaire!

B. Easy Opposition: The Horoscope of Mary Baker Eddy

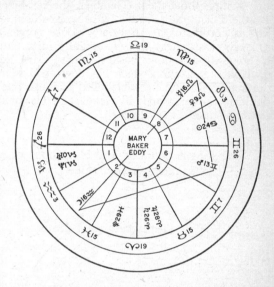

Diagram 16: Mary Baker Eddy's Chart.

The Easy Opposition occurs when a regular opposition exists between two planets while a third body is sextile to one end and trine the other. The challenge designated by the opposition can be resolved through the vibrations and affairs of the planet, sign, and House forming the third end of this planetary picture.

The example is the horoscope of Mary Baker Eddy, who founded the Christian Science Church. Mrs. Eddy has the Moon in opposition to her Venus and Mercury. This indicates some difficulty in general attempts at communicating with the people in the environment, and it further reveals some form of conflict in the personal, romantic, and emotional aspects of life. The way out is given by Mars in Gemini in the Sixth House.

Christian Science teaches that all ailments can be healed through prayer and the intervention of the cura-

tive forces of the Lord. The Sixth House is the House
of health and service. If Mrs. Eddy's personal drive
(Mars) is applied to the affairs of the Sixth House and
through writing about them (Gemini), she can help to
resolve the difficulties indicated by her opposition.

Mars is coruler of her Eleventh House (organizations, ideals, associates) as well as the Fourth House
ruler (homes, foundations, basic strivings). Mrs. Eddy
founded an organization which has developed a huge
international following and which also produces one of
the finest newspapers (ruled by Gemini) in this country
—the *Christian Science Monitor.*

C. The Finger of Fate: The Horoscope of Alexander Graham Bell

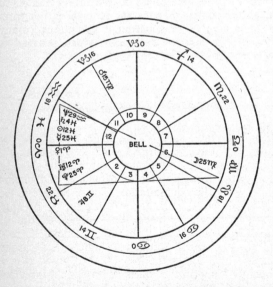

Diagram 17: Alexander Graham Bell's Chart.

The Finger of Fate is formed when one planet is
quincunx two others which are sextile to each other.

It points the way to some special task in life which can be most beneficial to an individual's evolution if the situation is handled wisely.

Alexander Graham Bell's chart provides a good example of this picture. Before Bell made his contribution to the invention of the telephone, he was a teacher of deaf children. The Finger of Fate in his map is formed by the Moon in Virgo in the Sixth, quincunx Neptune in Aquarius in the Twelfth, and Pluto in Aries in the First. The Moon's placement is definitely indicative of someone who fulfills himself through service, and this is further substantiated by Neptune's placement. Pluto, the element of regeneration in the chart, shows how Bell could infuse a new perspective on life into the lives of the deaf. If we view this planetary picture from a more universal perspective, we will see how Bell's inventiveness in the realm of sound (Neptune in Aquarius) affected the great mass of civilization. Pluto's function as the source of constant renewal is felt through the great number of subsequent inventions (many of which are yet to be developed) which resulted from Bell's personal efforts at serving humanity.

D. The T-Square: The Horoscope of Napoleon Bonaparte

The T-Square, one of the most commonly found planetary pictures, is formed when two planets are in opposition and both are square a third. The third body becomes the focal point of the tension and challenge embodied by the configuration. The T-Square is like a three-legged chair; constant pressure has to be applied by the individual to keep the energies of the three planets from unbalancing the life. Through its resolution, however, the T-Square can indicate the particular struggle which forces the individual to grow. It is very frequently found in the charts of prominent individuals, for it lends strength to a horoscope. *The position by sign and House of the degree of the Zodiac opposite to the planet square to both ends of the opposition indicates the area of life where such resolution and con-*

Diagram 18: Napoleon Bonaparte's Chart.

sequent growth may be found. We call this point the Karmic Degree.

In Napoleon's chart we find that Jupiter and Uranus are in opposition and square Mercury. The Karmic Degree is 6 Aquarius and falls in the Fourth House. The Mercury-Uranus square indicates a brilliant but erratic mind which, when mixed with the challenging vibrations of Jupiter, caused Napoleon to overextend himself in both his territorial objectives (Jupiter in the Second House) and in his idea of worldly position (Tenth House Leo Mercury). This configuration obviously gives difficulties in foreign places, as Mercury is the ruler of the Ninth House. If Napoleon had concentrated more on domestic issues and the resolution of certain quirks of his personality (Fourth House affairs) instead of planning world conquest (T-Square focused in the Tenth House), he might not have had such an ignominious end. (In this horoscope in particular, the question of destiny versus conscious choice becomes quite apparent. This is not, however, the proper place for such a discussion; we shall take up this matter in chap. 19, "Prognostication—Free Will or Destiny?")

E. The Grand or Cosmic Cross: The Horoscope of Empress Carlotta of Mexico

Diagram 19: Carlotta's Chart.

The Cosmic Cross is an extremely difficult pattern to master, although it leads to great strength and growth if used wisely by the individual in question. The configuration is an extension of the T-Square, as the point opposite the "short leg" of the T-Square is filled in by the position of another planet. Thus two oppositions and four squares are formed.

The Cosmic Cross calls for a very self-contained individual, possessing a great supply of inner strength and stamina. The square is the symbol for Saturn, and the Grand Square asks that the native learn lessons of consolidation, timing, limitations, and endurance. Some astrologers say that it is easier to handle a Cosmic Cross than the T-Square because the "fourth leg" stabilizes the picture. I have found this not to be the case, as the T-Square allows for more freedom of choice in the resolution of the problem area, while the Cosmic Square has the tendency to box one in. I should add, however, that one of my most respected teachers and colleagues has a Grand Cross in cardinal signs. This individual, who wishes to keep his anonymity, is a great teacher of the occult sciences, an author, and an accomplished musician.

The horoscope of Empress Carlotta, consort of Maximilian I of Mexico, is representative of the Cosmic Cross. Maximilian's role as a pawn in an international power game led to his execution by a revolutionary firing squad. During his confinement in prison, prior to his death, Carlotta sought aid for her ill-fated husband and reign through erratic and poorly timed visits to the various capitals of Europe. She finally went mad in her state of helplessness.

Her chart reveals a mutable Cosmic Cross in succedent Houses. This is an indication of tremendous restlessness and, with a Third House Gemini Sun opposing a Ninth House Sagittarius Saturn, of disastrous voyages. Uranus opposing the Moon indicates difficulty with the general public, especially with that segment that expresses revolutionary ideas. A mistaken sense of service and a general difficulty in political struggles is indicated by the position of the Moon by sign and House as well as by the Uranus-Saturn-Moon T-Square. Her general nervousness and erratic mental condition are revealed through Mercury's conjunction with the Sun and, therefore, its direct participation in the Cosmic Cross.

F. The Grand Trine: The Horoscope of Mahatma Gandhi

The Grand Trine is formed by the connection of three (or more) planets at 120-degree angles (within

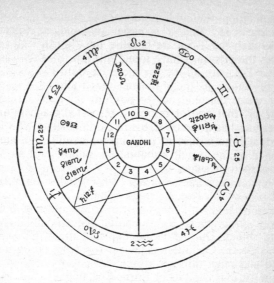

Diagram 20: Gandhi's Chart.

proper orbs), thus forming an equilateral triangle. This
configuration can be very auspicious and a tremendous
fount of potential creativity. If the energies contained
within the Grand Trine are not wisely directed, however, the result is much like what happens to a squirrel
in an exercise ring—it causes the individual to go
around in circles. Too many trines in a horoscope can
produce laziness and an inability to focus in on life's
challenges. The native sort of glides through things,
often too superficially to benefit from various experiences and contacts. The Grand Trine can be most helpful if it is connected in some way with squares and/or
oppositions (as in the case of Gandhi), which it modi-
fies through a lessening of tensions. In most cases the
Grand Trine can be said to be a bestower of benefits
which can manifest themselves as true blessings if the
abundant flow of harmonious energy is carefully channeled. In any case, there is an intensification of the
significance of the element in which the planets are
placed.

In Gandhi's horoscope this element is fire, as he has a Grand Trine between the Moon in Leo, Neptune in Aries, and Saturn in Sagittarius. This means that the idealization, imagination, scope of vision, and sympathy for human suffering which is significant of the Moon-Neptune trine is made most practical and concrete by Saturn's harmonious vibrations. In addition, Gandhi could use his Tenth House Leo Moon in order to make himself a symbol of a people's traditions (Saturn-Moon trine) and sufferings (Neptune-Moon trine), so that a social structure could be rebuilt (signified by the energies of the planets in the Grand Trine, modified by the tremendous regenerating force of his Scorpio Ascendant and strong First House Scorpio planets).

Among other manifestations, the T-Square with the Moon as the focal point reveals that Gandhi had to merge his personal with his political life and sacrifice his family life in order to bring about the changes he envisioned for India.

G. The Kite Formation: The Horoscope of Bobby Fisher[1]

The Kite Formation is an extension of the Grand Trine in that a fourth planet is in opposition to one corner of the triangle and therefore sextile the other two corners. This is a much more stable and powerful configuration than the Grand Trine, as the opposition gives a definite focal point for the direction of the abundant energy contained within this planetary picture.

Bobby Fisher's chart is as intricate as his chess. His natural Piscean strategy is activated and concretized through the powerful Saturn-Uranus-Mars trine. This configuration allows him to plan ahead with a great

---

[1] As Fisher's birth time was unavailable, we have used a solar horoscope. It is my opinion, however, that Fisher has an early degree of Leo rising with Pluto near or at the Ascendant, an Aries Midheaven closely conjoined Venus, and an Eighth or possibly early Ninth House Sun. The Moon is probably between 0° and 1° Taurus, giving a close, fixed T-Square between Mars-Pluto-Moon.

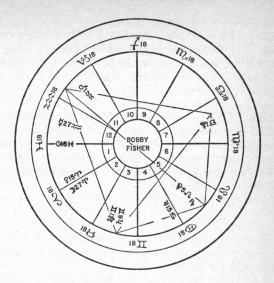

Diagram 21: Bobby Fisher's Chart.

sense of structure and formation. It also adds a certain daring to his character and is a contributing factor to his successful bouts with imposed authority and traditional behavior. In this respect Fisher has the ability to alter the political and economic circumstances surrounding chess for his own benefit as well as for the well-being of all chess players (Mars as well as Mercury are in Aquarius). Neptune's trines give a widened perspective to his strategy, allowing him to see all possible approaches, defenses, and attacks. Thus the combination of Uranus-Saturn, Mars, and Neptune provides Fisher with the ability to innovate original concepts resulting in his unpredictable and devastating style.

The focal point of his Kite Formation is the Mars-Pluto opposition. This is the undermining force which invisibly weakens his opponents, as the power of this particular opposition serves to drain other people's vital psychic energy. Through the inherent absorptive nature of his Pisces Sun (and what I believe to be his ascending Pluto), Fisher uses this energy for his own purposes. In other words, Fisher recharges his own "battery" by utilizing other people's "electricity."

It is doubtful that at this stage of his life Fisher has evolved to the point whereby he *consciously* applies the full extent of this undermining technique on others. He does not have to, actually, for Mars-Pluto to be effective; the nature of the Kite Formation would apply its energy to life through a type of "automatic-pilot" action. In other words, a great deal of Fisher's methodology, both in life and in chess, is instinctive, although recent observation reveals the individualization process gradually at work.

Fisher can become a truly powerful figure when and if he can transcend the chess board and consciously activate the vast energy potential at his disposal into other areas of life. The key to this process lies in the position of the Moon, which, among other manifestations, represents certain emotional fixations and obsessions that have to be overcome before balanced growth can take place.

EXERCISE.

Take out some blank index cards and draw the shapes of each of the planetary pictures discussed in this chapter, making sure that each is within a drawn circle. Contemplate these forms regularly until you really feel that you know them and can easily recognize them in a given horoscope.

17.

INTERPRETATION: THE FIRST STEPS

On page 279 is the third and last part of the Horoscope Calculation Sheet. You will find it convenient to reproduce Part III on the same page as or alongside Part II (A and B).

A. The Preliminary Synthesis

The present chapter will present the procedures for completing Part III of the Horoscope Calculation Sheet. I have decided to use the horoscope of John Lennon as the sample nativity for this phase of our work, as it is both interesting and illustrative of some major points in our interpretive system. Before proceeding further, let us study Lennon's map carefully.

Remember as you work your way through these first steps that we are in the process of tabulating information rather than interpreting its significance; this is the task in the second steps (chap. 18).

1. Elements. The horoscope shows only one planet and the Southern Node[1] in fire (Pluto in Leo); six planets and the Part of Fortune in Earth (Moon in Capricorn, Venus and Neptune in Virgo, and Jupiter, Saturn, and Uranus in Taurus); two in air (Sun and Mars in Libra), as well as the Ascendant and the

---

[1] In weighing preponderances, the order of importance is: luminaries, Ascendant, ruler, other planets, and Midheaven, while the nodes and fortuna are relatively unimportant in judgments of this nature.

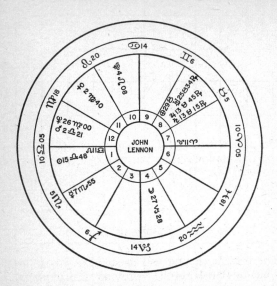

Diagram 22: John Lennon's Chart.

Northern Node; and one planet (Mercury in Scorpio) plus the Midheaven in water. We can therefore judge that there is a preponderance in Earth.

2. *Qualities.* Three planets (Sun and Mars in Libra and the Moon in Capricorn) as well as the Ascendant Midheaven and the Nodes) are in cardinal signs; five planets plus the Part of Fortune are in fixed signs (Mercury in Scorpio, Pluto in Leo and Jupiter, Saturn and Uranus in Taurus); and only two are in mutables (Venus and Neptune in Virgo). We therefore judge a preponderance in cardinal signs, with a secondary emphasis in the fixed quadruplicity.

Although the number of bodies in fixed signs is greater than those in cardinal signs, both the luminaries and the Ascendant are in signs of the latter quality; further, there is the fact that the Sun and Moon are *angular* while the majority of the fixed bodies are *succedent*. The relative strength of the Sun, Moon, and Ascendant shifts the balance of emphasis in this case.

Horoscope calculation sheet

Part III: Preliminary synthesis and aspectarian

A. Elements (Triplicities)	Declin.	☽	☿	♀	♂	♃	♄	♅	♆	♇	Asc.	MC
Fire:	☉											
Earth:												
Air:	☽											
Water:												
B. Qualities (Quadruplicities)	☿											
Cardinal:												
Fixed:	♀											
Mutable:												
C. Gender	♂											
Positive:												
Negative:	♃											
D. Overinfluence:												
E. Planetary Weights	♄											
Dignified:												
Detriment:	♅											
Exaltation:												
Fall:	♆											
Angular:												
Most Elevated:	♇											
Mutual Reception:												
Final Dispositor:		G. Planetary Pictures:										
Ruler:												
F. Critical Degrees:												

3. Gender.   Only two planets (Sun and Mars in Libra) plus the Ascendant are in positive signs, while eight bodies and the Midheaven are posited in female signs. This circumstance, of course, gives a negative preponderance.

4. Over-influence.   When we synthesize the results of our examination at this point, we find an over-influence of cardinal-earth-negative characteristics which correspond to the sign of Capricorn, which is Lennon's Moon sign. This tells us that, although Libra is both the Sun sign and Ascendant, the vibrations of Capricorn represent a very pervasive "tone," which should express itself in Lennon's motivations and activities.

5. Planetary Weights.   The chart reveals no planets in their own signs (dignity), although Neptune in Virgo, the Sun and Mars in Libra, and the Moon in Capricorn are in detriment. There are no planets in the signs of their exaltations, but Venus in Virgo, Pluto in Leo, and Uranus in Taurus are in fall. It cannot be said that Lennon is not successful (at least in his Earthly achievements), yet we find no planets in honor and seven bodies in dishonor, including both luminaries. This is a good example of Capricorn's making the best possible use of resources and its drive to succeed. We should also note that, although these seven bodies are in signs of detriment or fall, the Sun is in the First House and conjunct the Ascendant—a most powerful position; the Moon graces her own angular domicile (the Fourth), thereby strengthening her position while Pluto is in the Tenth, which brings its powerful and regenerative rays to what we term the "most elevated" position in the chart—closest to the cusp of the Tenth House. Thus the House positions of the luminaries, Pluto and Neptune (which is in its own domicile, the Twelfth), modify these ostensibly debilitating sign placements and add strength to the effects of the planetary rays.

6. Mutual Reception.   Planets are said to be in mutual reception when they are placed in each other's signs.

Thus, if Venus were in Capricorn and Saturn in Libra, they would be in mutual reception and be drawn together more closely in their influence on the total horoscope. Some mutual receptions can be quite beneficial, such as the Moon in Taurus and Venus in Cancer; others, such as Mars in Capricorn and Saturn in Aries, can be difficult to handle, since the energies are incompatible and are further aggravated by such an intense relationship. Your understanding of the planets, signs, and aspects is the key to the interpretation of mutual receptivity.

Lennon's chart does not contain any planets in this type of relationship.

7. *Final Dispositor.* The term *dispositor* refers to the ruler of the sign in which a planet is placed. For example, in Lennon's chart Pluto is the dispositor of Mercury in Scorpio; Venus disposits the Libran Sun, Saturn the Moon; and so forth. If a planet disposits all the others, it is said to be the *Final Dispositor.* There is no such planet in Lennon's chart, but to illustrate this point, if Venus were in Taurus in his nativity and not in its actual position in Virgo, Venus would be the Final Dispositor. All the planets in Taurus (Uranus, Saturn, and Jupiter) would be disposited by Venus, and as she is in her own sign, she disposits herself. Pluto in Leo is disposited by the Sun in Libra, which is disposited by Venus in Taurus. Neptune in Virgo is disposited by Mercury in Scorpio, disposited by Pluto in Leo, disposited by the Sun in Libra, and we come back to Venus in Taurus. If you were to treat all of the planets accordingly, you would always come back to Venus as Final Dispositor.

To save yourself the trouble of looking for the Final Dispositor where none exists, observe the following rules. There can be no Final Dispositor if there is no planet in its dignity. There can be no Final Dispositor if there are two or more planets in mutual reception. There can be no Final Dispositor if more than one planet is in its dignity.

The Final Dispositor (if any), along with the most elevated body and the ruling planet, are very important elements in any horoscope and must be given additional weight in the total interpretation of the chart.

8. The Ruler. The planet which is naturally associated with the ascending sign is said to be the ruler of the chart, but there are certain mitigating circumstances. If there is a planet which is within five degrees of the Ascendant, preferably in the First House rather than the Twelfth, it can vie for rulership over the chart. This is especially true if the conjoining planet is stronger than the ruler of the Ascendant.

In Lennon's case, Venus, ruler of Libra, is in a weak position, for she is both in detriment and not in an angular position. The Sun, however, is within orbs of the Ascendant to qualify for rulership. In addition, the Sun is especially powerful in the house of its exaltation, Aries.

What this means in Lennon's case is that the image he projects is a dominating solar type with a modifying influence of Libra; that is, he needs a partner or an audience to be truly effective, while the pervasive tone of Capricorn causes him to constantly strive toward the mastery of such an audience or partner(s).

9. Critical Degrees. When planets or major points are posited in the following degrees of the Zodiac, they are said to increase in their influence for either good or greater tension and stress, depending on their natal positions. These degrees are also called the Mansions of the Moon, as each Mansion represents the average diurnal motion of the Moon (12°51′ or approximately 13°). These segments begin at zero Aries (the Spring Equinox). The Critical Degrees are especially important in the Hindu, Chinese, and Arabic astrological systems but I am not fully convinced of the degree of their importance in our traditional Western system. They are given here because they are frequently mentioned in other texts and require further research. The Critical Degrees are:

Cardinal Signs: 0° 00′; 12° 51′; 25° 43′
Fixed Signs: 8° 34′; 21° 26′
Mutable Signs: 4° 17′; 17° 09′

I would advise using an orb of only one degree, although other astrologers have found a two- or even three-degree orb to be effective. Lennon's chart shows Mercury to be at one of these Critical Degrees.

10. Planetary Pictures. We can use this space to diagram any of these major configurations. Lennon's chart shows two such pictures: the very important Grand Trine (Moon-Uranus-Neptune conjunct Mars) and a wide T-square (Moon-Pluto-Mercury).

B. The Aspectarian

It will be helpful to list all the important aspects in the chart in this handy reference box. There is also a place for the planetary declinations and the resultant parallels and contraparallels.

When all the spaces of Part III of the Horoscope Calculation Sheet are filled in, the following tabulated results will emerge for John Lennon.

Now you may proceed to a detailed interpretation of this chart.

EXERCISES.

1. Make sure that you are completely familiar with the Table of Planetary Dignities and Detriments.
2. You should only continue at this point if you have thoroughly prepared yourself through a detailed study of the material presented so far. Now is the perfect time for a special review of the planets, signs, Houses, and aspects.

A. Elements (Triplicities)	Declin.	☽	☿	♀	♂	♃	♄	♅	♆	♇	Asc. MC.
Fire: 1 – ♀ + ☊ ✓	☉ 6S13	□(w)			△	⅄	⅄			Q	☌
Earth: 6 – ☽ ♃ ♄ ♅ ♆ + ⊕ ♐	☽ 15S27		□(w)					□		□	
Air: 2 – ☉ ♂ + Asc. ☋	☿ 15S50	‖		⊥				△	△·	∧	△
Water: 1 – ☿ + MC	♀ 10N20				∧			□		∧	
B. Qualities (Quadruplicities)	♂ 0S05	≠					☍			✶	
Cardinal: 3 – ☉ ☽ ♂ + Asc. MC ☋ ☍ ♐	♃ 14N37						‖				
Fixed: 5 – ☿ ♃ ♄ ♅ ♆ + ⊕	♄ 13N18							△	☌		
Mutable: 2 – ♀ ♇	♅ 18N53								△		
C. Gender	♆ 2N42										
Positive: 3 – ☉ ♂ ♀ + Asc. ☋ ☍	♇								△		
Negative: 7 – ☽ ☿ ♀ ♃ ♄ ♅ ♆ + MC ⊕ ♐											
D. Over-influence: Capricorn – ♑											
E. Planetary Weights:											
Dignified: None											
Detriment: ♂ ♎ ☽ ♑ ♆ ♍											
Exaltation: None											
Fall: ♀ ♍ ☉ ♎ ♅ ☿ ☿ ♌											
Angular: 3 – ☉ ☽ ♀											
Most Elevated: ♀											
Mutual Reception: None											
Final Dispositor: None											
Ruler: ☉ ☌ Asc.											
F. Critical Degrees: ☿ 7 ♏ 55											

Note:
☋ ☌ Asc.

G. Planetary Pictures:
T – □: ☽ – ☿ – ♀
⚼: ♆ ☌ – ☽ – ♅

18.

INTERPRETATION: THE SECOND STEPS

The method of interpretation becomes more highly individualized as one continues to study astrology. What follows, therefore, is a suggested systematic guide to delineation which may be used by the student and later adjusted to personal preferences. The given method will help to develop an understanding of the structure of the horoscope and the analytical processes involved in its interpretation:

1. Accurate erection of the natal chart
2. Completion of the Preliminary Synthesis and Aspectarian
3. Hemisphere emphasis (overview)
4. Synthesis of Elemental and Qualitative Preponderances
5. Sun, Moon, Ascendant, and their interrelationships
6. Weighing the planets
     a. The Ruler—planets in the First House
     b. Most elevated planet and other angular bodies
7. Major Configurations—Planetary Pictures
8. House-by-House analysis of planets and points not previously delineated
9. Prognostication
     a. (Secondary) Progressions
     b. Transits

At this point it should be stated that the horoscope makes no judgments (nor does the astrologer) as to "right" versus "wrong" actions. The good occult worker does not allow personal opinions to becloud judgment and sees character traits as shades and manifestations of energy polarities. It should also be said that the natal horoscope reveals the life tendencies and not the way an individual has modified and transcended certain characteristics through hard work and effort. It is left pretty much up to the intuition of the astrologer, therefore, to "fit" the life tendencies into the life structure of an individual at the moment when the horoscope is being read. The same holds true for prognostications; there too we must interpret energy patterns and fit these into the context of a given life.

With this in mind, let us proceed to the delineation of John Lennon's horoscope, beginning with the third step.

A. Hemisphere Emphasis (Overview)

Before studying the details of a given nativity, it is a very good idea to see in which of the quadratures the majority of the planets lie, regardless of the conditions of the planets themselves by sign, specific House, or aspect. For example, a position of the majority of the planets below the horizon (the north) indicates a personality structure which is usually subjective and in need of a means through which some form of social contribution may be made.

Planets in the south (above the horizon) will often point the way in which such self-expression may take place. If the majority of the planets were in the south, this would tend to make the individual seek some form of social approval for every action as well as contributing to a more objective approach to life. This position leads to a need to participate in social activities, but often there is also an inability to deepen oneself through an inner self-sufficiency (indicated by planets below the horizon).

A majority of the planets in the east (rising and culminating bodies) indicates a strong desire to initiate every phase of life activities. It shows the need to learn cooperation with others, but it bestows the ability to set up personal life circumstances.

Planets in the west (those setting or approaching the Nadir), however, cause natives to become extremely dependent on other people's activities in order to integrate their own motivations and drives. A western predominence gives a natural cooperative sense, but it is through such joint efforts that a western-oriented individual may succeed in life. The difference between east and west in the astrological sense, as Marc Edmund Jones puts it,[1] is like comparing an "à la carte" dinner with a "prix fixe" one. With the former, one can choose the dishes one prefers, but the expense is often greater than the "prix fixe" meal, which is already selected but costs less. We could say that the eastern preponderance represents Karmic sowing, while the western preponderence is indicative of Karmic reaping.

When we examine Lennon's horoscope with an eye to the establishment of a hemispheric propensity, we find an abundance of planets in the southeast. This nativity, therefore, reveals someone who aims to be appreciated and/or serve the public interest by his own efforts and initiative. The driving force and outer expression of these aims are conditioned by the strong Libran influence in such a way that it is Lennon's good fortune that his own desires and techniques of self-expression, personal growth and development are found to be synchronized and in complete harmony with tens of millions of others. In this respect we can see that this man is not just an individual undergoing his own evolution but is also the embodiment of a type of energy filtering through an entire generation.

B. Synthesis of Elements and Qualities

The preliminary synthesis has already established that this is a cardinal-earth-negative horoscope, corresponding to a Capricornian "overinfluence." This indicates that Lennon has a great need to be the dominating and directing force in whatever social sphere he finds himself. It is also indicative of a man with

---

[1] I strongly recommend studying the works of this eminent teacher, with special reference to Jones' system of the seven basic horoscope patterns, which he has discovered. The latter provide an excellent orientation to a primary overview of the horoscope before the detailed interpretation.

a strong drive to succeed, not just in the professional sphere, but also in positions of power, influence, and affluence. John's solar-lunar relationship will reveal his ability to feel the pulse of the people as a key to his popularity and notoriety.

C. Sun, Moon, Ascendant, and Their Interrelationship

With the Sun in the First House, John Lennon is constantly at work trying to project himself upon the environment. He has a tremendous amount of energy when it comes to his self-dramatization, and he wishes to assert his ideas, concepts, and personality at every instance. He is the type who will refuse any form of counsel unless it is in agreement with his own opinions. (This particular conclusion results from a mixture of three other influences: the Moon in Capricorn, Mercury's position in Scorpio, and Scorpio's opposition to Saturn in Taurus). In addition, this position—with the Sun in Libra and square the Moon, indicating a great restlessness—bestows the need to explore oneself in a multitude of social relationships. This square indicates that Lennon sees his actions and his very sense of being reflected through the eyes of the women in his life and by the general public. The only aspects the Sun makes is this wide square, so that one can conclude that when John is away from his wife or an audience, his sense of personal identity can waver and at times become lost in incertitude. Herein lies a crucial problem for a double-Libra (Sun and Ascendant): it is often extremely difficult for John to tell the difference between the essence of his being (the Sun) and the image of himself which he projects to others (the Ascendant). Thus he can easily confuse the man with the superstar.

John Lennon's Moon is strongly placed in the Fourth House in the sign of Capricorn. The Pluto opposition to the Moon (and Saturn's difficult placement) would seem to indicate a problematic early family life and a general stress in his relationships with women.

It should be noted, however, that the experiences gained through these difficulties plus the help he has definitely received from his second wife, Yoko Ono, have probably stabilized John's relationships with all people. The Moon in Capricorn usually means associations with older women and would point to Yoko's presence in his life, as she is about six years his senior (and as an Aquarian also ruled by Capricorn's planet, Saturn). Even the challenging aspects of Pluto and the Moon provide the ability to refine and regenerate emotional energy, though with more difficulty than when these two bodies are connected by flowing angles. The change in John's receptive nature (the lunar force) has to come about if he is to achieve the inner sense of peace so essential to Librans.

The Moon's position and her wide square to the Sun are indicative of John's inner motivations. These are geared toward a very personal fulfillment in life. He is quite eager for changes in his personal experiences, and if the life around him does not move quickly enough, he will create and force issues to change in a direction which is more gratifying and exciting for him. He is forever seeking to prove himself, and one would say that he has had to work out a great deal of personal insecurity having to do with certain obstinate fears about losing what has already been won and established.

The Capricorn Moon and overinfluence, however, contribute to the tendency to use people and his own public appeal to further his own aims and opinions (which, however, are not necessarily selfish). It is to a large extent the purpose to which he will gear his tremendous influence that will determine the course of the transmutation of the lunar force by Pluto's opposition.

D. Weighing the Planets

1. The Ruler—Planets in the First House. The Sun is the dominant force in John Lennon's horoscope. Two other factors, however, should be noted in connection with the Ascendant and the chart ruler.

With Libra as such a strong influence in his life, we must take the position of Venus very seriously in considering the predominant forces at work in this nativity, Venus is in Virgo in the Eleventh, square Uranus, and otherwise lacking any major aspects. The analysis of Venus tends to characterize John's relationships with others, a very important factor in the horoscope of a double Libra.

In this respect we can note two predominant manifestations: in the personal life the placement of Venus in Virgo leads to a very critical eye on personal relationships; apart from his wife, Lennon is likely to have very few, if any, close friends of long duration. Such friendships would have to entail a certain subservience to John's whims or "rules" about friendship or serve some pragmatic purpose in his life. It should be exceedingly difficult for most individuals to approach John on a truly intimate, personal, and equal level. The square of Venus to Uranus would bring John into contact with many experimental and unusual romantic, erotic, and creative experiences.

In terms of his public life, this square allows such experiences to be presented to the general public in the form of John's personal statement and creative self-expression. A case in point is the publication of the album cover in which John and Yoko pose completely nude. This endeavor was very helpful in allowing nudity of all forms to come into the arts without heavy censorship. Uranus, the planet of revolutions, is a very strong influence in this chart. Its square to Venus influences Lennon to lend his support to the present "sexual revolution." (One can further point out that his Libra Mars is also trine Uranus.)

Second, the Northern Node is exactly conjoined the Ascendant, giving Lennon the ability to make instant connections with other people, and as the Sun is also conjoined this point, John's means of self-expression have immediate reverberations on those around him. This explains in part his role as a pace-setter for a whole generation.

2. *Most Elevated Planets and Other Angular Bodies.*

Pluto in Leo is the most elevated planet and in this respect has the effect of making John's professional efforts a source of great change in the entertainment industry. The Beatles were the first and perhaps the biggest supergroup, and they became the idols of the same decade that produced the "flower-child" movement and all its associated manifestations.

The angular placement of the Sun and Moon have been adequately discussed.

E. Major Configurations—Planetary Pictures

John's Grand Trine is noteworthy for several reasons. The Moon is trine Uranus and the Neptune-Mars conjunction, bestowing the ability for tremendous influence upon the masses, which is certainly the case with Lennon. The Grand Trine also leads to a tremendous creative ability; as it occurs in Earth for the most part, it is also a way to build up an abundance of material resources. The Moon trine Neptune gives a poetic nature, and its trine to Uranus adds an understanding of all people and brings contact with the masses. The trine from Uranus to Neptune reveals an interest in the metaphysical and, in John's case, experimentation with hallucinogenic drugs. Most important, this planetary picture reveals that John's personal drive (Mars) and understanding (Moon) are directly related to the generation of which he is a part and show the effects his personal efforts have had on such a huge number of people.

John also has a very difficult T-Square between the Moon, Pluto, and Mercury. This means that he has had to keep changing his opinions and way of relating to life and to women in particular in order to grow in an evolutionary sense. Certain habits of thinking and some deeply ingrained fears have had to be released and transformed. This T-Square is further emphasized by Mercury's opposition to Saturn and Jupiter, which gives periods of great depression likely to result in lapses of good judgment and general indecisiveness. The Moon in opposition to Pluto is indicative of the difficulty his wife (Yoko) would have concerning children. She miscarried the child fathered by John and has had an agonizingly frustrating time trying to locate her daughter by her first husband.

F. House-by-House Analysis of Planets and Points Not Previously Delineated

1. Second House: Personal Finances.

For John Lennon, the ruler of this House is Pluto in Leo in the Tenth, indicating a great source of money to be made in a profession involving the arts. Pluto is also sextile Mars, the coruler of the Second, another factor contributing to the ability of resources to regenerate themselves (record royalties and the like). Mercury is in the Second and poorly aspected. This means that John's handling of his money is confusing for him and he will often make mistakes in his financial judgments. Some contracts may also prove tricky, and with Mercury's opposition to Saturn and Jupiter, certain litigations involving financial matters could go against him. The fears in regard to his T-Square are also related in part to financial anxieties. Pluto's sextile to Mars is a good counteracting force, however, for whatever is lost is sure to be replenished.

2. Third House: Communications and the Mental Faculties.

This House is ruled by Jupiter, as Sagittarius is on the cusp. The indications are that Lennon's work will be popularized in foreign countries and that he tends to have a philosophical nature but that there will be difficulties in several areas. First Jupiter opposing Mercury and conjunct Saturn does not allow the religious and philosophical inclinations to find a lasting and systematized discipline, even though interest in such matters is great. Lennon alternates between intensive periods of study and equally intensive periods of mental laziness, with a consequent lack of consistency in intellectual or philosophical matters. In addition, there is an interest in business and travel, but both of these areas are replete with delays, complications, and troubles with people in authority and governments (signified by the opposition).

3. Fourth House: Foundations and the Home.

The Moon's position here indicates many changes of government and difficulties in relation to foreign residences. The latter is signified by Saturn's position in addition to the Moon's square to Mercury. We can see, however, that there is a tendency for John Lennon to establish a beautiful home as a base of operations. The Moon in the Fourth shows a link with traditions, and though John will live in many places around the world, his home will always be England.

4. Fifth House: Creative Self-Expression, Romance.

Aquarius, Yoko's sign, is on the cusp; Uranus, ruler of the sign, is in Taurus and square Venus. Yoko also has Libra rising, so that the square of Uranus-Venus describes her and her type of artistic work quite well. The positions of these planets in relation to John's life is also quite revealing. Uranus in Taurus in the Eighth shows that wealth will come from the masses because of his creative work with a group of others. The fact that Uranus is in the Grand Trine also illustrates the extent that his artistry will affect his generation.

5. Sixth House: Jobs

This domicile is ruled by Neptune, which is in the Twelfth, conjoined with Mars. Neptune, of course, rules music; Lennon's contribution, success, and ability in this field are clearly shown by the connecting planets and aspects to Neptune: its conjunction to Mars equals personal drive; the Twelfth House indicates great resourcefulness and his connection with the "muses";

Neptune's connection by Grand Trine reveals his appeal to the masses.

6. Seventh House: Partnerships

The Seventh House is ruled by Aries, but Mars is in Libra. This means that John has to be a leader but works best in partnership with others. Mars in connection with Neptune shows music as the medium, and its linkage with the Grand Trine shows the public appeal of his group of partners, the Beatles.

7. Eighth House: Other People's Resources.

Venus is the ruler of the Eighth House, and its position in the Eleventh shows that the masses would contribute to Lennon's personal wealth. The difficult aspects of Jupiter and Saturn, plus the fact that Venus is square to Uranus, reveal that there are financial difficulties with partners' money and perhaps certain investments which will backfire and prove a constant source of financial drain.

8. Ninth House: Foreign Travel and Religion.

Mercury's rulership over this domicile and its position in the Second shows that money will be made through foreign travel. John's religious and philosophical tendencies have already been covered elsewhere.

9. Tenth House: Career.

The Tenth House is ruled by Cancer, and the Moon is in the Fourth House in Capricorn. This conjunction reveals success through public appeal. Other facets of this sphere of Lennon's life have already been covered.

10. Eleventh House: Friends, Associates, and Ideals.

The ruler of the Eleventh House is the Sun in the First. Thus all of John's ideals would be accompanied by some form of his creative self-expression. Friends have already been discussed.

11. Twelfth House: Karma.

The ruler of this domicile is Mercury in the Second House, showing that money is a sore spot with John Lennon. Virgo is the sign on the cusp of the Twelfth, indicating that John's Karma is such that it is quite possible for him to work out his personal difficulties through service to humanity, especially in those areas where money is needed. This could be done, perhaps, through setting up certain philanthropic works using his own vast financial and social resources. The Moon in Capricorn square the Second House Mercury will bring financial worries which can be cleared up when money is used unselfishly. Mars and Neptune in the Twelfth suggest that many of Lennon's activities are clandestine and that he will constantly surprise the public with his ideas concerning music and film (the participation of Mars and Neptune in the Grand Trine with Uranus and the Moon).

19

PROGNOSTICATION—FREE WILL OR DESTINY?

The question of predestination as against Man's ability to choose his own destiny has been the subject of endless treatises and the preoccupation of countless thousands of philosophers and theologians throughout the ages. Since one of the main reasons people are drawn to astrology is its predictive element, this question of the nature of fate is very important for us.

Very briefly stated, we can say that the more evolved people's consciousness, the more their destiny is in their own hands. Thus, a person who is familiar with the Laws and Structure of the Great Plan and has the understanding to apply this wisdom to his or her own life, can, in effect, direct a great deal of his or her destiny within the scope of Karma. Thus a person born a wealthy Oriental could never shape destiny in order to become a poor Caucasian, but a person inclined to be a thief can, through an expression of desire and an awareness of the steps necessary for a transformation, become an altruistic humanitarian.

It should always be remembered that *the purpose of the horoscope is to be able to work with it until it is transcended*. As one grows older (in both a chronological and spiritual sense), one evolves out of the pattern of one's natus and into a pattern of energy which one has consciously established with great effort and sacrifice. The means for making this transition is determined in great measure by the person's ability to transmute energy from one form or level of manifestation to another. A closer examination of the meaning of the higher-octave planets in relation to the lower-octave bodies will give the student some examples of this process of refinement.

The study of the planets is a study of cycles, and the aim of astrology is to match up the significance of these cycles with the various forms of terrestrial life. In natal work the task becomes more specific, as we are concerned only with the individual under consideration and that native's particular place in the scheme of the macrocosm. Since the majority of people are not consciously in tune with the motivating energies which govern our planet, they are in effect completely subservient to these greater forces. They have very little free choice in the larger issues of their destiny. They can and do choose between what suit to wear or what movie to see, but they do not consciously organize their activities with a view to complete compatibility with the great macrocosmic structure of which they are an unconscious part.

A few individuals, however, are chosen by the Master Energy Sources which guide the evolution of the Earth and Mankind to play a special role. These individuals—such as the last of the Romanovs, the last of the Hapsburgs, Hitler, Gandhi, and any number of other "people of fate"—are endowed with the power to alter history. Some of them have been in tune with these Great Centers of Cosmic Consciousness (both constructive and destructive), while others have been used as unconscious tools.

Then there are such people as you and me. These are the consciously working students who attempt to tread the Path of Light. Eventually we come into a greater perspective on life which allows us a larger degree of freedom of choice. Thus we can adjust ourselves to meet those situations, both pleasant and testing, which, as students of astrology, we can see coming as we chart the course of the planetary cycles in relation to our particular life styles. We cannot stop a planetary cycle from occurring, but we can place ourselves on a certain level of consciousness whereby the "deadly arrows" miss their mark and the "life-giving arrows" hit their target. We can and must gear our perspectives so that wisdom is gleaned from life's difficulties and blessings. Thus the total experiences of life can become integrated into each individual Sun, and its heavenly light can burn ever brighter.

There are at least half a dozen well-known prognosticatory techniques. We shall discuss the two that are most popular and in my opinion most consistently accurate. They are called Secondary Progressions and Transits. Before outlining these processes, I should like to make a few qualifying comments on their effectiveness.

All progressions and transits point the way toward *tendencies*. The exact form these tendencies take in a person's life is directly related to the native's chart, present life style, and level of consciousness. The astrologer must take all three factors into account at all times.

A progression or a transit works very closely with the structure and influences present in the natal chart. Thus, if a person has a natal trine between the Moon and Venus, all future celestial movements—transits and progressions—involving these two bodies tend to work in a harmonious way, *no matter what the angle of the transit or progression*. A square by transit might make these two forces work less beneficially than if the aspect of the transit were a trine, but the square would not rob these two planets of some form of harmonious interchange. This effect will become clearer through the examples provided in this chapter.

Planets affected simultaneously by transits and progressions will have their influences modified by the nature of the angles and bodies in passage and will act with great strength.

I. PROGRESSIONS

"I have appointed thee each day for a year."
Ezekiel, 4:6

According to occult philosophy, the life span of an individual is eighty-four years, which can be broken down into twelve seven-year cycles, one for each sign of the Zodiac. In addition, eighty-four years is the length of one orbit of Uranus around the Sun.[1] If we subtract 84 from 360 (the number of degrees of the ecliptic), we get 276, or the approximate number of days of the human gestation period. Thus we can say that from conception to birth, the Sun travels through 276 degrees of the ecliptic, but in order to complete its journey through all 360 degrees, 84 degrees, or days, are necessary. If we take each day after birth and equate that with a year of life, we have the symbolic basis for the predictive method known as Secondary Progressions. Aspects made from the Progressed Horoscope to the Natal (or Radical) Horoscope are also termed Directions.

A. The Progressed Horoscope

Part I of the Horoscope Calculation Sheet has a space marked "Adjusted Calculation Date." The ACD is the date corresponding to the year for which you have erected the progressed map. For example, Felissa Rose, my friend and assistant, was born in New York City on January 31, 1944, at 9:52 P.M. War Time (8:52 P.M. EST, 8:56 P.M. LMT, 1:52 A.M. GMT, February 1, 1944). In order to examine the positions of the planets by Progression for 1973, we have to take a day for a year in the ephemeris and, after determining the correct Adjusted Calculation Date, draw up her horoscope as if she had been born on that date at the same time her actual nativity occurred.

In order to find the ACD, we proceed as follows. First, we check an ephemeris for the year in question —in this case, 1944. Next, counting a day for a year and using the Greenwich Mean Time and Date of birth, we find that:

    2/1/44 = 2/1/44
    2/11/44 = 2/1/54
    2/21/44 = 2/1/64
    2/29/44 = 2/1/72
    3/1/44 = 2/1/73

[1] See *As Above, So Below*, chap. 28, for a fuller discussion of the astrological basis of Man's lifespan.

The positions of the planets on March 1, 1944, at 1:52 A.M. GMT correspond to events that will take place on or about February 1, 1973.

To erect the Progressed Horoscope, we calculate the House cusps for February 29, 1944, at the Local Mean Time of 8:56 P.M., New York City, and we adjust the planets for 1:52 A.M. GMT, March 1, 1944. Proceeding as if this were the birth data for the natal horoscope, we obtain the following completed map.

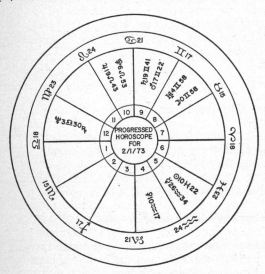

Diagram 23: The Progressed Horoscope.

We are not as interested in the aspects between the progressed planets as we are in the existing relationships between the progressed map and the natal horoscope. We therefore place the positions of the progressed planets, Midheaven, and Ascendant in their proper places around the wheel of the natal map.

B. Calculating the Progressed Moon

Now we are ready to interpret the influences except for the position of the Moon. Each of the planets moves

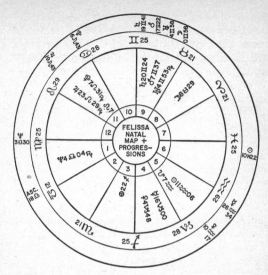

Diagram 24: Natal Map and Progressions.

very slightly from year to year (day to day). Uranus, Neptune, and Pluto move so little that even thirty or forty years after birth their passage can be quite negligible. We therefore concentrate on the passages of the faster-moving bodies when dealing with progressions and the slower-moving ones when interpreting transits (although the transits of the swifter planets are also important under certain circumstances).

Because the Moon travels an average of 13 degrees in one day, it can make many different aspects to several planets during the course of a year's progressions. We must therefore determine the position of the progressed Moon for each month of the year in question. The process is a relatively simple one.

First, calculate the position of the Moon for the Adjusted Calculation Date. In Felissa's case, this position is 0Ⅱ58.

Determine the position of the Moon for the following year using the same time of birth; ACD = 3/2/44 = 2/1/74 (1:52 A.M., GMT). This position is 13Ⅱ57.

Next, calculate the total movement of the Moon in

degrees and minutes between these two dates. The difference between 0♊58 and 13♊57 is 12°59′ of arc.

Divide 12 (months) into 12°59′ to arrive at the average monthly movement of the progressed Moon during 1973–1974:

$$
\begin{array}{r}
1 \\
\hline
12) \quad 12 \\
12 \\
\hline
\end{array}
\qquad
\begin{array}{r}
049 \text{ or } 1°\ 5′ \\
\hline
590 \\
\\
\hline
59 \\
48 \\
\hline
110 \\
108 \\
\hline
\end{array}
$$

Finally, make a table of this movement and note the directions of the Moon during each passage:

Lunar Progressions

```
 2/1/73 =  0 ♊ 58
 3/1/73 =  2 ♊ 03
 4/1/73 =  3 ♊ 08
 5/1/73 =  4 ♊ 13—p. ☽ △ r. ♆ ☌ r. ♅
 6/1/73 =  5 ♊ 18—p. ☽ ☌ r. ♅
 7/1/73 =  6 ♊ 23
 8/1/73 =  7 ♊ 28—p. ☽ ☌ r. ♂ ✶ r. ♀
 9/1/73 =  8 ♊ 33
10/1/73 =  9 ♊ 38
11/1/73 = 10 ♊ 43—p. ☽ △ r. ☉
12/1/73 = 11 ♊ 48—p. ☽ △ r. ☉
 1/1/74 = 12 ♊ 52
 2/1/74 = 13 ♊ 57
```

If you examine the positions of the progressed Moon in relation to the natal chart, you will see that in May 1973 the progressed Moon at 4♊13 will be conjunct the natal Uranus at 4♊53 and trine the natal Neptune at 4♎04. In August the progressed Moon will conjoin the natal Mars at 7♊37 and will sextile the natal Pluto at 7♌31. Finally, in November, the progressed Moon at 10♊43 will trine the radical Sun at 11♒06.

C. Orbs of the Progressed Moon

The effects of the Moon last for about two weeks before the precise moment of a given direction and for about two weeks afterwards. We should therefore allow an orb of approximately 30 minutes on either side of the exact position. If, however, the progressed Moon is aspecting a natal planetary picture or forming one by its passage, the orb can be extended. For example, in Felissa's chart there is a natal Grand Trine in air between Neptune, the Sun, and the Uranus-Mars conjunction. Thus the entire period between May and December is under the rays of the progressed Moon and her interchange with the Grand Trine. During this period the nature of this entire configuration will manifest itself in her life. The effects of the individual planet in the planetary picture, however, will be most noticeable when the Moon is within the orbs of exactitude to their specific position.

In order to calculate the exact week or day of the Moon's effects, it is only necessary to divide the lunar movement for a given month by 30 (days).

To determine when the progressed Moon will exactly conjoin the natal Uranus, divide the monthly travel of 1° 05' by the 30 days between May 1 and June 1, 1973: 65' ÷ 30 = 2.17' per day (approximately). To make calculations somewhat easier, use 2' per day.

We want to know how many days it will take the Moon to travel from 4♊13 (position on May 1) to 4♊53 (position of the natal Uranus). Subtracting 4♊13 from 4♊53 leaves 40', which equals about 20 days of movement.

Adding these 20 days to May 1, 1973, brings us to May 21, 1973, as the approximate day when the progressed Moon will make the exact conjunction with Felissa's natal Uranus.

Actually progressed aspects are not necessarily at their strongest when they are exact. In fact they color the whole period during which they are within proper orbs of exactitude; in most cases it is therefore sufficient to know where the progressed Moon is each month.

D. Orbs of the Other Planets

I suggest an applying orb of 1 degree and a separating orb of 30 minutes for the Sun, Venus, and Mercury, slightly less for Mars, and very close orbs for the progressed positions of Jupiter, Saturn, Uranus, Neptune, and Pluto.

To find the monthly positions of each of the progressed planets, proceed as for the lunar position. The Sun will move approximately 5 minutes of arc per month, as its average daily motion (yearly progression) is one degree (60 minutes). The monthly passage of Mercury, Venus, and Mars varies considerably. In Felissa's horoscope the progressed Venus is making a very important aspect—a conjunction to the Sun in the Fifth House (indicating some form of romance and abundant pleasures ahead). It may prove important to know more about the exactitude of this position, even though the entire year (1973–1974) will be colored by Venus' rays.

We have already determined that Venus' progressed position on February 1, 1973, is 10♒17. Similarly, we can determine that her position one year later will be 11♒31. Subtracting one from the other, we find that the yearly movement amounts to 1°14'. Dividing 74 by 12, we get approximately 6 minutes per month. Venus will therefore progress to the exact conjunction of the natal Sun (11♒06) in 8 months from February 1, or sometime during early October 1973 (8 × 6' = 48'; 10♒17 + 48' = 11♒05).

E. Duration of the Effects of the Progressed Directions

Aspects of the Sun, Venus, Mercury, and Mars will begin to be felt about a year prior to their exactitude and remain in effect for about six months afterwards. Aspects of Jupiter and Saturn last much longer, as their movement is slower, but their effects are not as sharp as those of the more swiftly moving planets. If, for example, you examine Felissa's progressed chart you will see that Saturn is pretty much where it was at her birth, twenty-nine years ago. When Saturn progresses to 23 ♐ (and it will do so about fifty years— fifty days in the ephemeris—from now according to Felissa's chart), she will reap to the fullest the material benefits of this passage and have something to help ease her old age. But because Saturn moves so slowly, I would use an orb of no more than 15 minutes. Even with such a small orb, the effects of the progressed Saturn making an exact sextile to the radical Jupiter last seven years. Since these two planets are natally sextile, the effects of such an aspect serve to reinforce or to bring into somewhat greater prominence the benefits which come regularly from this natal aspect.

F. Interpretation of Progressed Aspects

Progressed aspects must be interpreted in terms of planetary relationships existing in the natal chart. For example, in Felissa's natal map the Moon is closely square both Pluto and the Sun. Even though by progression it will come to these two bodies by sextile and trine respectively, she should not expect a completely flowing set of circumstances. These three bodies are natally found to be in challenging aspects, so that when they are "set off" by the progressed aspects of the Moon, the challenges indicated in the natal map will arise. The flowing aspects of the progressed directions will soften the effects, however, perhaps allowing Felissa to deal effectively with the situations indicated by her natal T-Square of Pluto and the two luminaries.

On the other hand, Venus and the Sun are not in mutual aspect in the natal map (aside from a semi-quintile, a very mild, flowing influence). When Venus comes to the Sun, therefore, some very positive events can be expected to occur. (Chances of this happening would be even greater if the two were natally semi-sextile.) In order to judge the entire effects of this progressed conjunction, we have to realize that Venus is natally square Neptune but trine the Moon. This means that if Felissa can see her romantic and social involvements (Venus in the Fifth House) clearly (removing the veil of illusion sent by Neptune's square) and practically (with the good sense of the Taurus Moon), she could be quite successful in some important liason during the year under consideration.

It would be most helpful to refer to the chapters on the aspects among the natal planets to determine their effects by progression. It should be kept in mind, however, that progressed aspects will trigger events signified by the planets in relation to the possibility for such events as evidenced by the natal map.

In interpreting Felissa's progressions for 1973 to get a broader idea of how they will affect her life, note that we only count the major aspects as having an importance in prognosticatory work.

The most important direction for her this year is, of course, the progressed Venus conjunct the radical Sun (written as p. ♀ ☌ r.☉). The implications are for an important relationship and for a varied social life. As Felissa has a natal Fifth House Aquarian Sun, she should be busier than ever and will definitely have to use discrimination in her choice of actions and associates.

The Moon is progressing through her Ninth House. This is an excellent position, which will trigger many uplifting experiences and will probably broaden her life through travel and study (the Moon is in Gemini). The ruler of her natal Ninth House is Venus, which is coming to the conjunction of the Sun. This indicates a positive linkage of the affairs of the Ninth with those of the Fifth, two strong domiciles natally.

When the progressed Moon comes to a conjunction with the natal Uranus in May, there is a strong possibility of travel in some working capacity (Uranus rules Felissa's Sixth) and/or with a group of people, one of whom is likely to be her new romantic interest. As the Moon is also trine Neptune, the experiences learned through work and travel will be of a sort to raise her level of consciousness, especially in regard to how to deal with (and serve) people properly.

The Moon's passage always refers to the daily events of life. As Felissa is an Aquarian, her relationships with people and in particular her service to them (Virgo rising) as an astrologer, will be the focal points of the progressions of the Moon and Venus in 1973. How she treats and integrates a personal romance into this picture is the issue being tested.

II. TRANSITS

Transits are much easier to find than progressions, since no calculations whatever are needed to determine their relationship to the natal map. *Transits are the daily movements the planets make in their orbits in the heavens.* By relating the daily celestial movements with the natal chart, we get quite a good portrait of how the microcosm of the natal map and the macrocosm of the solar system will react to one another on any given day.

Let us suppose that it is July 1, 1975. You want to take a vacation for a couple of weeks and need to determine the best time for this plan. All you have to do is to consult your ephemeris for the specific period and compare the positions of the planets with your natal horoscope. If your natal map shows that you are naturally a fortunate traveler (perhaps you have Mercury trine Jupiter or your Moon is in Gemini well aspected to Venus or Mercury), even transits which would indicate some challenging aspects could be overcome by your natal tendencies. Conversely, if you have, let us say, a T-Square in the cadent Houses, i.e. third, sixth, ninth, and twelfth, between Mercury, Uranus, and Saturn, any planetary transit to these positions, especially from the malefic planets or from planets with challenging aspects, could aggravate the natal difficulties.

The proper use of transits (and progressions) really requires an extensive understanding of the principles at work. It is often helpful to observe the effects of the planets by transit and progression as they are manifested in your own chart and in the charts of the people close to you over a considerable period. In this way you will obtain an intimate understanding of the celestial cycles and the many factors which, acting together, produce a certain set of circumstances at a given moment in time.

A. Orbs of the Transiting Planets

The orbs of the transiting planets should not be more than one degree, applying or separating for the Sun, Moon, Mercury, Venus, Mars, Jupiter, and Saturn, and perhaps 30 minutes for Uranus, Neptune, and Pluto. It is not unusual, however, to feel the influences of the transits of the outer bodies when they are 1 degree from exactitude.

B. Duration of the Effects of Transits

The Moon moves so quickly that she passes through one degree of the Zodiac in about two hours and transits an entire House in a matter of two and a half days. Her transiting aspects are therefore relatively unimportant by themselves and should be considered in association with other transiting bodies. Far more important is the House position of the transiting Moon, for this will signify the sphere of activities for a particular day. For example, it is a good idea (*if other factors warrant*) to handle business matters when the Moon transits through the Second, Sixth, or Tenth House.

The transits of the Sun last for about three days (one day applying, one day exact, and one day separating from the sensitive point to which it makes an aspect). The passages of Mercury and Venus are rather weak in their effects and need other factors to be of major consequence. It is far more important to note the Houses through which these two bodies pass. Mars is a little slower in its movements, and its passage over a sensitive point can take three or four days. Its transit through a House can last for two months or more. Mars has the tendency to instigate or "set off" other aspects; its combination with adverse angles from the Sun, Uranus, and Saturn, for example, can result in explosive conditions.

The transits of Jupiter and Saturn last for about one or two weeks, depending on speed. The passages of the three outer planets are very important, for they can last several months, even when the orb of influence is as narrow as 30 minutes. This is especially true for the movements of Neptune and Pluto.

C. Planetary Stations

The importance of retrograde planets is important in respect to transits. All the planets except for the Sun and Moon go through phases wherein they travel direct, become stationary, go retrograde, become stationary, and then go direct again. This process can occur three times over the same point, and if this particular degree is a sensitive one in a given horoscope, the strength of the transit is multiplied. It is not easy to have Uranus, for example, pass three times over your natal Mars, as the total passage and period of volatile sensitivity can take several months. Study the planetary movements in the ephemeris for a better idea of the nature and duration of these planetary stations.

D. Interpretation of Transiting Aspects

When in transit to sensitive points and other planets, the various bodies act as follows.

1. The Sun. This planet gives vitality and energy according to its position in the natal horoscope. In Houses, it points to the area of life in which activities will center.

2. The Moon. The Moon reveals the everyday activities and generalized feelings both emotional and physical. When in the Houses, it points to the area in life wherein events will occur within the cycle indicated by the Sun's transit.

3. Venus. This body indicates pleasures, romance, material matters, and the pattern of social life.

4. Mercury. This planet affects communications of all sorts, mental outlook, near relatives, and short-distance travels. When Mercury turns retrograde by transit, for example, there is usually a period of delays when it comes to the signing of contracts, the sending or receiving of letters, and so on. The severity of these delays depends on Mercury's relative importance in the natal chart.

5. Mars. Mars heightens the activities of any House through which it passes. It can also bring strife to those areas indicated by the other planets with which it makes a transiting and challenging aspect. Otherwise it can be a very stimulating influence, most helpful in eliminating difficulties.

6. Jupiter. This planet usually brings some measure of abundance, sometimes with the tendency to undo waste and laziness. When passing through a specific House, it can bring new opportunities and pleasant circumstances.

7. Saturn. The person learns lessons of consolidation and self-discipline from Saturn, which usually brings added responsibilities to the areas and planets in the chart which it transits.

8. Uranus. Uranus brings surprising circumstances to the area of life through which it is passing. Its action will be most noticeable when it aspects a natal planet from the domicile of its transit. Uranus can be an indication of great social gain and mental insight if the person can respond to its erratic vibrations in a positive way. It often breaks up established or existing circumstances so that new ones may follow.

9. Neptune. This planet brings about strange and mysterious occurrences and can cause certain fears and anxieties in the area through which it is passing. The nature of the planetary aspects it makes will bring out its specific tendencies. On a positive level, the transiting rays of Neptune can create feelings of great inspiration and creativity. Its passage can cause psychic openings and bring to light previously unknown opportunities for success or the discovery of hidden resources.

10. Pluto. Pluto has such long-lasting transits that they usually indicate the end of one phase of life and the beginning of another. Pluto square Venus by transit can end a long-lasting relationship, so that a better one can take its place (though this is not necessarily the outcome). If it conjoins Neptune, for example, and the person can respond to this vibration, it can elicit great understanding of metaphysical laws or cause dormant psychic powers to awaken. On the other hand, it can be the cause of nightmares and irrational fears. When planets of the higher octave aspect other higher-octave bodies, their effects on an individual's life are directly linked to the person's level of consciousness.

E. Transits to Felissa's Chart

Let us examine some of the major transits in Felissa's natal map and see how they correspond to the progressed aspects. Progressions usually work more internally than do the transits, and they indicate a type of inner unfolding or completion. For example, Felissa's natal chart shows a wide applying trine from the Sun to Saturn. By progression, this trine became exact when she was about nine years old (the Sun is nine degrees from an exact trine to Saturn). At that time, she says, she joined her first organization (the Girl Scouts) and through this social interchange came to the realization that she was different from the other little girls. This was quite traumatic for her, as Aquarians often identify and find security with their peers. This aspect caused Felissa to begin to establish herself as a separate being. Thus we can see the consolidating vibrations of Saturn and the integrating force of the Aquarian Sun at work. These two planets are basically unharmonious to each other, so that growth was achieved (the trine) with a great deal of difficulty.

Transits, however, work in the external environment, and we respond to them through the indications in the natal map. If we turn to the ephemeris for 1973, we can proceed to discuss some of Felissa's major transits for this period.

Jupiter enters Aquarius in late February 1973 and makes a Grand Trine with her Uranus and Neptune in March. It goes on to trine the natal Mars in April and makes a station on her Sun in May and June. Referring to her progressed Moon, we see that its aspects coincide with the indications of Jupiter's transits. Jupiter is passing through her Fifth House, indicating benefits with lovers and with pleasurable experiences in general. Its rulership over her natal Fourth House shows a broadening of inner values and a possibility of a change of residence which can take her traveling.

The transiting Uranus makes a trine to her natal Saturn at the same time that Jupiter makes its benevolent aspects. This indicates an end to existing circumstances, allowing for a greater expansion of herself and her relationships with people in general. It can bring her into contact with new social groups, especially if she takes advantage of Jupiter's rays and travels abroad.

In May Saturn returns to its own place, showing that a consolidation of life's directions has to be made. Natally Saturn is basically well-aspected, so that this consolidation should be most beneficial for her. This would be especially true if she is able to glean the wisdom coming from the many joyous and sensual activities that will arise as a result of the tremendous Fifth House influence.

These are just some of the many indications which point to a very positive year for her, one in which learning experiences coming from travel and a new romance can prove most beneficial. She will, however, have to make an effort to integrate these into the total structure of her being while at the same time working to transcend the somewhat undermining "rumblings" of her natal Moon-Sun-Pluto T-Square.

PART III

The Travelers: Seven Delineations

NOTE

The following seven delineations are examples of the method for horoscope analysis outlined so far. It includes technical terminology and assumes that the student is conversant with the principles of astrology previously discussed. In this respect these horoscopes provide a very good test, for should the reader fail to understand certain points of analysis all he or she need do is to *review* those sections and chapters which deal with the matter.

Before proceeding with any delineation, *make sure you study the natal chart of the person under discussion*. The more familiar you are with the various placements of the planets, the easier it will be to follow the course of the analysis. Take your time with each of these seven horoscopes and carefully note the symbolic use of language to express the astrological principles at work.

20.

CARL JUNG: VOICE OF THE COLLECTIVE UNCONSCIOUS

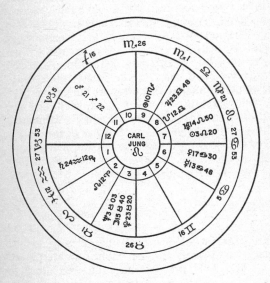

Diagram 25

"My life has been permeated and held together by one idea and one goal: namely, to penetrate into the secret of personality. Everything can be explained from this central point, and all my works relate to this one theme."

Leo is the sign in which Man has the greatest awareness of his creative potential. Carl Jung was able to use this strong sense of self to explore the depths of his being. He emerged with an understanding of Universal Man which he then passed on to humanity.

A. Hemisphere Emphasis

Insofar as its Oriental-Occidental orientation is concerned, Jung's is a balanced chart, since five planets are placed in the east and an equal number appear in the west. This indicates that Jung was a man whose activities were both self-initiated and stimulated and responsive to the actions and ideas of others. Although there are six planets in the north and four in the south, indicating a nature that is slightly more subjective than objective, the gathering of the planets, including the Sun at the Seventh House cusp, acts as a balancing agent between the hemispheres. It also demonstrates Jung's concern with the integration of the many parts of the Self into the whole (the universal consciousness) —a process he called "Individuation."

B. Synthesis of Elements and Qualities

The accentuation of the chart lies clearly in the fixed signs, as six planets and the Midheaven are placed in this quality. This predominance allowed Jung to pursue his work with great determination and persistence even in the face of widespread disapproval. Three planets in Taurus and his Capricorn Ascendant put the elemental emphasis in Earth. This foundation allowed Jung to make his theories about the invisible nature of the unconscious especially pertinent to the reality of daily life. He actively sought to make his beliefs not just textbook theories, but working practicalities, with the eventual aim of helping humanity (Sun conjunct Uranus). The Sun, Mars, and Uranus in fire signs endowed Jung with abundant creative power and vitality. Mercury and Venus in Cancer and a Scorpio Midheaven added great sensitivity, so that he could understand human feeling on a nonintellectual level. Jupiter and Saturn in air allowed Jung to abundantly communicate his ideas concerning man and his civilizations through his writing.

C. Sun, Moon, Ascendant, and Their Interrelationship

Jung's Leo Sun made him fully aware of the power contained within a single human entity. His concern for others and for the nature of human relationships in general is demonstrated by placement of the Sun in the Seventh House. Jung often found fulfillment when, as a consultant, he was in a position to help others realize their potential.

His Third House Taurus Moon gave him the ability to probe deeply into the area of human communications and emotions. The square between the dignified Leo Sun and exalted Taurus Moon brought a tension that caused a need for reconciliation between his inner drives and their external manifestation. In his personal life this discord was reflected in the disharmony between his parents. His mother, reflecting the Taurus Moon, was practical, jolly, a good cook, and rather plump. Jung states that she had a strong inner life which she rarely allowed to surface. His father reflects Jung's Sun-Neptune square; he was a clergyman who had lost his faith. Nevertheless, Jung's father managed to instill deep religious convictions into his son, which the latter incorporated into his understanding of Man and God. Thus Jung's parents (Sun and Moon)—the stern introspective father and the earthy, good-natured mother—never got along (the square aspect between the luminaries). The strength of their characters made a strong impression on Carl Jung and gave him the need to integrate the male and female—that is, the conscious and subconscious, assertive and passive—sides of his being.

In his work he refers to these in terms of animus (solar-male principle) and anima (lunar-female principle). Men also, of course, contain anima, which emerges from their emotions and which must be united with their stronger male principle. By contrast, all women obviously have the mental aspect animus, which, though weaker than the emotional drive, must also be integrated with their predominant anima and used for balance.

It is very interesting to note how Jung made such positive use of the exact square of Neptune to his Sun. In most cases this aspect leads to a decidedly deceptive nature. As Jung had a Seventh House solar position, the presumption is that social image will be quite important to him. After all, both Capricorn and Leo are extremely concerned with their presentation to and position in society. Yet Jung chose to write about his Neptunian influence by calling it "the shadow." Because Jung's Sun is conjoined Uranus, he could take a personal influence and see its common relationship in the human mass. He stated that most individuals repress their dark side (shadow) in order to conform to society and to be accepted. This continual repression more often than not results in increased tension, giving rise to periodic emotional explosions. On a mass level, wars arise as a formal release of this negativity. Thus, to avoid mental illness (and mass hysteria), people have to learn to recognize and integrate their "shadow" into the "light" of their existence.

Jung's Leo Sun opposes his Capricorn Ascendant. On a personal level this configuration contributed to certain economic hardships during his youth (a common manifestation of Capricorn rising, especially as Saturn is in the First House). He was forced to accept a series of scholarships and grants to complete his education. This reliance on outside assistance was damaging to both his Leo pride and his Capricorn sense of independence. The opposition, however, did bring him the awareness of the difficulties involved in adjusting his inner drives (Sun) to his environment (Ascendant). This particular situation is yet another facet of the question of individual versus society—individual consciousness versus collective consciousness—which seems to have preoccupied so much of Jung's thought.

D. Weighing the Planets

1. Ruler of the Chart.

The chart ruler, Saturn, is dignified in the First House in Aquarius, the sign of humanity. Aquarius governs science, and all of Jung's work was painstakingly researched (Saturn) so that it could be presented to the world in the prescribed scientific way. Saturn's trine to Jupiter in Libra shows that Jung's efforts would grow and have a large following, but not without certain difficulties. Saturn is also square Pluto, showing that the structure of his ideas and theories would destroy existing forms of thought, causing conflicts in the psychological community. In effect, much of Jung's work challenged Freud. In addition, Jung's interest in general occultism found disfavor with many people who could not relate to this aspect of Jung's involvement.

2. Most Elevated Planet.

The most elevated planet in this chart is Mars in Sagittarius, sign of religion, travel, and philosophical studies. It is placed in the Eleventh House—ideals; the natural and occult sciences and associates. Jung used astrology in his work, engaging in extensive astrological studies and erecting charts of his patients. He is also credited with revealing the true nature of alchemy to the modern world. Many of his friends were writers of mystically oriented literature, including Hermann Hesse and Richard Wilhelm; he even wrote the introduction to Wilhelm's version of the *I Ching*. Mars corules Jung's Ninth House of journeys and Tenth House of worldly achievement, and Jung traveled extensively, visiting the various cultures of Asia, North and South Africa, and the Indians of New Mexico. In these voyages Jung was seeking those symbols inherent to all people (he referred to them as "archetypes") to prove his theories of the collectivity of human consciousness. Mars in sextile to Jupiter activates these journeys, and Saturn sextile Mars brings them to completion. Jupiter is trine Saturn, enabling the quests of

Jupiter (in the Eighth House of occult research) to be accurately recorded and assimilated through the methodology of Saturn.

3. Other Angular Planets.

Although technically placed in the Third House, Pluto in Taurus is considered angular, since it is located on the Fourth House cusp. Pluto, ruler of man's collective unconscious, is located in the lowest part of the horoscope, sensitizing Jung to the deeper and often hidden aspects of human nature. Pluto co-ruling his Midheaven brought the exploration of these areas into his professional sphere.

Uranus is in Leo in the Seventh House of marriage and largely describes Jung's wife, Emma. Although she raised five children, she never lost her own identity and became an excellent analyst in her own right. A weaker individual would have found it easier to merge her identity with this powerful man's, but a strong-willed, independent, positive Uranian woman must insist on a life of her own, as did Emma Jung.

In his other personal relationships, this position of Uranus often brought sudden breaks with associates. The ruler of this house (Moon) is square to Uranus, causing sudden disruptions in personal ties as well as the nonacceptance of Jung's views by the contemporary public (which the Moon rules). Mars trine Uranus caused great dissatisfaction with established theories, leaving Jung with the need constantly to invent new concepts. For example, he introduced the terms "extrovert" and "introvert" into psychological parlance.

E. Major Configurations

The most prominent planetary picture in this horoscope is the fixed cross between Saturn, Uranus, Pluto, Moon, and the Midheaven. Fixed signs govern inherent values and ideals, and the opposition between Saturn (past) and Uranus (future) forced Jung to challenge established beliefs and present new concepts to the world. The conjunction of the Moon (personal subconscious) with Pluto (collective unconscious) was

the focal point for Jung's ability to develop and artic-
ulate his theories concerning the collective unconscious.
As the Midheaven (profession) completes the grand
cross, Jung used his career as his tool to present his
views to the world.[1]

F. House-by-House Analysis

1. Second House: Finances.

Much of Jung's income was earned from the publication of his various writings (Pisces on the cusp, while
its ruler, Neptune, is placed in the Third House of
writing). Neptune square the Sun shows the necessity
to associate with emotionally disturbed people, but
additional income is earned when the latter became
his patients.

2. Third House: Communications, Writing.

Neptune conjunct the Moon shows the importance
of dreams as a factor in Jung's basic understanding
of both himself and mankind. Jung's memory was
very precise about his dreams, and he refers to them
frequently in his writings. Neptune square the Ascendant brought pressure in reconciling his personal
faith with his environment; he believed that a man's
religious feelings cannot be ignored and must be applied to his daily existence if strong tensions are not
to emerge, and cause difficulties for the individual in
relating to life.

3. Fourth House: Home.

Venus, ruler of Taurus, governs this unoccupied
House. Jung's home was quite beautiful, located next
to a lake in Switzerland (Venus in Cancer—water).

---

[1] Here is a very good example of the inability of the masses to
respond in a personal sense to the vibrations of the outer planets—
in this instance Pluto. If they could, everyone would reach the
same enlightenment concerning the relationship between the collective unconscious and the individual. Jung was a highly developed
soul who could respond to his Pluto-Moon conjunction in a personal way and relate his findings to Mankind.

Peace, harmony, and solitude (Pluto near the cusp) were essential to him, and he rarely entertained visitors. As Venus is placed in the Sixth House of work, he did a great deal of his labors at home, especially during his later years.

4. Fifth House: Creativity, Children, Pleasure.

Mercury, ruler of this House, is conjunct Venus (planet of beauty), revealing Jung as a highly talented individual. Along with writing his many books, he painted exquisite mandalas and made unusual stone carvings. Since Mercury is located in the Sixth House of health and is well aspected in Cancer, Jung enjoyed exercise in the form of walking, boating, and fishing. In addition, Mercury indicates that his five children would tend to bring him great joy.

5. Sixth House: Employees, Employment, Health.

Venus and Mercury conjoined here in Cancer made Jung extremely concerned with helping emotionally afflicted people. The placement of these two bodies sextile to the Moon brought great devotion from co-workers. Jung was basically physically very healthy and full of vitality all his life.

6. Eighth House: Death.

Jupiter's placement in this House is a very protective influence, bringing long life and death from natural causes in old age. Mercury (ruler of this house) conjoined with Venus indicates an extremely peaceful end. His death resulted from a heart failure—quite a natural end for someone with a Leo Sun.

7. Ninth House: Higher Education, Distant Lands.

Mars, ruler of the Ninth House, is sextile Jupiter (awards). Jung was the recipient of many honorary degrees from various institutions of higher learning. His writings are published all over the world and translated into many languages.

8. Twelfth House: Confinement, Occult Research.

The ruler of the Twelfth House, Saturn, is placed in the First House, the area of personal approach to the world. Before presenting his beliefs to the public, Jung did a great deal of reflection and meditation. Intensely interested in the occult, Jung is credited with reintroducing alchemy to the world of the twentieth century. This can be understood astrologically if we note that the ruler of metals (Saturn) is square Pluto (planet that transforms matter from one form into another). The urge to delve into alchemy emerged in dreams (Pluto conjunct the Moon, Saturn square). These recurring dreams concentrated on events in the seventeenth century (the time when alchemy was at its height). Jung finally concluded that his task was to bring alchemy out of the darkness of superstition and into the light of understanding.

G. General Analysis of Major Events in the Life

This section can explore the astrological indications at work in the relationship between Carl Jung and Sigmund Freud. In 1903, when Jung's progressed Midheaven (career) conjoined his natal Mars (ruler of the Tenth House), he started working at the Burghölzli Psychiatric Clinic. At that time his progressed Sun entered Virgo in the Seventh House, showing employment through public service. It was there that Jung's interest in the subconscious began to surface as his progressed Moon passed through the Fourth House (psychological foundations). He also became interested in the work of the Taurean Freud as progressed Venus (ruler of Taurus) trined his natal Midheaven and entered the Seventh House of partnerships.

In 1907 Jung's progressed Moon passed through the Seventh House and he traveled to Vienna to meet with Freud, with whom he had been corresponding for several years. In addition to the positive transits of Mercury (mind) and Neptune (all psychological work), Jung's transiting Jupiter trined his Midheaven. This configuration symbolizes that Jung would learn a great deal from Freud.

In 1913, however, Jung broke off the relationship—a difficult event for Freud, as he had looked upon Jung as the foremost exponent of his teachings and had hoped that Jung would carry on his work. At that period Jung's progressed Venus was trine his natal Neptune, pulling him toward more spiritual interests. The transiting Neptune was also trine his Midheaven, which gave even further importance to the mystical tendencies inherent in his chart. It now becomes quite understandable why Jung felt that he had become too limited by Freud's sexually oriented doctrines. Completing Jung's astrological portrait at the time of the break with Freud, we find that his progressed Ascendant entered Aries, and his progressed Midheaven entered Capricorn. These cardinal signs stress the importance of individual actions and reveal the desire to go one's own way to explore one's own theories.

Jung viewed the Age of Pisces as a period in which Man was unconscious of his own divinity (the Christ within, as the occultist would say). He saw the Age of Aquarius, however, as the time when Mankind would understand its true nature. As we approach the New Age, Jung's work is beginning to be understood and accepted by more and more people. Jung was a harbinger of the coming era, a man who attempted to guide Mankind to its enlightenment through the painful and difficult realization of his own being.

21.

ISADORA DUNCAN: VOICE OF THE MUSES

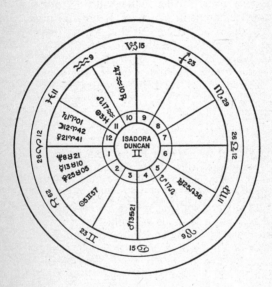

Diagram 26

"To rediscover in its ideal form the beatific movements of the human body, in harmony with the highest beauty of physical form, and to resuscitate an art that has lain dormant for two thousand years: this is the serious purpose of my school."

Isadora Duncan was a woman immersed in the rhythms of life, who flowed with the pulse of nature and danced to the joy of motion. This fluid and ethereal character enabled her to enunciate a new approach to her art. Isadora found beauty and inspiration in all those around her, but tragic death was always a close companion.

A. Hemisphere Emphasis

With the exception of Uranus, all the planets in Isadora Duncan's horoscope are located in the eastern half of the map. This almost completely Oriental preponderence reveals her as someone whose desires were brought into manifestation through her own efforts. She was a very independent woman and found it extremely difficult to take direction from anyone. The Occidental position of Uranus in her chart shows a great sensitivity to the vibrations and cycles of this planet and can be considered her Achilles' heel. The sudden eruptions which characterize Uranus brought great chaos and sorrow into her life. Uranus is in the Fifth House of children and is exactly square to Pluto. Isadora was to suffer the deaths (Pluto) not only of her two natural children but also of an adopted one.

B. Synthesis of Elements and Qualities

Duncan's chart shows five planets in fixed signs, indicating her to be very determined in the pursuit of her ideals (fixed signs govern values). The cardinal placement of four planets, the Ascendant, and Midheaven demonstrate that she actively worked to achieve her goals rather than sitting back and waiting for things to happen. This is further emphasized by the cluster of planets around her Aries Ascendant.

As four planets and the Ascendant are placed in fire, Isadora can be considered a passionate individual. The highest manifestation of a fiery temperament lies in creative activity, and Isadora certainly embodied this element. The placement of the Midheaven in Capricorn and three planets in Taurus in the First House reveal the tendency to manifesting her often unrealistic dreams. Her Gemini Sun and the strong Aries influence made her quite an outspoken woman. She often lacked tact and, like many Aries natives, was sometimes unaware of her effect on others. This trait is further emphasized by her lack of water, a feature which can give rise to an insensitivity to other people's feelings.

C. Sun, Moon, Ascendant, and Their Interrelationship

The Aries Ascendant is clearly indicative of Isadora's impulsive approach to life. Aries is the pioneer, and Isadora Duncan is one of the founders of modern dance. This Ascendant enabled the rapid initiation of projects but the lack of patience to complete them. This tendency is emphasized by the placement of the Sun in Gemini. Such a combination can give an irresponsible attitude, exhibited by the inherent duality of Duncan's nature. At times she was completely involved with her work, then suddenly shifted the emphasis of her energy toward a new lover. Then she kept her whereabouts secret, abandoned rehearsals, and sometimes did not show up for scheduled performances. The placement of the Moon in Aries in the Twelfth House gives the tendency for secretive love affairs; it also indicates a person with a very active emotional life which, partly because of the close square to Mars, could and did bring about many upsetting personal experiences. This position of the Moon is another indication of the sorrow which would come to Isadora through children. A Twelfth House Moon brings with it a dislike of solitude and a fear of imposed confinement; but it also carries with it the need to run away from people and seemingly to disappear on occasion.

The lack of any major aspect between Duncan's Sun, Moon, and Ascendant shows the difficulty of integrating these forces into a cohesive whole. This can be summarized by the following pattern: as Isadora would jump into new activities (Aries Ascendant), there would be an equally strong pull between work and pleasure (Sun in Gemini), and she would either seclude herself in the intense pursuit of her art or run away with a lover (Moon in Aries in the Twelfth House).

D. Weighing the Planets

1. Ruler of the Chart.

Venus in Aries placed on the Ascendant is the chart ruler, and in her autobiography, Isadora made note of her birth under the "star of Aphrodite." Searching for harmony and love in her surroundings, the physically beautiful Isadora always sought to express these ideals through her personal magnetism and her art.

2. Planets in the First House.

Neptune, the planet of illusion and ruler of dance, and Mercury, ruler of the mind, are joined here in Taurus. This conjunction demonstrates her difficulty in separating reality from fantasy. Neptune's placement in her chart gives a strong love of the sea and water. "As a child, I danced on the sea beach, by the waves . . . the movement of the waves rocked my soul . . . could I dance as they—their eternal message of rhythm and harmony." Both Neptune and Mercury are square Jupiter. This aspect shows the rash and stubborn opinions she held, many times exhibited in her speech (Mercury), as well as the surrounding nebulous aura (Neptune) which caused her to be generally misunderstood by most people.

Pluto's placement in the First House has a great deal to do with her reshaping of the existing structure of dance into a new form. She sought to do this through the inspiration of the rhythms of nature (Pluto in Taurus), as well as by the modes of ancient Greek theatrics. We must remember that Pluto represents the collective unconscious of mankind: Isadora (whose First House Pluto conjoined her Sun) could search out the past (she tried to revive the Greek chorus) and bring to the present those ideas which would be accepted in the future.

3. Most Elevated Planet.

The most elevated planet in this chart is Jupiter, the philosopher. This noble body is placed in Aquarius, sign of social ideals, reformation, and the masses. Its location in the Tenth House (career) made her a popular performer because of her uniqueness (Aquarius rules the unusual). Jupiter in Aquarius contributed to her dreams of disseminating her beliefs to the children of the world (Jupiter rules education, and its dispositor, Uranus, is in Leo in the Fifth, the sign and house of children).

4. Other Angular Planets.

Mars, though actually placed in the Third House, is so close to the cusp of the Fourth that it can be considered angular. Mars is square the Moon and in a very negative mutual reception. This reveals how sudden temper flare-ups would act to Duncan's disadvantage. Disruptive and rash feelings would rush into her conscious mind from the subconscious, and she would brush everything aside to give in to these impulses (Moon in Aries). Mars, square Venus, demonstrates the great difficulties she encountered with lovers. Mars' placement in the Third House indicates her restlessness and danger from accidents during travel. Its proximity to the cusp of the Fourth House shows a deep insecurity, an inability to establish permanent roots, and a constant change of residence.

E. Major Configurations

Isadora Duncan's chart shows no major planetary pictures such as T-Squares or Grand Trines. The major configuration is the mass of planets on the Ascendant, which has already been discussed.

F. House-by-House Analysis

1. Second House: Finances, Resources.

The location of the Sun in this house made Isadora fond of comfortable surroundings and good food. Jupiter trine the Sun brought her into contact with wealth but gave her an extremely extravagant nature. Thus she continually spent all the money she earned and always provided for an entourage of friends wherever she went. An extravagant nature is further demonstrated by the square of the Second House ruler Venus to Mars. This influence contributes to living beyond one's means. The elevated position of Jupiter is extremely protective, and Duncan was able to emerge out of her resultant financial difficulties with the help of friends, lovers, and her own ingenuity.

2. Third House: Brothers, Sisters, Travel, Communication.

The placement of Mars in this house (ruler of the Ascendant, demonstrates that Isadora Duncan worked on many projects with her brothers and sisters. Mercury, the house ruler, is square Jupiter, showing many journeys, sometimes difficult ones, taken with them. When Mercury is sextile to Mars, it is also an indication of travel, a sharp tongue, and a quick mind.

3. Fourth House: Home and Roots.

The ruler of this house (Moon) is square Mars, showing the tendency to broken homes (Duncan's father left her mother shortly after Isadora's birth). Mars, ruler of her Ascendant, is square the Moon (representing her birthplace) and reveals her alienation from the United States and her subsequent wanderings across Europe and South America.

4. Fifth House: Children, Pleasure, Romance, Creative Expression.

Uranus' placement in this house is extremely important. Ruling the Eleventh House of ideals, Uranus in the Fifth House is the vehicle for their expression.

To dance without any set of established rules, according to her own beliefs in natural rhythms, was a totally unconventional concept for the era in which she lived. The motivating factor throughout her life was to create a school in which children could be taught to move according to their natural inclinations. Venus trine Uranus shows the financial aid given to her in this project by a millionaire lover, Paris Singer. (Saturn sextile the Sun and Sun trine Jupiter are also indications of wealthy patronage by admirers, as the Sun rules the Fifth House of lovers.) Her romantic attachments were completely Uranian; she refused to marry the fathers of her children. Isadora always sought to remain independent and felt that she did not want to abandon her art for the sake of marriage and convention. Finally, Pluto in exact square to Uranus indicates the unpopularity of her "revolutionary" art form in most circles.

5. Sixth House: Health, Employment.

Mercury (ruler of the House) conjunct Neptune demonstrates that Isadora Duncan's thinking and imagination had much to do with her state of health; the square to Jupiter shows illness stemming from excessive sensual activities. The placement of Mercury in the First House and her Aries Ascendant show her preference for solo performance or recitals with her protegées.

6. Seventh House: Marriage.

Venus is ruler of this house, and its trine to Uranus indicates Duncan's preference for unconventional relationships. It would seem that she was more comfortable relating to a man as a lover than as a wife. Her only marriage was to a Russian revolutionary poet (the quintessence of Uranus trine Venus), Serge Essenin, but this marriage took place solely to enable Serge to enter the United States. This marriage was the cause of great unhappiness, indicated by the square of Mars (coruler of the Eighth House of death) and Venus (ruler of the marriage partner). Serge eventually committed suicide.

7. Eighth House: Death.

Deaths played a major role in Isadora's life. We have already mentioned the passing of her husband. The drowning of her children eventually led to her own demise, as she was never able to recapture her spirit after this tragedy. Uranus rules mechanical inventions (and sudden accidents) and is placed in the Fifth House of children, exactly square Pluto (coruler of the Eighth House). The Moon, which governs motherhood and water, is exactly square Mars (the other ruler of the Eighth). Thus, we can see the indications demonstrating the accident which took the children's lives. Isadora's own death occurred through a freak automobile accident, when the scarf she was wearing caught on one of the wheels of a car, causing asphyxiation.

8. Ninth House: Travel, Philosophy.

Jupiter, ruler of this house, is trine the Sun, showing that Isadora reached her real success in foreign countries. The placement of Jupiter in Aquarius indicates an interest in astrology and the occult. She often studied her own chart (but obviously either did not see or did not apply its warnings to her life). Incessant travel is shown by the square of Jupiter to Mercury-Neptune and Jupiter's trine to the Sun.

9. Tenth House: Career, Mother.

The ruler of this house is Saturn, which is sextile the Sun and indicative of the great influence her mother held in Isadora Duncan's life. The mother, an accomplished musician, helped to train Isadora in her early years. Neptune trine the Midheaven shows that her career would involve music and the dance, while Mercury trine this same point illustrates a consciousness of purpose while quite young. The square of the Moon to the Midheaven demonstrates how moodiness and premature action (Mars square the Moon opposite the Midheaven) caused Isadora to lose bookings and her popularity. Venus, her ruling planet, square Mars and the Midheaven shows that her life style was the reason for her downfall.

G. General Analysis of Major Transits and Progressions

Isadora Duncan left the United States in 1899 to achieve acclaim in Europe. Her progressed Mars had squared the natal Venus, and Isadora left her position with the Augustin Daly Dance Company, with which she had long been dissatisfied. The entrance of the progressed Moon into the Ninth House made this naturally restless individual seek her livelihood in a foreign land. Upon her arrival in London, she and her family spent a great deal of time studying ancient Greek art at the British Museum. This is signified by a conjunction of the progressed Mercury to the natal Sun (meaning a new field of study). As progressed Venus (her ruler) also conjoined Mercury, this interest led to her recognition as a dancer when during the course of the next five years the progressed Moon entered the Tenth House of career and Eleventh House of hopes and dreams.

A critical time for Isadora came in 1925. The progressed Sun squared Venus (ruler of the Second House), and she was forced to sell her house to pay her debts. Progressed Mars squared Mercury, and one of her adopted children died, followed by the suicide of her husband. By transit Neptune squared Pluto (coruler with Mars of the Eighth House of death), showing the unnatural condition surrounding Serge's death. In addition, Uranus was squared by transiting Saturn in Scorpio (again connecting children and death).

In true Aries fashion, Isadora planted a seed which others cultivated. Today her ideas are expressed in modern dance, the field she largely brought into existence. Personal tragedy prevented Isadora from seeing the fruition of her dreams, but she can be credited with turning the dance into a form of art relatively unlimited within the scope of its expression.

22.

JOSEPH STALIN: VOICE OF THE EGO

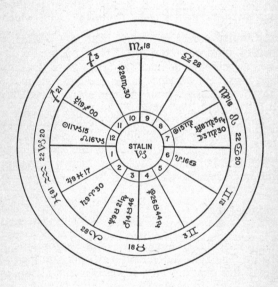

Diagram 27

"The state will die out, not as the result of the relaxation of state power, but as a result of its maximum consolidation, which is necessary for the purpose of crushing the remnants of the dying classes and for organizing the defense against capitalist encirclement, which is far from being annihilated and will not soon be annihilated."

Speech, January 1933

The vast majority of human beings pass through this world affecting only the people in their immediate environment. A very small number, however, are endowed with the destiny to shape and mold the lives of millions, even of the entire world. Joseph Stalin was such a man; he had the power to transform the macrocosm of Russia into the microcosm of his personal horoscope.

A. Hemisphere Emphasis

Seven of the planets in Stalin's chart are posited in the Eastern portion of the map. This topography indicates that activities initiated by Stalin were the ones that had major consequence in his life and thus in the national life of Russia. Four of these seven planets are placed in the north, including the very important ruler of the chart, Saturn in Aries. The latter helped to create a cult of personality around him as his associates and the general populace revered him as the embodiment of Soviet Russia. Stalin placed his pictures and his totalitarian doctrine everywhere.

B. Synthesis of Elements and Qualities

The predominant quality of this horoscope is cardinality. The Sun, Ascendant, and Ruler are located in signs of this quadruplicity. Fixity is also a feature of this natus, with four planets and the Midheaven so placed. Thus we can see that once Stalin entered on a course of action, he could never be dissuaded from changing his direction. The Moon and three other planets are posited in common signs, giving him the ability to adjust the external environment to suit his own purposes.

The predominant element of the chart is clearly earth, as there are six planets and the Ascendant in this triplicity. Stalin was a complete Saturnian pragmatist— that is, a man who worked to systematize all the resources of his land and its people. The lack of any planets in air contributed to his great sense of insecurity in personal relationships and his lack of objectivity in understanding his own public image.

C. Sun, Moon, Ascendant, and Their Relationship

In Stalin's chart the Sun, which represents the Will of an individual, is placed in the Twelfth House in Capricorn. This House denotes those things which are usually hidden from view. A Capricorn influence in this sector manifests itself as a subtle and crafty form of self-expression. Stalin's true desires were not easily apparent to those around him, and he employed any means necessary to insure this position.

Stalin often invited his associates to a night of drinking. After pressuring them into a state of complete intoxication, he prodded them into revealing their true feelings. If perchance his guests were unlucky enough to say something Stalin did not like to hear, the poor unfortunates could find themselves on the following day in a prison cell or worse.

As the welfare of Russia was inexorably related to his own position, Stalin took a stern, paternal, Capricornian hand in making sure that the country would endure according to his envisioned plan. Individual sacrifices are very minor to a Capricorn mind when it is dealing with the historic and economic collectivity of a nation. This particular factor may help to explain two other Capricorn world leaders—Mao Tsetung and Richard M. Nixon.

Stalin's Virgo Moon is trine the Sun. This position bestows great versatility in handling all the bureaucratic details with which a head of state must concern himself. The trine facilitates the union of inner drives with the conditions of surroundings and associates. In a chart such as this, it can also bring about the approbation of the masses. In this instance the Russian people were so undermined and controlled by the powers at work through Stalin's Twelfth House Capricorn Sun that they had little influence on affairs of state. Nevertheless, the Sun trine the Moon indicates the ease with which Stalin could make manifest his surreptitious plans and desires.

D. Weighing the Planets

1. Ruler of the Chart.

Saturn is clearly the ruler of this horoscope, since it governs both the Ascendant and the Sun sign. Placed in Aries, it is in close square to the Sun. This planetary relationship is particularly significant and can be considered a symbolic synopsis of Stalin's real character.

Born Iosif Vissarionovich Dzhugashvili, he later changed his name to Stalin, which in Russian means "man of steel." Like steel, a strong Saturn influence in a chart confers great strength, powers of endurance, perseverance, and sustainment. Aries is the sign of constant self-projection. The placement of Saturn in the sign of the Ram made Stalin extremely concerned with the continual growth of his status in the world and the adoption of his own set of laws and restrictions (Saturn is called "the planet of limitation"). The placement of Saturn in his Second House further emphasizes this drive, as it is the House of "Fixed Values."

2. Planets in the First House.

It is of great interest to note that, though Stalin's ruler is Saturn, Jupiter, the planet governing expansion and outward growth, is placed in the Ascendant. Jupiter sextile the Sun and semi-sextile Saturn gives him two angles of opportunity. Stalin therefore tended to nurture his acquisitive nature by expanding his influence wherever possible. During his regime Russia acquired an enormous amount of territory and became increasingly imperialistic, for Stalin desired to make Russia (and thereby himself) the strongest power in the world. (This is a fine example of Capricornian identification with worldly position.) The ability to successfully balance a policy of consolidation (influence of Saturn) with acts of expansion (influence of Jupiter) is a most important factor in the comprehension of Stalin's modus operandi. We can see this process at work by noting that, during the various Five-Year Plans, he enforced a great many restrictions on consumer goods. His actions were based on the idea that such temporary limitations would result in a greater and more permanent economic expansion for the Russia of tomorrow (Capricorn truly at work).

3. Most Elevated Planet and Other Angular Planets.

Since Venus in Scorpio is placed in the Midheaven, it is the most elevated planet in the chart. One can see in this position an indication of Stalin's great personal magnetism. In addition, Venus is opposed and in mutual reception with Pluto in Taurus, a combination which can easily bend others to one's will. As these two bodies are also in a T-Square configuration with the Moon, they reveal Stalin's ability to influence the subconscious of the masses. In other words, Stalin's chart gives the portrait of a man in complete possession of a nation's potential for self-expression.

Venus' placement in Scorpio, the sign of its detriment, adds to Stalin's possessive and jealous nature. It also caused him to be especially suspicious of anyone close to him. Thus he sought to annihilate (Pluto) those individuals he considered dangerous to the state (of Stalin). Venus in the Tenth House opposing Pluto accounts for the purge of people in high governmental positions. If we add the factor of Uranus conjunct the Moon, we can expand this purgative methodology to include entire populations and races.

Pluto is located in the Fourth House in Taurus. This is the astrological causal factor behind Stalin's attempt to reorganize the age-old Russian family structure by taking babies away from their parents and sending them to state nurseries. Thus the state would be the sole parent to whom these future citizens would owe their loyalty (here is an excellent example of the Capricornian expression of responsibility to the family-state). Children already living at home were rewarded for spying on their parents and denouncing them if the little ones thought that the parents were against the government's policies.

The Moon and Uranus are conjoined in Virgo in the Seventh House, which added to Stalin's complete control over the masses. Their square to the Fourth House Pluto contributed to Stalin's drive for complete power and helps us to understand his mastery of the order and structure of Soviet society. Stalin was able to move millions of people quite suddenly from one geographical location to another (Uranus conjoined Moon) according to his personal understanding of economic and social desirability (Virgo).

E. Major Planetary Configurations

We have already mentioned the T-Square between Pluto, Venus, and the Moon, but this configuration is such a pervasive influence that we should look at it also from another point of view.

Stalin initiated a large spy network and a powerful secret police system which permeated all levels of society (KGB). Each floor in an apartment house, for example, would have its informer, responsible to the agent for the entire building. The latter reported to the chief informer of the block, and so on. This system pyramided until it eventually reached Stalin himself. Thus we see the workings of Pluto in the Fourth House as the underground subterfuge within the community. The other end of the opposition, Venus in Scorpio in the Tenth House, represents the regular national police. Both the underground and the overt networks are directed to the masses, signified by the Moon. The great detail of this frightening web can best be described by the Moon's placement in Virgo.

Stalin allowed the tension indicated by his T-Square to be released negatively, so that what might have been a positive polarization of Venus, Pluto, and the Moon —the ability to infuse a constantly renewable sense of economic and social harmony—became instead an extreme force for cruelty and devastation. Instead of harmony as the unifying force of his people Stalin brought fear.

Stalin had a Grand Trine in Earth involving six planets. Here we see his resourcefulness and his ability to use the abundant material resources at his disposal. His Sun is trine Neptune and Mars from the Twelfth House of confinement. This aspect, plus the third trine to Uranus, helped Stalin to escape from prison many times. In addition, it helped him to root out individuals who plotted against him, as this Grand Trine endows the native with a strong sixth sense. It also made it easy for Stalin to succeed in his own deceptions. (This is a fine example of the negative channeling of energy from a nominally harmonious configuration, the Grand Trine.)

F. Analysis of Houses and Planets Not Previously Delineated

1. Third House: Communication, Education.

There is a Mars-Neptune conjunction in Stalin's Third House, adding to his personal drive and imagination. The energy exchanged between the Sun and the Moon helped Stalin to impose his views (Sun) on the people (Moon) through the press (Third House) with great success (all bodies connected by trines). Stalin held complete control over the media and was well aware of the importance of propaganda (Mars-Neptune trine Moon-Uranus).

2. Fifth House: Creative Expression.

Mercury is the ruler of this unoccupied House. Stalin was a prolific writer and poet, whose works were widely published in many languages (Mercury is the Sign of Sagittarius, ruler of international publication.)

3. Sixth House: Health.

Mercury is also the ruler of the Sixth House. Although he was basically a healthy man, Stalin did contract tuberculosis while young. Gemini placed on the cusp of this House rules the lungs and chest. In addition, individuals with Capricorn Ascendants are often ill as children, though their health improves as they grow older. Mercury is also placed quite close to the Twelfth House cusp (area of imprisonment), indicating a worsening of the tubercular condition while he was incarcerated in Siberia.

4. Seventh House: Marriage.

Stalin's first wife, Ekaterina Svanidze, is reported to have died of natural causes after three years of marriage. Little is known about her except for the fact that she did not completely support her husband's revolutionary doctrine, although she was extremely loyal to him in all other ways. (Virgo Moon in the Seventh House is indicative of a supportive helpmate, though a conjunction to Uranus may indicate a difference in ideologies.)

Stalin's second wife, Nadezhda Alleluieva (Svetlana's mother), was also loyal to her husband. During her lifetime she was employed as a secretary in Lenin's office (Moon in Virgo, sign of clerical duties) and used this position to spy for Stalin (Moon trine a Twelfth House Sun).

Stalin, however, was not a faithful husband. Pluto opposite Venus is indicative of a tendency toward excessive sexuality. His emotional responsiveness in general was noted for its violent extremes. This tendency is seen in the horoscope through two configurations of Jupiter (excesses) opposite Uranus (sudden, sometimes violent actions) conjunct the Moon (subconscious forces and the women in one's life) and Pluto (annihilation) square the Moon opposing Venus. Nadezhda Alleluieva was to learn the impact of this configuration during a party celebrating the fifteenth anniversary of the Russian Revolution, when she and Stalin had a violent argument over another woman with whom Stalin was involved. In a sudden fit of anger Stalin shot and killed her.

5. Eighth House: Death.

Mercury is also the ruler of the Eighth House. Stalin's death is reported to have occurred from a cerebral hemorrhage (Mercury has a strong affinity with the workings of the mind and brain). There is, however, a very strong indication that before his death Stalin grew increasingly insane. At this time he was in the midst of preparing another purge of intellectuals (especially those of Jewish origin). This move posed some danger to his close comrades, many of whom feared they might be on this new list. This circumstance gave rise to the speculation that Stalin's death was effected "with a little help from his friends." As Mercury is in the House of friendships (the Eleventh), unaspected and close to the Twelfth House cusp (hidden enemies), the chart supports the theory of assasination. At the very least, it indicates some mystery surrounding his demise.

6. Ninth House: Foreign Travel.

Venus, ruler of Libra, the sign of treaties and peace agreements, governs the Ninth House. Stalin traveled outside of Russia only in pursuit of such accords. Venus' placement in the Tenth House of national standing and government adds to the necessity of travel abroad for international conferences and meetings. Venus is also square the Moon, while Jupiter is opposing the Moon. These positions reveal a great many journeys but a certain dislike about having to make them.

G. General Analysis of Major Transits and Progressions

The following events were chosen for our purposes on the basis of their historical importance: Stalin's initial meeting with Lenin, the time of his assumption of total power within the Soviet Union, and the signing of the nonaggression pact with Hitler.

Stalin first met Lenin while he was a delegate attending the Bolshevik Conference in Tampere, Finland. Stalin's progressed Moon was passing through the Seventh House, a period when close associates and partnerships were especially important to his life. Uranus was trine the natal Moon by transit and was thus instrumental in bringing this revolutionary team together. Stalin's natal Moon-Uranus conjunction is indicative of someone who forms alliances with political figures, and the trine aspect set this inherent tendency in motion. His progressed Mercury (planet of meetings) was also forming two important aspects: sextile Venus in the Tenth House, symbolizing that this meeting would have an important effect upon his eventual position in the world, and trine Pluto, indicating that the meeting in Finland would eventually undermine existing social structures. Mars was also trine the Ascendant by progression, giving Stalin additional drive for power and opportunities for personal advancement.

Stalin assumed supreme control of Russia after the death of Lenin in April 1923. At that time the progressed Ascendant was trine Venus at the Midheaven, indicating the merger of his personal image with national life. In addition, his progressed Jupiter was trine the Midheaven, placing him in a position to govern. At the time Jupiter was also exactly conjunct the Midheaven by transit.

On August 23, 1939, Stalin signed a nonaggression pact with Hitler. At that time his progressed Mars was square his natal Uranus. This aspect reveals a break with tradition as an alignment was contracted between Russia and her former enemy. It also indicates war, and the fact that this pact would end as suddenly as it had begun. Mars square Uranus does not make for any degree of stability.

Stalin's progressed Midheaven was trine Mars, however, illustrating the sagacity of such a play in the strategy of war—which is, of course, an affair of the Red Planet. In addition, transiting Mars sat on Stalin's Ascendant for a month, trine to Pluto. This was a definite help to Stalin's war effort, as World War II was a battle of Plutonian proportions (Pluto is connected with mass annihilations). Perhaps an even more important factor, in the historical sense, was that Stalin's participation in the war led to Russia's dominance of Eastern Europe, which resulted in the complete polarization of East and West.

It is interesting to note that from a period beginning many years before the end of World War II until the present day a state of cold war has existed between the forces of Western and Eastern imperialism. Pluto is said to be the planet of "frozen fire," its energies working for many years under the surface of physical manifestation before erupting. In effect Pluto can be said to be very closely associated with those aspects of subterfuge and spying which have categorized the relationships of the great world powers since the first rumblings of World War II were heard in the early 1930s, the time of Pluto's discovery.

23.

ANGELA DAVIS: VOICE OF THE REVOLUTION

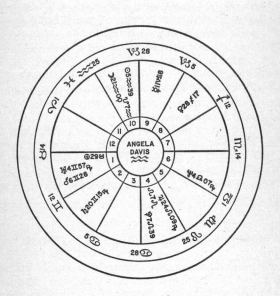

Diagram 28

"You don't see your life, your individual life, as being so important. . . . I have given my life for the struggle. My life belongs to the struggle."

Angela Davis serves as a perfect example of our revolutionary age: she is black, a woman, and an

Aquarian. Angela is an idealist, expressing in her unique way her personal concept of today's reality and her vision of tomorrow's. As we carefully delineate her natal chart, the astrological reasons behind her historical role as well as her personal drives become increasingly evident.

A. Hemisphere Emphasis

Although a majority of the planets are in the northern hemisphere of Angela Davis' chart, the nature of the bodies in the south tend to throw the emphasis of the map to this sector of the chart. Thus, in spite of numerical preponderance (six to four), the balance of the life energies is shifted, so that her personal life (planets in the north), though extremely important to her, is overshadowed and sublimated by her public life (planets in the south).

There are five planets in the west, an indication that other people's actions will have a great effect on her own; but as five others, including the luminaries, are in the east, we can conclude that an Oriental prevalence is established. Angela personifies her ideologies and relationships through her activities.

B. Synthesis of Elements and Qualities

Although the number of planets is evenly split between the common and the fixed signs, the importance of those in the latter quality (the oppositions from the Sun and Moon in Aquarius to Jupiter and Pluto in Leo) as well as the fixed nature of the Ascendant, Taurus, clearly shows the predominance of this quadruplicity.

Out of the total of ten planets, six are in air, including the luminaries. This combination of fixity and air causes Angela Davis to be firm in maintaining her opinions and strengthens her Aquarian nature. Once decided upon a course of action, she is willing to undergo many hardships rather than yield her position.

The emphasis in air gives her a strong intellect and contributes to her talent as a writer, speaker, and teacher. There are no planets in water; while this does not, of course, indicate that she is without emotions, the absence of water does make it difficult for her to "feel" (as opposed to "understand") other people's personal emotions. This shortcoming can result in a certain tactlessness. On another level, a lack of water in her chart can contribute to the sacrifice of personal emotional relationships and a rechanneling of this energy into the service of her political causes. The placement of Venus, Jupiter, and Pluto in fire aids her in her purposes through a generally optimistic nature and a great deal of social charisma (Venus, her ruler, is trine Jupiter).

C. The Sun, Moon, Ascendant, and Their Interrelationship

Both Sun and Moon are in Aquarius, indicating a merging of the inner drives and the external instrument through which they are expressed. The luminaries are placed in the Tenth House, revealing a life which will have some impact upon the general public. This is especially so as they are in Aquarius, the sign of the mass media.

The Sun in the Midheaven makes Angela quite conscious of her goals, and the proximity of the Moon channels all personal interests and emotions toward their realization. She becomes in effect a champion of social causes (Sun in Aquarius in the Tenth) which are directly related to herself, her roots, and her heritage (Moon in Aquarius, ruler of the Fourth House in the Tenth). Thus, in her own words, she can "merge the personal with the political when they're no longer separate."

Her Taurus Ascendant gives her an abundance of physical beauty and magnetism. It also reinforces her determination and stubbornness. The fact that her Sun and Moon are square the Ascendant gives her a public image quite different from either what she is really trying to represent or how she sees herself. She is thought of by many as the glamor girl of the radical left, but personal acclaim or "stardom" is very far from her true motivation.

D. Weighing the Planets

1. Ruler of the Chart.

The ruler of this natus is Venus in Sagittarius, a sign concerned with the laws and mores governing the whole of society. It is therefore another natal and impersonal influence contributing to the "tone" of Angela Davis' chart. Sagittarius rules foreign places, journeys of the mind and body, while Aquarius rules the masses and the applications of these laws upon daily life. This combination of influences gives her cause a worldwide perspective, so that her activities are not limited to her native land. The importance of Venus in Sagittarius is evidenced by her travels abroad for university study (Sagittarius rules higher education). In addition, Angela first came into prominence as a philosophy teacher on the college level.

2. Planets in the First House.

Mars in the First House can be a great source of inspiration and leadership. When it is combined with Uranus, the masses are easily attracted to the native's ideologies. This is especially true in Davis' horoscope, as the two planets are placed in Gemini. In addition, Angela has this combination trine her Aquarius Sun, giving her words and actions even further strength, since the entire force of her being is behind her beliefs and actions.

The Mars-Uranus conjunction is dynamic and embodies the energy of the revolutionary. Since the First House rules personal approaches to the immediate environment and Gemini is the sign of communications, this configuration results in quickness of speech and great alacrity in the handling of most matters. Angela

Davis can never be at a loss for words, and thoughts come to her with lightning speed.

Mars-Uranus in this position also indicates rash, dramatic, and often precarious and violent actions. The conjunction can make Davis quite nervous and can give her so much energy so suddenly that at times she may act too hastily, without adequate consideration of the outcome. When this influence is combined with Taurus Ascendant, her release of energy becomes erratic in yet another sense. There are times when she is completely taken over by lethargy, while at other times she can appear to be a superwoman.

3. *Most Elevated Planet and Other Angular Planets.*

We have already discussed some of the significance in Angela Davis' chart of the Sun and the Moon in the Midheaven. We should also say, however, that the Moon in this position makes her a favorite with the general public. She had a great deal of support during her imprisonment, and she is likely to continue attracting a large following. Not only ordinary citizens from all over the world, but also several foreign dignitaries demanded her release from prison (the Moon trine Saturn is indicative of this reaction, as Saturn represents people in government). The Sun brings her before the public, and the Moon makes people identify and sympathize with her.

Pluto, located in the Fourth House in opposition to the Sun, brings Davis into frequent contact with danger and violence. She has often found it necessary to have personal bodyguards in response to threats on her life.

The placement of Jupiter, also in the Fourth, indicates occasional residence in foreign countries (especially as Jupiter is trine Venus in Sagittarius). These changes of residence are, however, forced on her at times, and she may find herself an exile during certain intervals during her life. Because Cancer is ruler of the Fourth, she is especially concerned with her roots and will tend to return to her country of birth in order to continually seek improved conditions for Black Americans.

E. Major Planetary Configurations

Angela Davis' Grand Trine in air (Sun, Neptune, Mars-Uranus) aids her ease and agility of self-expression. She is a brilliant writer and speaker, and the inclusion of Neptune in this configuration endows her with sympathy for human suffering. This configuration also gives her great imaginative powers and makes her a very romantic figure in the eyes of the public.

The squares of Mercury and Venus to Neptune indicate that at times she may find herself enmeshed in impractical personal involvements; she is apt to misjudge people close to her. Venus square Neptune makes it difficult to distinguish between the real and the unreal in relationships and causes suffering in the personal romantic sphere. Mercury's square demands that she establish a greater sense of objectivity, especially in relation to the state of the world outside her personal interests.

F. Analysis of Planets and Houses Not Previously Delineated

1. Second House: Personal Finances.

Angela Davis may encounter some difficulties in handling her own and other people's resources. She will earn money through her writing and lectures (Mercury rules her Second House), but the placement of Saturn in the Second is a test and often takes away that which has been given. Extremely generous, she will share her money with those in need. Venus in the Eighth House indicates a capacity for obtaining resources by working with others in foreign countries and from previous publication. Her books will sell quite well in other lands, but Venus square Neptune can bring financial deception.

2. Sixth House: Health.

Neptune in Libra in the Sixth House adds to Davis' sensitivity and probably made her prison confinement quite injurious to her mental and psysical health. The absorptive nature of this planet would make her especially prone to personalizing the pains of fellow prisoners, even though she was for a large portion of her term physically isolated from them. Further, the fixed star Ascella, located on her Pluto, has a detrimental effect upon the eyes. The opposition to Angela's Sun is indicative of her myopic condition, which was aggravated during her prison term. Another indication of ill health resulting from confinement is that the ruler of her Sixth House, Venus, is square to Neptune within it.

G. General Analysis of Important Events in the Life

The September 1963 tragedy in which four young Black girls were murdered in a Birmingham church must have been a major shock to Angela, since she had known them since childhood. When this incident occurred, transiting Uranus was exactly square her natal Mars, indicating danger, explosive conditions, and possibly an accident. At the same time, by progression, Uranus went direct and progressed Mercury trined natal Neptune. This configuration set off her Grand Trine and is symbolic of a major change in consciousness.

In 1967 Angela received a scholarship and went abroad to study for a second time. This event is consonant with her progressed Sun sextile her natal Venus in Sagittarius. The scholarship is a result of one who has Venus trine Jupiter natally, as this combination often bestows awards and prizes.

In May 1967 Angela paid her first visit to a Communist country, East Germany. This must have been of major significance, as her transiting Uranus now squared natal Saturn, giving a confrontation with a social structure at variance with that of her own nation. It can also indicate a radical change in personal political beliefs.

By early 1970 Angela Davis' progressed Moon

reached the conjunction of the Midheaven, and she became more active in public, working for the release of George Jackson and the other Soledad Brothers. In the spring of that year the Regents of UCLA refused to renew her teaching contract (progressed Midheaven opposed her natal Jupiter, signifying a challenge from those in authority, especially to her philosophical beliefs. In addition, transiting Jupiter was also square her natal Midheaven).

On August 7, 1970, Jackson made a fatal attempt to rescue his brother, and Angela was alleged to have played some role in this event. At that time transiting Jupiter once again came to the square of her natal Midheaven, indicating a flight from those in authority, for at the same time Saturn was also square her Moon.

In October 1970, with Saturn still square the Moon (signifying restrictions on personal freedom), Angela was arrested in New York. In December of that year Saturn came close to the conjunction of her Ascendant by transit (restriction of self-expression), and Jupiter squared the Moon (causing difficulties in travel). Jupiter is also the ruler of courts of law, and with the above configurations in effect, Angela was extradited from New York to California to stand trial.

During 1971 she remained in prison as Saturn continued to transit her First House. She was placed under great personal restriction and wrote that she "didn't see the sky or sun for 85 days in the winter and spring of 1971." During that time Jupiter by transit opposed her natal Mars-Uranus conjunction, while Saturn once again squared her Moon, thus preventing her release.

On February 23, 1972, she was finally freed on bail after sixteen months in prison. During that time Saturn conjoined her Part of Fortune and trined her Midheaven. Jupiter conjoined her natal Venus (an aspect of great good fortune) and set off her natal trine between these two bodies.

On June 4, 1972, Angela Davis was completely acquitted. Pluto then made its final trine to her Midheaven, releasing her from a previous state of Being and giving her the chance for renewed activity (Pluto here acting as the planet of regeneration). In addition, her progressed Moon had passed the square of Uranus and Mars, indicating a release of tension. Finally, Saturn left her First House, ending personal restrictions.

Aquarius was free to continue its revolution.

24.

HARRY HOUDINI: VOICE OF ILLUSION

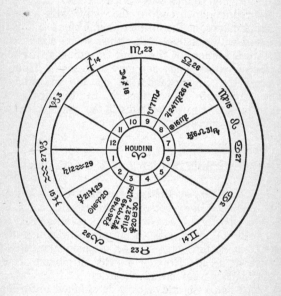

Diagram 29

"I am induced to take this step for the manifest reason that the public of both hemispheres may, through ignorance of the real truth, give credence to the mendacious boasts and braggadoccio of the horde of imitators who have sprung into existence with mushroom rapidity of growth and equal flimsiness of vital fibre, who with amazing effrontery and pernicious falsity seek to claim and hold the credit and honor, such as there may be, that belongs to me."

A. Hemisphere Emphasis

The majority of the planets appear in the northeastern quadrature in the horoscope of Harry Houdini (whose original name was Erich Weiss). This particular predominance endows the native with a highly subjective nature, as the northern hemisphere is directly concerned with personal rather than social affairs, and the eastern section of the chart is indicative of self-initiated activities. Thus one may deduce that Houdini instigated the circumstances of his life in order to achieve complete self-satisfaction. In this respect he constantly strove to make himself the center of attention—and he succeeded.

B. Synthesis of Elements and Qualities

The preliminary synthesis of the map reveals a fixed-fire emphasis. A fiery person, in the astrological sense, must be constantly active; such people are usually filled with an inner type of inspiration, which they seek to express through some sort of personal creativity. Throughout his life Houdini traveled in pursuit of new stunts to incorporate into his theatrics.

A fixed emphasis indicates a determined individual, someone with set ideas and values. Together, fixed-fire gives a Leo overtone to the horoscope. We can see this in the showmanship which characterized Houdini's public life. He was a proud man, abhorring all forms of deceit and malpractice—marked Leonian traits. Houdini's "magic" was most often the result of his ability to control his breathing, muscles, and limbs. If, however, some form of artifice was employed in a particular act, Houdini would reveal the trick to the audience after he had entertained them with the illusion.

A secondary influence in this chart is in Earth (three planets and the Ascendant). This contributed to his need to demonstrate the practical foundation of his various stunts and his desire to bring mystical theatrics down to Earth.

All four elements are represented in the chart by planetary placements, but only one planet lies in each of the air and water triplicities. The former element is represented by Saturn, the ruler of the chart. This planet's position in Aquarius is a contributing factor to Houdini's tendency to communicate his discoveries to his audiences. With Uranus in opposition to Saturn, this man was loath to obey any established set of rules. This opposition, plus the individualizing drive of his Aries Sun, gave Houdini the need to set himself apart from others in his field, even at the cost of other performers' reputations.

C. Sun, Moon, Ascendant, and Their Interrelationship

Once again we see the importance of fire in Houdini's chart. The Aries Sun indicates his constant drive toward finding new devices to incorporate into his form of magic. In addition, he thoroughly investigated all areas of the occult and of spiritualism (Sun conjunct Neptune, ruler of psychic phenomena).

Houdini's Sagittarius Moon further emphasized his Aries audacity, the Archer is the sign of the adventurer and gambler, while Aries is not afraid to take chances. The harmonious trine linking the two made it easy for Houdini to combine these characteristics, as the fire of one constantly feeds the flames of the other.

Capricorn Ascendant was indeed a fortunate position for Houdini; it helped to crystallize his ambitions and enabled him to bring projects to completion. Capricorn is tenacious and is not satisfied until it has achieved its many goals. When this influence is added to Aries, the result is someone who must establish himself as the best in his field. In this respect Houdini was always trying to top himself, so that his position as "the

greatest of the great" would remain constant throughout history. This is a sterling example of the Aries-
Capricorn ego trip.

D. Weighing the Planets

1. Ruler of the Chart.

The ruler of Houdini's chart is Saturn in Aquarius;
Aquarius rules science, and Houdini sought to treat
magic as science, bringing it out from behind the cur-
tain of superstition. Saturn's rule of obligations and
restraint is reflected in his choice of material, for he
always appeared in tricks which seemed to restrain
him in some way: handcuffed, submerged in a box,
tied up with cords and chains, and the like. Houdini's
ability to release himself from the bondage of near-
death was his best-known feat.

The First-House position of Saturn in Houdini's
horoscope placed a series of heavy burdens upon him
during his early life. After the death of his father,
Houdini had to become the family's major provider.
He therefore began performing before the public at a
very early age and did not stop until he died.

2. Most Elevated Planet and Other Angular Planets.

The Moon is the most elevated planet in the chart.
Houdini therefore obtained his greatest satisfaction
from activities and people associated with the vibrations and affairs of this body. This circumstance largely
explains his devotion to (and from) his mother, his
wife, and the general public (all of which are ruled
by the Moon). His wife, Beatrice, his closest companion, also served as his assistant in his act. The
special prominence of women is further emphasized by
the placement of his Moon in the Tenth House (public
image and social contribution).

Uranus is located in the Seventh House (signifying
close associates, marriage, and public enemies). Houdini's marriage was extremely sudden (Uranus rules
quick and surprising events), but it was harmonious
(Uranus is trine the Moon, ruler of this House) and

lasted for more than thirty years. Uranus is also square Mars (contests, disputes), endowing Houdini with the urge to challenge all his opponents, not merely with enthusiasm, but also with vindictiveness. If Uranus contributed to his contests, it also helped him in his triumphs. This is due in large measure to his inventiveness and his sheer genius of self-expression, indicated by the trine of Uranus to the Sun and Moon.

Another important planet in this chart is Pluto. Although its actual location is in the Third House, its proximity to the Nadir qualifies it as angular. The Fourth House rules those aspects of life which are under the surface of the personality, while Pluto is definitely connected with underground activities. Pluto is also the regenerator of matter, the annihilator of old forms so that they may be replaced by new. Many of Houdini's tricks involved submergence under Earth or water. Through these demonstrations he sought to dissolve preconceived ideas about magic. He desired to present it in a new form, bearing his personal signature.

E. Major Planetary Configurations

Houdini's chart holds two major planetary pictures: a T-Square in fixed signs and a Grand Trine in fire. (There is also a Grand Trine in Earth involving the Ascendant, but that is not a matter of planetary energies.)

Several factors must be considered in any examination of Houdini's angular T-square. As we know, squares bring out obstructions and tensions. These must be worked out if the problems are not to recur and cause additional difficulties. The fixed signs are concerned with will, deep-seated desires, and personal values. Planets placed in angular Houses impel the native to act upon the energy of those bodies within the situation symbolized by these planetary configurations. Such activity usually occurs through external events. We can, therefore, summarize the above configuration by stating that the angular placement of the

T-square put Houdini under considerable tension, challenged his deeply rooted opinions of himself and the world in which he lived, and forced him to compensate for these internal conflicts through the unique expression of his public life.

The planets involved in this planetary picture are Mars, Saturn, and Uranus. Saturn rules the past, the established way. Uranus rules the future, the breakthrough of the new. Thus the opposition between these bodies brought about a constant conflict, as Houdini continually had to question and challenge things formerly held to be unshakable and absolute in the eyes of history and the public. Thus, after finding out that Robert Houdin, the man he had always regarded so highly and from whom he had adopted the name Houdini, was not the great magician he had professed to be, Houdini publicly exposed this fact by writing a book on Houdin's life. He showed how Houdin had stolen his ideas from other magicians and had fooled people into believing that he possessed supernatural powers.

The placement of Mars in the T-square adds to the strength of the Saturn-Uranus opposition. It gave Houdini the necessary force to act upon his beliefs, as Mars is the planet of direct actions and irrevocable conclusions.

The Grand Trine in fire instilled in Houdini enormous self-confidence, as well as the necessary good fortune and vital energy to realize his ambitions. Trines bring forth gains without much personal effort, and fire is the element ruling creative activity. The placement of the Moon in this configuration gave Houdini easy success in demonstrating his special talents to the general public while winning their approval.

F. Analysis of Planets and Houses Not Previously Delineated

1. Second House: Finances and Material Resources.

The placement of the Sun and Mercury in the Second House endowed Houdini with a special interest in his earning capacity. The placement of Mercury in Pisces explains the income from his writing about magic and his appearances in movie serials (also ruled by Neptune-Pisces). His investments were probably not always wise, as there is a tendency to extravagance. (Mercury rules his Fifth House—speculation—and is in opposition to Jupiter. Both Mercury and Jupiter are placed in detriment, an indication of a person who overspends and makes financial misjudgments).

The trine from the Sun to Uranus in the Seventh and Mercury's placement also reveal the importance of publicity to Houdini's financial well-being.

2. Third House: Communications.

The third is a heavily tenanted House. Houdini was a widely published author, who wrote many articles and several books. (Venus is located here and rules the Ninth House of publication in his chart.) The conjunction of Venus (personal magnetism) and Neptune (hallucinations) made Houdini a master of illusion. As these two are in the sign of Aries and conjoin his Sun, his personal interest in the occult is easily explained.

3. Fourth House: Father, Foundation of One's Being.

Taurus on the cusp of this unoccupied House gives Venus the rulership over it. Venus is conjoined with Neptune and indicates that Houdini's father was deeply involved with religion and mysticism. This conjunction also tells much about Houdini's own interests in this subject. When we also see that this conjunction is square the Capricorn Ascendant, we can note that it was the pressure of Houdini's early life—the absence of the father—which forced him to make a living out of his Neptunian involvements.

4. Sixth House: Employment.

The Moon in Sagittarius as ruler of this House shows that Houdini's employment is likely to involve the general public and take him abroad. During his various journeys Houdini constantly studied magic and collected data concerning various aspects of occultism.

5. *Eighth House: Death.*

Houdini's death did not occur through a mishap during one of his tricks. Actually he died as the result of a serious but accidental blow to his abdomen, after which he developed peritonitis (inflammation of the abdominal wall) and other fatal complications.

The whole of Houdini's map leads one to assume that he was constantly involved with danger. Sudden and accidental death should therefore come as no surprise. Virgo, however, is the ruler of his Eighth House and is, of course, directly related to the intestines and to the abdomen in general.

6. *Eleventh House: Hopes, Wishes, and Ideals.*

Jupiter's rulership over the Eleventh House adds to the fact that Houdini's goals did not become actualized until he set off on his international travels. As Sagittarius is the philosopher, Houdini was not afraid to question either the status quo or his own beliefs. The placement of Jupiter in Virgo makes him critical of himself and others in this respect.

7. *Twelfth House: Secrets, Hidden and Restricted Things.*

Saturn, ruler of the Twelfth House, is placed in the First. This configuration inclines Houdini to bring to the public things that were previously hidden from them. (Saturn in Aquarius is the sign of mass distribution of knowledge.) He believed that nothing should be kept from the public, and he constantly revealed those "mysteries" he had painstakingly researched (the Twelfth House equals secret investigations).

G. General Analysis of Events in Houdini's Life

The year 1900 serves as a very good example of the importance of transits and progressions on Houdini's life. At this time he rose to the fame he was seeking through his brilliantly executed and well-publicized

"Scotland Yard Escape."[1] At that period his progressed Moon was in the Ninth House of foreign travel. His progressed Midheaven was also trine his Sun, indicating the beginning of personal success in the chosen career. In addition, his progressed Sun conjoined his natal Mars, indicating that his success would come from a dangerous and daring act. Jupiter was in Sagittarius that year, activating the Grand Trine in fire which resulted in a four-year European tour.

The death of Houdini's mother in 1913 led to his investigation of mediums and spiritualism. Scorpio rules the Tenth House (mother) and accounts for his devotion and desire to reach her in the invisible realms. At the time of her passing, his Sun opposed the Midheaven and his progressed Mercury conjoined Mars, a very important aspect. (Mercury, ruler of communication, is the ruler of Houdini's Eighth House, while Scorpio, sign of death, rules the Tenth. This aspect induced him to try to communicate with his deceased parent and led to subsequent investigations of this area of psychic work.)

Ironically, Houdini died on Halloween eve, October 31, 1926. At that time transiting Saturn filled in the "fourth leg" of the T-Square in fixed signs, setting off a fixed cross. This configuration indicates a very dangerous time of life. The fact that Houdini was born when the Sun was in Aries and died when it was in Scorpio brings to mind the interesting relationship which exists between these two signs, as well as the dual rulership of Mars and the magic which surrounded Houdini's life.[2]

---

[1] Although thoroughly searched before being placed in an escape-proof cell in Scotland Yard, Houdini managed to escape, as always, from his confinement. He did this by having a wire file sewn underneath the upper layers of his abdominal skin. When he was alone, he removed the file by breaking the skin with his fingernails and using the wire to effect his release. (A strong interest in devices of torture and the infliction of pain upon oneself in a dramatic sense can be seen in his horoscope by the conjunction of Mars and Pluto, as well as by the square from Saturn to Mars-Pluto and from Mars to Uranus.)

[2] The reader may wish to review those passages in this text dealing with Aries, Scorpio, and Mars.

25.

GRETA GARBO: VOICE OF A WOMAN

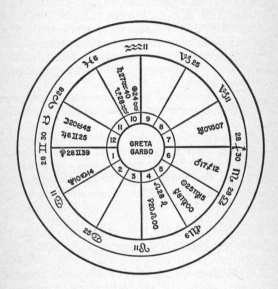

Diagram 30

"Even when I was a tiny girl, I preferred being alone. . . . I could give my imagination free reign and live in a world of lovely dreams. . . . My moods were changeable. Happy one moment—the next plunged in despair."

A. Hemisphere Emphasis

Greta Garbo was chosen by destiny to personify the essence of a film goddess. She was perfectly cast, for the intensity of her beauty and limitless depth of her emotions created the image of a woman whose realm of experience seemed to go far beyond ordinary human consciousness.

When we first examine her chart, we find that both its eastern and western halves are equally balanced by the presence of the heavenly bodies. This circumstance would seem to indicate that Garbo is an individual who not only initiates a great deal of her own activities but who is also highly responsive to situations created by others.

Although her work was directed to the enjoyment and enrichment of the public (four planets in the south), it is well known that Garbo placed extraordinary importance on her privacy. She is quoted as having said, "There are many things in your heart you can never tell another person. They are you, your private joys and sorrows, and you can never tell them. You cheapen yourself, the inside of you, when you tell them."

B. Synthesis of Elements and Qualities

The emphasis of this chart is in the common signs, with five planets and the Ascendant so placed. The mutables cause the native to fluctuate, and Garbo was notorious for her changing moods. One could never be sure, least of all Garbo herself, whether she would be happy or despondent from one moment to the next.

As for the elemental preponderance, we can see a strong placement of planets, including both the luminaries, in Earth signs. The strength of the Moon is further enhanced by its placement in Taurus. This combination of factors gives Garbo a strong sense of practicality and a certain dedication to her work (Fifth House Virgo Sun and Mercury). But there are also three planets, plus the Ascendant and Midheaven, in air, resulting in a conflict between mutable-air and fixed-Earth signs: on the one hand we find a woman of great irresponsibility, and on the other a person consistently working to control the many mutations of her will.

The presence of air in the horoscope contributes to a great facility for oral self-expression. Garbo's Taurus Moon adds earthy magnetism to her voice and the emotions it conveys, aptly demonstrated by her film portrayals.

C. Sun, Moon, Ascendant, and Their Interrelationship

Garbo's Sun is placed in Virgo, the sign of perfection. Through a proper sense of order and organization, Virgo can make the native extremely fussy and conscious of time. This is especially so in relation to jobs.

Garbo was never willing to work overtime. She would arrive on the set promptly at 8:00 A.M. and stop working at exactly 5:00 P.M. When she was forced to work overtime, Garbo arrived at the studio the following day as late by the exact amount as she had worked over the normal schedule the night before.

Garbo's Gemini Ascendant made the word the medium through which she reached the world. The square between her Fifth House Sun and the Ascendant brought about a constant pressure for her to express her opinions clearly. Although she was a master of gesture, voice, and movement, this square brought about many misunderstandings in her personal life.

The Moon is in its exaltation in Taurus, but it is posited in the Twelfth House; this placement causes the Moon's energy to become somewhat restrained. As the Moon largely rules emotional nature, Garbo internalized many of her feelings; this factor contributed to the depth of her inner life. The trine to the Sun allowed these repressions to become easily manifested through Twelfth and Fifth House affairs—the theater, film, and the arts. It also made her an extremely practical and resourceful person, since both Sun and Moon are found in the Earth signs.

D. Weighing the Planets

1. The Ruler of the Chart and Planets Located in the First House.

The ruler of Garbo's chart is Pluto, which is exactly conjunct the Ascendant. This position reveals a great deal about Garbo's true nature. Pluto is the loner, as well as a force exuding great mystery. It represents the untapped and unknown energies simmering beneath the surface of an individual's consciousness. Pluto's influence can be seen in many of Garbo's roles. She projects a strange elusiveness in all her films, an aura of deep emotions that are not allowed to emerge, else they would bring havoc and destruction upon herself and the environment.

The Ascendant represents projected image; Pluto's proximity to this most important point endows Garbo with a fascinating and hypnotic power over people. It also gives her the desire to control her surroundings, as is aptly demonstrated by her refusal to allow anyone on the set while she was working. At times even the director was forced to stand behind a screen drilled with peepholes in order to observe a particular scene. Pluto conjunct the Ascendant also explains to a large extent much of her insistence on solitude and secrecy. It is interesting to note that Garbo's most famous quotation is a deep, Taurus-throated, "I want to be alone."

Garbo often goes bargain-hunting in thrift shops. Her usual appearance is anything but glamorous: dark glasses, an old coat, a scarf over her head, no make-up. The duality of Pluto conjunct a Gemini Ascendant is such that this very same recluse was able to (and no doubt still could) make every person who saw her on the screen feel as if he, too, were undergoing the emotional traumas she personified.

A square exists between the Ascendant-Pluto conjunction and the Virgo Sun. Any relationship between Pluto and the Sun requires an individual to undergo a constant metamorphosis; a dissolution of old ways is required, so that new energies may emerge from the unconscious. Since the Ascendant is involved, these changes are reflected in the world of appearances and are often brought about through lovers (Fifth House Sun). One such complete transformation occurred before Garbo acted in films. Her first important director (and lover), Stiller, a Swede like herself, dictated what clothes she was to wear, how she was to move, and with whom she was to associate.

Neptune is placed in the First House. When Neptune is in Cancer, the sign of its exaltation, its powers are strengthened. Neptune's influence therefore adds to Garbo's elusiveness, desire for seclusion, and dreamy quality. Neptune is the ruler of film, and Garbo projected her personal mystique through this medium.

2. Most Elevated Planet and Other Angular Planets.

Saturn placed in dignity in the Tenth House in Aquarius is the most elevated planet in the chart. This position usually brings great gains and/or severe restrictions to the professional life. After the failure of her last film, *Two-Faced Woman*, Garbo decided to retire. Although at the time she did not think of this move as permanent, Saturn's placement in a fixed sign proved that such was not to be the case. When at times she did seriously consider returning to films, either a suitable property was not available or the backers would not provide the needed capital. The phenomenon of her retirement, however, contributed to her legend.

Venus in Leo in the Fourth House makes Garbo adept at dramatizing emotion. This placement also contributes to her great need to express herself artistically and to be surrounded by beauty, especially in her own home. (Today she resides in a large seven-room apartment in one of New York City's most fashionable neighborhoods—indicative of the luxurious surroundings brought by a Fourth House Venus in Leo.) As the Fourth also rules the latter part of life, Venus in Leo, square the Moon and opposing Saturn, is expressive of her life at this time—luxurious but solitary. It must be added, however, that this condition is completely self-imposed and definitely in keeping with her personality.

The last angular planet under discussion is Uranus in Capricorn in the Seventh House. The planet of independence is placed in the house of partnerships and further explains Garbo's refusal to marry. It also says much about her relationships with people in general that Uranus is in opposition to the Ascendant. The Seventh House reveals how natives get along with others. Uranus can contribute to a nervous temperament and can create erratic and irritable moods. Thus Uranus in this position tends to make Garbo fanatical in getting her own way. She is not one to cooperate with too many demands.

E. Major Configurations

The major planetary picture in this chart is a T-Square in fixed sign, a configuration which indicates great anguish in Garbo's romantic life. An exact square to the Moon by Venus in Leo denotes many fluctuations and conflicts in personal relationships. A Twelfth House Moon can bring unusual and often clandestine relationships. (The unconventional side of her love affairs is emphasized by the placement of Uranus in the Seventh House.) Saturn completes the T-Square and puts a cold, restricting aura upon the release of emotions in the personal sense. Saturn is not a completely negative influence, for it adds permanence and depth to feelings. However, Venus is placed at the Nadir of the chart, forcing the personal love nature to simmer underneath the surface of public life. The strong vibrations of Saturn so sublimated Garbo's romances that most of the energy of her love had to be transformed into her acting. The general public, represented by the Moon, became the fortunate recipient of these feelings. A Saturn-Venus opposition is often indicative of someone who has to choose between duty and personal desire. When Maurice Stiller was forced to leave this country, Garbo had to choose between her lover and her career. She chose Saturn—

her career. A few of her lovers were taken from her by death. This is indicated by several aspects: the Sun in the Fifth House (representing the men in her life) is square both Mars and Pluto; Uranus is both in the Seventh House of marriage and in opposition to Pluto and square the Sun.

We should also note the major connections among the higher-octave planets (Pluto, Uranus, Saturn). Saturn in late Aquarius and Uranus in early Capricorn are in sextiled and mutual reception. This relationship can make the native a bridge between the generations and a strong influence on the customs of the general public. The added vibration of Pluto trine Saturn from the First House (physical appearance) caused the public to emulate Garbo. Women of the 1920s and 1930s tried to look and speak like Garbo; they wore her type of slouched hats and raincoats. "Garbo" hairstyles were "in," as was her seductive, aloof, and mysterious manner. Few were able to forget Garbo once they had seen her.

F. Analysis of Planets and Houses Not Previously Delineated

1. Second House: Finances and Material Resources.

The Moon is the ruler of this House and clearly shows that Garbo earned her money by working with the public. Neptune (movies) is exactly on the cusp of this House and is sextile Mercury. The latter is in the House of speculation (Fifth) and shows the opportunities she had for very wise investments. The placement of the Moon in Taurus (land) in the Twelfth House indicates that her investments were probably in real estate and were kept and made in great secrecy.

2. Third House: Brothers, Sisters, Communications.

The Moon also rules the Third House. Garbo had a brother and a sister to whom she was very close. The death of her sister, Alva, from tuberculosis was a tragic event in her life. Alva's death and the profound effect it had on Garbo can also be seen by her Saturn-Moon-Venus T-Square.

As for communications, Garbo despised interviews, which she usually refused. As a rule she never gave her autograph to anyone. This attitude is emphasized by placement of the Third House ruler in the Twelfth, indicating once again a person who does not easily reveal her ideas and opinions. In addition, Garbo never confirmed or denied what was said about her, thus adding to the mystique which surrounds her.

3. Fifth House: Pleasure, Creativity, Love Affairs.

The ruler of the Fifth House, Mercury, is in dignity and placed within it. A square aspect between Mercury and Jupiter indicates that Garbo traveled a great deal in pursuit of her craft, her lovers, and her varied pleasures. (The square aspect often leads to incessant travel and wasted movement.) Although she was often reclusive, her Fifth House Sun and Mercury plus Gemini Ascendant brought her in touch with many different people. She attends many parties, especially in Europe, and she can be frank and outspoken at times (Mercury square Jupiter). Once again we see the pervasive dualism inherent in Gemini in particular and in mercurial people in general.

4. Sixth House: Employment, Clothing, Health.

Mars is placed in the Sixth House in Sagittarius and is trine Venus in Leo. This aspect contributed to Garbo's great sex appeal and to the personal magnetism which she used in her work. It also reveals her interest in health, a tendency which she manifests through addiction to special diets and health foods. The square from the Sun to Mars can, however, indicate a tendency to go to extremes in life. This is especially true in terms of her health, work, and creative self-expression. A short phrase that could be used to categorize Garbo is "intense extremist."

5. Eighth House: Death.

Saturn is the ruler of the Eighth House. Its positing by sign, House, and aspect indicates someone who will live to an advanced age. As previously mentioned, the square of Saturn to the Moon and its opposition to Venus brought many upsetting deaths into Garbo's life.

6. Ninth House: Travel, Higher Education.

Saturn is also the ruler of this House because Capricorn is on the cusp. Capricorn, the sign governing a desire for achievement, could indicate that Garbo would move to a foreign country to pursue her career. Garbo was discovered while she was attending the Royal Dramatic Academy in Sweden on a scholarship (one of Saturn's benefits).

7. Eleventh House: Friendships.

Neptune and Jupiter corule this domicile. Neptune brings friends who are artists, film makers, and musicians (Garbo had a long-lasting friendship with Leopold Stokowski), while Jupiter's influence gives her many friends of foreign birth (not Swedish). Neptune rules secrecy, and Garbo's friends refuse to discuss her, for fear of losing her favor (she has been known to cut people out of her life entirely if they publicly speak about her). Jupiter in the Twelfth House adds to this emphasis on closely guarded intimacies.

8. Twelfth House: Things Hidden, Occult Study, Confinement.

Both the Moon and Jupiter are placed in the Twelfth House. Jupiter is trine the Midheaven, indicating that Garbo could achieve success in a country foreign to her birth. A Twelfth House Moon bestows an interest in things of a hidden nature, but judging by the general "tone" of the horoscope, I doubt Garbo's serious involvement with the occult or metaphysical.

G. General Analysis of Events in Garbo's Life

A major time in a movie star's life is the period of first discovery. In the spring of 1923, when Garbo's progressed Moon was passing through the Ninth House, she was enrolled as a student at the Royal Academy in Sweden. At that time her progressed Midheaven had entered Pisces (sign of film) and exactly sextile Uranus (ruler of her Midheaven and to a large extent her career) in the Seventh House of partnerships. Maurice Stiller was in search of an actress for a new picture. He immediately spotted Garbo and decided that she was perfect for the film. Not only did this meeting lead to her eventual success in the United States, but Stiller also became her lover. Astrologically we can see these events indicated in three ways: the ruler of her House of Partnerships (Jupiter) was trine Neptune by transit; Neptune was also conjoined with Venus in Leo (the fusion of film with a personal romantic attachment); this conjunction occurred in the Fourth House, thereby causing a very deep change in Garbo's being. It was no surprise that, with all these important aspects, the film *The Atonement of Gosta Berling* opened to good notices the following year, launching her career.

Another important period in Garbo's life came late in 1926. At that time her first American film, *The Temptress*, was released, and she was widely accepted as a new star. Mars by progression conjuncted natal Uranus (ruler of the Tenth) in the House of Public Approval (Seventh), indicating sudden success. In addition, the Moon was passing through the Tenth House by progression (bringing her before the public) into the Eleventh House (realizing her hopes, bringing rewards from public efforts, meeting new friends) in the sign of Pisces (film). The explosiveness of the Mars-Uranus combination also brought about the end of her affair with Stiller. The break in their relationship occurred while Saturn, transiting through Scorpio, opposed the Moon and squared Venus, accentuating the nature of Garbo's T-Square configuration.

Greta Garbo left Hollywood and pictures in 1942,

after *Two-Faced Woman* had opened to bad reviews on December 31, 1941. Several aspects indicate a break with the film medium. Her progressed Sun had entered Scorpio that year, indicating a complete change of direction and a dissolution of what had already been established—her career. Progressed Mercury was approaching a square to Neptune, showing a loss of interest in making films and perhaps a certain lack of mental clarity. By transit, Saturn was in the Twelfth House conjoining the Moon. This position added to Garbo's desire for seclusion and lent a rather depressive note to her feelings. At the same time Saturn was square Venus in Leo, restricting her means of self-expression. Uranus was also transiting the Twelfth and squaring Saturn. Both of these planets being corulers of her Midheaven, this aspect of Uranus could indicate a sudden move to end her career. Finally, Neptune in Virgo was squaring her Ascendant-Pluto conjunction by transit. This aspect could lead to dissatisfaction with her own image and the feeling that it was no longer necessary to expose herself to criticism. The break she made was fixed and irrevocable. It is very unlikely that Garbo will ever return to films.

26.

EDGAR CAYCE: VOICE OF THE SPIRIT

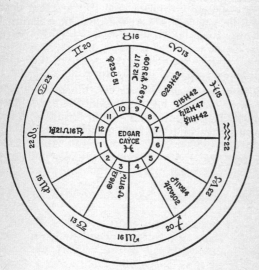

Diagram 31

"This body is controlled in its work through the psychical, or the mystical or spiritual. It is governed by the life that is led by the person who is guiding the subconscious when in this state. As the ideas given the subconscious to obtain its information are good, the body becomes better. The body should keep in close touch with the spiritual side of life if he is to be successful mentally, physically and financially."

Edgar Cayce, a reading on himself.

A. Hemisphere Emphasis

When he was a child, Edgar Cayce was visited by a beautiful and maternal Spirit who offered him one wish. The boy asked that he be allowed to be helpful to people, especially to those who were ill. Fortunately for humanity, his prayer was answered, and Cayce went on to serve Mankind to such an extent that he is known as the most important Western seer, prophet, and healer to appear so far in the twentieth century.

If we examine the chart as a whole, we note that most of the planets are posited in the southwestern quadrature. Eight bodies are placed in the west, demonstrating Cayce's natural tendency to act on situations presented to him for consideration, rather than initiating his own avenues for self-expression. All but two of the planets are located in the south, illustrating a universal rather than a personal approach to life. Thus we find Cayce to be a man who was not primarily concerned with the development of his personality, his ego structure, but a being evolving through service and the enrichment of other people's lives.

B. Synthesis of Elements and Qualities

The synthesis of this chart reveals a fixed-Earth emphasis. This was a fortunate combination for Cayce, a man whose work lay in the delivery of messages coming from unseen spiritual forces. His Pisces Sun and secondary water emphasis sensitized his receptivity of such subtle energies. The placement of five planets in Earth and the strong fixed quality of the map (five planets, Ascendant, and Midheaven), however, gave the necessary "grounding" for Cayce to work in the invisible without losing himself on the thin line which exists between the material and the various so-called higher mental, astral, and etheric spheres of consciousness. An absence of planets in the air signs shows his ability to bypass the logical, restrictive forces of mind in order to create a direct connection with the universal or collective mind of Man.

C. Sun, Moon, Ascendant, and Their Interrelationship

In its highest manifestation Pisces is concerned with the sacrifice of self for the well-being of others (hence the symbolism of the fish for the martyrdom of the Christ). Cayce's Pisces Sun is placed in the Eighth House. This astrological domicile is particularly concerned with the regeneration of energy; therefore positively oriented people with a strong placement of planets in Pisces are potential healers. Cayce is, of course, a primary example of this tendency. The multi-leveled nature of Pisces in connection with the Eighth House (and a strong Pluto) enabled Cayce to probe deeply into the true nature of a person's being, to find the root of his or her illness, and to prescribe a cure.

Cayce's Moon is in the generous sign of its exaltation, Taurus.[1] Because the Moon is only 4 degrees from an exact conjunction with the Midheaven, Cayce's work put him in touch with the general public. Because the Moon is the ruler of his Twelfth House, his career entailed a knowledge of humanity's "underside"—the collective unconscious. The Twelfth House is also associated with hospitals and healers, and of course Cayce could be put in this category. The conjunction of the Moon with Neptune increased Cayce's mystical union and his ability to communicate with all humanity, regardless of social class or ethnic distinctions. This trait is furthered by the conjunction of Uranus with the Ascendant.

Leo is rising, giving Cayce a warm and open nature. The Taurus-Leo combination of the Moon-Ascendant lends him great determination and abundant energy. The Sun-Moon are not, however, in an aspect which can lead to a dissipation of vital energy through a lack of union between inner drives and external circumstances. A good example is the duality of Cayce's

---

[1] We are dealing with a human being who represents the positive side of almost every configuration in his chart. In its highest aspect Taurus can be a most generous sign, offering nourishment, protection, and material goods to all people. All in all, Taurus is the sign of "Mother Nature" and is closely associated with our planet, Earth.

life structure: an "ordinary" citizen with comparatively little psychic power while awake (Sun), but a seer, prophet, and healer while asleep (Moon).

D. Weighing the Planets

1. Ruler of the Chart.

Uranus, Cayce's chart ruler, governs electricity; its exact placement on the Ascendant (physical body) enabled Edgar Cayce to use his body as a radio receiver, picking up and transmitting electrical impulses from higher planes of consciousness. Uranus square the Moon, however, results in a tendency to overstrain and overwork. During World War II, when families inquired about the life or death of their children overseas, Edgar Cayce exhausted himself by increasing his little psychic power while awake (Sun), but a seer, reading from two to ten hours a day. His premature death in 1945 (just after the end of the war) has sometimes been attributed to this factor.

2. Most Elevated Planet.

Pluto in Taurus is elevated in the Tenth House and is a true focal point of the chart, especially because it is configurated with the Moon and the Midheaven. Since Cayce always gave his messages and prognostications while in a state of complete trance, it can be said that he was "asleep" and unaware of what he was saying during these sessions. The alignment of Pluto, Moon, and Midheaven allowed the universal forces of the collective mind of Man (Pluto)[2] to express themselves through the vehicle of Cayce's personal subconscious (Moon). The subconscious is, of course, most fully in operation during sleep, when the rational mind is put to rest. Cayce's pronouncements while in

---

[2] The term invented by Jung, "collective unconscious of Man," is also applicable here. What is meant is basically the source and memory of all stages of evolution past, present, and future which have been, are, and will be manifested on Earth. Compare the functions of Pluto in the charts of Jung, Stalin, and Cayce.

this state brought him world prominence (Midheaven), especially after his own death (Pluto elevated).

Uranus is square Pluto in angular Houses. This influence made many of Cayce's prophecies extremely disturbing; they foretold of cataclysmic events and social upheavals. In a personal sense Cayce was a victim of such a world catastrophe—World War II— since his extreme efforts during that period may be said to have killed him. The square of Pluto to the Ascendant illustrates his ability to bring light to various mysteries through the submergence of his own identity (Ascendant) when he was in trance.

3. Other Angular Planets.

Located on the cusp, Mercury and Saturn in Pisces have a great deal of influence on the affairs of the Eighth House. They are, however, technically placed in the Seventh and also influence this domain. Pisces, governing the limited and afflicted, is the sign of the sufferer and the server. The Seventh House is the area of the consultant and rules the other people in one's life. Cayce worked as a psychic diagnostician. People came to him who were unable to get help elsewhere, and he served them. He was able to communicate with his fellows (Mercury) by concentrating fully (Saturn) on their problems. In this way he could free them from their afflictions (Pisces). The prominence of Saturn shows a deep sense of responsibility and commitment.

E. Major Configurations

The reader will note the lack of planetary T-Squares, Grand Trines, and oppositions in Edgar Cayce's chart. The absence of oppositions especially enabled him to view objectively the conflicts and problems of the people who came to him for help, without his personally becoming involved in these difficulties. This ability left the equilibrium of his own life in his own hands; he was given the opportunity to control the use of his vital energy, a factor contributing to the success of his work. However the lack of oppositions also led to an unbalanced state, resulting in his total and fatal exhaustion. (Compare the absence of oppositions in this chart with Isadora Duncan's.)

F. House-by-House Analysis

1. Second House: Finances.

Mercury is the ruler of this unoccupied House; before discovering his vocation, Edgar Cayce earned money in several mercurial positions: insurance salesman, bookstore clerk, and photographer (Mercury in Pisces is a sign of photography). Mercury conjoined Saturn is reasonably well-aspected at the cusp of the Eighth. This indicates that Cayce acquired funds at the right time through serving the needs of others.

2. Third House: Brothers, Sisters, Education, Communications.

A well-aspected Venus rules this unoccupied House, showing the harmony which existed between Edgar Cayce and his four sisters. He remained close friends with them and their families throughout his life, and there was great love and loyalty among them. (Venus is sextile the Moon and both bodies are in their sign of exaltation.) Venus in Pisces can bring an inclination toward laziness, and Cayce was not overly fond of school. He often needed the aid of his Spirit Teachers (Saturn in Pisces) to pass his courses. Venus conjoined Mercury gave him a fondness for mystical literature, and the location of Saturn between these two planets contributed to the manifestation of this interest in the traditional area of the Bible, which he read and reread many times.

3. Fourth House: Father, Family, Foundations.

Edgar Cayce's father, Leslie, is designated by Scorpio on the cusp of this House; he was a justice of the peace and a man with connections in local politics. (Mars is in Capricorn, sign of government, and Pluto is in the Tenth House of government.) Pluto is square the Ascendant, revealing an underlying friction between the two. In spite of the lack of closeness with his father, Cayce had a relatively harmonious family life (Mars in Capricorn trine Moon in Taurus).

4. Fifth House: Speculation, Children.

Jupiter, ruler of the Fifth House, is in its fall and square the Sun. This position shows Edgar Cayce's inability to speculate on money matters. Even when he attempted to solicit funds for his school and hospital, he was severely reprimanded and arrested. (Jupiter square the Sun brings legal difficulties.) An exalted and well-aspected Mars in this house, however, demonstrates the great affection between Cayce and his sons. One son, Hugh Lynn, worked alongside his father during his life and currently heads the Edgar Cayce Foundation, ARE (Association for Research and Enlightenment).

5. Sixth House: Employees.

Saturn, planet of loyalty, is the ruler of the Sixth House. It can be said to describe Gladys Davis, Cayce's secretary, who worked for him from the time she was eighteen years old until Cayce's death, almost twenty-two years later. Gladys was very devoted to Cayce (Saturn conjoined with Venus) and was considered part of the family. The placement of Saturn in Pisces shows the subjugation of her personal life (she did not marry until after Cayce's death) to continued work with him.

6. Seventh House: Partnerships, Marriage.

Independent Uranus corules the Seventh House; accordingly, Edgar Cayce found great difficulty in working with others. It was therefore necessary for him to be a loner in this respect. His solitude is further emphasized by the placement of Saturn in the Seventh House.

In marriage, however, Cayce was most fortunate

(the Venus-Moon sextile certainly indicates his successful relationships with women). Gertrude Evans Cayce, his wife, shared his life and was completely devoted and loyal to him (Saturn conjunct Venus). They were married while they were quite young, and she passed away only a few months after Cayce's own death.

7. Eighth House: Regeneration, Other People's Resources.

Edgar Cayce was primarily a healer, his Sun (center of Being) being placed in the Eighth House. Venus placed here in Pisces and sextile the Taurus Moon shows that he obtained material goods in strange and wonderful ways. During the time of greatest want his family's needs were met; mysterious checks appeared in the mail, and firewood was miraculously available. His ability to generate life extended to plants as well as to people; he found great joy in gardening—another influence of this particular Venus-Moon sextile.

8. Ninth House: Dreams, Visions.

The conjunction of the Moon with Neptune in this House shows an ability to contact higher planes of consciousness while in a sleeplike state. Neptune is sextile the Sun, permitting some of Cayce's psychic powers to manifest themselves while he was awake; he had the ability to see other people's auras.

9. Eleventh House: Ideals, Friendships.

Mercury, the ruler of the Eleventh House, is in Pisces and many of Edgar Cayce's playmates as a child were Beings of the invisible realms. (Pisces rules the unseen.) His ideals were directly connected with the betterment of humanity through the use of the forces of Light. In a practical sense, Cayce envisioned the founding of a hospital (Pisces rules hospitals) and an institute where his findings could be made useful. Cayce met many distinguished people (Mercury conjoined with Saturn) during his lifetime, but his true friends were few and usually younger than himself (Mercury rules youth).

10. Twelfth House: Hidden Part of Life, Occult Research.

Placement of the House ruler (Moon) on the Midheaven shows that Cayce made a major impact on the world by bringing his occult findings before the public.

G. General Analysis of Events in the Life

A significant event in Edgar Cayce's life was his initial discovery of his own gift of healing. For several months he had been afflicted with a throat condition that did not permit him to speak above a whisper. Several physicians and hypnotists had tried to effect a cure, but none had succeeded. On March 31, 1901, when Al Layne hypnotized Cayce, he made a completely detailed medical prognosis of his own condition, suggesting a cure for himself which effectively relieved the condition.

At this period Cayce's progressions and transits are truly extraordinary. The intuitive powers of Uranus were brought to the surface of Cayce's consciousness as the progressed Sun formed a trine to its position at the Ascendant. At the same time progressed Mercury conjoined the Sun in the Eighth House, and the progressed Ascendant formed a Grand Trine in Virgo with Mars in Capricorn and the Taurean Moon. These aspects indicate a practical link between mind and matter. Transiting Mars trined Pluto, awakening the hidden energy which effected the cure and, more important, opened Cayce's channel to the collective mind. In addition, Jupiter sextiled Mercury, giving the opportunity to raise his consciousness, and Mercury conjoined Saturn, effecting the deep probe of the mind whose secrets were now unlocked.

A difficult time in Edgar Cayce's life was connected with his arrest for fortune telling in New York City. On February 28, 1931, Cayce was taken into custody by an undercover policewoman after he had given her a reading. He had come to New York to raise funds for his hospital and university, since his major benefactor had been impoverished by the stock-market crash. At that time his progressed Venus (ruler of his Midheaven) was square his Ascendant, while his progressed Sun was square Uranus and the Ascendant. The net effects of these aspects were to bring about sudden incidents which would question and challenge his public image. Its manifestation as a conflict with the authorities is shown by transiting Jupiter (law) opposing Mars, indicating a personal confrontation with the former. The case was immediately dismissed. Cayce's natal chart shows no serious conflict with the law (the Moon and Neptune are trine Jupiter and Mars and Venus are in exaltation). This is, therefore, a very good example of how the development of natural tendencies can work to modify seemingly adverse transits and progressions.

The study of Cayce's life, work, and methodology should be investigated by the student. This beautiful soul is an outstanding example of a highly developed clairvoyant and worker for the cause of humanity. The greatest Master is always the most devoted Servant.

APPENDIX: ANSWERS TO EXERCISES

The following are those answers which the reader cannot find directly within the body of the text:

Part II, Chapter 11

page 146

A. New York = EST; Los Angeles = PST; Paris = GMT; Rome = CET; Amsterdam = GMT; London = GMT; Madrid = GMT.
B. London = 1:00 a.m.; New York = 8:00 p.m.; Los Angeles = 5:00 p.m.
C. Denver = 1:15 p.m.; San Francisco = 12:15 p.m.; Geneva = 9:15 p.m.; Philadelphia = 3:15 p.m.
D. 1. 3/1—8:07 A.M. GMT
    2. 3/1—5:19 P.M. GMT
    3. 3/2—3:01 A.M. GMT
    4. 3/1—11:40 A.M. GMT
    5. 2/28—11:14 P.M. GMT

page 149
1. 10:23 P.M. LMT
2. 9:23 A.M. LMT
3. 4:19 P.M. LMT
4. 1:50 A.M. LMT

page 151
1. 8:19 A.M. CST
2. 3:48 P.M. MST
3. 4:17 A.M. GMT
4. 12:21 P.M. EST

Chapter 12

page 163

1.   12:08:09
    + 3:56
    +   39
    +   55
    ─────────────
     15:64:103 = <u>16:05:43</u>

2.   13:22:06
    − 2:42
    −   27
    ─────────
     10:39:39
    + 1:22
    ─────────────
     10:40:61 = <u>10:41:01</u>

3.   16:30:24
    − 9:22
    −   1:34
    ─────────
     7:07:50
    +   58
    ─────────────
     7:07:108 = <u>7:08:48</u>

page 165

1a.   May 22, 1947
     New York City
     Long. 74W—Lat. 40N43

     3:00 P.M. EDST
    − 1:00
    ──────────────
     2:00 P.M. EST
    + 04
    ──────────────
     2:04 P.M. LMT

     3:57:04
    + 2:04
    +   21
    +   50
    ──────────────
     5:61:75 = <u>6:02:15</u> (Local Sidereal Time)

House Cusps

Asc. = 0 ♎ 52	7th. = 0 ♈ 52
2nd. = 27 ♎	8th. = 27 ♈
3rd. = 27 ♏	9th. = 27 ♉
4th. = 1 ♑	M.C. = 1 ♋
5th. = 5 ♒	11th. = 5 ♌
6th. = 5 ♓	12th. = 5 ♍

(♐ intercepted in the 3rd; ♊ intercepted in the 9th.)

1b. December 12,1958
   Denver, Colorado
   Long. 105W—Lat. 39N45
   3:00 A.M. MST (exactly on time zone meridian so
      3:00 A.M. also = LMT)
      17:22:43
   −9
   −   1:30
      ‾‾‾‾‾‾‾‾
      8:21:13
   +   1:10
      ‾‾‾‾‾‾‾‾
      8:22:23 = Local Sidereal Time

House Cusps

Asc. = 28 ♎ 07	7th. = 28 ♈ 07
2nd. = 26 ♏	8th. = 26 ♉
3rd. = 28 ♐	9th. = 28 ♊
4th. = 3 ♒	M.C. = 3 ♌
5th. = 6 ♓	11th. = 6 ♍
6th. = 5 ♈	12th. = 5 ♎

(♑ intercepted in 3rd; ♋ intercepted in 9th.)

Chapter 13

page 190

1a. Moon = 24 ♐ 17 = 264° 17′
    + Asc. = 10 ♉ 14 = 40   14
                      ‾‾‾‾‾‾‾‾‾‾
                       304   31
                    + 360   00
                      ‾‾‾‾‾‾‾‾‾‾
                       664   31
    − Sun = 19 ♓ 20 = 349   20
                      ‾‾‾‾‾‾‾‾‾‾
                       315   11
    Fortuna (⊕)   = 15 ♒ 11

Note: 360° has to be added to the sum of the Asc. and
Moon as the Sun's longitudinal position is greater
than that sum.

1b. Moon = 19 ♓ 20 = 349°   20′
 · + Asc. = 24 ♐ 17 = 264   17
                       613   37
  − Sun = 10 ♉ 14 = 40   14
                       573   23
                 − 360   00
                       213   23
  Fortuna (⊕)   =   3 ♏ 23

Note: In order to ascertain the zodiacal long. of the Part
of Fortune, 360° had to be subtracted from the
total as this figure is greater than 360.

1c.   Moon = 19 ♓ 20 = 349°   20′
   + Asc. = 10 ♉ 14 = 40   14
                       389   14
   − Sun = 24 ♐ 17 = 264   17
                       125   17
   Fortuna (⊕)   =   5 ♌ 17

Chapter 14

page 215
1. 1.   9 ♊ — 9 ♍
   2.   6 ♋ — 6 ♎
   3. 21 ♋ — 21 ♎
   4.   4 ♍ — 4 ♐

2. 1.   1 ♈ — 1 ♊
   2. 12 ♉ — 12 ♋
   3. 27 ♊ — 27 ♌
   4.   0 ♋ — 0 ♍

Chapter 13, page 192

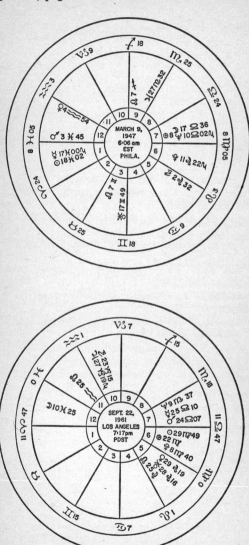

BIBLIOGRAPHY

Durgnat, Raymond and Kobal, John, *Greta Garbo*, E. P. Dutton, New York, 1965.

Gibson, Walter B., and Young, Morris N., *Houdini on Magic*, Dover, New York, 1954.

Jung, Carl G., *Memories, Dreams, Reflections*, Pantheon Books, New York, 1973.

MacDougall, Alan Ross, *Isadora, A Revolutionary in Art and Love*, Thomas Nelson and Sons, Nashville, Tenn.

New York Committee to Free Angela Davis, *A Political History of Angela Davis*.

Oken, Alan C., *As Above, So Below*, Bantam Books, New York, 1973.

Payne, Robert, *The Rise and Fall of Stalin*, Simon & Schuster, New York, 1965.

Stearn, Jess, *Edgar Cayce, The Sleeping Prophet*, Doubleday & Co., New York, 1967.

Steiniger, Klaus, *Free Angela Davis—Hero of the Other America*.

Sugrue, Thomas, *There Is a River: The Story of Edgar Cayce*, Dell, New York, 1970.

Terry, Walter, *Isadora Duncan, Her Life, Her Art, Her Legacy*, Dodd, Mead & Co., New York.

Zierold, Norman, *Garbo*, Popular Library, New York, 1971.

INDEX

Acceleration of the interval, 154
Adjusted Calculation Date, 299
Age of Aquarius, 7, 325
Age of Pisces, 325
Air (element), 65, 366
Alaska Standard Time, 143
Alleluieva, Nadezhda, 342
Angular Houses, 102–8
A/P Table of Houses, 24
Applying aspects, 209
Approximate solar chart, 19
Aquarius, 65, 66, 81–82, 110, 204, 293,
  320, 349, 354
  Age of, 7, 325
  and Aries, 204
  in First House, 107
  Jupiter in, 96, 312, 330, 333
  and Leo polarity, 79–82
  Mars in, 94
  Mercury in, 91, 101
  Moon in, 89, 209, 348
  Pluto in, 101
  Saturn in, 98, 101, 320, 357, 362,
    368, 370
  Sun in, 88, 101, 306, 348
  Uranus in, 101, 204
  Venus in, 92–93
Arabian astrology, 185
ARE (Association for Research and
  Enlightenment), 381
Aries, 35, 66, 67, 107, 202, 204, 207,
  294, 328, 334, 357, 358
  and Aquarius, 204
  Ascendant in, 325, 327, 328, 329, 332
  and Cancer, 202
  and Capricorn, 202
  in First House, 104
  and Gemini, 204
  Jupiter in, 95
  and Leo, 203
  and Libra, 200
  and Libra polarity, 67–70
  Mars in, 93, 101
  Mercury in, 89–90
  Moon in, 88, 328, 329, 330
  and Sagittarius, 203
  Saturn in, 96, 101, 336, 338
  and Scorpio, 206
  Sun in, 87, 101, 357, 363
  and Taurus, 207
  Venus in, 91, 101, 329, 361
  and Virgo, 206
Arthur, Gavin, 206
Ascella, 352
Ascendant, 188, 277, 288–89, 327, 328,
  336, 357, 365, 368, 376, 377, 378,
  379, 383
  in Aries, 325, 327, 328, 329, 332
  aspects of, 263–64

  in Capricorn, 317, 319, 342, 357, 361
  in Gemini, 366, 367, 371
  Jupiter in, 338
  and Mars trine, 344
  and Moon opposition, 264
  and Neptune square, 322
  and Pluto conjunction, 367, 374
  and Pluto square, 367, 381
  and Sun square, 384
  in Taurus, 348, 350
  and Uranus conjunction, 377
  and Uranus opposition, 369
  and Venus square, 384
  and Venus trine, 344
  in Virgo, 383
Ascendant House, 103–7
Aspectarian, The, 283–84
Aspects, 86, 193, 212
  applying, 209
  of Ascendant, 263–64
  of challenge, 194
  dynamic, 200
  of flow, 194
  of Jupiter, 252–53, 261–62, 304
  major, 193, 198–205
  of Mars, 247–51, 304
  measuring of, 209–11
  of Mercury, 234, 241, 304
  of Midheaven, 263–64
  minor, 193, 205–8
  of Moon, 225–34
  progressed, 305–7
  of promise, 207
  safe, 204
  of Saturn, 256–60, 304
  separating, 209
  of slower-moving planets, 252–62
  of Sun, 218–25, 304
  of swifter-moving planets, 218–51
  of Uranus, 260–61
  variable, 198–99
  of Venus, 241–47, 304
Associates, 294
Association for Research and Enlightenment (ARE), 381
Astrologer, the, 9
Astrologer's Astronomical Handbook
  (Mayo), 27, 139
Astrological affinities, 42
Astrological Aspects (Carter), 218
Astrology, 4, 5
Astrology (Mayo), 39n.
Astrology: The Cosmic Science
  (Hickey), 218
Atlantic Standard Time, 143
Atonement of Gosta Berling, The
  (film), 373

391

Attraction, 47
Augustin Daly Dance Company, 334

Baudelaire, Charles, 265–66
Basic character traits, 42
Beatles, The, 291, 294
Bell, Alexander Graham, 268–69
Bonaparte, Napoleon, 269–71
Brahe, Tycho, 11
Brothers, 331, 370, 380
Burghölzli Psychiatric Clinic, 324

Cadent Houses, 110–11, 307
Calculated Sidereal Time, 155, 163
Cancer, 66, 107, 294, 350
    and Aries, 202
    and Capricorn polarity, 76–79
    in First House, 105
    Jupiter in, 95, 101
    Mars in, 93, 101
    Mercury in, 90, 323
    Moon in, 88–89, 101
    Neptune in, 101, 368
    Saturn in, 97, 101
    Sun in, 87
    Venus in, 91–92, 322
Capricorn, 65, 66, 78–79, 108, 202,
    319, 338, 339, 357, 358, 372, 381
    Ascendant in, 317, 319, 342, 357, 361
    and Aries, 202
    and Cancer polarity, 76–79
    in First House, 106
    Jupiter in, 96, 101
    Mars in, 94, 101, 204, 383
    Mercury in, 91
    Midheaven in, 325, 328
    Moon in, 89, 101, 277, 294, 295
    Neptune in, 99, 101
    rising, 319
    Saturn in, 97–98, 101
    Sun in, 88, 337
    Uranus in, 369, 370
    Venus in, 92
Cardinal qualities, 66, 67
Career, 294, 333
Carlotta, Empress of Mexico, 271–72
Carter, Charles E. O., 218
Cayce, Charles E. O., 218
Cayce, Edgar, 59, 375–84
Cayce, Gertrude Evans, 382
Cayce, Hugh Lynn, 381
Cayce, Leslie, 380
Central European Time, 143
Central Standard Time, 143
Challenge, aspects of, 194
Character traits, 42
Children, 323, 331, 381
Christian Science, 267–68
Circle, the (as symbol), 31
Clothing, 371
Collin, R., 39n.
Commerce, The Part of, 185n.
Communication(s), 292–93, 322, 331,
    341, 361, 370, 380
    and Consolidation, 237
    and Expansion, 236
    and Feelings, 225
    and Illumination, 239
    and Intuition, 238
    and Personal Drive, 235
    and Personal Magnetism, 234
    and Regeneration, 240
    and Will, 219
Configuration, planetary, 217–64

Confinement, 324, 372
Conjunction, 193n., 198–200, 210,
    214–15
Consolidation, 54
    and Communication, 237
    and Expansion, 252
    and Feelings, 229
    and Illumination, 257
    and Intuition, 256
    and Personal Drive, 248
    and Personal Magnetism, 243
    and Regeneration, 259
    and Will, 221
Constellations, Zodiac of, 15n.
Correction for Longitude, 154–55
Correspondences, Law of, 5n.
Cosmic Cross, 271–72
Cosmobiological Institute
    (W. Germany), 10
Creative expression, 293, 323, 331, 341
Critical degrees, 282–83
Cross, the (as symbol), 32
Counter-parallels, 208
Cusps, 16

Dalton's Table of Houses for
    Northern Latitudes, 24
Darling, H. F., 10
Davis, Angela, 346–54
Davis, Gladys, 381
Daylight Savings Time, 140, 149–50
De Vore, 187
Death, 323, 333, 343, 362, 372
Declination, 208
Destiny vs free will, 296–312
Detriment (planetary), 86, 101
Deutsche Ephemeride, Die, 24
Dignity (planetary), 86, 101
Directions, 299
Dishonor (planetary), 86, 101
Dispositor, 281
Distant lands, 323
Diurnal Motion Tables, 168–79
Divorce, The Part of, 185n.
Doane, Doris Chase, 26, 149
Dobyns, Zipporah, 10
Dot, the (as symbol), 32
Double Summer Time, 140
Dove (Scorpio type), 72
Dragon's Head (Moon), 63, 169n.
Dragon's Tail (Moon), 63, 169n.
Dreams, 382
Dynamic aspects, 202
Dzhugashvili, Josif Vissarionovich
    (see Stalin, Joseph)

Eagle (Scorpio type), 72
Earth (element), 65, 341, 357, 365, 376
Earth (planet), 377n.
Eastern European Time, 143
Eastern Standard Time, 143
Easy Opposition, 267–68
Ebertin, Reinhold, 10
Ecliptic, the, 15n.
Eddy, Mary Baker, 267–68
Edgar Cayce Foundation, 381
Education, 341, 380
Eighth House, 109, 294, 321, 323, 333,
    343, 362, 363, 372, 377, 382
    Jupiter in, 125, 323
    Mars in, 123
    Mercury in, 119–20

ighth House *(continued)*
Moon in, 118
Pluto in, 134
Sun in, 116, 382, 383
Venus in, 121, 351
lements (in nature), 65, 277–78,
287–88
leventh House, 109–10, 294, 334, 362,
372, 373, 382
Jupiter in, 125
Mars in, 123
Mercury in, 120
Moon in, 118–19, 334
Neptune in, 132
Pluto in, 134
Saturn in, 127–28
Sun in, 116
Uranus in, 129–30
Venus in, 121–22
mployees, 323, 381
mployment, 323, 332, 361, 371
ncyclopedia of Astrology (De Vore),
187
ndocrine glands, 36
phemeris, 19
qual House method, 153, 160–63
soteric teaching, 5
ssenine, Serge, 332
volutionary potential, 208
xact sunrise chart, 19
xaltation (planetary), 87, 101, 366,
368, 377, 380, 384
xotic teaching, 6
xpansion, 51
and Communication, 236
and Consolidation, 252
and Feelings, 228
and Illumination, 254
and Intuition, 253
and Personal Drive, 247
and Personal Magnetism, 242
and Regeneration, 255
and Will, 221

aculty of Astrological Studies, The
(London), 161n.
all (planetary), 87, 101
amily, 380
eelings:
and Communication, 225
and Consolidation, 229
and Expansion, 228
and Illumination, 232
and Intuition, 231
and Personal Drive, 227
and Personal Magnetism, 226
and Regeneration, 233
and Will, 218
ifth House, 109, 293, 323, 331, 333,
341, 370, 371, 381
Jupiter in, 124
Mars in, 122
Mercury in, 119, 370, 371
Moon in, 117–18
Neptune in, 131
Pluto in, 133
Saturn in, 126
Sun in, 115–6, 306, 365, 370, 371
Uranus in, 129, 327, 330, 331, 339
Venus in, 121, 306
nal dispositor, 281–82
nances, 322, 331, 360, 370, 380
nger of Fate, The, 206n., 268–69

Fire (element), 65
First House, 103–7, 338–39, 349, 370
Aquarius in, 107
Aries in, 104
Cancer in, 105
Capricorn in, 106
Gemini in, 105
Jupiter in, 124
Leo in, 105
Libra in, 105–6
Mars in, 122, 349
Mercury in, 119
Moon in, 117
Neptune in, 130, 368
Pisces in, 107
Pluto in, 132, 325
Sagittarius in, 106
Saturn in, 126, 320, 324, 353, 362
Scorpio in, 106
Sun in, 115, 294
Taurus in, 104, 328
Uranus in, 128
Venus in, 120
Virgo in, 105
Fischer, Bobby, 274–76
Fixed Cross, 321, 363
Fixed qualities, 66
Flow, aspects of, 194
Foreign travel, 294, 343
Form (Soul-Moon), 195
Fortuna, 185
Fortune, The Part of, 185–90, 278, 353
Foundations, 293, 361, 380
Fourth House, 107–8, 293, 321, 322,
331, 361, 380
Jupiter in, 124, 350
Mars in, 122
Mercury in, 119
Moon in, 117, 294
Neptune in, 130–31
Pluto in, 339, 340, 350
Saturn in, 126
Sun in, 115
Uranus in, 128–29
Venus in, 121, 368
Franklin, Benjamin, 149
Free will *vs* destiny, 296–312
Freud, Sigmund, 324, 325
Friends, 294
Friendships, 372, 382

Gandhi, Mahatma, 272–74
Garbo, Greta, 364–74
Gemini, 65, 66, 73–75, 111, 204, 341,
371
and Aries, 204
Ascendant in, 366, 367, 371
in First House, 105
Jupiter in, 95, 101
Mars in, 93, 349
Mercury in, 90, 101
Moon in, 88, 306, 307
and Sagittarius polarity, 73–76
Saturn in, 97
Sun in, 87, 328, 329
Uranus in, 349
Venus in, 91
Gender, 66, 280
Geniture, the, 14
Geometry of the spheres, 193–216
Grand Cross, 271–72
Grand Trine, 272–74, 291, 293, 294,
295, 312, 351

Great Centers of Cosmic
    Consciousness, 297
Greenwich Mean Time, 140–47
Gustafsson, Alva, 370–71

Hatha yoga, 35
Health, 323, 332, 341, 351, 371
Hemisphere emphasis, 286–87
Hesse, Hermann, 320
Hickey, Isabel, 218
Hidden and restricted things, 362, 383
Higher education, 323, 372
Home, the, 293, 322, 331
Honor, (planetary) 86, 101
Hopes, 362
Horoscope Calculation Sheet, 165–67,
    169, 176, 186, 279
Houdin, Robert, 360
Houdini, Beatrice, 358
Houdini, Harry, 355–63
House cusps, 153
House of Death, 109
House of Friends and Associates, 110
House of Immediate Family, 110
House of Others, 107
House of Self, 107
House structure, 16
Houses, The, 112–13
    Angular, 102–8
    Ascendant, 103–7
    Cadent, 110–11
    pattern of the, 102–13
    Placidean, 160
    planets in the, 115–35
    Succedent, 108–10
    Table of, 156–57

I Ching, 320
Ideals, 294, 362, 382
Illumination:
    and Communication, 239
    and Consolidation, 257
    and Expansion, 254
    and Feelings, 232
    and Intuition, 260
    and Personal Drive, 250
    and Personal Magnetism, 245
    and Regeneration, 261
    and Will, 223
Inconjunction, 193, 206–7
Individuality, 41
Inner temple, 5, 7
Intercepted signs, 159
International Meridian Conference
    (1884), 141
Interplanetary relationships, 217–64
Intuition, 56
    and Communication, 238
    and Consolidation, 256
    and Expansion, 253
    and Feelings, 231
    and Illumination, 260
    and Personal Drive, 249
    and Personal Magnetism, 244
    and Regeneration, 261
    and Will, 222

Jackson, George, 353
Jackson, Jesse, 353
Jobs, 293–94
Jones, Marc Edmund, 287
Jung, Carl G., 10, 316–25

Jung, Emma, 321
Jupiter, 38, 111, 174, 209, 292, 294,
    309, 310, 312, 331, 342, 350, 353,
    361, 362, 372, 381, 384
    in Aquarius, 96, 312, 330, 333
    in Aries, 95
    in Ascendant, 338
    aspects of, 252–53, 304
    in Cancer, 95, 101
    in Capricorn, 96, 101
    in Eighth House, 125, 323
    in Eleventh House, 125
    in Fifth House, 124
    in First House, 124
    in Fourth House, 124, 350
    in Gemini, 95, 101
    in the Houses, 124–26
    in Leo, 95
    in Libra, 95, 320
    and Mars configuration, 247–48
    and Mars opposition, 213, 384
    and Mars sextile, 320, 323
    and Mars trine, 312
    and Mercury configuration, 236–37
    and Mercury opposition, 292, 361
    and Mercury sextile, 383
    and Mercury square, 329, 331, 332,
        333, 371
    and Mercury trine, 307
    and Midheaven conjunction, 344
    and Midheaven opposition, 353
    and Midheaven trine, 324, 344, 372
    and Moon configuration, 228–29
    and Moon conjunction, 342
    and Moon opposition, 343
    and Moon square, 353
    and Moon trine, 384
    and natal chart, 52
    and Neptune configuration, 254–55
    and Neptune square, 329, 333
    and Neptune trine, 312, 373
    in Ninth House, 125
    orb of, 304, 308
    in Pisces, 96, 101
    and Pluto configuration, 255–56
    in Sagittarius, 96, 101, 350, 363
    and Saturn configuration, 252–53
    and Saturn conjunction, 292
    and Saturn semi-sextile, 338
    and Saturn trine, 320
    in Scorpio, 95–96
    in Second House, 124
    in Seventh House, 125
    in the signs, 95–96
    in Sixth House, 124–25
    and Sun configuration, 221
    and Sun parallel, 208
    and Sun sextile, 338
    and Sun square, 381
    and Sun trine, 208, 331, 332, 333
    in Taurus, 95, 277
    in Tenth House, 125
    in Third House, 124
    transitory, 312
    in Twelfth House, 125–26, 372
    and Uranus configuration, 253–54
    and Uranus opposition, 342
    and Uranus trine, 312
    and Venus configuration, 242
    and Venus conjuction, 353
    and Venus square, 213
    and Venus trine, 348, 350, 352
    in Virgo, 95, 101, 362

Karma, 12, 295
Kepler, Johann, 11
Key phrases, 68, 70, 71, 73, 74, 76, 78, 80, 82, 85
Key words, 68, 70, 71, 73, 75, 76, 78, 80, 82, 85
Kite Formation, 274–76
Kundalini yoga, 35

Law of Correspondences, The, 5n.
Law of Karma, 12
Laws of Motion (Newton's), 12
Layne, Al, 383
Lennon, John, 64, 214, 277–78, 283–84, 287, 289, 291, 292, 293, 294, 295
Leo, 65, 66, 79–80, 109, 317, 319, 356, 377
    and Aquarius polarity, 79–82
    and Aries, 203
    in First House, 105
    Jupiter in, 95
    Mars in, 93
    Mercury in, 90, 101
    Moon in, 89
    Pluto in, 101, 277
    rising, 377
    Saturn in, 97, 101
    Sun in, 87–88, 101, 318, 319, 323
    Uranus in, 101, 203, 291, 292, 321, 330
    Venus in, 92, 368, 369, 371, 373, 374
Libra, 65, 66, 69, 108, 343
    and Aries, 200
    and Aries polarity, 67–68
    in First House, 105–6
    Jupiter in, 95, 320
    Mars in, 94, 101, 277, 294
    Mercury in, 90
    Moon in, 89
    Neptune in, 351–52
    Pluto in, 99–100
    Saturn in, 97, 101
    Sun in, 88, 101, 277
    Uranus in, 98–99
    Venus in, 92, 101
Life (Spirit-Sun), 195
Local Mean Time, 140, 147–48, 153, 167
Local Sidereal Time, 153–60
Longitudes and Latitudes in the United States, 27
Longitudes and Latitudes through the World, 27
Longitudinal correction, 154–55
Longitudinal divisions, 141
Love, Universal, 59
Love affairs, 371
Lowell, Percival, 61

Major aspects, 193, 198–205
Manifested Universe (Matter-Ascendant), 195
Mansions of the Moon, 282
Mao Tse-tung, 337
Marriage, 332, 342, 381
Marriage, The Part of, 185n.
Mars, 38, 107, 109, 177, 178, 179, 184, 197, 201, 209, 308, 310, 332, 333, 354, 360, 363, 381
    in Aquarius, 94
    in Aries, 93, 101

    and Ascendant trine, 344
    aspects of, 247–51, 304
    in Cancer, 93
    in Capricorn, 94, 101, 204, 380–81, 383
    in Eighth House, 123
    in Eleventh House, 123
    in Fifth House, 122
    in First House, 122, 349
    in Fourth House, 122
    in Gemini, 93, 349
    in the Houses, 122–24
    and Jupiter configuration, 247–48
    and Jupiter opposition, 213, 384
    and Jupiter sextile, 320, 323
    and Jupiter trine, 312
    in Leo, 90, 93, 101
    in Libra, 90, 94, 277, 294
    and Mercury configuration, 235
    and Mercury conjunction, 363
    and Mercury sextile, 331
    and Mercury square, 334
    and Midheaven conjunction, 324
    and Midheaven opposition, 333
    and Moon configuration, 227–28
    and Moon conjunction, 302
    and Moon square, 209, 328, 330, 331, 333, 381
    and natal chart, 50
    and Neptune configuration, 250
    and Neptune conjunction, 293, 294, 341
    and Neptune trine, 384
    in Ninth House, 123
    orb of, 304, 308
    in Pisces, 94
    and Pluto configuration, 250–51
    and Pluto sextile, 292
    and Pluto trine, 344, 383
    in Sagittarius, 94, 320, 371
    and Saturn configuration, 248–49
    and Saturn conjunction, 199
    and Saturn sextile, 320
    in Scorpio, 94
    in Second House, 122
    in Seventh House, 123
    in the signs, 93–94
    in Sixth House, 122–23, 371
    and Sun configuration, 220–21
    and Sun conjunction, 363
    and Sun square, 370, 371
    and Sun trine, 341
    in Taurus, 93, 203, 209
    in Tenth House, 123
    in Third House, 122, 330, 331
    in Twelfth House, 123–24, 295
    and Uranus configuration, 249
    and Uranus conjunction, 208, 341, 349, 351, 353, 373
    and Uranus sextile, 204
    and Uranus square, 344, 352, 359
    and Uranus trine, 203, 321
    and Venus configuration, 241–42
    and Venus parallel, 208
    and Venus square, 202, 213, 330, 331, 332, 333
    and Venus trine, 203, 371
    in Virgo, 93–94
Master Energy Sources, 297
Material resources, 360, 370
Matter-Ascendant (Manifested Universe), 195
Mayo, Jeff, 27, 139

Maximilian I, Emperor of Mexico,
  272
Measurement of aspects, 209–11
Mental faculties, 292–93
Mercury, 38, 111, 177, 178, 184, 209,
  291, 292, 294, 307, 308, 310, 323,
  324, 329, 331, 341, 342, 343, 344,
  351, 361, 363, 371, 379, 382, 383
  in Aquarius, 91, 101
  in Aries, 89–90
  aspects of, 234–41, 304
  in Cancer, 90, 323
  in Capricorn, 91
  in Eighth House, 119–20
  in Eleventh House, 120
  in Fifth House, 119, 370, 371
  in First House, 119
  in Fourth House, 119
  in Gemini, 90, 101
  in the Houses, 119–20
  and Jupiter configuration, 236–37
  and Jupiter opposition, 292, 361
  and Jupiter sextile, 383
  and Jupiter square, 329, 331, 332,
    333, 371
  and Jupiter trine, 307
  and Mars configuration, 235
  and Mars conjunction, 363
  and Mars sextile, 331
  and Mars square, 334
  and Midheaven trine, 333
  and Moon configuration, 225–26
  and Moon square, 293, 295
  and Neptune configuration, 239–40
  and Neptune conjunction, 329, 332
  and Neptune square, 351, 374
  and Neptune sextile, 370
  and Neptune trine, 302, 352
  in Ninth House, 120
  orb of, 304, 308
  in Pisces, 91, 101, 361, 379, 380, 382
  and Pluto configuration, 240–41
  and Pluto trine, 344
  retrogradation of, 173
  in Sagittarius, 90–91, 101
  and Saturn configuration, 237–38
  and Saturn conjunction, 380, 382,
    383
  and Saturn opposition, 292
  in Scorpio, 90, 278
  in Second House, 119, 295, 360
  in Seventh House, 119
  in the signs, 89–91
  in Sixth House, 119, 323
  and Sun configuration, 219
  and Sun conjunction, 334, 365, 383
  in Taurus, 90, 329
  in Tenth House, 120
  in Third House, 119
  in Twelfth House, 120
  and Uranus configuration, 238
  and Venus configuration, 234–35
  and Venus conjunction, 323, 334,
    380
  and Venus sextile, 344
  in Virgo, 90, 101
Middle European Time, 143
Midheaven, 278, 317, 321, 322, 327,
  336, 365, 376, 378
  aspects of, 263–64
  in Capricorn, 325, 328
  and Jupiter conjunction, 344
  and Jupiter opposition, 353

  and Jupiter trine, 324, 344, 372
  and Mars conjunction, 324
  and Mars opposition, 333
  and Mercury trine, 333
Moon in, 350, 383
  and Moon conjunction, 352–53
  and Moon square, 333
  and Neptune trine, 325, 333
  in Pisces, 373
  and Pluto configuration, 378
  and Pluto trine, 353
  progressed, 324
Sun in, 348
  and Sun conjunction, 263–64
  and Sun opposition, 363
  and Sun trine, 363
  and Uranus sextile, 373
Venus in, 339
  and Venus square, 333–34
Minor aspects, 193, 205–8
Minor variables, 208
Moon, 34, 107, 177, 178, 183, 188, 209,
  288–89, 291, 293, 295, 305, 308,
  309, 312, 321, 333, 336, 339, 340,
  341, 342, 350, 354, 358, 365, 369,
  370, 371, 377, 378
  in Aquarius, 89, 209, 348
  in Aries, 88, 328, 329, 330
  and Ascendant opposition, 264
  aspects of, 225–34
  in Cancer, 88–89, 101
  in Capricorn, 89, 101, 277, 294, 295
  in Eighth House, 118
  in Eleventh House, 118–19, 334
  in Fifth House, 117–18
  in First House, 117
  in Fourth House, 117, 294
  in Gemini, 88, 306, 307
  in the Houses, 117–19
  and Jupiter configuration, 228–29
  and Jupiter conjunction, 342
  and Jupiter opposition, 343
  and Jupiter square, 353
  and Jupiter trine, 384
  in Leo, 89
  in Libra, 89
  Mansions of the, 282
  and Mars configuration, 227–28
  and Mars conjunction, 302
  and Mars square, 209, 328, 330, 331,
    333
  and Mars trine, 381
  and Mercury configuration, 225–26
  and Mercury square, 293, 295
  in Midheaven, 350, 383
  and Midheaven conjunction, 352–53
  and Midheaven square, 333
  and natal chart, 43
  and Neptune configuration, 232–33,
    377
  and Neptune conjunction, 322, 382
  and Neptune trine, 302, 306
  in Ninth House, 118, 306, 334, 363,
    373
  nodes of, 63, 169n., 277, 278
  Northern Node of, 63
  orb of, 308
  in Pisces, 89, 373
  and Pluto configuration, 233–34, 378
  and Pluto conjunction, 324
  and Pluto square, 305, 340, 342
  progressed, 300–2, 303
  in Sagittarius, 89, 357, 361

Moon (*continued*)
  and Saturn configuration, 229–31
  and Saturn conjunction, 374
  and Saturn opposition, 373
  and Saturn square, 353, 372
  and Saturn trine, 350
  in Scorpio, 89, 101
  in Second House, 117
  in Seventh House, 118, 334
  in the signs, 88–89
  in Sixth House, 118
  Southern Node of, 63
  and Sun configuration, 218–19
  and Sun square, 305
  and Sun trine, 302, 337–38, 342, 366
  in Taurus, 88, 101, 318, 365, 370,
    377, 381, 382, 383
  in Tenth House, 118, 334, 348, 373
  in Third House, 117
  in Twelfth House, 119, 328, 329,
    366, 370, 372
  and Uranus configuration, 231–32
  and Uranus conjunction, 302, 306,
    339, 340, 344
  and Uranus square, 321, 378
  and Uranus trine, 344, 358
  and Venus configuration, 226–27
  and Venus conjunction, 199
  and Venus sextile, 380, 382
  and Venus square, 343, 368, 369
  and Venus trine, 305
  in Virgo, 89, 340, 342
Mother, 333
Motion, Laws of (Newton's), 12
Mountain Standard Time, 143
Mutable qualities, 66
Mutual reception, 280–81

Nadir:
  and Pluto, 359
  Venus in, 369
Natal astrology, 14
Natal chart, 14, 139
  Jupiter's function in, 52
  Mars's function in, 50
  Mercury's function in, 45
  Neptune's function in, 59
  Moon's function in, 43
  Saturn's function in, 54
  Sun's function in, 41
  Uranus' function in, 56
  Venus' function in, 47
Natal figure, 14
Natal horoscope, 14
Natal map, 14
Nativity, the, 14
Natural chart, 19
Natus, the, 14
Nearest Sidereal Time, 163, 165
Negative character traits, 42
Negative key words, 69, 70, 71, 73, 75,
  76, 78, 80, 82, 85
Neptune, 38, 111, 174, 209, 293, 295,
  301, 309, 310, 324, 351, 357, 361,
  370, 372
  in Aries, 111
  and Ascendant square, 322
  aspects of, 261–62
  in Cancer, 101, 368
  in Capricorn, 99, 101
  in Eighth House, 131
  in Eleventh House, 132
  in Fifth House, 131

  in First House, 130, 368
  in Fourth House, 130–31
  in the Houses, 130–32
  and Jupiter configuration, 254–55
  and Jupiter square, 329, 333
  and Jupiter trine, 312, 329, 373
  in Libra, 351–52
  and Mars configuration, 250
  and Mars conjunction, 293, 294, 341
  and Mars trine, 384
  and Mercury configuration, 239–40
  and Mercury conjunction, 329, 332
  and Mercury sextile, 370
  and Mercury square, 351, 374
  and Mercury trine, 352
  and Midheaven trine, 325, 333
  and Moon configuration, 232–33
  and Moon conjunction, 322, 377, 382
  and Moon trine, 302, 306
  and natal chart, 59
  in Ninth House, 131
  orb of, 304, 308
  in Pisces, 101, 361
  and Pluto configuration, 261–62
  and Pluto square, 334, 374
  in Sagittarius, 99
  and Saturn configuration, 257–58
  in Second House, 130
  in Seventh House, 131
  in the signs, 99, 101
  in Sixth House, 131, 351–52
  and Sun configuration, 223–24
  and Sun conjunction, 357, 361
  and Sun sextile, 382
  and Sun square, 318, 322
  and Sun trine, 341
  in Taurus, 329
  in Tenth House, 131–32
  in Third House, 130, 322
  in Twelfth House, 132, 295
  and Uranus configuration, 260–61
  and Venus configuration, 245–46
  and Venus conjunction, 361, 373
  and Venus square, 305, 351, 352
  and Venus trine, 325
  in Virgo, 101, 277, 374
Newton, Isaac, 11, 12
Ninth House, 111, 294, 320, 323, 333,
  343, 372, 382
  Jupiter in, 125
  Mars in, 123
  Mercury in, 120
  Moon in, 118, 306, 334, 362–63, 373
  Neptune in, 131
  Pluto in, 134
  Saturn in, 127
  Sun in, 116
  Uranus in, 129
  Venus in, 121
Nixon, Richard M., 337
Nodes of moon, 63, 169*n.*, 277, 278
Noon Sidereal Time, 154
Northern Node of Moon, 63, 169*n.*
Novile, 194

Occult research, 324, 372, 383
Ono, Yoko, 289, 293
Opposition, 194, 200–1, 210, 215
  Easy, 267–68
Orbs:
  planetary, 211–14, 304
  of progressed Moon, 303
  of transiting planets, 308

Other people's resources, 294, 382
Outer temple, 6
Overinfluence, 280

Pacific Standard Time, 147
Parallel of declination, 208
Parallels, 208
Pars Fortuna, 185
Part of Commerce, The, 185n.
Part of Divorce, The, 185n.
Part of Fortune, The, 185-90, 278, 353
Part of Marriage, The, 185n.
Part of Spirit, The, 185n.
Partnerships, 294, 381
Perfection of Values, 59
Permanent logarithms, 182
Personal Drive, 49
    and Communication, 235
    and Consolidation, 248
    and Expansion, 247
    and Feelings, 227
    and Illumination, 250
    and Intuition, 249
    and Personal Magnetism, 241
    and Regeneration, 250
    and Will, 220
Personal finances, 292, 351
Personal Magnetism:
    and Communication, 234
    and Consolidation, 243
    and Expansion, 242
    and Feelings, 226
    and Illumination, 245
    and Intuition, 244
    and Personal Drive, 241
    and Regeneration, 246
    and Will, 219
Personality, 43
Philosophy, 333
Pisces, 35, 66, 83-85, 111, 322, 373, 379
    Age of, 325
    in First House, 107
    Jupiter in, 96, 101
    Mars in, 94
    Mercury in, 91, 101, 361, 379, 380, 382
    Midheaven in, 373
    Moon in, 89, 373
    Neptune in, 101, 361
    Saturn in, 98, 379, 380, 381
    Sun in, 88, 376, 377
    Venus in, 93, 101, 380, 382
    and Virgo polarity, 82-85
Placidean Houses, 160
Placidean system of House division, 153, 160
Planetary detriment, 86, 101
Planetary dignity, 86, 101
Planetary dishonor, 86, 101
Planetary exaltation, 87, 101
Planetary fall, 87, 101
Planetary honor, 86, 101
Planetary Honors and Dishonors, 101
Planetary orbs, 211-14
Planetary stations, 309
Planetary weights, 280
Planets:
    aspects of, 218-64
    configuration of, 217-64
    in the Houses, 115-35
    orbs of, 304, 308
    retrograde, 309

transiting, 308
unaspected, 262-63
Pleasure, 323, 331, 371
Pluto, 35, 38, 109, 174, 209, 291, 301, 305, 309, 310, 312, 321, 323, 333, 334, 339, 340, 359, 367-68, 377, 378, 379
    in Aquarius, 101
    and Ascendant conjunction, 367, 374
    and Ascendant square, 367, 381
    in Eighth House, 134
    in Eleventh House, 134
    in Fifth House, 133
    in First House, 132, 329
    in Fourth House, 133, 339, 340, 350
    in the Houses, 132-34
    and Jupiter configuration, 255-56
    in Leo, 101, 277, 291, 292
    in Libra, 99-100
    and Mars configuration, 250-51
    and Mars sextile, 292
    and Mars trine, 344, 383
    and Mercury configuration, 240-41
    and Mercury trine, 344
    and Midheaven configuration, 378
    and Midheaven trine, 353
    and Moon configuration, 233-34, 378
    and Moon conjunction, 324
    and Moon square, 305, 340, 342
    and Nadir, 359
    and natal chart, 62
    and Neptune configuration, 261-62
    and Neptune square, 334, 374
    in Ninth House, 134
    orb of, 304, 308
    and Saturn configuration, 259-60
    and Saturn square, 320, 324
    and Saturn trine, 370
    in Scropio, 101
    in Second House, 133
    in Seventh House, 133-34
    in the signs, 99-100, 101
    in Sixth House, 133
    and Sun configuration, 224-25
    and Sun opposition, 350
    and Sun square, 370
    in Taurus, 101, 321, 329, 339, 378
    in Tenth House, 134, 378
    in Third House, 133, 359
    in Twelfth House, 134
    and Uranus configuration, 261
    and Uranus opposition, 370
    and Uranus square, 327, 332, 333, 340, 379
    and Venus configuration, 246-47
    and Venus opposition, 339, 342
Positive character traits, 42
Positive key words, 69, 70, 71, 73, 75, 76, 78, 80, 82, 85
Polarities, 67-85
Polarity, 37
Predestination, 296
Prime Meridian, 142
Progressed aspects, 305-7
Progressed horoscope, the, 299-301
Progressed Midheaven, 324
Progressed Moon, 300-2, 303
    orbs of, 303
Progressions, 298-307
Promise, aspect of, 207
Proportional Logarithm Method, 170, 179-92

Qualities, 278, 287–88
Quincunx, 193, 206–7
Quintile, 194, 208, 211, 215

Raphael's Ephemeris, 23
Raphael's Table of Houses for Northern Latitudes, 24
Rational Mind, The, 45
Regeneration, 61, 282
  and Communication, 240
  and Consolidation, 259
  and Expansion, 255
  and Feelings, 233
  and Illumination, 261
  and Intuition, 261
  and Personal Drive, 250
  and Personal Magnetism, 246
  and Will, 224
Religion, 294
Resources, 331
Retrogradation, 173
Retrograde planets, 309
Rising sign, 103
Rod, the (as symbol), 33
Romance, 293, 331
Roots, 331
Rose, Felissa, 299, 301, 304, 305, 306, 311–12
Rudhyar, Dane, 9
Ruler, The, 282, 289–90, 336

Safe aspect, 204
Sagittarius, 65, 66, 75–76, 111, 292, 341, 362
  and Aries, 203
  in First House, 106
  and Gemini polarity, 73–76
  Jupiter in, 96, 101, 350, 363
  Mars in, 94, 320, 371
  Mercury in, 90–91, 101
  Moon in, 89, 357, 361
  Neptune in, 99
  Saturn in, 97, 358
  Sun in, 88, 352
  Venus in, 92, 349
Saturn, 38, 110, 174, 209, 211, 293, 294, 305, 309, 310, 311, 312, 320, 321, 333, 338, 350, 353, 354, 357, 360, 362, 363, 369, 371, 372, 379, 380, 381
  in Aquarius, 98, 101, 320, 357, 362, 368, 370
  in Aries, 96, 101, 336, 338
  aspects of, 256–60, 304
  in Cancer, 97, 101
  in Capricorn, 97–98, 101
  in Eighth House, 127
  in Eleventh House, 127–28
  in Fifth House, 126
  in First House, 126, 320, 324, 353, 362
  in Fourth House, 126
  in Gemini, 97
  in the Houses, 126–28
  and Jupiter configuration, 252–53
  and Jupiter conjunction, 292
  and Jupiter semi-sextile, 338
  and Jupiter trine, 320
  in Leo, 97, 101
  in Libra, 97, 101
  and Mars configuration, 248–49
  and Mars conjunction, 199
  and Mars sextile, 320
  and Mercury configuration, 237–38
  and Mercury conjunction, 380, 382, 383
  and Mercury opposition, 292
  and Midheaven trine, 353
  and Moon configuration, 229–31
  and Moon conjunction, 324
  and Moon opposition, 373
  and Moon square, 353, 372
  and Moon trine, 350
  and natal chart, 54
  and Neptune configuration, 257–58
  in Ninth House, 127
  orb of, 304, 308
  in Pisces, 98, 379, 380, 381
  and Pluto configuration, 259–60
  and Pluto square, 320, 324
  and Pluto trine, 370
  in Sagittarius, 97, 358
  in Scorpio, 97, 373
  in Second House, 126, 127, 338, 351
  in the signs, 96–98
  and Sun configuration, 221–22
  and Sun sextile, 332, 337
  in Taurus, 96–97, 277
  in Tenth House, 127, 368
  in Third House, 126
  in Twelfth House, 128, 374
  and Uranus configuration, 256–57
  and Uranus opposition, 211, 357, 360
  and Uranus square, 334, 352, 374
  and Venus configuration, 243–44
  and Venus conjunction, 381, 382
  and Venus opposition, 211, 368, 369, 372
  and Venus square, 373, 374
  in Virgo, 97
Scorpio, 66, 72–73, 109, 207, 363, 380
  and Aries, 206
  in First House, 106
  Jupiter in, 95–96
  Mars in, 94, 101
  Mercury in, 90, 278
  Moon in, 89, 101
  Pluto in, 101
  Saturn in, 97, 373
  Sun in, 88, 363, 374
  and Taurus, 200
  and Taurus polarity, 70–73
  Uranus in, 101
  Venus in, 29, 101, 339, 340
Scorpion (Scorpio type), 72
Second House, 108–9, 292, 322, 331, 338, 351, 360, 370, 380
  Jupiter in, 124
  Mars in, 122
  Mercury in, 119, 295, 360
  Moon in, 117
  Neptune in, 130
  Pluto in, 133
  Saturn in, 126, 338, 351
  Sun in, 115, 331, 360
  Uranus in, 128
  Venus in, 120
Secondary progressions, 299
Secrets, 362
Semicircle, the (as symbol), 32
Semi-quintile, 194
Semi-sextile, 194, 207, 210, 215
Semi-square, 194, 207, 210, 215
Separating aspects, 209
Septile, 194

Sesquiquadrate, 193–94
Seventh House, 107, 294, 317, 332,
    342, 358, 369, 370, 373, 381
  Jupiter in, 125
  Mars in, 123
  Mercury in, 119
  Moon in, 118, 344
  Neptune in, 131
  Pluto in, 133–34
  Saturn in, 127
  Sun in, 116
  Uranus in, 129, 358, 369, 370
  Venus in, 121
Sextile, 194, 201, 204–5, 210, 215
Sidereal Time, 151–52
Signs, Zodiac of, 15
Simplified Astronomy for Astrologers
    (Williams), 27, 139
Simplified Scientific Ephemeris, 23
Simplified Scientific Table of Houses,
    25
Singer, Paris, 332
Sisters, 331, 370, 380
Sixth House, 111, 293–94, 332, 341,
    351, 361, 371, 381
  Jupiter in, 124–25
  Mars in, 122–23, 371
  Mercury in, 119, 323
  Moon in, 118
  Neptune in, 131, 351–52
  Pluto in, 133
  Saturn in, 127
  Sun in, 116
  Uranus in, 129
  Venus in, 121
Solidad Brothers, 353
Soul-Moon (Form), 195
Southern Node of Moon, 63, 109n.,
    277
Speculation, 381
Spheres, geometry of the, 193–216
Spirit, The Part of The, 185n.
Spirit-Sun (Life), 195
Square, 194, 201–3, 210, 215, 359
Stalin, Joseph, 335–45
Standard Time, 141, 147–48, 167
Stellitium, 265–66
Stellium, 265–66
Sternzeit, 151
Stiller, Maurice (Mauritz), 368, 369,
    373
Stokowski, Leopold, 372
Structure, 54
Succedent Houses, 108–10
Summer Time, 140
Sun, 34, 109, 177, 178, 183, 188, 288–
    89, 308, 309, 311, 312, 317, 336,
    341, 350, 351, 352, 367–68, 377,
    378, 382
  in Aquarius, 88, 101, 306, 348
  in Aries, 87, 101, 357, 363
  and Ascendant square, 384
  aspects of, 218–25, 304
  in Cancer, 87
  in Capricorn, 88, 337
  in Eighth House, 116, 377, 382, 383
  in Eleventh House, 116
  in Fifth House, 115–16, 306, 365,
    368, 370, 371
  in First House, 115, 294
  in Fourth House, 115
  in Gemini, 87, 328, 329
  and Jupiter configuration, 221

and Jupiter parallel, 208
and Jupiter sextile, 338
and Jupiter square, 381
and Jupiter trine, 208, 331, 332, 333
in Leo, 87–88, 101, 318, 319, 323
in Libra, 88, 101, 277
and Mars configuration, 220–21
and Mars conjunction, 363
and Mars square, 370, 371
and Mars trine, 341
and Mercury configuration, 219
and Mercury conjunction, 334, 365,
    383
in Midheaven, 348
and Midheaven conjunction, 263–64
and Midheaven opposition, 363
and Midheaven trine, 363
and Moon configuration, 218–19
and Moon square, 305
and Moon trine, 302, 337–38, 342,
    366
and natal chart, 41
and Neptune configuration, 223–24
and Neptune conjunction, 357, 361
and Neptune sextile, 382
and Neptune square, 318, 322
and Neptune trine, 341
in Ninth House, 116
orb of, 304, 308
in Pisces, 88, 376
and Pluto configuration, 224–25
and Pluto opposition, 350
and Pluto square, 305, 370
in Sagittarius, 88, 352
and Saturn configuration, 221–22
and Saturn sextile, 332, 333
in Scorpio, 88, 363, 374
in Second House, 115, 331, 361
in Seventh House, 116
in the signs, 87, 88
in Sixth House, 116
in Taurus, 87
in Tenth House, 116, 348
in Third House, 115
in Twelfth House, 116–17, 337, 342
and Uranus configuration, 222–23
and Uranus conjunction, 317, 319
and Uranus square, 370, 384
and Uranus trine, 341, 361, 383
and Venus configuration, 219–20
and Venus conjunction, 305, 306,
    361
and Venus sextile, 352
and Venus square, 334
in Virgo, 88, 365–66, 367
Svanidze, Ekaterina, 342
Symbols, 30–33

Table of Diurnal Planetary Motion, 27
Table of Houses, 24, 156–57, 158
Table of Proportional Logarithms, 170
Taurus, 65, 66, 70–71, 109, 207, 322,
    361, 370, 377
  Ascendant in, 348, 350
  and Aries, 207
  in First House, 104, 328
  Jupiter in, 95, 277
  Mars in, 93, 101, 203, 209
  Mercury in, 90, 329
  Moon in, 88, 101, 318, 365, 370, 377,
    381, 382, 383
  Neptune in, 329

Taurus (*continued*)
 Pluto in, 101, 321, 329, 339, 378
 Saturn in, 96–97, 277
 and Scorpio, 70–73, 200
 Sun in, 87
 Uranus in, 101, 277, 293
 Venus in, 91, 101
Temptress, The (film), 373
Tenth House, 108, 294, 320, 333, 334, 363, 373
 Jupiter in, 125
 Mars in, 123
 Mercury in, 120
 Moon in, 118, 334, 348, 373
 Neptune in, 131–32
 Pluto in, 134, 378
 Saturn in, 127, 368
 Sun in, 116, 348
 Uranus in, 129
 Venus in, 121, 339, 340, 344
Theory of Celestial Influence, The (Collin), 39n.
Things hidden, 372
Third House, 110, 292–93, 331, 341, 361, 370, 380
 Jupiter in, 124
 Mars in, 122, 330, 331
 Mercury in, 119
 Moon in, 117
 Neptune in, 130, 322
 Pluto in, 133, 359
 Saturn in, 126
 Sun in, 115
 Uranus in, 128
 Venus in, 120–21, 361
Third Law of Motion (Newton), 12
Time, 140–52
Time Changes in Canada and Mexico, 26
Time Changes in the United States, 26
Time Changes in the World (Except Canada, Mexico and the U.S.A.), 26
Time-factor tables, 26
Time Standard, 142
Time zones, 141, 142, 145
Transiting planets, orbs of, 308
Transits, 307–12
Travel, 331, 372
Trine, 194, 201, 203, 210, 215, 272–74, 291
True Local Time, 147
T-Square, 211, 213, 269–71, 291, 292, 305, 307, 312, 339, 360, 371
Twelfth House, 111, 293, 295, 324, 341, 362, 372, 377, 383
 Jupiter in, 125–26, 372
 Mars in, 123–24, 295
 Mercury in, 120
 Moon in, 119, 328, 366, 370, 372
 Neptune in, 132, 295
 Pluto in, 134
 Saturn in, 128, 374
 Sun in, 116–17, 337, 342
 Uranus in, 130, 374
 Venus in, 112
Two-Faced Woman (film), 368, 374
Unaspected planets, 262–63
Unification, 47
Universal Love, 59
Uranus, 36, 110, 174, 209, 211, 295, 301, 306, 309, 310, 321, 327, 331,
 333, 342, 354, 360, 373, 378, 381, 383
 in Aquarius, 101, 204
 and Ascendant conjunction, 377
 and Ascendant opposition, 369
 aspects of, 260–61
 in Capricorn, 369, 370
 in Eighth House, 129
 in Eleventh House, 129–30
 in Fifth House, 129, 327, 330, 331, 333
 in First House, 128
 in Fourth House, 128–29
 in Gemini, 349
 in the Houses, 128–30
 and Jupiter configuration, 253–54
 and Jupiter opposition, 342
 and Jupiter trine, 312
 in Leo, 101, 203, 321, 330
 in Libra, 98–99
 and Mars configuration, 249
 and Mars conjunction, 208, 349, 351, 353, 373
 and Mars sextile, 204
 and Mars square, 344, 352, 359
 and Mars trine, 203, 321
 and Mercury configuration, 238
 and Midheaven sextile, 373
 and Moon configuration, 231–32
 and Moon conjunction, 302, 306, 339, 340, 341, 344
 and Moon square, 321, 378
 and Moon trine, 344, 358
 and natal chart, 56
 and Neptune configuration, 260–61
 in Ninth House, 129
 orb of, 304, 308
 and Pluto configuration, 261
 and Pluto opposition, 370
 and Pluto square, 327, 332, 333, 340, 374
 and Saturn configuration, 256–57
 and Saturn opposition, 211, 357, 360
 and Saturn square, 334, 352, 374
 in Scorpio, 101
 in Second House, 128
 in Seventh House, 129, 358, 369, 370
 in the signs, 98–99, 101
 in Sixth House, 129
 and Sun configuration, 222–23
 and Sun conjunction, 317, 319
 and Sun square, 370, 384
 and Sun trine, 341, 361, 383
 in Taurus, 101, 277, 293
 in Tenth House, 129
 in Third House, 128
 transiting, 312
 in Twelfth House, 130, 374
 and Venus configuration, 244–45
 and Venus square, 290, 293, 294
 and Venus trine, 332
 in Virgo, 340

Values, Perfection of, 59
Variable aspect, 198–99
Variables, minor, 208
Venus, 35, 108, 109, 177, 178, 184, 197, 201, 209, 211, 294, 304, 306, 307, 308, 310, 322, 332, 334, 340, 343, 361, 371, 380, 384
 in Aquarius, 92–93
 in Aries, 91, 101, 329, 361
 and Ascendant square, 384

Venus (*continued*)
  and Ascendant trine, 344
  aspects of, 241–47, 304
  in Cancer, 91–92, 322
  in Capricorn, 92
  in Eighth House, 121, 351
  in Eleventh House, 121–22
  in Fifth House, 121, 306
  in First House, 120
  in Fourth House, 121, 368
  in Gemini, 91
  in the Houses, 120–22
  and Jupiter configuration, 242
  and Jupiter conjunction, 353
  and Jupiter square, 213
  and Jupiter trine, 348, 350, 352
  in Leo, 92, 368, 369, 371, 373, 374
  in Libra, 92, 101
  and Mars configuration, 241–42
  and Mars parallel, 208
  and Mars square, 202, 213, 330, 331, 332, 333
  and Mars trine, 203, 371
  and Mercury configuration, 234–35
  and Mercury conjunction, 323, 334, 380
  and Mercury sextile, 344
  in Midheaven, 339
  and Midheaven square, 333–34
  and Moon configuration, 226–27
  and Moon conjunction, 199
  and Moon sextile, 380, 382
  and Moon square, 343, 368, 369
  and Moon trine, 305
  in Nadir, 369
  and natal chart, 47
  and Neptune configuration, 245–46
  and Neptune conjunction, 361, 373
  and Neptune square, 305, 351, 352
  and Neptune trine, 325
  in Ninth House, 121
  orb of, 304, 308
  in Pisces, 93, 101, 380, 382
  and Pluto configuration, 246–47, 339, 342
  in Sagittarius, 92, 349
  and Saturn configuration, 243–44
  and Saturn conjunction, 381, 382
  and Saturn opposition, 211, 368, 369, 372
  and Saturn square, 326, 373
  in Scorpio, 92, 101, 339, 340
  in Second House, 120
  in Seventh House, 121
  in the signs, 91–93
  in Sixth House, 121
  and Sun configuration, 219–20
  and Sun conjunction, 305, 306, 361
  and Sun square, 334
  and Sun sextile, 352
  in Taurus, 91, 101
  in Tenth House, 121, 339, 340, 344
  in Third House, 120–21, 361
  in Twelfth House, 122
  and Uranus configuration, 244–45
  and Uranus square, 290, 293, 294
  and Uranus trine, 332
  in Virgo, 92, 101, 277, 290
Virgo, 65, 66, 82–83, 111, 207, 340, 342, 362
  and Aries, 206
  Ascendant in, 383
  in First House, 105
  Jupiter in, 95, 101, 362
  Mars in, 93–94
  Mercury in, 90, 101
  Moon in, 89, 340, 342
  Neptune in, 101, 277, 374
  and Pisces polarity, 82–85
  Saturn in, 97
  Sun in, 88, 365–66, 367
  Uranus in, 340
  Venus in, 92, 101, 277, 290
Visions, 382

War Time, 140, 149–50
Water (element), 66
Weiss, Erich, 356
Wheel of Life, The, 153–65
Wilhelm, Richard, 320
Will:
  and Communication, 219
  and Consolidation, 221
  and Expansion, 221
  and Feelings, 218
  and Illumination, 223
  and Intuition, 222
  and Personal Drive, 220
  and Personal Magnetism, 219
  and Regeneration, 224
Williams, David, 27, 139
Wishes, 362
Writing, 322

Zodiac, 9
Zodiac of the Constellations, 15*n*.
Zodiac of Signs, 15, 36